PRINCIPLES OF
AMERICAN
GOVERNMENT

PRINCIPLES OF AMERICAN GOVERNMENT
Third Edition

Kenneth Prewitt
Social Science Research Council

Sidney Verba
Harvard University

HARPER & ROW, PUBLISHERS, New York
Cambridge, Hagerstown, Philadelphia, San Francisco
London, Mexico City, São Paulo, Sydney

1817

Sponsoring Editor: *John Michel*
Rewrite Specialist: *Carolyn Smith*
Project Editor: *Lois Lombardo*
Designer: *Frances Torbert Tilley*
Production Manager: *Marion A. Palen*
Photo Researcher: *Myra Schachne*
Compositor: *Progressive Typographers Incorporated*
Printer and Binder: *Halliday Lithograph Corporation*
Art Studio: *Vantage Art Inc.*

Principles of American Government, Third Edition

Library of Congress Cataloging in Publication Data
Prewitt, Kenneth.
   Principles of American government.

   Includes index.
   1.   United States—Politics and government—
Handbooks, manuals, etc.   I.   Verba, Sidney, joint
author.   II.   Title.
JK274.P762   1980   320.4'73   79-19712
ISBN 0-06-045278-1

Credits for Chapter Opening Photographs

Chapter 1, Beckwith Studios; Chapter 2, Culver; Chapter 3, Franken, Stock, Boston; Chapter 4, Conklin, Monkmeyer; Chapter 5, Sapieha, Stock, Boston; Chapter 6, Anderson, Woodfin Camp; Chapters 7, 8, 9, UPI; Chapter 10, Wide World; Chapter 11, UPI; Chapter 12, Holland, Stock, Boston; Chapter 13, De Wys; Chapter 14, Smolan, Stock Boston; Chapter 15, UPI; Chapter 16, Pines, Woodfin Camp.

Other Photo Credits

Beckwith Studios: 60*(bottom)*. Brown Brothers: 18, 21, 54, 225*(left)*, 268. DPI: 304; Beame, 241. Library of Congress, 272. Magnum: Erwitt, 138; Manos, 183; Webb, 297. Monkmeyer: Conklin, 197; Forsyth, 124; Rogers, 105; Shelton, 239, 300*(bottom)*; Zimbel, 300*(top)*. Stock, Boston: Alper, 242; Brody, 123; Franken, 8; Grace, 41; Gross, 37, 111; Herwig, 44, 143; Menzel, 319, 331; Southwick, 6, 51, 83, 195; Vandermark, 4; Wolinsky, 39. Taurus: Kroll, 60*(top)*. UPI: 27, 28, 56, 76, 85, 88, 101, 137, 146, 152, 164, 170, 173, 192, 216, 225*(right)*, 229, 249, 270, 282, 285, 286. Wide World: 7, 108, 136, 155, 209, 219, 274, 292, 311, 317, 334.

Contents

Preface

Principles of American Government, Third Edition is a substantially abbreviated and rewritten version of the third edition of *An Introduction to American Government*. It is suitable for courses in American government taught on the quarter basis or for other courses in which a less detailed book is desirable. This book maintains the same basic approach to American government as that of the larger volume.

The book does not adopt any single theoretical approach—there being none that we believe deals adequately with the complexities of American government. We are theoretically eclectic. As scholars, we have learned much from the various frameworks for the study of American politics; we use these frameworks to guide us in the organization of our argument. We have, however, attempted to keep the theoretical scaffolding to a minimum so that the student can gain a more direct understanding of American politics.

We attempt to use examples and issues drawn from recent political events, but we are aware of the disadvantage in focusing only on the most recent political controversy. Such a current events approach diverts attention from the serious long-term problems facing America. Furthermore, the latest headlines are soon irrelevant. We have tried to understand the underlying patterns in American politics so that our analysis will be relevant not only to yesterday's headlines and today's headlines, but to tomorrow's as well.

We try to provide students with the basic facts they need to know about American government and to place such facts in context so that their broader meaning can be understood. It is not our purpose to provide the student with an encyclopedia of facts about events, institutions, people, and issues.

We draw upon many sources: upon the latest research in political science and also upon political history. We use these materials, not for their own sake, but to further our goal of revealing the workings of the political process.

Politics inevitably involves evaluations. Our goal is to aid students to make their own evaluations of the American political system. It is not our purpose to celebrate American politics, as do some tests, nor condemn it, as do others. Rather we attempt to show both strengths and weaknesses. We provide the student with materials to be used for evaluation and with alternative evaluations.

We recognize that politics involves controversy, and the theme of controversy permeates our text. An example of such controversy is the issue of inequality that occurs in many of the chapters in the book. The way in which the government and the economy interrelate to affect the allocation of benefits across social groups is one way in which inequality is dealt with; value conflicts and dilemmas of policy is another way.

Our book is divided into several sections. The first set of chapters deals with the context of American politics. After a brief introduction, we review the Constitution as basic to the government of the United States. Then we continue with an analysis of the relationship between the polity and the economy, a consideration that is followed by a discussion of the way in which the coexistence of a democratic polity and a capitalist economy creates problems in the allocation of benefits in society.

The next section of the book moves to the actual political behavior of citizens in the United States. We consider the political beliefs of Americans, the basis of political conflict in America, political participation, and the process of leadership recruitment.

In the next two chapters we consider the major links between the citizen and the government: interest groups as they serve to link the interests of citizens to the government and political parties as they operate in the electoral process.

We center our attention on the major governmental institutions in the next four chapters. We deal with Congress, the Presidency, the American bureaucracy, and the Supreme Court.

The last few chapters deal with the way in which the institutions interact to affect different policies of importance. Attention is given to the issue of individual rights and governmental power when we consider the issue of civil liberty in America. We follow that by a consideration of federalism. Our last chapter is devoted to a discussion of the policy process. This allows us to tie together the various themes of the earlier chapters and to show how the actors in the political process interrelate. We develop some general themes about policy making and illustrate them with several examples of domestic and international policies.

KENNETH PREWITT
SIDNEY VERBA

PRINCIPLES OF
AMERICAN
GOVERNMENT

Government and Politics

1

BASIC QUESTIONS

In this book we will be concerned with four basic questions. Here are those questions, along with some preliminary answers:

1. Q: Why have a government at all?
   A: Because without government people would lack the security they need to go about their normal lives. Also, government forces citizens to contribute to collective goods. (For example, it requires us to pay taxes, which are used to pay for things like public parks or the postal service.)

2. Q: If the governments are necessary, why is there so much conflict about what they do?
   A: People disagree about how much the government should do. (Should it provide medical care? Should it force people to wear seat belts?) They also disagree about who should pay for government programs and who should benefit from them. (Should the cost of providing medical care for the aged be paid for by the old as well as the young, and the poor as well as the rich?) Out of disagreements like these comes political conflict.

3. Q: If government is necessary and political conflict is unavoidable, how does democracy fit in?
   A: In the United States, democratic *government* protects the rights of citizens against the powers of government. This is partly because democratic *politics* emphasizes open political participation, the right to criticize the government, regular elections in which unsatisfactory leaders can be replaced, and the equal right of all citizens to play a role in self-government.

4. Q: Do we have democratic government and politics in the United States?
   A: This question cannot be answered with a simple yes or no. The Constitution provides for a democratic government, but the nation faces social problems and international challenges that seem to demand a government with strong powers of management and control. While the Constitution promises political equality, it also supports a free-enterprise system that results in economic inequality. At times, great inequalities of wealth and living conditions threaten to undermine the promise of political equality.

Of course these four issues are not the only subjects that will interest us. But they are at the core of any study of government, politics, and democracy.

WHY GOVERNMENT?

We tend to take government for granted and rarely ask why we have it. In fact, there is a good argument against government: It makes us do things—pay taxes, drive at certain speeds, respect other people's property, and so on.

We have to do these things; if we do not, we are likely to be punished. Thus by forcing people to do certain things governments limit individual freedom. If we value freedom, then, why do we put up with government?

Maintaining Social Order

One answer to this question is that government is necessary to maintain social order. Without government, civilized life would be impossible. We support government because it provides law and order. It provides an environment in which a citizen can raise a family, work at a job, get an education, and plan for the future. It does this in just about every area of life. Take, for example, economic activities. Working for a salary, investing savings, buying or producing a product all depend on contracts—between worker and manager, lender and borrower, seller and buyer. Someone has to make sure people honor such contracts—to make sure the car buyer does not drive off and stop making payments, that the employer does not suddenly decide not to pay the workers, that the bank does not close its doors and keep people's savings deposits. That "someone" is the government: People honor their contracts because the government makes sure they do and may punish those who do not.

Providing National Security

The government is also expected to protect the nation's borders against foreign invasion and international outlaws. Today, however, nuclear weapons, worldwide business investments, international terrorism, and huge armies and navies stationed throughout the world mean that "national security" involves a lot more than simply protecting national boundaries. It involves maintaining international order, including participation in the United Nations and such defense organizations as the North Atlantic Treaty Organization (NATO).

Providing Collective Goods

The usual justification for government, then, is that it provides national security and maintains the social order necessary for civilized life. But the government does many things that are not aimed at providing law and order, such as repaving an interstate highway in Nevada; supporting a graduate student writing a dissertation on the tools used by prehistoric people in Central Africa; raising the tax on gasoline in order to conserve energy; publishing a booklet naming the trees and plants along a trail in the Smoky Mountains; or sending a monthly check to a blind pensioner in New York. Obviously we must look beyond law and order to answer the question, why government?

Governments often make *binding* decisions that cannot be made by individuals. For example, all drivers are interested in having everyone drive on one side of the road or the other. It does not matter which side is chosen as long as everyone drives on the same side. In such a case all will benefit if they give the government the power to make a rule requiring people to drive on a particular side.

To understand why social goals may require *binding* decisions by government, we must understand what is meant by *collective goods.* Collective goods are benefits that are available to every person whether or not he or she has worked for them. If the government creates a national park, I can use it even though I did not help create it. But if I benefit from the park whether I work for it or not, why should I help create the park? Why not sit back and let

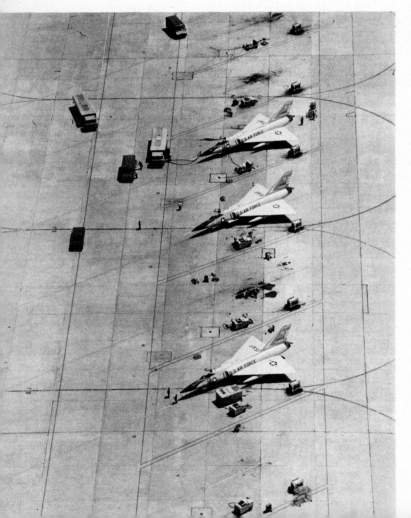

An extensive, and expensive, military force protects American interests.

others do the work? On the other hand, if I wanted to create a public park on my own I would probably not succeed because I could not contribute enough labor or money.

Thus for any individual it makes sense to wait until others have created a collective good, and then take advantage of it. In that case, however, collective goods would never be created. Only a binding governmental decision that forces people to contribute to collective goods through taxes will lead to the creation of such goods.

WHY POLITICS?

Government would be a simple matter if all governmental decisions were like the decision that people must drive on the right-hand side of the road. What is important is having a single rule that everyone can agree with and which is not unfairly costly to a particular group. Many traffic rules are like this, such as a rule (in the United States) which says that drivers must stay on the right side of the road or (in England) that they must stay on the left side.

Different Preferences

Government, however, is not always a matter of achieving goals that all citizens approve of and that do not cost anything. In fact, governmental decisions nearly always lead to conflict. People do not agree on what collective goods the government should provide or who should pay for them. People do not benefit equally from such goods, nor do they pay equally. Thus government involves competition among individuals and groups for the greatest benefit at the lowest cost.

Public highways are an example. They are a collective good, since no individual could afford to build one and because they are open to any adult who is licensed and willing to obey the traffic laws. Yet they are a subject of intense political conflict. Downtown merchants may want an expressway to come directly into the central city; apartment dwellers who are about to lose their homes to the bulldozers will fiercely oppose such a plan. Truckers and automobile manufacturers will call for more and faster expressways; conservationists insist that cities would be more livable if the money was spent on mass transit and public parks instead. Another group, favoring lower taxes, does not want the expressway no matter where it is located and opposes mass transit and parks as well. Still another group, perhaps the largest one, simply does not care.

The first important point about politics and government, therefore, is that individuals and groups have different preferences. These different pref-

erences lead to arguments over what collective goods the government should provide and who should pay for those goods. These arguments also result in struggles to control and influence government.

Differences in Impact

The political struggle begins with different preferences, but it is spurred on by a second major factor: *Governmental decisions do not affect all citizens equally.* Any policy is likely to benefit one group a lot, another group a little, and a third group not at all. It may even hurt some people. The decision to build a highway next to my house benefits the highway builders a lot, commuters a

Citizens differ not only in their view but in the intensity with which they hold their views.

little, and most citizens not at all, but it may hurt me and a few of my neighbors. As a result of such differences in impact, on any particular issue we will find not only different preferences but also different levels of intensity. Differences in intensity lead to differences in political involvement. The citizens who are most severely affected will be concerned and active; those who are not affected will not care about the outcome.

GOVERNMENT AND POLITICS IN THE UNITED STATES

At this point we need to think about how some of our definitions explain present-day government and politics in the United States. In doing so it is important to realize that we are living in a time of rapid governmental expansion. This expansion itself is a source of serious political conflict.

Collective Goods and the Growth of Government

The idea of collective goods can help us understand why governments expand. When benefits become defined as collective goods, the powers of government increase. Creating a collective good requires laws, programs, and agencies. As these are added, the government grows. The more benefits become defined as collective goods, the greater the powers and responsibilities of government become. As we enter the last part of the twentieth century, more and more social goals or benefits are being defined as collective goods.

National defense has always been thought of as a collective good. It is almost impossible to defend some citizens without defending others—you can hardly let an enemy bomber fly across the country and bomb only the homes of people who do not contribute to the national defense system. Added to national defense are several things that have only recently been defined as collective goods, such as a clean environment, medical research, a national highway system, public parks, and a stable economy.

You may wonder why there is conflict over whether the government should provide collective goods. Where would we be without national security or clean air and water or a highway system? But there *is* conflict. There is conflict over priorities—should taxpayers' money be spent on developing better missiles, cleaning polluted rivers, or improving the highway system? There is also conflict over what should be defined as a collective good. Some economists argue that the tendency to redefine certain benefits as collective goods is really the tendency of government bureaucrats to try to expand their powers. They claim that the free-market system is more likely to produce the kind of society Americans want without creating a bureaucracy that spends taxpayers' money and regulates the lives of individuals. (For example, when enough citizens prefer clean air to fast cars they will use their purchasing power to punish the polluters. The market will respond, and cars that pollute will no longer be produced.)

How far should the government go in deciding how citizens can use their private property?

In this book we will discuss the growth of governmental powers and responsibilities, but we will also be concerned with the conflict over how these powers are used and over whether government should take on even more responsibility.

Planning for Scarcity

Another trend that is contributing to the growth of government is the trend toward planning for the future. Will there be enough doctors in the year 2000? If not, start spending more on medical education now. Will there be too few wilderness areas for wildlife in the year 2000? If so, now is the time to stop the developments that destroy such areas. Will there be enough energy to heat homes, drive cars, fly planes? If not, now is the time to plan future energy supplies.

Who is responsible for planning? The only institution large enough, rich enough, and powerful enough to try to control events that will affect the future is the government. The government's planning role has increased in recent years because of a shift from abundance to scarcity. In the years between the end of World War II and the early 1970s, American society was a society of abundance. The purchasing power of many Americans increased greatly, and American technology mass-produced nice things for them to buy and enjoy. Working hours became shorter and vacations longer. There was an increase in the number of "high-status" professional and technical jobs available in government, education, and industry. The result was a growing and satisfied middle class.

Few Americans realized that the "American way of life" was based partly on cheap labor—the labor of underpaid blacks and the rural poor in this country, as well as cheap labor in foreign lands. Some of the minerals needed by American industry were mined by cheap labor in South America and parts of Africa; the fresh fruit enjoyed by Americans was picked by migrant workers in California or local workers in Honduras. Even fewer Americans recognized the importance of a constant supply of cheap energy, energy that filtered swimming pools and lit theaters, that heated offices and libraries in the winter and air-conditioned them in the summer, that drove motor boats and campers, that brought big-time sports into everyone's living room. The source of this cheap energy was cheap oil.

Labor and energy are no longer so cheap, and it is clear that the world does not have an endless supply of the resources that are needed to support the way of life many Americans have become used to. It is also clear that other nations, such as the oil producing countries, are going to charge as much as the market can stand. Abundance has turned into scarcity. At the very least, we can no longer assume that our standard of living will continue to increase. Now we are growing concerned about how to hold on to what we already have. One result is increased emphasis on planning—especially in the area of future energy needs and sources—and further growth of the government.

The expansion of the government's planning role contributes to social conflict. In a time of scarcity those who are well off struggle to keep what they have, to increase their wealth and security if possible, and to pass it along to their children. Those who are not so well off shout "foul!" When there is not enough to go around, it does not seem fair to them that the rich should remain rich while the poor become even poorer.

The government is in the middle of this conflict. It must try to plan for the future while satisfying competing and contradictory demands for benefits right now. Once again we find conditions that seem to stimulate both increased governmental power and greater political conflict.

The Demand for Equality

Still another factor encouraging the growth of government is the demand for citizenship equality. Americans are proud of the principles of equality on which our nation is based: equal political rights, equality in the eyes of the law, and equal opportunity. But these principles are not always carried out in practice. Many groups have been denied equal treatment and equal opportunity—Irish immigrants, American Indians, blacks, women, and the handicapped, to list only a few examples. What do such groups do when they are treated unfairly? In recent years they have been turning to the government for help. The government has responded with laws and programs and agencies, and the government has grown.

Equality of Opportunity vs. Equality of Condition   Equality of opportunity means that everyone should have an equal chance to compete for unequal rewards. There should be no arbitrary barriers—such as skin color or sex—that keep some people out of the competition. Equal opportunity is lacking if blacks cannot go to the same schools as whites, if women cannot become corporate executives, or if a Jew cannot become President.

Equality of opportunity does not guarantee equality of condition. Some people will succeed while others fail. The government's role is to make sure that everyone has an equal chance to succeed, not that everyone succeeds to the same extent. During the past few years, however, the emphasis on equality of opportunity has been giving way to an emphasis on equality of condition. No longer is it enough for every child to have the opportunity to go to school; all schools must be equally good. No longer is it enough to bar sex discrimination; affirmative-action programs are needed to make sure women and men are represented equally in medical schools or law firms or business offices.

Equality and Conflict The government's efforts to protect equality of opportunity and to provide equality of condition generate political conflict. Some citizens are opposed to the growth of government. They feel that in trying to help disadvantaged groups the government may do as much harm as good. For example, a government medical program might provide decent health care for people who are too poor to pay the high costs of hospitals and doctors, but such a program would create a new and costly government bureaucracy and might even lower the quality of medical service.

Another source of conflict in this area is the tension between the principles of equality and freedom. Protecting the rights of one group may limit the freedom of another. Busing schoolchildren, for example, may increase equality of educational opportunity, but it also limits the freedom of parents to choose the kind of school they want for their children. Thus as the government takes on more and more responsibility in the area of equal treatment, it becomes involved in more battles over the principles of equality.

Here we see a pattern that will be found in many other areas of social and political life in the years ahead. A problem, such as inequality of opportunity, is identified. The government is expected to create policies and programs to deal with the problem. The government grows: It hires more people, requires a larger share of the national income, and makes more laws and regulations. As the main agency for dealing with America's problems, the government becomes the arena in which differences of opinion about those problems are expressed and political conflict takes place.

DEMOCRATIC PRINCIPLES

There is more to politics than conflict. Politics is also about *principles,* the basic law and rules of political conduct. In the United States the basic political principles are, of course, democratic principles.

Limited Government

Because the nation's founders feared political tyranny, they set up a government based on the principle of *limited government;* that is, government was defined in terms of what it could *not* do as well as what it *could* do. With this goal in mind, the founders divided the powers of government so that they would not be in the hands of any single group of leaders. This was done in the following ways:

1. *Federalism.* Power was divided between the states and the national government.
2. *Separation of Powers.* The national government was divided into three separate branches.
3. *Checks and Balances.* Each branch was given ways of limiting the actions of the other two.
4. *A Bill of Rights.* The basic political rights of citizens were guaranteed, thus creating a balance of power between the elected leaders and the citizens.

Individual Liberty

An even more basic democratic principle is *individual liberty*. Every citizen should be allowed to make his or her own way without interference by the government. The government was expected to protect equality of opportunity, but beyond that there was to be no governmental action that would limit individual freedom. Among other things, this meant a minimum of governmental intervention in the economy.

Our book will have much to say about democratic principles, but here we need to mention two themes that will run throughout our discussions of American politics: the contrast between principles and practice and the fact that an activist state exists alongside a limited government.

Principles vs. Practice

A major theme in American politics is the contrast between *principles* and *practice*. As we saw in our discussion of equality, it is not easy to translate principles into practice. School busing programs are a good example of this problem—the principle (equal educational opportunity) is clear, but the practice (busing children to other neighborhoods) interferes with the freedom of parents to choose their children's school. Much of American politics is a trade-off between principles such as equality of opportunity and freedom of choice.

A Limited Government vs. an Activist State

Another important theme is the contrast between *limited government* and *governmental activism*. The nation's founders wanted a limited government, but clearly we do not have such a government. Instead, we have a large and expanding government. National security alone seems to demand a strong central government. Providing collective goods such as a clean environment or a stable economy requires governmental action. The government is also expected to satisfy demands for equal opportunity and equal treatment. Finally, planning for scarcity leads to further expansion of government.

In short, we will have a better understanding of American politics if we add to the idea of limited government the somewhat contradictory idea of an activist state. Seeing government only in terms of what it does *not* do would blind us to the many things it *is* doing: regulating, managing, planning, and intervening.

What, then, has happened to our democratic principles? Do they count for nothing? In this book we will see that they continue to count in important ways. We must, however, keep in mind the fact that there is constant tension between the principle of limited government and the reality of an activist state.

HOW WE FIND OUT ABOUT POLITICS: I

Our understanding of politics is based on two kinds of knowledge: facts and explanations of facts. We cannot study politics without knowing something about the two major parties, the role of interest groups, and the importance of federalism. It is also useful to have some information about public policies.

But not all facts are equally important. The child who has memorized all the state capitols knows some political facts but does not understand much about politics. Even the adult who can name his or her representative in Congress and all the members of the President's Cabinet does not have very useful knowledge. Such facts do not answer important questions about the operation of government: Why do the President and his Cabinet often favor one kind of legislation while Congress favors another? Why are there shifts in the portion of the vote won by the Democratic and Republican presidential candidates from one election to the next? Why does a Congress dominated by Democrats sometimes give as much support to a Republican President as to a Democratic one?

To answer questions like these we need much more than the names of members of Congress and the Cabinet. We need to know about their social backgrounds and careers. We need to know about voters' party loyalties. We need to know about the organization of Congress and the party ties of its members. Some of these facts can be linked to others to help us understand how our nation's leaders act in office. Even more important, they help us understand how public policy is made.

This explains why we have chosen certain facts and not others to discuss in this book. We cannot describe all the facts of American politics and connect them together. Nor can we keep up with the political events reported in the news. Instead, we must choose the facts that will help us gain some general knowledge about politics.

Facts and explanations of facts are not enough, however. Those who write about politics in newspapers, magazines, and books usually describe politics from a particular viewpoint. Their interpretations of the facts differ widely, depending on their point of view. It is difficult, if not impossible, to be neutral about politics.

In this book we will pay attention to the various possible interpretations of American politics. We will not present one interpretation as gospel truth, but will try to focus on some of the major controversies in the interpretation of political facts. Understanding political controversies may well be the first step toward understanding politics.

The Constitutional Framework

2

WHAT IS A CONSTITUTION?

When a group of people form an organization in order to achieve some common goal or goals, they often begin by writing a constitution. A constitution states the basic principles shared by the members of the organization. But since those principles will not always be interpreted in the same way by every member of the group, the constitution must also contain rules and procedures for settling disputes.

The Constitution of the United States is often called the basic rule from which all other rules are derived. Any act by the government or by an individual that violates the principles contained in the Constitution is said to be "unconstitutional" and will be punished. The criminal and civil codes are designed to be "constitutional," that is, to be in accord with the principles contained in the Constitution.

In this chapter we will describe how the U.S. Constitution came into being, as well as the principles and procedures for resolving disputes set forth in the Constitution.

UNDERSTANDING THE CONSTITUTION

In 1790, farmers could grow whatever crops they wanted to, pay their help any wages they agreed to, and set their own prices. Today, dozens of regulations affect what crops are planted and in what amounts, what fertilizers and insecticides are used, what wages are paid for farm work, and what prices are charged for farm products.

In 1790, farmers who were well off sent their children to private schools. If a farmer was sick, other family members or neighbors took care of the farm until he could go back to work. As he grew old and could no longer run the farm, he lived off his savings and the good will of his children. Today, by contrast, most farmers send their children to public schools and depend on public-health services and social security as protection against sickness and old age.

The relationship between the citizen and the government has changed greatly over the past 200 years. Yet the same basic rule—the Constitution— that governed American society in 1790 governs it today. The tremendous increase in governmental regulation of the affairs of citizens, and in the services provided by the government, has taken place within the framework hammered out during a hot summer in Philadelphia nearly 200 years ago.

How has the Constitution survived two centuries of growth and change? To understand the Constitution we need to review a bit of American history. Then we will discuss how the Constitution handles the nation's basic needs:

procedures for defending itself, means of settling conflicts between its members, ways of making and carrying out rules, and a method for choosing the rule makers. Finally, we will look at how the Constitution has managed to adapt to the political, economic, and social changes that have taken place since 1787.

THE NATION'S FOUNDING

The 1770s and 1780s were a critical period in American political history. Figure 2.1 lists some of the major events of that period. The process of creating a new nation was carried out in two stages. During the first stage the ties between the American colonies and Great Britain were broken and a new government was set up under the Articles of Confederation. This government had many weaknesses, however, so there was a second stage in which a new government was designed and adopted. A loose league of states was transformed into a strong federal union.

The War for Independence

During the Revolution the American colonists did not agree on the wisdom and justice of the war. The Tories, who were opposed to the war, believed the colonies should remain loyal to Great Britain. The Patriots argued that because of his tyrannous actions the king of England had no claim on the

1774	The First Continental Congress, in which delegates from 12 colonies meet in Philadelphia to discuss problems shared by all of the colonies.
1775	Military action between Britain and the colonies increases.
1776	Thomas Paine publishes *Common Sense*, a radical call to break all ties with Great Britain. Signing of the Declaration of Independence.
1777	Drafting of the Articles of Confederation, which link the 13 states in a loose "League of Friendship."
1781	Adoption of the Articles of Confederation.
1782	The War for Independence comes to an end.
1786	Shays' Rebellion, an attack by Massachusetts debtors on their creditors.
1787	The Constitutional Convention meets in Philadelphia.
1788	Enough states ratify the new Constitution so it can be adopted.
1789	George Washington is elected first President of the United States.
1791	The Bill of Rights is added to the Constitution.

FIGURE 2.1 *American Political History, 1774–1791*

loyalty of the American people. As Thomas Jefferson put it in the Declaration of Independence,

> Prudence, indeed, will dictate that Governments long established should not be changed for light and transient causes; and accordingly all experience hath shown, that mankind are more disposed to suffer, while evils are sufferable, than to right themselves by abolishing the forms to which they are accustomed. But when a long train of abuses and usurpations, pursuing invariably the same Object evinces a design to reduce them under absolute Despotism, it is their right, it is their duty, to throw off such Government, and to produce new Guards for their future security. Such has been the patient sufferance of these Colonies and such is now the necessity which constrains them to alter their former Systems of Government.

Other Patriots felt that the colonists would benefit politically and economically from a break with Great Britain. Thomas Paine expressed this view in his pamphlet *Common Sense*:

> I Challenge the warmest advocate for reconciliation to show a single advantage that this continent can reap by being connected with Great Britain. I repeat the challenge; not a single advantage is derived. Our corn will fetch its price in any market in Europe, and our imported goods must be paid for, buy them where we will.[1]

However, the strongest arguments against remaining loyal to Great Britain were based on a belief in individual freedom and in the right to rebel against a tyrannous government.

---

[1] Nelson F. Adkins, ed., *Common Sense and Other Political Writings* (Indianapolis: Bobbs-Merrill, 1953), p. 22.

Designing a Government

The Articles of Confederation   The Articles of Confederation, ratified in 1781, lasted less than ten years. The Articles were a compromise between the states and the central government. They reflected the belief that the freedom gained in the war could best be preserved by local self-rule, but that some coordination among the states was needed in areas like national defense, foreign affairs, and commerce.

Under the Articles Congress consisted of delegates from the 13 states who served only as long as their home state allowed them to. Each state had only one vote, and nine votes were required to pass major legislation. In such conditions deadlock is almost unavoidable. Since there was no separate executive branch, public policy had to be carried out by various committees, panels, and individuals—a disorderly and inefficient system.

There were, in addition, many limits on the powers of Congress. For one thing, it had no direct power over individuals; people were citizens only of their state. No congressional law was binding on an individual unless the state chose to enforce it. Moreover, Congress did not have the power to tax but had to request contributions from the states. The states were unwilling to comply with such requests, and as a result the confederation was practically bankrupt. Finally, Congress could neither regulate commerce nor impose tariffs. This not only closed off an important source of revenue, but also led to economic warfare among the states.

The Critical Period   It soon became clear that the Articles of Confederation were a failure. During the War for Independence the national government did not deal effectively with the problems of war. In foreign affairs the situation was no better: The United States seemed to speak with 13 voices instead of one; some states even conducted formal negotiations with European nations. Since Congress did not have the power to set tariffs on imported goods, it could not make commercial treaties with other nations. To many people, however, the most serious weakness of the confederation was the fact that Congress did not have the power to regulate domestic commerce. Tariffs imposed by the states often crippled small industries in neighboring states and generally hampered the flow of goods among the colonies. The national economy suffered as a result.

Commercial interests were not the only ones that suffered under the Articles. People who had lent money for the war effort would lose everything if the government went bankrupt. Those who wanted to open up the land west of the Appalachians to settlement and trade were hurt by the central government's inability to protect settlers from Indians and to dislodge the British from their trading posts.

But some groups—particularly debtors—were *not* hurt by the weakness of the central government under the Articles. Debtors benefited from the cheap paper money issued by state governments and were able to get state legislators to pass laws delaying the collection of debts. They also benefited from the central government's lack of police power. Open rebellions against creditors, like the one in Massachusetts led by Daniel Shays, were fairly common. Many citizens became concerned about the weakness of the central government.

The Constitutional Convention   By the mid-1780s there was widespread agreement that something had to be done. Congress asked the states to send delegates to Philadelphia "for the sole purpose of revising the Articles of Confederation." But the 55 delegates who met in Philadelphia in May of 1787 did much more than revise the Articles. As soon as they arrived they agreed on two things: first, that their meetings would be held in the strictest secrecy, and second, that the Articles were so inadequate that it was necessary to create an entirely new Constitution.

It is not easy to write a constitution. Political leaders are often strong willed, and if they disagree sharply they are unlikely to write a document that will be accepted by all. Yet in a single summer the delegates to the Constitutional Convention produced what may be the most effective constitution ever written.

The fact is, those delegates were a remarkable group. The Constitution reflects their vast political experience. Many of the delegates had helped write state constitutions; many were serving in state legislatures at the time of the convention, and a majority had been members of Congress under the Articles of Confederation. Among them were George Washington, Alexander Hamilton, James Madison, and Benjamin Franklin.

The delegates drew not only on their experience but also on their knowledge of political theory. They were familiar with John Locke's *Two Treatises on Government* and James Harrington's *Commonwealth of Oceana,* both written in the seventeenth century, as well as Montesquieu's *Spirit of the Laws,* written 40 years before the Philadelphia convention. These writings contained many of the basic ideas that found their way into the Constitution. More than half of the delegates were trained in law, particularly English common law, on which our legal system is based.

Despite all their knowledge and experience, the writers of the Constitution faced a difficult task. Any constitution must balance freedom and authority—the freedom of citizens from arbitrary or unjust rule and the authority of the government to manage the society and settle disputes. The political climate of the time played as important a role in the balance between freedom and authority as the personal traits of the founders. Three political factors contributed to the success of the Constitutional Convention: (1) The delegates agreed on certain basic issues; (2) they skipped the toughest issue; and (3) they were willing to compromise.

AGREEING ON BASIC ISSUES Missing from the convention were both the most conservative and the most radical political leaders in the nation. They either chose to ignore the convention or were not sent as delegates. (Patrick Henry, for example, refused to attend and said, "I smelt a rat.") The men who dominated the convention reflected solid financial interests. They shared a philosophy that included mistrust of human nature, respect for property, concern about possible abuses of democracy, and the belief that they had the right to design a new government. At the same time, they were committed in varying degrees to the idea of self-government.

SKIPPING THE TOUGHEST ISSUE The strongest political feelings of the time centered on the issue of state versus national sovereignty. *Federalism,* in which sovereignty is shared between the states and the central government, was a brilliant compromise. Yet the Constitution avoided the toughest issue of all, namely, whether states had the right to secede from the Union. If the right to secede had been written into the Constitution, it is unlikely that the Union would have lasted very long. If it had been forbidden, there might not have been a Union at all. The nation's founders simply passed this question along to a later generation, and it was finally settled by the Civil War.

WILLINGNESS TO COMPROMISE The delegates compromised on many

issues besides sovereignty. For example, some of the delegates recognized that slavery was inconsistent with a government based on individual liberty. George Mason of Virginia warned that slavery "would bring the judgment of heaven on a country." However, other delegates said that their states would not join the Union if the Constitution banned slavery. The compromise on this issue is contained in Article I: Congress could not outlaw the slave trade until 1808.

The most famous compromise in the Constitution has to do with the makeup of Congress. The issue was whether the states would be represented in Congress on the basis of population (which would give larger states an advantage) or on an equal basis (which would give smaller states an advantage). This problem was solved by the "Connecticut Compromise." There would be a House of Representatives in which each state would be given a number of seats based on its population. There would also be a Senate in which each state, no matter how small, would have two seats. Most important legislation must be passed by both the House and the Senate.

Ratification: Federalists vs. Anti-Federalists

In September of 1787 the new Constitution was presented to the nation for ratification. Special conventions for this purpose were elected in each state; nine of those conventions had to ratify the Constitution for it to be adopted. Those who were opposed to the Constitution—the Anti-Federalists— thought the delegates to the Constitutional Convention had gone too far. They admitted that reforms were needed: The government should have some limited taxing power and the power to regulate domestic and foreign commerce. However, the government that would be set up under the Constitution went much further: It had unlimited taxing power; it could raise and maintain a large army; it included an independent executive who would command the armed forces; and it created an independent judiciary that could dictate to the state courts. This government, the Anti-Federalists claimed, would dominate the state governments, which were the true homes of democracy, and threaten the individual liberty for which the Revolution had been fought at such great cost.

The Federalists, who supported the Constitution, argued that the states had not been effective in protecting the rights of citizens. They criticized the states for the "multiplicity," "mutability," and "injustice" of state laws. Only a strong Union would guarantee individual liberty. The Constitution, said the Federalists, would provide a competent government while at the same time preventing abuses of power.

Some of the most difficult battles over the Constitution were fought during the two years after it had been written. It was not until 1789 that the required nine states had ratified the document and the new government went into effect.

CONSTITUTIONAL PRINCIPLES

John Adams once wrote to his cousin Samuel Adams as follows:

> Human appetites, passions, prejudices and self-love will never be conquered by benevolence and knowledge alone. . . . "The love of liberty," you say, "is interwoven in the soul of man." So it is (also) in that of a wolf; and I doubt whether it be much more rational, generous, or social in one than in the other. . . . We must not, then, depend alone upon the love of liberty in the soul of man for its preservation. Some political institutions must be prepared, to assist this love against its enemies.

Adams was saying that human nature is not to be trusted. Without social and civil institutions, human beings break their contracts. Their passions and ambitions would dominate their reason and self-restraint. If a minority gained control, it would tyrannize and rob the majority; if the majority was unrestrained, it would ignore the rights of minorities and force them to conform to the majority will.

This negative view of human nature, together with a positive view of human institutions, is the philosophical basis of our Constitution.

But if there must be authority, it too must be restrained. No single group must have final control. The nation's founders feared the ambitions of leaders as much as they feared the possible excesses of the people. Therefore they were careful to impose restraints on those in authority. These restraints took three forms: (1) a representative form of government, (2) division of power, and (3) limited government.

A Representative Form of Government

The nation's founders were strongly opposed to arbitrary rule and believed that no government was legitimate without "the consent of the governed." As Madison put it, "A dependence on the people is, no doubt, the primary control on the government."

One of the first acts of the founders was to abolish titles of nobility and inherited positions of power. No arbitrary standard, especially birth, should give some people the right to rule and deny it to others. The founders did, however, believe that the "best" people should rule. Not everyone has the moral and intellectual qualities necessary for political leadership. The electoral process was designed to put these individuals in the nation's top political positions. Yet no one could claim a *right* to rule based on personal qualities or social position. The people were completely free to choose their own leaders.

Regular Elections "Consent of the governed" was to be expressed through regular elections. But the right to vote went only so far. For one thing, the states could pass their own voting laws. For another, only members of the House of Representatives were directly elected by citizens. Senators were chosen by the state legislatures (until 1913, when the Seventeenth Amendment to the Constitution was ratified). The President and Vice-President were elected in an even more indirect way: They were chosen by the Electoral College, which, in turn, was appointed by the state legislatures. And of course all judges were appointed, not elected.

Yet elections played a major role in the development of representative government. Regular elections mean that leaders serve for a limited time. At the end of that time they must face the group that gave them power in the first place (that is, the people or an agency chosen by the people). This, according to *The Federalist* (No. 57), creates in political leaders an "habitual recollection of their dependence in the people."

Representative Government Today we think of representative government as a compromise between "perfect" democracy, in which people participate directly in making the laws that govern them, and the realities of huge, complex nations in which such direct participation is impossible. In a representative government a selected group of people meet and decide on the issues facing the nation, but they always keep in mind the wishes of those whom they represent, namely, the people. Figure 2.2 is a diagram of this view.

What the nation's founders had in mind, however, was quite different. Because they feared arbitrary rule, they believed that those in power must be kept from abusing that power. Representative government was not a compromise with a commitment to democracy; rather, it was a cautious move away from the tradition of hereditary rule. Compare Figure 2.3 with Figure 2.2 and you will see how different these two views are.

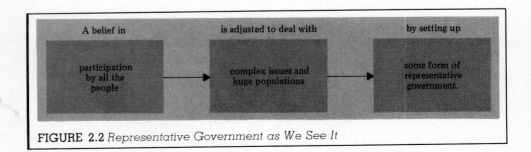

FIGURE 2.2 *Representative Government as We See It*

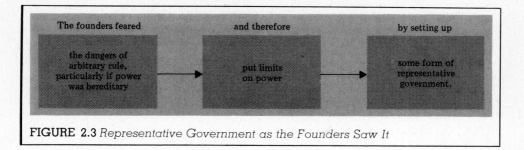

FIGURE 2.3 *Representative Government as the Founders Saw It*

This point can also be looked at from another angle. Today we think of representative government as a means by which the people can express their preferences on political issues. The founders, by contrast, saw it as a way of *limiting* the influence of the people. Elected representatives would be wiser and more cautious than the general public. In Madison's words, representative government would "refine and enlarge the public views by passing them through the medium of a chosen body of citizens."

Division of Power

In addition to external checks on those in authority, the founders designed a system of internal checks in which those in authority restrained one another. This was accomplished by the division of power *within* the government.

Federalism To begin with, power was divided between the layers of government: Some went to the national government, some to the states. This was a brilliant piece of political engineering because it served two seemingly contradictory purposes. The first of these was the creation of a strong, effective central government. Nothing less would guarantee social order, pay the public debt, and make it possible to develop the country's resources. But it was also necessary for the state governments to remain independent, since this would act as a check on the central government. Out of the tension between these two goals grew the federal system, which we will describe in detail in Chapter 15.

Separation of Powers In addition to being divided between the *layers* of government, power was divided across three different *branches* of government—legislative, executive, and judicial. This was done for three reasons.

First, the powers of government would be fragmented. According to *The Federalist* (No. 51),

> In the compound Republic of America, the power surrendered by the people is first divided between two distinct governments (Federal government and the States), and then the portion allotted to each subdivided among distinct

and separate departments. Hence, a double security rises to the rights of the people. The different governments will control each other, at the same time that each will be controlled by itself.

Second, each branch of the government would be able to check the actions of the other two branches using the *system of checks and balances* built into the Constitution. Congress passes laws—but the President can veto those laws. The President appoints judges—but those appointments must be confirmed by the Senate. Judges serve for life—unless they are removed by Congress for misconduct in office. So it goes throughout the federal government, and every state government as well.

The third reason for the separation of powers is that under such conditions various units of government must cooperate to reach common goals. As a result government policy reflects a wider range of interests; moreover, the blending of different interests should lead to better policies. In addition, each unit of government must make a greater effort to communicate with others.

Limited Government

As mentioned earlier, one of the main concerns of the nation's founders was to create a government with enough authority to govern, but one that would not interfere with individual freedom. Friedrich Hayek's definition of liberty comes close to what the founders wanted to achieve. Hayek writes that liberty is "that condition of man in which coercion of some by others is reduced as much as possible in society."[2] The writers of the Constitution tried to guard against coercion in various ways.

The Bill of Rights   The Bill of Rights, the first ten amendments to the Constitution, protects the rights of the individual citizen. The government cannot deny citizens the right to practice the religion of their choice, to say and write what they please, to assemble for political purposes, and to bear arms. It cannot take life, liberty, or property without due process of law, which includes the right to a speedy, public, and fair trial and in some cases to a trial by jury.

"Government of Laws"   Another important protection against coercion is *constitutionalism*—"government of laws, not of men." There is a basic law, the Constitution, against which all other laws should be measured. Since it is based on the consent of the governed, all lesser laws should have the same basis. The basic law as well as lesser laws regulate the operation of govern-

---

[2] Quoted in the *New York Times,* 21 September, 1977.

The courts offer citizens the means to check arbitrary government.

ment. No one is "a law unto himself" or may "stand above the law," not even the President of the United States.

The Court System The court system provides a way of testing the constitutional character of the government. A citizen who has been hurt by an act of the government can challenge that act in court; the government must show that its act was authorized by law. A police officer cannot arrest a citizen for no reason; the officer must be able to show that the arrest has a legal basis. Welfare officials cannot refuse to issue checks to people whose hair styles they dislike; they must be prepared to show in court that any applicant who is denied welfare is not entitled to it by law. Thus in principle, if not always in practice, the courts offer citizens a means of checking arbitrary actions by the government.

But the courts play an even more important role in American politics. Even if a government official can show that he or she has acted in accordance with a local, state, or national law, that action can still be reversed if the court rules that the *law itself* is unconstitutional. In this way the judicial branch of the government can limit the activities of the legislative and executive branches. Only an amendment to the Constitution can reverse the Supreme Court's interpretation of the Constitution (though the Court can reverse its own decisions).

A FLEXIBLE CONSTITUTION

Early in this chapter we asked, How has the Constitution survived two centuries of growth and change? Part of the answer is that the Constitution was and is a political document, and at least some of the political conflicts of the 1780s are still with us. A document that was workable then must therefore remain workable today. Another part of the answer is that the principles of representative government, division of power, and limited government are as attractive today as they were 200 years ago. The only serious challenge to the U.S. Constitution was the attempt by the Confederacy to secede from the Union, an attempt that failed.

More important than these partial answers, however, is the flexibility of the Constitution. "The Constitution belongs to the living and not to the dead," Jefferson wrote. "As new discoveries are made, new truths disclosed, and manners and opinions changed . . . institutions must advance also, and keep pace with the times." The Constitution has kept pace with the times— if it had not, it would have been abandoned long ago. Three factors have made the Constitution flexible: (1) its language, (2) its silences, and (3) the amendment process.

The Language of the Constitution   The Constitution seems purposely ambiguous in places. This ambiguity has allowed later generations to interpret it in various ways to meet their needs. For example, the Constitution neither states nor denies the power of the Supreme Court to declare acts of Congress unconstitutional, but the Supreme Court soon ruled that it did have this power. The President's executive power is not clearly spelled out in the Constitution either, but the tremendous growth of the federal bureaucracy has been justified by the statement that the President "shall take care that the laws be faithfully executed."

In addition to being ambiguous at times, the Constitution uses language that allows new meanings to be given to old words. For example, the Fourth

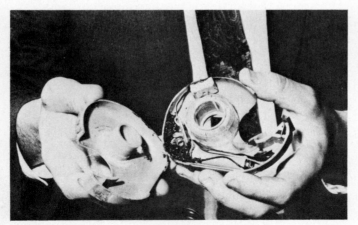

The language of the Fourth Amendment, prohibiting unreasonable searches, is used to challenge the use of hidden microphones.

Amendment states that "the right of the people to be secure in their persons, houses, papers, and effects, against unreasonable searches and seizures, shall not be violated." What the writers of the Constitution had in mind was the way colonial officers searched private homes at will, but the amendment uses such general language that it can still be applied today. The right of government agents to use wiretaps, hidden microphones, and the like has been challenged on the basis of the Fourth Amendment's ban on unreasonable searches.

Constitutional Silences A good example of a constitutional silence is the matter of political parties. The Constitution does not mention parties, yet who could imagine American politics without parties of some sort? All major elected officials, and most appointed ones, are backed by a political party. The parties do most of the work of organizing and managing elections, including primaries and nominating conventions. This takes place outside the framework of the Constitution—indeed, largely outside any type of federal law.

The Amendment Process The nation's founders knew that changes in American society would require changes in the Constitution, so they provided for a formal amendment process. This is a two-step process—proposing an amendment and then ratifying it—and it is somewhat complicated because there are two ways of proposing amendments and two ways of ratifying them. An amendment is usually proposed by a two-thirds vote in both the Senate and the House of Representatives. It is ratified when the legislatures of three-fourths of the states vote in favor of the amendment. Amendments may also be proposed by a special convention called by Congress at the request of two-thirds of the state legislatures. This has never happened. And they may be ratified by special conventions in three-fourths of the states. This has happened only once—in the case of the Twenty-first Amendment, which repealed Prohibition.

Besides the Bill of Rights, only 16 amendments have been passed since the Constitution went into effect. Among them are the famous "Civil War Amendments": the Thirteenth, which outlawed slavery; the Fourteenth, which defined national citizenship and limited state interference with equal protection and due process; and the Fifteenth, which gave the right to vote to all men regardless of race, color, or prior servitude. Other amendments have provided for direct election of senators, given women the right to vote, repealed the poll tax, and lowered the voting age to 18. One of the most important amendments, the Sixteenth, authorized the income tax. The proposed Twenty-seventh Amendment, known as the Equal Rights Amendment, would require equal treatment of males and females.

Types of Constitutional Change

The genius of the Constitution is also its weakness. A document that divides power among different political institutions will sooner or later be caught in a squeeze when the interests of those institutions clash. Four types of conflicts have led to constitutional change: (1) conflicts between the federal and state governments, (2) conflicts over the authority of a particular branch of the government, (3) conflicts over the separation of powers, and (4) conflicts over the rights of citizenship.

Conflicts Between the Federal and State Governments   In Chapter 15 we will see how easy it is for conflicts to arise over which level of government is responsible for what. The Civil War was fought over this question, but it did not put an end to conflicts between different levels of government. The principle of federalism is still being tested today.

Conflicts over Governmental Authority   Many of the problems that the government has faced during the past 200 years have been handled within the framework of the Constitution. But some of those problems have been so new and so complicated that they could be solved only by a shift in the interpretation of the Constitution. Sometimes the courts have been willing to do this; sometimes they have not. For example, the Great Depression of the 1930s seemed to call for action by the government to get the economy rolling again. However, the Supreme Court declared several new laws unconstitutional, claiming that Congress and the President were trying to increase their authority in illegal ways. At other times the Court itself has stimulated constitutional change. Thus citizenship rights and liberties were greatly expanded in a series of Court decisions in the 1950s and 1960s.

Conflicts over the Separation of Powers   As we have seen, the writers of the Constitution designed a government in which each branch would be able to keep the others in their proper place. This situation has led to many conflicts between the Presidency and Congress, between Congress and the courts, or between the courts and the Presidency. Most of these disputes have been settled without major constitutional change, but the Watergate affair, in which Richard Nixon was forced to resign from the Presidency, was a significant separation-of-powers conflict. It will be discussed in detail in Chapter 11.

Conflicts over the Rights of Citizenship   The hardest test of the Constitution has been the problem of defining what is meant by equal citizenship, both in principle and in practice. In later chapters we will see how the principle of equal citizenship has been transformed over the years since the nation's founding. This has been a long and often painful process. Today we face an entirely new issue: Should the results of past discrimination and inequality be corrected through affirmative action? How well the Constitution guides us through the complexities of affirmative action is discussed at several points in the text.

CONCLUSION: LIMITED GOVERNMENT VERSUS THE ACTIVIST STATE

A continuing tension in American political life focuses on the size of government. How much of the nation's resources should be in the public sector, and how much left to the private sector? How active should government be in solving social problems such as pollution, unemployment, racial conflict, urban decay, and energy shortages? Is there too much, or not enough, regulation of airline safety, potentially harmful food additives, unsafe working conditions, industry-caused water pollution, and similar risks to society? Do Americans want a government big enough to solve major social problems and protect against most social risks?

The Constitution is a weapon in the hands of those interests that would further expand government and those that would place restrictions on government. As we enter the 1980s there is debate over a constitutional amendment that would require the government to operate with a balanced budget. On one side are those who feel that the best way to control the growth of government is to control the amount of money it can raise through taxes. The most effective way to limit the taxing power of government is to require that it operate with a balanced budget or at least work within a budget that grows no faster than the economy as a whole. On the other side are those who feel that such an artificial limit on government would hamper the ability of society to defend itself and to deal with pressing social issues.

Echoes of this political debate appear throughout our text. What is interesting to observe here is that the Constitution itself, a document nearly 200 years old, is at the center of the debate. When a basic conflict over whether to limit the size of government is the issue, the fundamental rules of the society will be called into play. In the United States, this necessarily involves a Constitutional debate.

The Structure of the U.S. Government

What Is the Basis of the General Structure of the Government?

The general structure of the U.S. government is based on the Constitution, especially the principles of federalism and separation of powers. In the federal system the powers of government are divided between the central, or federal, government and the states. Then the authority given to the central government is divided among three separate branches: legislative, executive, and judicial. (See Figure 2.4.)

What Are the Agencies and Institutions of the Government?

Legislative. Laws are made by a Congress that consists of two houses, the Senate and the House of Representatives. The Senate has 100 members (2 from each state) and the House 435 (with the number from each state based on its population). The Constitution does not say how Congress is to be organized, but both houses have chosen a committee system.

Executive. Laws are to be carried out by the President; no other executive unit is called for in the Constitution. However, an enormous bureaucracy has grown up around the President. The Executive Office serves the President's managerial needs and includes the White House Office, the Office of Management and Budget, and the National Security Council. The executive branch also includes the 12 Cabinet departments (State, Defense, Treasury, and so forth). In addition, there are a number of independent government agencies of two general types: independent executive agencies and government corporations (such as the CIA and the U.S. Postal Service) and independent regulatory commissions (such as the Interstate Commerce Commission and the Federal Power Commission). These agencies are formally part of the executive branch, but they are independent of the President.

Judicial. The Constitution gives judicial power to the Supreme Court and any lower courts established by Congress. Over the years Congress has created a system of lower federal courts that includes the U.S. circuit courts of appeals and the U.S. district courts.

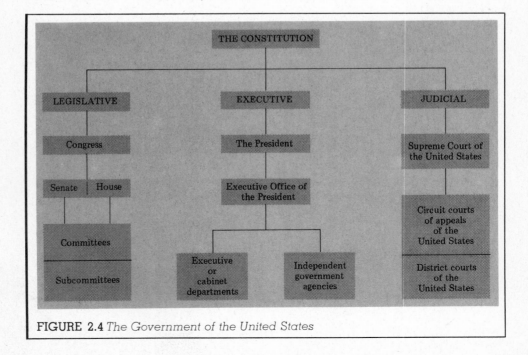

FIGURE 2.4 The Government of the United States

The American Economy
and Political Life

Why do we include a chapter about economics in a book on American government? This is a fair question, and it deserves an answer. The answer has two parts.

First, the things the government does are largely economic, as may be seen in the following recent headlines:

Energy Program to Cost Taxpayers Billions

Labor Department Acts to Head off Coal Strike

Federal Program for Unemployment Provides City Jobs

Government Investigates Soaring Prices

Balance-the-Budget Amendment Debated in Congress

Each of these headlines refers to an *economic* issue or problem, and each refers to a *governmental* action or program.

Here are some more headlines:

Parents of College Students Demand Tax Relief

Taxpayer Revolt Predicted If Social Security Taxes Increased

Auto Workers Support Congressmen Who Promise Higher Tariffs on Foreign Cars

Defense Plant Employees out of Work, Claim Unemployment

Again we see the connection between economics and politics: In each of these headlines a citizen's *economic* role—as worker, taxpayer, or consumer—leads to a *political* act.

The second reason for including a chapter on economics is that any book about American government is a book about *power:* who has it and how it is used. We have already discussed the growth of the government's power. This growth has not gone unnoticed by the groups that might benefit or be hurt by the way that power is used. This is especially true of economic interests. Indeed, we may go further and say that the power of wealth—of large corporations and private property—is not too different from the power of government. In the United States there are not two distinct sources of power, one economic and one political, struggling against each other. Rather, there is an active partnership between powerful economic and political institutions.

In short, there is no way to separate politics from economics, and no way to describe the powers of government without describing important aspects of our capitalist economy.

WHAT IS ECONOMICS?

Economics is the study of how a society chooses to use scarce resources such as land, labor, and capital to produce various goods and to distribute those goods, now and in the years ahead, among the society's members. This definition suggests some difficult questions. For example, how should resources be used? (Should limited oil supplies be used to heat homes or keep gasoline prices down?) How much should be used to meet current needs and how much to meet long-term goals? (Should a Gary, Indiana factory be closed down, putting some people out of work, or should it be allowed to go on operating even though it is helping to pollute Lake Michigan?) And how should goods be distributed among the many groups in society? (Should the government provide free medical care for the elderly or spend the money on research on children's diseases?)

Behind all of these questions is the toughest question of all: Who will make the decisions about the use of limited resources, the balance between current needs and long-term goals, and the distribution of goods in society? Should these decisions be made by the government?

Until fairly recently it was out of the question for the government to make economic decisions. The American economy was based on the principle of free enterprise—in other words, the government was expected to stay out of economic affairs. A healthy, growing economy should result from the free interplay of workers and owners, sellers and buyers, producers and consumers.

Things never quite worked out in practice the way they were supposed to in principle. In fact from the very beginning the government was called upon to perform certain economic functions, and its economic role has expanded steadily ever since. We will discuss the government's involvement in the economy under the headings "A Supported Economy," "A Regulated Economy," and "A Managed Economy."

The government's growing economic role has not destroyed the free-enterprise system, however. Many important aspects of capitalism remain, though they have been changed by government involvement. We will discuss those aspects under the heading "A Capitalist Economy." In so doing we will try to show that while the government plays a major role in the economy it does not actually control the economy.

A SUPPORTED ECONOMY

The American economy is supported by the government in at least three ways: (1) The government provides the legal framework of a free-enterprise economy; (2) it directly subsidizes many economic activities; and (3) it is a major consumer of goods and services.

The Legal Framework

Modern democracy began as a reform movement led by the European middle classes against the oppressive rule of kings and nobles. The special privileges and status of the nobility hampered the activities of merchants, traders, and craftsmen. These early "capitalists" knew that free enterprise depends on the right to enter contracts that are backed by law, to sell products and labor in a free market, and to use personal abilities to gain material goods and, thus, social advancement. Free enterprise cannot survive when the exchange of goods and labor is restricted and when social position is inherited.

In the process of freeing commerce and trade from arbitrary restrictions, the democratic reform movement gave rise to the principles of due process of law, protection from arbitrary arrest and unfair seizure of property, and the right to vote. As the reformers expected, a constitution that guaranteed these rights would also make possible a free-enterprise economy.

Thus the legal framework of a free-enterprise economy was fairly well established by 1800. It included a police force to protect private property, a court system to deal with contract violations, and a monetary system to provide the bills and coins used in economic exchanges. Today the government continues—on a larger scale—to provide the legal framework that allows a free-enterprise system to operate smoothly, at least most of the time.

Direct Subsidy

Direct support of private enterprise by the government is as old as the nation itself. Alexander Hamilton, the first Secretary of the Treasury, persuaded the new government to set up a national bank to stimulate commerce. "Industry is increased" in this way, he said; "commodities are multiplied, agriculture and manufacturers flourish; and herein consists the true wealth and prosperity of a state." Today federal-government subsidies amount to more than $100 billion a year. Every person or business, from Lockheed Aircraft Corporation to the sick and the hungry, has been subsidized in one way or another.

Government subsidies are of four major types:

1. *Cash Payments*. Medical-school scholarships are cash payments; so are government payments to support artists, move people off welfare and into jobs, or build airports.
2. *Tax Subsidies*. Tax subsidies do not involve actual transfers of cash. Instead, certain individuals or corporations pay a smaller tax than they would otherwise. A

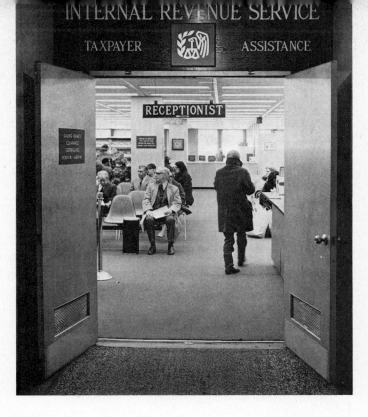

good example is the tax deduction on mortgage interest. Every homeowner who makes mortgage payments benefits from this subsidy. While the government does not actually spend anything on such subsidies, it pays for them by giving up potential tax revenues.

3. *Credit Subsidies*. In this type of subsidy the government makes loans at lower interest rates than those charged by banks or other lending agencies. Examples are student loans and loans by the Small Business Administration.

4. *Benefit-in-Kind Subsidies*. Food stamps and Medicare are examples of benefit-in-kind subsidies, in which a product or service is paid for by the government and provided to individuals.

The Government as Customer

A society's gross national product (GNP) is the total, in dollars, of all the goods, services, and investments produced by its land, labor, and capital. GNP is the yardstick that tells a society how well it is doing. When more goods are being produced (e.g., apples, tanks, and medicines), more services are available (e.g., health care and police protection), and more investments are being made (e.g., new factories and training programs), a society's GNP rises. When there is a slowdown in the production of goods, services, and investments, GNP falls.

    Government spending accounts for a large portion of GNP—in the case of the federal government, more than one-fifth. (See Figure 3.1.) A large percentage of the government's contribution to GNP is in the form of salaries—for the military; for teachers, judges, clerks; for the FBI and for medical researchers. But the government is also a consumer of goods produced by private industry—food for school lunches; typewriters, paper, cars; military hardware. Since World War II the U.S. government has become the largest single purchaser of American products and services.

    The government's role as a consumer is especially important to the industries that supply the military. Many of the nation's largest and most powerful corporations hold direct contracts with the Pentagon. Not only do these contracts involve huge amounts of money, but some corporations, such as General Dynamics and Lockheed Aircraft, depend on government contracts for almost all of their business. Yet direct defense contracts are only the tip of the iceberg. The companies that provide raw materials (e.g., aluminum and plastics) and manufactured parts (e.g., airplane tires and gaskets) also depend on the government's defense spending for much of their business.

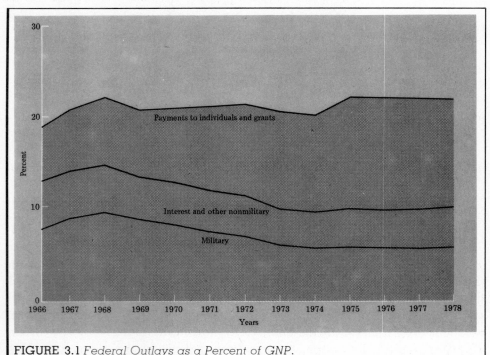

FIGURE 3.1 *Federal Outlays as a Percent of GNP.*
Source: *The Budget of the United States* (Washington, D.C.: U.S. Office of Management and Budget, 1966–1978).

The government is the single largest customer for American industrial products and goods, especially for those industries which supply the military.

In 1977 government expenditures at the local, state, and federal levels amounted to about $715.7 billion. This comes out to almost $10,000 for every household in the United States!

A REGULATED ECONOMY

Government regulation of the economy dates from the late nineteenth century. At that time a nation of farmers and traders was slowly being transformed into a nation of factory workers and industrialists. The country was crisscrossed by railroads. Canals and harbors were opened up. Factories began to mass-produce everything from shoes to stoves. The telegraph and then the telephone came into widespread use. American exports were shipped around the world.

This growth and change had some harmful effects, but the government took little notice of them. As mentioned earlier, it was expected to stay out of economic affairs. So it did not do very much for those who were hurt by an unregulated economy—small businesses forced out of the market by monopolies like Standard Oil, farmers gouged by the high prices charged by the railroads that shipped their crops, workers who worked long hours in unsafe and unsanitary factories for very little pay. Not only were judges and politicians unsympathetic to the idea of government regulation; they often owed their jobs to industrialists. In the words of Henry Adams, "Capitalists, seeking land grants, tariffs, bounties, favorable currency policies, freedom from regulatory legislation, and economic reform, supplied campaign funds, fees, and bribes and plied politicians with investment opportunities."[1] Few resisted the temptation.

Correcting the Flaws

It was not until the 1890s that various groups—angry farmers, middle-class reform groups, labor leaders—began to call for government regulation of the economy. They were not very successful, but they did create a political climate in which the flaws of a capitalist system, such as child labor, price fixing, shoddy merchandise, and unsafe working conditions, could be seen and corrected.

In addition, the industrialists themselves began to see the advantages of regulation. An unregulated economy was hard to manage. The federal government could bring some order to the economy if business could define the limits of governmental activity in this area. Regulation, therefore, was not a "triumph of small business over the trusts" but a "victory of big business in achieving the rationalization of the economy that only the government could provide."[2]

"Trust-Busting"

It is often claimed that the force behind the expansion of the U.S. economy was the small businessman. Not so. It was industrial corporations, not small businessmen, that put together the capital and the know-how to build railroads, cut timber, mine coal, drill for oil, invent new production techniques, and experiment with new products. The early "captains of industry" are remembered for their industrial empires: Rockefeller (oil), Carnegie (steel), Pillsbury (milling), Vanderbilt (railroads), Morgan (banking).

Sometimes a single company (e.g., Standard Oil of New Jersey) could monopolize a particular industry (e.g., oil), setting prices at will. No other company was big enough to compete. This situation was believed to be the source of the flaws that the late-nineteenth-century reformers wanted to correct. "Trust-busting" became a political slogan, and Supreme Court Justice

[1] Richard Hofstadter, *The American Political Tradition* (New York: Vintage, 1954), p. 170. The quotation from Henry Adams appears in this work as well, p. 107.
[2] Gabriel Kolko, *The Triumph of Conservatism* (New York: Quadrangle, 1967), p. 284.

Louis D. Brandeis warned of the danger of "industrial absolutism." Regulatory legislation was passed, including the Sherman Antitrust Act of 1890 and the Federal Trade Commission Act of 1914; in addition, laws were passed dealing with working conditions and hours of work, especially for women and children.

From Monopoly to Oligopoly

Today whenever a single corporation, such as IBM or ATT, takes over a large share of the market for its products, the Attorney General's office will investigate its activities and perhaps bring suit against it for violations of anti-trust law. But such actions cannot prevent a few corporations from gaining control of a particular part of the economy. This situation is called *oligopoly,* and an example is the automobile industry, which is dominated by three giant corporations—Ford, Chrysler, and General Motors.

Concentration of economic power and resources can occur even when there are many firms producing the same goods or service. For example, 33 of the 67,000 corporations in the utilities and communication industry control half of that industry's assets. Of the nearly 14,000 commercial banks in

It requires massive concentrations of capital resources to maintain technological growth.

the United States, the 50 largest control about half of all banking assets. Economic concentration is greatest in the key sectors of the economy—transportation, iron and steel production, banking, and communication. It has not been reduced by government regulation.

Regulation and Freedom

The relationship between government regulation and individual freedom is an important issue. Some people believe government regulation is stifling free enterprise. They point out that there are 77 different federal agencies that regulate some aspect of private activity. Other people believe that we live in a "dense society" in which every part is interdependent with every other part. In such a society a comfortable, civilized life is possible only if certain activities are regulated. The conflict between these two points of view will crop up several times in this book. It is one of the central issues of democracy.

A MANAGED ECONOMY

Regulating the economy is not the same thing as managing it. The purpose of regulation is to correct flaws in the economic system such as deceptive advertising or monopolistic business practices. It was not until the Great Depression of the 1930s that the government began trying to manage the economy.

Before the Depression, most U.S. economists believed that a capitalist system was self-adjusting. Full employment and stable prices would result if workers freely traded their labor for pay, if prices were regulated by supply and demand, and if the rate of investment was guided by profits. This view was challenged only by a few "radical" economists and business leaders, who claimed that capitalism is by nature unstable—that every "boom" is followed by a "bust."

During the 1930s, as unemployment rose, banks failed, and factories closed, many people began to doubt that the economy would straighten itself out. Government leaders began to pay attention to the ideas of John Maynard Keynes. Keynes believed that the government could use certain economic tools, such as taxes, government spending on public projects, and the money supply to stop the boom–bust cycle.

The government began to use these tools in the 1930s. In this way it became responsible for the health of the economy—for trying to keep unemployment at a low level while at the same time preventing prices from rising too fast. Thus, while the economy remains privately owned, it is increasingly being managed by the government.

This management has not been entirely successful, however. There are still business cycles, though they are less severe than in the past. In recent years unemployment has risen to levels well above what government economists consider "safe." At the same time inflation has become a major problem. Prices have been increasing by as much as 6 to 10 percent a year, much faster than wages. The dollar is buying less and less. Responding to the demand that it "do something," the government has tried various things— even wage and price controls—but so far nothing has worked. Carter made the fight on inflation a major part of his program in 1979.

Whether it succeeds or not, the fact that the government is trying to manage the economy represents a major change in attitude. In 1929, when the stock market closed and many banks failed, J. P. Morgan, the nation's leading banker, called a meeting in New York City of major bankers and financiers. They issued a statement saying that *they* would solve the problem. Few people thought of an economic crisis as something for the government to deal with. Today, on the other hand, we look to government leaders to solve economic problems. The responsibility for managing the economy has shifted from Wall Street to the White House.

A Planned Economy?

The question of whether the economy should be planned by the government has been a subject of political debate since the 1930s. On one side of the debate is the argument that planning is necessary. Various industries should have production targets; prices and wages should be based on long-range planning. In an unplanned economy there is too much wasted effort and too much risk of boom–bust cycles. On the other side of the debate is the argument that government planning would discourage investment, destroy initiative, and create so much government bureaucracy that individual freedom would be threatened.

Specific plans can be found throughout the economy, but they are limited to particular goals. The Ford Motor Company may have a detailed plan for the introduction of a new car. This plan takes many factors into consideration. For example, the company cannot afford to spend millions of dollars designing, testing, and then mass-producing a car that does not meet federal safety standards. It must know what those standards are as much as five years in advance. At this level, then, there is a lot of planning by both government and industry.

The government has not yet tried to plan at a more general level, though during the 1970s people started talking about creating an economic planning agency. Such an agency would coordinate all the activities of the government that affect the economy: taxation, the federal budget, the money supply, energy policy, international trade policy, and so on. If such an agency was formed, the connection between economics and politics would become stronger than ever before.

A CAPITALIST ECONOMY

If the government supports, regulates, and manages the economy, is the United States still a capitalist society? In answering this question we will touch on three aspects of capitalism: (1) private ownership, (2) individual choice, and (3) material incentives.

Private Ownership

The nation's founders believed that the job of government is to protect life, liberty, and property. Citizens own property, and the government must make sure citizens can buy, use, and sell property as they choose. This idea is as important today as it was 200 years ago. What has changed is not the principle of private ownership but the kind of property that is privately owned.

In the nation's early years the most valuable form of property was land. While land is still valued, many other forms of property have become equally important. This is especially true of natural resources and the processes by which those resources are transformed into consumer goods.

In the United States, natural resources, production processes, patents, means of transportation, and the like are privately owned. They are used in such a way as to earn a profit for their owners. In this sense the American economy is still a capitalist economy.

In this sense, also, the United States is unusual. We expect that in socialist nations such as the Soviet Union or East Germany much of the economy is

Natural resources, though often developed with government assistance, remain under private ownership in the United States.

owned by the state. But it is easy to forget that even in Western democracies such as France or Great Britain many economic enterprises are publicly owned. Take airlines, for example. Germany, France, Britain, and Canada all have government-owned airlines; the United States does not. Consider utilities: Gas and electricity are wholly state owned in Germany, France, and Britain and 80 percent state owned in Canada. In the United States they are almost entirely privately owned.

Americans tend to resist the idea of public ownership of major businesses. The railroads are a good example. In recent years they have been operating at a loss, especially in the Northeast. In a free-enterprise system a business that cannot make a profit usually closes its doors. But if the product of that business is a collective good such as rail transportation, closing down the business would be harmful to society. In most countries a bankrupt transportation system would be taken over by the government—unless it was state owned in the first place. But in the United States a government agency, the U.S. Railway System, was formed to restructure rail service in 17 states. In 1975 this agency announced a long-term recovery plan that would cost $7 billion. The new rail system will be managed by a private corporation with the aid of large amounts of federal money.

Individual Choice

We live in a society in which many economic activities result from thousands and even millions of uncoordinated individual decisions. Think about New York City, where 8 million people live and thousands more come to work each day. How are all those people fed? Obviously they do not grow their own crops or fatten their own livestock. Instead, they depend on the supply of food that pours into the city each day from 50 states and dozens of foreign countries: milk from Wisconsin, beef from Iowa, cheese from France, coffee from Brazil.

The process that puts food on the tables of New Yorkers depends on a huge network of food producers and processors, packagers and transporters, marketers and sellers. This network functions without being directed or coordinated by any central agency. It is a result of millions of individual economic activities.

If an economy is capitalist when it allows citizens to choose what they will buy, what jobs they will seek, how much they will save, and so on, then the American economy is capitalist. The feeding of New Yorkers is only one of many examples showing that much of our nation's economic life does not depend on either governmental or corporate decisions. True, there are a variety of ways in which the government and big business control economic activities, but it would be unrealistic to ignore the role of individual choice.

Material Incentives

It is generally agreed that people will work only if they are given suitable rewards. If they are not rewarded, they will not work, or at least they will work less. What are those rewards? In a capitalist society the reward is money. A person's worth is measured by what he or she can earn. A shop foreman earns twice what an assembly line worker earns because the foreman's job requires more experience, skill, and responsibility. The factory owner earns several times what a foreman does because the owner took the risk and created the business.

The use of unequal wages to get talented people to do certain jobs, and to encourage them to work hard, is basic to capitalism. Most Americans support this principle. They believe that initiative and hard work should be rewarded and that laziness and incompetence should be punished. As we will see in the next chapter, this leads to huge differences in income—though it should be recognized that those differences are not due only to differences in talent and effort.

THE ECONOMY AND THE GOVERNMENT

Two facts are now clear. First, the government is heavily involved in economic affairs. It supports private enterprise, regulates economic activities, and tries to manage general economic conditions. Second, our system is still a capitalist one. Private citizens, often organized as corporations, own the mines, trucks, chemicals, factories, and land of America. These assets are used to make a profit for their owners. Thus on the one hand we have a government that intervenes in the economy, while on the other hand we have huge privately owned corporations that can be influenced, for better or worse, by the activities of the government. What is the outcome of this situation?

Most writers on capitalism today agree that the government and the economy form a partnership. This partnership includes not only corporations such as General Motors or Sears but also organized labor. It is held together by some important shared goals. Economist John Kenneth Galbraith describes the government's goals as follows: "The state is strongly concerned with the stability of the economy. And with its expansion or growth. And with education. And with technical and scientific advance. And, most notably, with the national defense."[3] Corporations and organized labor share these goals—stability is necessary for long-term planning; economic growth brings profits and promotions; training and research are required in a mod-

---

[3] John Kenneth Galbraith, *The New Industrial State* (Boston: Houghton Mifflin, 1967), p. 304.

ern industrial system; and, as we have seen, defense spending directly supports a large part of the economy.

Critics of the partnership between the economy and the government believe that it is making it difficult for citizens to control their own lives. Milton Friedman, who won a Nobel Prize for his studies in economics, calls freedom "a rare and delicate plant," one that must be carefully guarded. "Our minds tell us, and history confirms, that the great threat to freedom is the concentration of power," he writes. According to Friedman, the truly free person will ask, "How can we keep the government from becoming a Frankenstein that will destroy the very freedom we establish it to protect?"[4]

In this view it is concentration of power in the hands of the government that must be avoided. The government has developed into a huge bureaucracy because of its interference in the economy. If the economy were allowed to take care of itself, there would be less need for government bureaucracy—and less risk that the government would limit individual freedom.

Other critics are more concerned about the concentration of economic power. They point out that wealth can be converted into political control. If this is the case, it is hard to see how all citizens can have equal political influence, as they are supposed to in a democracy. Indeed, the Marxist economists Paul Baran and Paul Sweezy claim that the United States is *not* a democracy. In this country, they write, "the propertyless masses have never been in a position to determine the conditions of their lives or the policies of the nation's government." Instead, a tiny group "resting on vast economic power and in full control of society's political and cultural apparatus makes all the important political decisions. Clearly to claim that such a society is democratic serves to conceal, not to reveal, the truth."[5]

The fears of these critics seem to be supported by the evidence. For example, Friedman's concern over the threat to individual liberty is supported by the sheer size of the government bureaucracy and the number of government regulations that affect the lives of citizens. Baran and Sweezy's claim that the political system is controlled by the wealthy class of owners and managers is supported by evidence showing how economic inequality affects political participation and recruitment and by the role of interest groups in the policy-making process. We will discuss this evidence at several points in this book.

On the other side of the debate over modern capitalism are those who believe that the partnership between the government and the economy is healthy. In this view the government, giant corporations, and organized labor have joined forces to achieve desirable goals: a steady growth in production, higher standards of living, larger world markets for American prod-

---

[4] Milton Friedman, *Capitalism and Freedom* (Chicago: University of Chicago Press, 1962), p. 2.
[5] Paul A. Baran and Paul M. Sweezy, *Monopoly Capital: An Essay on the American Economic and Social Order* (London: Pelican, 1968), p. 327.

ucts, and continual improvement in public education. Those who take this view are aware of the problems of poverty, unemployment, and inflation, but they think the best way to solve these problems is to strengthen rather than weaken the partnership between the government and the economy.

CONCLUSION

The picture of the American economy that we have presented in this chapter is the context within which we will study many aspects of American politics. In the next chapter, for example, we will look more closely at the tension between citizenship equality and economic inequality, and in later chapters we will see how political participation and the choice of political leaders are affected by economic inequality.

The economy is also the context for many political conflicts. For example, interest groups compete for federal money—a truckers' association may want more money spent on the federal highway program, while a citizen action group wants the money to be spent for improvements in mass transit. Thus the making of public policy is closely linked with the economy.

It is safe to conclude from our discussion of the connection between politics and the economy that neither government nor business can exist without the other. The government must provide the legal framework in which businesses operate. It provides the currency used in economic exchanges, the police force that protects private property, and the courts that hold people to their contracts. Yet the government could not operate without the support and cooperation of business. Businesses pay taxes, which are used to pay government salaries and fund government programs. They produce the goods and services desired by citizens and provide jobs for those citizens. If they did not provide these things, the government would face a lot more political and social unrest than it does now.

The most important job of government, therefore, may be to keep the economy healthy. Both Democrats and Republicans understand this. Political leaders are blamed when jobs are scarce and when prices increase faster than wages. So it is in the interest of those leaders to encourage economic growth and to listen to the demands of business.

Political Equality, Social Inequality

A basic principle of American democracy is political equality—"one person, one vote." At the same time, a capitalist economic system leads to economic and social inequality—"one person, one vote" does not translate into "one person, one dollar." In this chapter we will be concerned with the contradiction between political equality and social inequality and its effects on American society.

DEMOCRACY AND EQUALITY

"We hold these truths to be self-evident," says the Declaration of Independence, "that all men are created equal." The signers of the Declaration were not trying to say that everyone is equal in ability, intelligence, or ambition. They wanted to go on record against a political system in which members of society are *legally* unequal.

In this respect the nation's founders were making a bold break with the past. Traditionally members of society had been assigned to different legal classes with different rights and privileges. Only members of the nobility were allowed to hold positions of authority; the commoners or serfs were legally inferior. This system is known as *aristocracy,* or rule by the best. Its supporters justified it as follows:

> The lot of the poor, in all things which affect them collectively, should be regulated for them, not by them. They should not be required or encouraged to think for themselves, or give to their own reflection or forecast an influential voice in the determination of their destiny. It is the duty of the higher classes to think for them, and to take responsibility for their lot. . . . The rich should be [like parents] to the poor, guiding and restraining them like children.[1]

Democratic theory rejects the idea that people who are richer, more intelligent, or of nobler birth than others are somehow "better." It elbows aside the traditional beliefs that served as a basis for monarchies, aristocracies, class systems, and racial prejudice. True, the principle of equal worth is not completely accepted even today, and probably never will be. But it is deeply rooted in Western political systems: In those systems all citizens are *legally* equal.

LEGAL CITIZENSHIP

Early American history was dominated by constitutional issues. These included the definition of citizenship rights and the grantings of those rights to

---

[1] John Stuart Mill, *Principles of Political Economy, II* (Boston: Little, Brown, 1848), pp. 319–320. Here Mill is summarizing the aristocratic viewpoint, not endorsing it.

One person, one vote does not produce one person, one dollar.

the entire population. Legal citizenship, or *civil rights,* includes the basic freedoms of speech, religion, and assembly. It also includes economic rights, especially the right to buy and sell property, to choose one's place and type of work, and to enter into contracts knowing that they will be upheld by the courts.

The courts are central to legal citizenship. Under the principle of *due process of law* a citizen is innocent until proved guilty. He or she has the right to be tried by a jury of fellow citizens and may not be kept in jail unless there is reasonable evidence of guilt. Due process also includes the right to legal counsel and the protection against self-incrimination (a citizen cannot be forced to testify against himself or herself), as well as the right to question witnesses and the protection against unreasonable searches (e.g., telephone taps).

POLITICAL CITIZENSHIP

A second major form of citizenship is political participation. According to democratic theory, all members of society have an equal right to participate in choosing their rulers. This is what is meant by "the consent of the governed." The principle of equal political citizenship is stated in *The Federalist* (No. 57):

> *Who are to be the electors of the federal representatives?*
> Not the rich, more than the poor; not the learned, more than the ignorant; not the haughty heirs of distinguished names, more than the humble sons of obscurity and unpropitious fortune. The electors are to be the great body of the people of the United States.

Despite the founders' emphasis on equal participation, the Constitution they wrote placed many barriers between the voter and the government. For one thing, it did not actually guarantee the right to vote. For another, it provided for direct election only in the case of representatives. Senators were to be chosen by the state legislatures, and the President by the Electoral College. Supreme Court justices were to be appointed, not elected.

Moreover, the Constitution did not answer the question of who may vote and under what conditions. It has taken four amendments to do this.

The Growth of Voting Rights

At first the Constitution left voting laws to the states. People who could not vote in state elections could not vote in federal elections. Most states restricted the vote to white male property owners; in some states only about 10 percent of the white males could vote. However, during the Presidency of Andrew Jackson (1829–1837) most property standards were dropped. In this respect America served as a model for the democratic world. It was 50 years before Britain followed its example.

Still, as Figure 4.1 shows, less than 40 percent of the adult population could vote at the time of the Civil War. Blacks were forbidden to vote in the South and generally unable to vote in the North. After the Civil War the Fifteenth Amendment was passed, stating that "the right of citizens of the United States to vote shall not be denied or abridged by the United States or by any State on account of race, color, or previous condition of servitude." But when white southerners regained control of their state governments, they made it impossible for blacks to vote by requiring them to pay a poll tax or pass a phony literacy test, as well as using outright violence to prevent them from registering to vote.

During the late 1800s new states were added to the Union and large numbers of immigrants came from foreign countries. The number of voters grew rapidly. But although blacks could vote in some areas and women were gaining the right to vote a little at a time, in the early twentieth century most voters were white males.

The next step was the addition of women to the voting public. In the

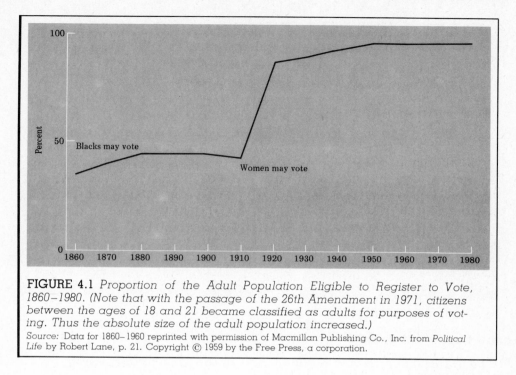

FIGURE 4.1 *Proportion of the Adult Population Eligible to Register to Vote, 1860–1980. (Note that with the passage of the 26th Amendment in 1971, citizens between the ages of 18 and 21 became classified as adults for purposes of voting. Thus the absolute size of the adult population increased.)*

Source: Data for 1860–1960 reprinted with permission of Macmillan Publishing Co., Inc. from *Political Life* by Robert Lane, p. 21. Copyright © 1959 by the Free Press, a corporation.

1800s several states, mostly in the West, had given women the right to vote. The drive for women's suffrage on a nationwide scale began in the early 1900s, led by Susan B. Anthony and Elizabeth Cady Stanton. In 1917 the "suffragettes" began marching in front of the White House; they were arrested and jailed. But they triumphed in 1920 with the ratification of the Nineteenth Amendment, which states that the right to vote cannot be denied on account of sex.

In recent years the government has acted to remove the barriers to voting that have been set up in certain areas. In 1964 the Twenty-fourth Amendment banned the use of poll taxes in federal elections, and the Voting Rights Act of 1965 did the same for state elections. This act also gave federal examiners the power to register voters. The effect of this legislation was dramatic: Between 1964 and 1970 black voter registration in the southern states increased by over 50 percent.

In 1970 Congress expanded the Voting Rights Act to forbid the use of literacy and character tests as a requirement for voting. It also set a residency requirement of 30 days for voting in federal elections. In 1971, with the ratification of the Twenty-sixth Amendment, the voting age was lowered to 18, adding about 10.5 million people to the voting public.

Second-Class Citizenship

The history of citizenship rights starts with the principle that all citizens are to be treated equally. There is to be no such thing as first- and second-class citizenship, with first-class citizens having rights and privileges that are denied to second-class citizens. This principle has not always held up in practice, however. Blacks and other minority groups, as well as women of all races, have found that their legal and political rights are not equal to those of white males.

Blacks Slavery—which amounts to the denial of citizenship—was protected by law until after the Civil War, and of course in the eighteenth century most American blacks were slaves. Slaves could not say what they wanted to say or be with people they wanted to be with. They could not sell their labor or enter into contracts. Despite the promises of the Declaration of Independence, the Constitution gave one group of people rights and privileges that were denied to another group.

The legal separation of slaves from free people was not intended to separate blacks from whites. Prior to the Civil War period nearly 100,000 blacks had obtained their freedom and lived in the North and West much like other citizens. They paid taxes, voted, and in a few cases even held public office. But in 1857, in the Dred Scott case, the Supreme Court ruled that blacks, free or slave, "had no rights which the white man was bound to respect."

Long after the Civil War had officially ended slavery, blacks continued to be treated as second-class citizens. The Fourteenth Amendment declared that "all persons born or naturalized in the United States, and subject to the jurisdiction thereof, are citizens of the United States. . . . No state shall make or enforce any law which shall abridge the privileges or immunities of citizens." However, the meaning of this amendment was changed by later court decisions and blocked by "Jim Crow" laws.

Jim Crow laws separated blacks from whites. They applied to "waiting rooms, theaters, boardinghouses, water fountains, ticket windows, street-cars, penitentiaries, county jails, convict camps, institutions for the blind and deaf, and hospitals for the insane,"[2] as well as to schools, businesses, clubs, churches, and the armed forces. The facilities provided for blacks were always inferior to those provided for whites, though equal prices had to be paid for the unequal services.

Racism was even backed by the Supreme Court. In *Plessy* v. *Ferguson* (1896), Justice Brown remarked that "if one race be inferior to another socially, the Constitution of the United States cannot put them upon the same plane." So much for the Fourteenth Amendment! This decision, which expressed the "separate but equal doctrine," remained in force until 1954. In later chapters we will describe the long, slow process by which this doctrine was reversed.

Women The proposed Equal Rights Amendment (ERA), which will become the Twenty-seventh Amendment to the Constitution if it is ratified, states that "equality of rights under the law shall not be denied or abridged by the United States or by any state on account of sex." Two hundred years after the Declaration of Independence, women are trying to gain the same rights as men.

Women have long been second-class citizens. They were not allowed to vote until 1920. Certain government jobs, especially in the military, were reserved for men until quite recently. Women have been discriminated against in property ownership, in employment, and in the terms of marriage and divorce. In addition, women face many informal barriers. For example, they are paid less than men, even for doing the same work, and they find it hard to reach high positions. (Very few women are doctors, directors or officers of large corporations, or members of Congress.)

ERA is only one of many legal and political challenges to second-class citizenship for women. In 1978 over 100 bills and resolutions were introduced in Congress that, if passed, would affect women's rights. Under the Pregnancy Disability Act, for example, employers would have to cover pregnant workers under health insurance and temporary-disability plans.

---

[2] Commission on Civil Rights, 1963.

Other bills call for improvement of day care facilities and for more flexible work hours for working mothers with small children.

One of the most hotly debated questions in the area of women's rights is the issue of abortion. In the past ten years legal barriers against abortion have gradually been removed, but economic barriers remain. In the mid-1970s as many as 300,000 women a year were having abortions that were paid for with medicaid funds. However, in 1977, under pressure from "right to life" groups, the Supreme Court considered this issue and ruled that neither the Constitution nor federal law requires states to use federal funds to pay for abortions. Nor are public hospitals required to provide abortions. In short, women can have abortions, but the taxpayer is not required to pay for them.

Minors In 1971, after a series of racial demonstrations, nine students were suspended from high schools in Columbus, Ohio without formal hearings. The students challenged this action, claiming that they were deprived of liberty and property (their legal right to an education) without due process of law, in violation of the Fourteenth Amendment.

The case reached the Supreme Court in 1975, and in a five to four decision the Court ruled in favor of the students.[3] It held that public schools cannot suspend students without giving formal notice of the charges against them, explaining the evidence, and allowing the students to tell their side of the story. In other words, students had rights that could be upheld in federal courts.

Note that the Court did not give students full rights of due process. Suspended students cannot hire counsel, cross-examine witnesses, call their own witnesses, or be tried by a jury. However, the Court left open the possibility that more formal proceedings might be required if students are expelled or suspended for long periods.

Minors have always been "second-class" citizens in that they do not vote, cannot run for office, cannot enter contracts without their parents' permission, and so on. They also get special protection; for example, a minor convicted of a crime, even murder, is treated much less harshly than an adult convicted of the same crime. The issue of citizenship rights for minors is a new one, and it is too soon to know what the outcome will be. It is clear, however, that, just as there have been major changes in the citizenship rights of minority groups and women, there will be changes in the way minors are treated in the United States.

SOCIAL-RIGHTS CITIZENSHIP

The Constitution is concerned mainly with legal and political rights. It is generally assumed that if these rights are truly available to all members of society, then democracy will have kept its promise. Today, however, a third form of citizenship is demanding more attention than either of the others. This is social-rights citizenship.

President Roosevelt's 1944 State of the Union Address contained a new definition of citizenship. Roosevelt began on a familiar note: "The Republic," he said, "had its beginning and grew to its present strength, under the protection of certain unalienable political rights—among them the right of free speech, free press, free worship, trial by jury, freedom from unreasonable searches and seizures. They were our rights of life and liberty." But he went on to say,

> As our Nation has grown strong in size and stature, however—as our industrial economy has expanded—these political rights proved inadequate to assure us equality in the pursuit of happiness. . . . We have come to a clear realization of the fact that true individual freedom cannot exist without economic security and independence.

---

[3] *Goss* v. *Lopez,* 73-898 U.S. (1975).

Roosevelt was saying that the citizenship rights guaranteed by the Constitution were not enough. Other rights should be guaranteed as well, such as a useful job, decent housing, an adequate diet, medical care, education, and security against the threats of sickness, unemployment, and old age.

When Roosevelt used the word *right,* he was describing a new concept of citizenship that went far beyond due process of law. This theme was echoed by President Carter in 1978:

> While civil and political liberties are good in themselves, to have sufficient food to live and to work, to be adequately sheltered and clothed, to live in a healthy environment and to be healed when sick, to learn and be taught — these rights too must be the concerns of our Government.

In the modern social-welfare state the basic rights listed by Roosevelt are provided by direct governmental action. In the past 40 to 50 years there has been much action of this sort. The government programs in the area of social welfare include social security, unemployment insurance, urban renewal and housing, food stamps for the poor, medicare and medicaid, job training, and the welfare program. These programs are the subject of much debate and criticism, but today even their strongest critics accept the need for some form of welfare state.

Social-Rights Citizenship and the Market System In a traditional market system supply and demand are in balance, with prices based on what people are willing to pay. Those with more money can buy more and better goods and services than those with less money. This is one reason people are willing to work hard in order to earn more.

The idea of social-rights citizenship does not destroy the market system, but it certainly affects it. It separates social services from the price system. People who are strongly committed to a free-enterprise system do not like this. Medical care, housing, food, and even education have always been priced according to what the market will bear. Those who could pay the price got better medical care, housing, food, and education, while those who were "worth less" got less. Social-rights citizenship makes a decent standard of living a right rather than a privilege to be paid for, and the social benefits involved are provided by the government, not the market system.

Social-Rights Citizenship and Economic Inequality We might expect the idea of social-rights citizenship to affect economic inequality. The poor would use their political rights to manipulate the social-welfare system and thus reduce the great differences in wealth and income that exist in the United States. In reality, however, as we will see in the next section, there is as much economic inequality today as there was in Roosevelt's time. We then turn to the issue of political attempts to reduce inequality.

ECONOMIC INEQUALITY IN THE UNITED STATES

We mentioned earlier that one of the basic principles of capitalism is unequal economic rewards. In a capitalist system people sell their labor to the highest bidder. The more valuable their labor is, the more they can earn. Unequal rewards are viewed as fair: Talented, hardworking people should earn more than lazy, less talented people. Moreover, society needs a way of getting qualified people to do important jobs. Unequal rewards operate like a grading system—the most deserving get the "A's," the least deserving the "F's," and those in between the "B's," "C's," and "D's."

Distributive Justice

Capitalism tells us that economic inequality is fair, but it does not tell us how much inequality is necessary. Table 4.1 shows some of the higher salaries paid in our capitalist system. Is it "fair" for the chairman of General Motors to earn about 100 times as much as an assembly-line worker? Maybe he should earn only 50 times as much or 20 times as much; maybe he should earn 200 or 300 times as much. Whatever difference is "fair," is it really necessary to pay someone almost $1 million a year to be chairman of General Motors? Is it impossible to find a talented person to do that job for a half-million or even a quarter-million a year? These are the kinds of questions we ask when we talk about *distributive justice*.

In the next chapter we will see that different groups have different ideas about how much inequality is fair. Here we will get an idea of how much inequality there actually is in the distribution of wealth in the United States.

Income and Wealth

Income is the money people receive from various sources. Most income comes from wages and salaries, but people also have investments, such as

TABLE 4.1 Salaries and Bonuses of Leading Executives, 1977

Company	Name and Title	Amount
International Harvester	Archie R. McCardell, President	$1,076,666
Ford	Henry Ford II, Chairman	992,420
ITT	Harold S. Geneen, Chairman	986,054
General Motors	Thomas A. Murphy, Chairman	975,000
ABC	Leonard H. Goldenson, Chairman	750,000
Mobil	Rawleigh Warner, Jr., Chairman	724,610
ATT	John D. deButts, Chairman	721,763
IBM	Frank T. Cary, Chairman	669,845

SOURCE: Based on data in *U.S. News & World Report*, 12 June 1978.

Capitalism stresses the need for economic incentives but does not answer the questions of distributive justice—how much inequality is necessary or fair?

stocks and bonds, that provide them with income. The rent received by owners of apartment buildings and the like is also income. Income is what people report on their tax return each year; it is "How much I made."

Wealth is the value of the property that people own. A family's house, car, and furniture are included in its wealth. Also included is the market value of any stocks and bonds it owns. A farmer's wealth would include land, livestock, and equipment. Wealth is the amount of cash a family would have if it sold everything it owned; it is "How much I am worth."

How are income and wealth distributed in the United States? One way of

TABLE 4.2 Hypothetical Distributions of Income

PERFECT EQUALITY		SUBSTANTIAL INEQUALITY	
Population Ranked by Quintile	*Percent of Income Received*	*Population Ranked by Quintile*	*Percent of Income Received*
Highest	20%	Highest	60%
Next highest	20	Next highest	20
Middle	20	Middle	10
Next lowest	20	Next lowest	7
Lowest	20	Lowest	3
	100%		100%

getting a picture of the distribution of income and wealth is to think in terms of *quintiles*. A quintile is 20 percent of the population. If income is equal throughout the population, any 20 percent of the population will receive 20 percent of the total income earned, as in the left-hand side of Table 4.2. If income is distributed unequally, the top 20 percent will have earned most of the income and the rest of the population will receive much less, as in the right-hand side of Table 4.2.

Table 4.3 shows the actual distribution of income in the United States. Three things are clear:

1. The richest 20 percent of the families in the United States receive about 8 to 10 times as much income as the poorest 20 percent.
2. From 1930 to 1950 there was a marked drop in the percent of income received by

TABLE 4.3 Percent Distribution of Family Personal Income by Quintiles, Selected Years, 1929 to 1970

Families Ranked from Highest to Lowest Income	*1929*	*1941*	*1950*	*1960*	*1970*
Highest fifth	54.4%	48.8%	42.6%	42.0%	41.6%
Next highest	19.3	22.3	23.5	23.6	23.5
Middle fifth	13.8	15.3	17.4	17.6	17.4
Next lowest	9.0	9.5	12.0	12.0	12.0
Lowest fifth	3.5	4.1	4.5	4.9	5.5
	100.0%	100.0%	100.0%	100.0%	100.0%

SOURCE: U.S. Bureau of the Census, *Current Population Reports*, Series P–60, no. 80 (4 October 1971), Table 14, p. 28, for 1950, 1960, 1970. For 1929 and 1941, Edward C. Budd, ed., "An Introduction to a Current Issue of Public Policy," in *Inequality and Poverty* (New York: Norton, 1967), pp. x–xix.

the richest families (from 54 percent to 42 percent) and a slight increase in the percent received by the poorest families (from 3.5 percent to 4.5 percent).

3. For the past 20 or 30 years there has been almost no change.

The Distribution of Wealth The distribution of wealth is much more unequal than the distribution of income. In the United States a very large share of the personal wealth is owned by a very small percentage of the population. In fact, throughout the nation's history the richest 1 percent of the population has owned between 20 and 30 percent of the personal wealth; and a 1962 study estimated that the richest quintile owned 77 percent of the wealth while the poorest quintile owned less than 0.5 percent.[4]

Of course these figures do not take into account different forms of wealth. The most common form of wealth is personal possessions. Houses, cars, and appliances produce pleasure for their owners, but such wealth is not influential. Influential wealth is wealth that produces more wealth: rental property, stocks and bonds, patents and royalties. Almost 100 percent of this income-producing wealth is owned by the richest 20 percent of the population; indeed, most of it is owned by a very small number of families.

To sum up, it is clear that there is tremendous economic inequality in the United States. It is also clear that this inequality means huge differences in standards of living. Some Americans live in big, comfortable houses; have jobs that they enjoy doing; can take vacations and send their children to college; and can save enough money to protect themselves against sickness or unemployment. Others live in crowded, shabby housing; have dull, dirty jobs; worry more about how to feed their children than about what college to send them to; are always in debt; and are never secure against sickness or unemployment.

EFFORTS TO END ECONOMIC INEQUALITY

When the idea of equal political rights was first proposed many people were against it. They were afraid the poor would use their voting power to redistribute wealth. This fear was expressed in 1821 by Chancellor James Kent of New York in a debate over whether the right to vote should be granted to all white males. According to Kent,

> There is a constant tendency in human society, and the history of every age proves it; there is a tendency in the poor to covet and to share the plunder of the rich—in the debtor to relax or avoid the obligation of contracts—in the

[4] Robert J. Lampman, *The Share of Top Wealth-Holders in National Wealth, 1922–1956* (Princeton, N.J.: Princeton University Press, 1962).

indolent and the profligate to cast the whole burthens of society upon the industrious and the virtuous.[5]

The same argument can still be heard today. In the spring of 1977, for example, there was much discussion of the idea of universal voter registration. Supporters of the proposal claimed that by increasing the number of Americans who could vote it would be taking a further step toward citizenship equality. Opponents argued that the nonvoters include a large number of poor people who, if voting were made easier, would support programs that would result in a radical redistribution of wealth in the United States. As political writer Patrick J. Buchanan put it,

> Universal registration . . . may be the method through which the nation's tax consumers and nonproducers set about the systematic plunder of the tax-paying and producing majority. . . .
> [Members of the welfare class are] parasitic slugs who pay no taxes, who show such disinterest in the political process that they will not get off their duffs to register, have no business at the ballot box election day, casting a vote in ignorance and canceling out the ballot of some conscientious citizen.[6]

This argument has the same weakness today that it did in 1821: Increasing the number of people who can vote has not resulted in a radical redistribution of wealth. The following sections explain why.

The Progressive Income Tax

The principle behind the progressive income tax is that the more money a person earns, the higher the percentage he or she should pay in taxes. The progressive income tax would be an easy way to redistribute wealth—the poorer citizens would vote for a system that takes a very low percentage from people with low incomes and a very high percentage from people with high incomes. In this way political equality ("one person, one vote") would lead to economic equality ("one person, one dollar").

In practice this has not happened. Table 4.4 shows the difference between the percentage required by law and the percentage actually paid by families in various income groups. If there were no deductions or loopholes in the tax system, the richest family would pay 60.5 percent of its income in taxes while the poorest would pay only 1.9 percent. The average percentages actually paid by the richest and poorest families are 30.4 percent and 0.5 percent, re-

---

[5] Quoted in Alpheus T. Mason, ed., *Free Government in the Making,* 2d ed. (New York: Oxford University Press, 1956), p. 399.

[6] Patrick J. Buchanan, "Reform Aids Welfare Class," a nationally syndicated column that appeared in the *Chicago Tribune,* 3 March, 1977.

TABLE 4.4 Portion of Family Income Paid in Income Taxes

Family Income	Payment Required by Tax Law	Average Paid After Deductions	Average Amount Saved via Loopholes
$ 2,500	1.9%	0.5%	$ 35
5,000	7.5	2.8	235
10,000	12.4	7.6	480
20,000	20.8	12.1	1,740
75,000	46.0	26.8	14,400
250,000	58.0	29.6	71,000
1,000,000	60.5	30.4	301,000

SOURCE: Based on data from Philip M. Stern, *The Rape of the Taxpayer* (New York: Random House, 1974), p. 11.

spectively, Clearly the progressive income tax is not as "progressive" as it is supposed to be. Why is this so?

The Sixteenth Amendment to the Constitution allows Congress to tax income "from whatever sources derived," but this principle has been greatly affected by tax legislation. Dollars earned from some sources, though they are worth just as much as dollars earned from other sources, are not taxed at the same rate. The dollars that are most heavily taxes are earned as wages and salaries; those that are least heavily taxed are earned from investments such as real estate, stock options, and state and local bonds. Thus a family of four with an income of $10,000 pays the following tax:

$905 if the income is all in the form of wages and salaries

$98 if the income is all in the form of profits from selling stocks or land

$0 if the income is all in the form of interest on state and local bonds

In other words, people who earn their income by working pay a greater share of that income in taxes than people who receive income without lifting a finger. Since most of the income of the wealthy comes from nonwage sources, it is the wealthy, not the wage earners, who benefit from lower tax rates.

In addition, the government loses a lot of money through tax deductions and loopholes. This money amounts to a gift to those who are able to take advantage of such deductions—usually the wealthy. The annual budget of the antipoverty program is less than three percent of the loss from this "tax welfare" program.

The progressive income tax does result in a more even distribution of income at the lower end of the scale. For example, it brings a family with an income of $16,000 closer to a family with an income of $8,000. However, it has a much smaller effect on the top of the scale. The average income of the richest 20 percent of the population is about 10 times that of the poorest 20 percent before taxes; after taxes it is about 9 times that amount. Thus the progressive income tax does not do much to close the gap between the rich and the poor.

Other kinds of taxes are even less progressive than the income tax. The sales tax, for example, takes a much larger share of income from the poor than from the rich. A family that earns $5000 and pays a 5 percent sales tax on the $4000 it spends on consumer goods pays $200, or 4 percent of its total income, in sales taxes. A family that earns $25,000 and spends $8000 on consumer goods spends $400, or 1.6 percent of its total income, in sales taxes.

Students of the American tax system have come to the conclusion that it is not very progressive. Almost everyone, rich or poor, pays from one-quarter to one-third of his or her income in taxes. This situation has not changed much since World War II. The amount of economic inequality in the United States has not been greatly affected by the various taxes the government uses to pay for its programs.

There is another way of looking at taxes, however. The fact is, people who earn more money *do* contribute more to government programs than people who earn less money. In 1976, for example, about half of the households in the United States earned less than $10,000 and the other half more than $10,000. The wealthier half earned 81 percent of the income and got most of the tax breaks (88 percent). They also paid 94 percent of all federal income taxes collected in 1976.

Programs to Reduce Economic Inequality

The major social-welfare programs are social security, unemployment compensation, public education, and medicare. It can be argued that these programs have made citizens more equal. To understand this argument we must first understand what is meant by the terms inequality of distance and inequality of scope.

Inequality of distance refers to the size of the gap between the rich and the poor. In a society where the richest group earns 20 times as much as the poorest group, there is great inequality of distance. In a society where the richest group earns only five times as much as the poorest group, inequality of distance has been reduced. Social security and unemployment compensation do not greatly reduce the distance between the rich and the poor; they are simply government-managed insurance programs to which workers contribute during their working years. Other programs, such as medicare, help citizens in times of financial need, but they do not "level" society by redistributing wealth from the rich to the poor.

Inequality of scope refers to the number of ways in which the rich are better off than the poor. This can best be explained by comparing two imaginary societies.

First, imagine a society in which every social benefit is available only in the free market and at a price that gives its owners the highest profit possible. Education, medical care, recreation, transportation and communication, and even personal safety are available only to those who can pay for these services. Therefore they are more available to the rich than to the poor. The less money you have, the less of any of these services you can get. At the bottom of the scale there is no public education, no free medical care, no public parks, no transportation or communication systems (except those used by the rich), and no police force. In such a society inequality of scope would be enormous.

Now imagine a society in which no social benefit has a price; all are equally available to all citizens. All children can go to public schools of equal quality; all citizens are protected equally against sickness and accident; public parks are available to all; the transportation and communication systems may be used by every citizen; and the police protect every citizen equally. In such a society there would be very little inequality of scope. The rich could still buy things that the poor could not afford, but they could not buy better social services.

There is much disagreement over whether it is fair to reduce inequality of scope—to increase the number of services for which wealth is unnecessary. This would reduce the number of ways in which the rich are better off. Julius Nyerere, president of Tanzania, made this point when he called for

> the provision of social services which are available to all, regardless of income; for a man who suddenly has new medical services available to him and his family, or a new house, or a new school or community center, has had an improvement in his standard of living, just as much as if he had more money in his pocket.

Social-welfare programs have reduced inequality of scope, but not as much as either their supporters or their critics claim. For one thing, the benefits of such programs are not always received by the poorest groups in society. Free higher education, for example, has benefited the middle class and to some extent the working class, but it has not done much for really poor families. The impact of welfare programs has also been reduced by the methods used to pay for them. The taxes that raise the money for those programs are paid by the whole population, which means that the poor are actually paying for the services that are designed to increase their income.

To sum up, even though social-rights citizenship has done less to equalize income than some people hoped and others feared, there is no doubt that by providing decent social services, either free or at a low cost, the government reduces inequality of scope. The rich can still send their children to private universities, but excellent public universities are available as well. Thus government programs tend to equalize opportunities to receive a quality education.

The War on Poverty

In the mid–1960s President Johnson declared a War on Poverty that was to have an annual budget of around $2 billion and include programs like Head Start, the Job Corps, and VISTA. How have these programs affected economic inequality in America?

The purpose of antipoverty programs is to raise the "floor level" of society. The poor are those who are living below a level that is considered tolerable. In a society as rich as ours there should not be people who are so poor that they cannot have a decent standard of living. A successful antipoverty program would raise every citizen above the tolerable level.

Note that antipoverty programs increase the number of people who are able to compete in a free-enterprise system. They do not redistribute wealth. The only way such programs can affect inequality is by reducing the gap between the rich and the poor. They would achieve this not by making the rich less wealthy but by making the poor better off. The War on Poverty did not close the gap between the rich and the poor by very much.

A more recent idea, the "negative income tax," would attempt to help the poor in a more direct way. Under such a plan families at a certain income level, say $5000, would pay no taxes. A family earning less than that amount would receive a payment that would raise its income to $5000. Only families earning more than $5000 would pay income taxes. This idea has been tried out in a few areas but is not yet a national program. If it were carried out on a national scale it would help the poorest families in America live a little more decently, but it still would not do much to close the gap between the very rich and the very poor.

Affirmative Action

In the 1970s a new debate over citizenship arose in the United States. Like many earlier ones, this one is about equality. At the center of the debate is the phrase "affirmative action": Should society take affirmative action to make up for past discrimination? Affirmative action is sometimes called "reverse discrimination" because it discriminates in favor of groups that have been discriminated against in the past.

It is no accident that the issue of affirmative action came up in the 1970s. It followed a period of very successful civil-rights activity. Many forms of racial discrimination have been ended. Blacks and other minority groups are no longer prevented from voting or holding office or excluded from jobs, housing, good schools, restaurants, and so on. In short, an enormous social transformation has taken place.

Despite its many achievements, the civil-rights movement has not ended segregation: In Chicago the public schools are 70 percent nonwhite; in Baltimore, 75 percent; in Detroit, 81 percent; in Washington, D.C., 96 percent. Nor has it erased the great economic inequalities that separate whites from blacks. In 1970 the median income of white families was $9961; for black families it was $6067. This difference was due not only to the fact that whites have better jobs but also to the fact that blacks are paid less than whites for similar jobs.

The civil-rights movement of the 1960s tried to make the law "color-blind" and rid society of a tradition of discrimination. But ending discrimination did not eliminate the effects of past discrimination—poverty, broken homes, inferior schools, and so on. Affirmative action tries to put color back into the picture. But now it is the "haves" who are, in effect, discriminated against so that the "have-nots," especially blacks and other minority groups, can have a better chance to go to good schools and get good jobs.

Affirmative-action programs have "targets," "goals," or "quotas." For example, if a college does not admit a percentage of blacks that is proportional to the percentage of blacks in the total population, this is seen as evidence of discrimination. The government then suggests guidelines for the college, guidelines that must be met if it wants to receive federal funds.

Affirmative action represents a shift from an emphasis on equality of opportunity to an emphasis on equality of condition. A college admissions program is not expected to give everyone an equal chance at admission; it is expected to achieve a certain outcome. Because of past discrimination, a colorblind admissions program would probably admit very few blacks. Only if the college takes color into account and tries to meet a particular goal is it likely to admit a large number of blacks.

The political issues stirred up by affirmative action are complicated ones. They include the following:

1. *Career Advancement.* Because of past discrimination most black workers do not have as much seniority as white workers. If career advancement is based on seniority, it will take a long time for blacks to become union leaders or police chiefs or school principals. But is it fair to advance blacks faster than whites who have worked hard to earn their seniority?
2. *Housing.* Because of both segregation and poverty, few blacks can afford to live in the suburbs. Should low-income housing be built in white suburbs? This would help blacks escape unemployment, poverty, and poor schools, but it would also reduce the freedom of a community to plan its own land use.
3. *Busing.* Large numbers of black children go to poor-quality inner-city schools

while white children go to good schools in the suburbs. Black children cannot be expected to compete with white children unless the schools are integrated. But is it fair to bus children to other neighborhoods in order to create integrated schools?

Affirmative action is a new and troublesome phase in the history of citizenship. It goes beyond equal protection of the law and even equal opportunity to a new concept: the right to be treated unequally and favorably in compensation for unequal and unfavorable treatment in the past. Such treatment is bound to be labeled "reverse discrimination." People who have struggled to succeed under the old rules will resent any change in the rules that takes away the benefits they won in that struggle.

CONCLUSION

We have found out three things about equality in the United States: (1) The demand for equal treatment has resulted in the achievement of considerable legal, political, and social equality. (2) Economic inequality has been reduced only slightly by government programs such as the progressive income tax, social-welfare programs, and the War on Poverty. (3) American society is characterized by a major contradiction: The democratic creed promises political equality while the capitalist creed supports economic inequality.

This is not to say that politics makes no difference. Indeed, political action has produced some major changes in the meaning of citizenship. The phrase "equality of opportunity" has taken on new meaning as a result of the civil-rights movement of the 1960s and the women's movement of the 1970s. Political action has also gone a long way toward raising the standard of living of the poor to a decent level. The idea that each person should get only what he or she earns has been softened to take account of sickness, old age, unemployment, and other situations that make it hard for a person to earn much.

On the other hand, political action has not done much to redistribute wealth. Large differences in income and wealth will continue to result in different standards of living for different groups in American society. For while Americans accept the democratic creed of equality, they also accept the capitalist principle that economic inequalities are not only fair but necessary.

CONTROVERSY

In 1978 the U.S. Supreme Court had to decide one of the most difficult civil rights cases ever before it. This case raised the complicated issue of affirmative action. The medical school at the University of California, Davis, had reserved a number of places for minority students. Candidates for these places were reviewed by a special admissions committee. The committee used less demanding criteria than those that were used in the regular admission process. A white applicant to the medical school was turned down. His name was Allan Bakke, and he later learned that minority students with lower grade point averages and test scores had been admitted to the medical school. Bakke felt that this "affirmative action" program with its use of a quota system discriminated against him. He initiated a court test of the medical school's practice, which reached the Supreme Court as the *Regents of California v. Bakke*. The Court's decision was mixed. It rejected the specific California program because the program reserved a given number of places for racial minorities, but it granted to schools the right to take race into account in considering applicants.

The Bakke case was aggressively debated in the nation's newspapers and on university campuses. A large number of organizations filed what are called "friend-of-the-court" briefs with the Supreme Court. These briefs are statements that attempt to influence the Court's decision by providing legal and constitutional reasons for one side or the other. We can summarize a few of the main arguments presented in the Bakke case in order to pose the difficult controversy that surrounds the issue of affirmative action.

One Side

The University of California vigorously defended its special admissions program, arguing in its brief to the Supreme Court that "there is, literally, no substitute for the use of race as a factor in admissions, if professional schools are to admit more than an isolated few applicants from minority groups long subjected to hostile and pervasive discrimination." Various studies supported the University's assertion. The Association of American Medical Colleges said in its brief:

> Without special admissions programs it is not unrealistic to assume that minority enrollments could return to the distressingly low levels of the early 1960's. This would mean a drop from the present level of 8.2 percent enrollment of underrepresented minorities . . . to slightly over 2 percent.[7]

In the absence of special admissions programs, similar drops in minority enrollment would occur in law schools, according to the Association of American Law Schools. In its brief it cited a study by the Educational Testing Service that showed that without such programs the number of blacks admitted to American law schools in the previous year would have dropped by 60 percent and the number of Chicano students by 40 percent.

The argument for affirmative action proceeds not only from the type of facts just cited but also from considerations of justness and equity. Equal protection of the law is not enough to overcome centuries of racial and sexual discrimination and unequal treatment. To simply apply equal criteria at this stage in history is as if there were a race between two people, one of whom had been in training for ten years while the other had been in chains for ten years. If the chains were removed, both runners started at the same point on the track, and the rules of the race were applied to the runners equally, would we say that each runner had an equal chance to win? Affirmative action, supporters argue, is intended to help the chained runner get in condition so that the race will be fair.

---

[7] Cited in *The Chronicle of Higher Education*, 15, no 3. (September 19, 1977), 4.

The Other Side

The arguments against affirmative action frequently start by pointing out how quota programs are unfair to blacks and other minorities. The assumption is made that "blacks will not succeed in rising more or less on their own merits, as other minorities have. Nothing could more surely handicap able blacks further than the assumption that they have become doctors or lawyers not by individual merit but by a preference based on skin color."[8]

Moreover, affirmative-action programs turn innocent people into victims. Though his grade point average and test scores were good enough to enter medical school, Bakke was denied admission. Similar things happen whenever there are quotas or special selection procedures. Some qualified applicants cannot enter college or a professional school or a training program or find employment in "reserved" jobs. As Supreme Court Justice Brennan wrote in a previous case, "We cannot ignore the social reality than even a benign policy of assignment by race is viewed as unjust by many in our society, especially by those individuals who are adversely affected by a given classification."[9]

The case against affirmative action is also made on straightforward constitutional grounds. Two well-known professors of constitutional law state the issue forcefully:

> If the Constitution prohibits exclusion of blacks and other minorities on racial grounds, it cannot permit exclusion of whites on racial grounds. For it must be the exclusion on racial grounds which offends the Constitution, and not the particular skin color of the person excluded.[10]

These professors argue that if someone is denied admission to a medical or law school *because* he or she is white, this is racial discrimination and therefore is unconstitutional. "Discrimination on the basis of race is illegal, immoral, unconstitutional, inherently wrong and destructive of democratic society."

---

[8] Editorial, *Wall Street Journal*, 15 September, 1977, p. 20.
[9] Quoted by Anthony Lewis, "Racial Quotas Will Come Again Before High Court," *New York Times*, 13 March, 1977.
[10] Philip Kurland and Alexander M. Bickel, quoted in Nina Totenberg, "Discrimination to End Discrimination," *New York Times Magazine*, 14 April, 1974. © 1974 by the New York Times Company. Reprinted by permission.

The Political Beliefs
of Americans

To understand American politics we must understand more than the formal structure of the government. We must understand the beliefs and feelings of the American people about the political system in which they live. For those beliefs and feelings have a major effect on how the system works.

This lesson has been learned the hard way by nations that have tried to borrow their constitutions from Britain or the United States. The new constitutions have provided for periodic elections, the right to criticize the government, and other institutions of democracy. In many cases, however, the democratic governments have been replaced by military regimes or one-party states. The democratic structure was there, but the democratic beliefs were not. Democracy must have roots in the "hearts and minds" of the people.

CALCULATION VS. CULTURE

There are two ways of explaining political behavior. On the one hand, a person can calculate the benefits of a particular act, compare them to the costs, and do whatever produces the greatest benefit at the least cost. This is the way a careful shopper purchases a major appliance. On the other hand, a person can act on the basis of beliefs and values, often learned in early childhood, without questioning them. This is the way people acquire their religion. Most people do not usually choose a religion on the basis of costs and benefits; rather, their religion is the religion of their parents, and they would never think of changing it.

The difference between calculation and culture is basic to one theory of how democracy works. According to this theory, democracy will survive if citizens acquire fundamental democratic beliefs as part of their culture but make calculated choices when it comes to specific issues. In this view it is necessary for citizens to believe, without question, that the government is *legitimate* (i.e., that it deserves the support and obedience of citizens). They must also believe in the "rules of the democratic game" (e.g., freedom of speech, periodic elections, and so on). If there is widespread agreement on the legitimacy of the government and on the rules of the democratic game, the nation can stand the strain created by disagreements over specific issues. For example, citizens may calculate which presidential candidate will act in their interest if elected. Or they may calculate whether a stiff tax on gasoline to encourage conservation is in their interest. But they should not calculate whether to accept the outcome of the election or not or whether to pay the gasoline tax or not.

This last point is an important one. Democracy allows people to express their political preferences. Citizens can try to persuade the government to act in their interest by supporting particular candidates or by pressuring government officials. Since citizens have different preferences, some will support one candidate and others another, and some will favor a particular policy while others oppose it. As a result some will win and others will lose.

Why should people who voted for a Republican candidate accept the election of a Democrat? Because they believe in the rules of the game. They believe in free elections even if they sometimes lose. Besides, if both winners and losers agree on the rules, the losers will have another chance to win because the winners will not use their political power to abolish elections. Similarly, those who oppose a gasoline tax will obey the law and pay the tax because they believe the government that passed the law is legitimate. When you consider a government to be legitimate, you obey its laws even if they are not in your immediate interest. You obey the new tax law not because a cost-benefit calculation tells you that you will gain from it, but because it was passed by a legitimate government.

AMERICAN POLITICAL BELIEFS: THE EVIDENCE

The Legitimacy of the Government

Do Americans consider their government legitimate? One way to answer this question is to find out how they feel about the symbols of American democracy. Over the years studies have found that most Americans have a deep respect for such symbols as the flag and the Constitution. Reverence for the flag and the Constitution is taught in the schools and maintained throughout the life of the average American.

A major study done in 1959 compared the political beliefs of Americans with those of citizens in four other countries. Citizens were asked what aspects of their country they were proud of. Table 5.1 shows the results. Notice that few Americans—only 4 percent—said that there was nothing they

TABLE 5.1   What Aspects of Their Country Are Citizens Proud of?

	United States	Great Britain	Germany	Italy	Mexico
Percent who are proud of "nothing"	4%	10%	15%	27%	16%
Percent who are proud of political institutions	85%	46%	7%	3%	30%

SOURCE: Based on data from Gabriel Almond and Sidney Verba, *The Civic Culture: Political Attitudes and Democracy in Five Nations* (Princeton, N.J.: Princeton University Press, 1963).

Citizens accord the government legitimacy out of long-term habit.

were proud of. More interesting, however, is what they were proud of. Americans were much more likely than citizens of other countries to be proud of political aspects of their society: the Constitution, political freedom, democracy.

American politics has changed a lot since 1959, but these political attitudes of Americans have not changed much. In 1976 a sample of Americans was asked to choose between two statements: "I am proud of many things about our form of government" and "I can't find much about our form of government to be proud of." Most of the respondents (80 percent) chose the first statement. When asked whether there is a need for major change in our form of government, only 25 percent said that a big change is needed.[1]

Trust in the Government When it comes to the way the government is run, the public seems much less satisfied. Over the years researchers have asked citizens questions like "Do you think the government is run for all the people or for a few special interests?" and "Do you trust the government to do what is right?" In the past ten years or so there has been a large increase in the percentage of respondents who show dissatisfaction. (See Figure 5.1.) In

[1] University of Michigan, Center for Political Studies, 1976 election study.

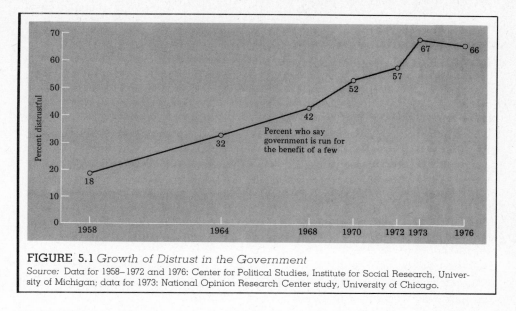

FIGURE 5.1 *Growth of Distrust in the Government*

Source: Data for 1958–1972 and 1976: Center for Political Studies, Institute for Social Research, University of Michigan; data for 1973: National Opinion Research Center study, University of Chicago.

1958, 18 percent of the public thought the government was run for the benefit of a few; by 1976 this figure had risen to 66 percent.[2]

There has also been a general decline in optimism among Americans. One group of researchers has been studying the hopes and fears of Americans for many years. In 1959 and 1964 they found that Americans saw the present as better than the past and believed the future would be even better. But in the 1970s they found a striking change. People saw the late 1960s as a time of decay, not progress. They still hoped for a better future, but they no longer saw progress as a steady, uninterrupted process.[3] This change was due not only to the Watergate scandal but also to a belief that the government could not cope with the many serious problems it faced during the late 1960s and early 1970s—racial tension, Vietnam, pollution, and the like.

It is not clear whether the decline in confidence in the government will continue. Some people believe it is a temporary reaction, while others argue that it is a major trend that threatens democracy. So far the evidence shows that the public is dissatisfied with the nation's leaders but not with its form of government. People seem to be saying, "The system is all right; it's just working badly." A long period of dissatisfaction with the way the system works could lead to a general loss of belief in the legitimacy of that system.

[2] Data from University of Michigan Survey Research Center election study and from National Opinion Research Center study.

[3] William Watts and Lloyd A. Free, *The State of the Nation, 1974* (Washington D.C.: Potomac Associates, 1974).

But there is little evidence that this is happening—in fact, under Presidents Ford and Carter there has been an increase in confidence in the government, though not to the level of the early 1960s.

Political Efficacy   Another citizen attitude that is closely related to belief in the legitimacy of the government is the feeling of *political efficacy* —the belief that every citizen has a voice in the government. Democratic government is supposed to be responsive to the people. If the people do not believe they can influence the government, they are unlikely to believe that it deserves their support.

Do Americans have a feeling of political efficacy? In general, yes; but the number who feel this way has decreased in recent years. Most Americans believe that the vote is an effective means of controlling government officials and that those officials are basically responsive to the people. A 1959 study found that Americans are more likely than citizens of other nations to feel that they have some political influence. Those who feel that they are able to influence the government are likely to try. Americans also believe that a citizen has a duty to try to influence the government.

How have things changed since 1959? There is evidence that feelings of efficacy rose in the 1950s and fell in the 1960s and early 1970s. In 1952, 69 percent of a sample agreed that "people have some say about what the government does"; by 1960 the figure had risen to 72 percent. But by 1973, during the Watergate scandal, it had fallen to 49 percent. By 1976 it was back up to 56 percent.[4] Thus citizens' sense of efficacy, after falling sharply, appears to be rising again.

The Rules of the Game

Agreement on the "rules of the game" means agreement on the basic procedures of democracy, such as fair elections and freedom of speech. As we said earlier, agreement on the rules of the democratic game is important. If a democracy is to work, opposing groups must be able to organize and to express their views; there must be control over public officials through periodic elections; government leaders must be willing to step down when the voters choose other leaders; and so on. These rules are written into the Constitution and the law. However, they survive only because the people believe in them. The Constitution states that the winning presidential candidate will become the new President. But the changeover takes place not only because it is in the Constitution, but also because people agree that this is the way things should be. Similarly, while the Bill of Rights formally guar-

---

[4] Data from University of Michigan Survey Research Center studies.

antees freedom of speech, if the public does not believe in this right, the Bill of Rights will be meaningless.

If Americans agree on these basic rules, we are told, they will be able to disagree on other issues. Should there be laws against abortion? Should the government establish wage and price controls? Americans disagree on such issues, sometimes quite strongly. But as long as they agree that people have the right to express their views, and as long as they accept the outcome of the dispute when it is settled according to the rules of the game, democracy survives.

Several studies have shown that more than nine out of ten Americans agree with the principles of democratic government. They agree that freedom of speech should be guaranteed for all citizens, that all citizens should have the right to vote, that political leaders should be responsive to the people, and that democracy works best when there is strong competition between political parties.[5] But other research shows that belief in the rules of democratic procedure is not as firm in particular cases as it is in the abstract. The same people who say that freedom of speech is a good thing are not sure certain groups should have that freedom. When asked whether groups with unpopular views (e.g., communists) should be allowed to make speeches, Americans are not sure speech should be *that* free. Many Americans are opposed to letting such groups make speeches in their community, and many would like to remove their books from the local library.

In theory, people who believe in the rules of the democratic game should favor freedom of speech no matter how they feel about the speaker or about the content of the speech. In 1971 a National Opinion Research Center study asked questions such as "Should a group be allowed to circulate a petition to stop a factory from polluting the air?" and "Should a group be allowed to circulate a petition calling for the legalization of marijuana?" Table 5.2 shows the results. It is clear from this study that many citizens would allow freedom of speech for things they favor but not for things they oppose.

Similarly, people would allow freedom of speech for people they like but not for those they dislike. Most of the sample—95 percent—said yes when asked if "a group of your neighbors" should be allowed to circulate a petition, but only about 70 percent thought "black militants" or "radical students" should be allowed to do so.

The rules of the democratic game would be meaningless if people supported them in theory but not in practice. Fortunately, however, we can go a step further. We have seen what citizens say when they are asked questions about freedom of speech, but how do they act? It turns out that they act dif-

---

[5] James W. Prothro and Charles M. Grigg, "Fundamental Principles of Democracy: Bases of Agreement and Disagreement," *Journal of Politics,* 22 (Spring 1960), 276–294; Herbert McClosky, "Consensus and Ideology in American Politics," *American Political Science Review,* 58 (June 1964), 361–382.

TABLE 5.2   Citizens Are More Likely to Favor Free Speech When They Approve of the Views of the Speakers

	Percent Saying Yes
Should a group be allowed to circulate a petition . . .	
to stop a factory from polluting the air?	93%
expressing concern with crime in their community?	95%
calling for the legalization of marijuana?	52%
calling on the government to make sure that blacks can buy and rent homes in white neighborhoods? (asked of whites only)	70%
calling on the government to prevent blacks from buying or renting in white neighborhoods? (asked of blacks only)	51%

SOURCE: National Opinion Research Center study, University of Chicago, 1971.

ferently than we would expect them to on the basis of some of their answers. For example, in Tallahassee, Florida, 42 percent of a sample said that a black should not be allowed to run for mayor.[6] But a few months earlier a black *had* run for mayor and no one had tried to stop him. In communities where citizens said that certain unpopular speakers should not be allowed to speak and that their books should be removed from the library, no one was actually barred from speaking and no books were removed from the library.

In short, when you ask Americans about the rules of the democratic game, they show support for those rules. When you ask about specific cases, they are less likely to show strong support for the rules of the game; but when you ask about what they actually *do*, you find that they do not act on those views. They are not consistent.

There is one fact, however, that helps explain why free speech survives even though many Americans oppose freedom of speech for certain groups. The same study that found many citizens opposing freedom found that the most politically active citizens are much more likely to support freedom of speech for such groups. (See Table 5.3.) Another study found that while almost one-third of all Americans believe the majority has a right to deny freedom of speech to minority groups, only 7 percent of the nation's political leaders feel this way.[7] These studies suggest that support for the rules of the democratic game may be stronger among people who are likely to have a voice in how the political system is run—those who are active in politics.

---

[6] Prothro and Grigg, p. 294.

[7] Herbert McClosky, "Consensus and Ideology in American Politics," *American Political Science Review,* 58 (June 1964), 361–382.

TABLE 5.3   Political Activists Are More Tolerant of Unpopular Views Than Ordinary Citizens

	Among a Cross-Section of Citizens	Among Political Activists
Percent saying they would allow an admitted communist to speak in public	58%	88%
Percent saying they would allow an atheist to speak in public	65%	95%

SOURCE: Kay Lehman Schlozman and Kristi Andersen, "Changes in the Level of Tolerance for Dissent, 1954–1974," unpublished paper based on National Opinion Research Center data.

Beliefs About Equality

We have been discussing the beliefs of Americans on matters related to liberty. The other great democratic ideal is equality. Most Americans would agree with the Declaration of Independence that it is "self-evident that all men [and women] are created equal." But this does not stop them from arguing about what equality means and what the government should do to create equality.

Equality can have many meanings. To Americans it has almost always meant equality of opportunity, not equality of condition. They do not believe everyone should have an equal income or standard of living. Rather, they believe everyone should have an equal chance to get ahead.

This belief is illustrated by a recent study in which leaders from all areas of American life were asked what they think about equality. Some (e.g., black leaders) represented groups that have been demanding more equality. Others (e.g., business leaders) represented more conservative groups. All were asked whether they believe in "equality of opportunity: giving each person an equal chance to get a good education and to develop his or her ability" or "equality of results: giving each person a relatively equal income regardless of his or her ability." As Table 5.4 shows, most of the leaders chose equality of opportunity.

The fact that most leaders agree on the ideal of equality does not mean that they agree on the reality of inequality. The study just described also asked whether poverty is the fault of the poor or whether it is caused by "the system." On this issue business leaders and Republican party leaders take a sharply different stand from labor leaders, black and feminist leaders, and Democratic leaders. Table 5.4 shows large differences among these groups on how much the government should do to reduce inequality. For example,

TABLE 5.4   Agreement and Disagreement on Equality

	AGREEMENT ON IDEALS	
Type of Leader	Prefer Equality of Opportunity	Prefer Equality of Condition
Business leaders	98%	1%
Labor leaders	86	4
Black leaders	86	7
Feminist leaders	84	7
Democratic leaders	84	8
Republican leaders	98	0
	DISAGREEMENT ON REALITY	
Type of Leader	Believe Poverty Is the Fault of the Poor	Believe Poverty Is Caused by the System
Business leaders	57%	9%
Labor leaders	15	56
Black leaders	5	86
Feminist leaders	9	76
Democratic leaders	5	68
Republican leaders	55	13

SOURCE: Sidney Verba, Gary Orren, and Donald Ferree, "The Meaning of Equality: A Leadership Survey," unpublished manuscript, Center for International Affairs, Harvard University, 1977.
Percentages do not add up to 100 percent because some had no opinion or took a middle position.

only 14 percent of the business leaders think the government should do more to reduce the income gap between the rich and the poor, while 82 percent of the black leaders feel this way.

As we saw in Chapter 4, the American economic system gives very different rewards to people who do different jobs. Do Americans think such differences are fair? The same set of leaders were asked what they believe people earn for doing various jobs and what they *should* earn. They agreed that the top executive of a large corporation probably earns about 30 times as much as an elevator operator. When asked whether such a large difference is fair, the business leaders said yes, while the labor leaders and black and feminist leaders said no. But those who said that a large difference is not fair do not think that the executive and the elevator operator should earn the same amount. They think the executive should earn about 12 times as much as the elevator operator rather than 30 times.

Thus there is widespread agreement in America that equality means the right of each person to do the best he or she can. However, there is much less agreement on whether that ideal is matched by reality.

WHERE DO POLITICAL ATTITUDES COME FROM?

Political Socialization

The term *political socialization* refers to the process by which young people learn basic political beliefs. This takes place in the family and in the school. In kindergarten, for example, children learn to prefer the American flag over other flags, and during the elementary-school years they are taught to identify "America" with the rules of the democratic game—with "freedom" or "the right to vote." At the same time they learn what it means to be a "good citizen"—voting, understanding current events, and so on.

The President plays an important role in political socialization. Young children identify the government with the President. They also see him as a wise, supportive father figure. Only later do they develop a more realistic understanding of what the President actually does.

Thus children are first exposed to the symbols of government—the flag, the President—and develop a supportive attitude toward the political system long before they understand anything about how that system works. This attitude is a matter of culture, not calculation: Children quickly learn to believe without question in the legitimacy of the government.

Socialization in Later Life

Political beliefs are affected not only by socialization during childhood but also by experiences in later life. For example, as mentioned earlier, the trust

Practice in political participation starts in the school.

of adult Americans in their government declined during the Watergate scandal and the Vietnam War. Their experience with politics led them to become more cynical than they had been as children. Yet their early trust in the government kept them from rejecting the political system itself along with its leaders. As we would expect, with the end of the Vietnam War and Nixon's Presidency came greater confidence in the government.

Another reason why political learning continues during adult life is that children cannot develop views on specific political candidates or issues that will carry over into adulthood. The candidates and issues will have changed by the time they grow up.

Other Sources of Political Attitudes

When people are trying to form an opinion on a specific issue or decide how to vote, they are likely to look to others for guidance. Who are these "others"? They include peer groups, political authorities, the political party, and the mass media.

Peer Groups Groups of people who are in contact with one another are likely to have similar opinions. This is especially true of *primary groups*— friends, families, neighbors, and the like. The opinions of members of these groups are similar partly because they are in similar situations: They live near one another, have similar jobs, and face similar problems.

In addition, members of groups will change their own opinions to match those of other members. This helps them become accepted by the group, reduces conflict with friends and relatives, and gives them the feeling that their opinions are "right"—after all, other people agree with them.

Political Authorities Many Americans turn to political authorities such as the Supreme Court when they are uncertain about their opinions. If the Court has taken a stand on an issue, they feel that it must be the right one. The same goes for the President, though he represents only one opinion and one political party. The President is well covered by the news media, so that his views are widely known and usually respected.

The influence of the President may be illustrated by public opinion on the Vietnam War. Over time there was a steady decline in the number of people who thought the President was doing a good job in relation to Vietnam. But whenever he did something dramatic—such as increasing the bombing *or* stopping it—the percentage of the population that thought he was doing a good job went up, only to drop again later. The increase in support for the President whenever he made a dramatic announcement was due largely to the willingness of the American people to be guided by him in matters that they did not understand.

The Political Party For a long time the political party played a major role in the formation of opinions. People's party identification was inherited from their parents and served as a guide to their political behavior. As we will see in Chapter 9, the importance of party identification has faded in recent years. The party still serves as a guide on many issues, however. Since issues are often complicated and are changing all the time—and since candidates' views on issues may be unclear—many citizens use the party's position on an issue as a basis for their own views.

The Mass Media The major source of information for the average American is television news—the network evening news is watched by people from all walks of life. Newspapers are also widely read, but educated and politically active citizens are more likely to read news about national and international affairs than less well educated and less active citizens, who may skip to the sports page with hardly a glance at the news. As a result, the bulk of the American public gets a much more limited view of the news than citizens who are politically concerned and active. Television news provides little variety or depth, whereas news magazines and newspapers offer greater depth and a variety of views on any given issue.

There is much debate in America as to whether the media are biased. The media are constantly attacked for slanting the news. They are criticized both for being too conservative and for being too liberal. Both criticisms are partly true. Newspapers and television stations are owned by businessmen, usually Republicans, who tend to be more conservative than the general public and to support Republican candidates. On the other hand, many reporters, especially for national newspapers such as the *New York Times* and the *Washington Post,* are liberal in their views.

Americans from all walks of life follow the news on TV.

It is hard to tell whether the media really are biased. It is true, however, that the media tend to criticize whatever government is in power. As Theodore H. White has written, "The national media have put themselves into the role of permanent critical opposition to any government which does not instantly clean up the unfinished business of our time."[8] Of course this means that no government can ever satisfy the media.

THE SOCIAL BASES OF POLITICAL BELIEFS

So far we have been discussing the American people as if they were all alike. This is not the case, of course. When we look more closely at American opinion we see great variety. All (or at least most) Americans agree with the general principles of democracy, but when it comes to specific cases "most" becomes one-third, one-half, or two-thirds, depending on the groups we are talking about.

In the United States there are many bases for disagreement among groups. People who live in different regions, have different jobs, are of different races, ages, or religions, or come from different ethnic backgrounds are likely to have different political views. In fact the struggle among opposing groups is at the heart of American politics. This point is so important that we will devote the next chapter to it. Here we will look at some of the different viewpoints of such groups toward such matters as basic freedoms, political efficacy, and trust in the government.

The American population can be divided by region or sex or age or income or race, and in many other ways as well. Most of these divisions reveal very little difference in attitude as far as basic democratic principles are concerned. The division that makes the most difference is between the better-educated citizens and the rest of the population. We have already seen that commitment to democratic principles is strongest among those who are politically active. This is probably because such commitment usually comes with education, and educated people are more likely to be politically active. Education also makes a difference in the extent to which people feel that they are able to influence the government. In 1972 a sample of citizens was asked whether they could do anything about an unjust or corrupt public official. Among those with only a grade-school education 35 percent said yes, while among the college educated 71 percent said yes.[9]

---

[8] Quoted in Samuel P. Huntington, "Postindustrial Politics: How Benign Will It Be?" *Comparative Politics,* 6 (January 1974), 184.

[9] U.S. Senate Subcommittee on Intergovernmental Operations of the Committee on Governmental Operations, *Confidence and Concern; Citizens View Their Government,* 3 December, 1973.

BLACK AMERICANS AND WHITE AMERICANS

What if we turn from the average middle-class white American to those who have generally been denied the full benefits of citizenship—the blacks, the Chicanos, the poor? What are their political attitudes? It is hard to get detailed information on some minority groups, but we know quite a bit about the political attitudes of blacks.

In some ways blacks and whites have similar political attitudes. Their general views on the American political system do not differ much. But the views of blacks on how the government affects them are much more negative than those of whites. Almost 90 percent of all white Americans expect equal treatment by the government; fewer than half of the blacks expect such treatment.

Differences between the races are most dramatic when it comes to attitudes toward the police. Urban blacks have less confidence in the honesty of the police, are less likely to expect fair treatment by them, and have had less favorable experiences in dealing with them. Also, blacks are less satisfied with public services in their neighborhoods and complain more about high prices and low-quality goods in neighborhood stores.

Do the different outlooks of blacks and whites mean that the agreement among "average" Americans on democratic principles covers up some basic differences? Let's look at some evidence before answering this question.

Racial Hostility

If you compared the newspapers of the 1950s with those of the 1970s you would conclude that blacks and whites have become more hostile toward each other. There is much more news about racial conflict today than there was 20 years ago. But this does not mean that bitter race hatred has developed. It only shows that racial differences have come out into the open.

In the past 20 years white attitudes toward blacks have changed. In general, whites have become more favorable toward blacks and more responsive to their demands. In 1949 the National Opinion Research Center asked people whether Negroes were as intelligent as whites. Only 42 percent of whites thought so. By 1956 this figure had risen to 78 percent. In 1942 only 30 percent of whites thought white and black children should go to the same schools. By 1956 this figure had risen to 48 percent, and by 1968 it was 60 percent. In 1972 the Harris poll found that 71 percent of whites believed schools should be desegregated.

Note, however, that many whites still oppose integration. Furthermore, while whites support the goals of blacks, they sometimes dislike their tactics.

We have seen that they reject militant tactics. They also generally reject direct action by black groups even when it is peaceful and within the law. In 1968, for example, the Harris poll found that 80 percent of blacks favored Martin Luther King's Poor People's March while only 29 percent of whites did.

Thus the picture is quite mixed: More favorable attitudes are coupled with less favorable attitudes. This may be due at least partly to the American belief in "rugged individualism." Most whites no longer believe blacks are inferior, but they still think people should get ahead on their own steam and can do so if they try hard enough. Many whites see the lower levels of education or income achieved by blacks as resulting from lack of effort—if blacks do not succeed, it is because they do not try hard enough. They tend not to favor programs aimed at improving the situation of blacks.

Figure 5.2 compares the attitudes of whites and blacks on racial issues. Citizens were asked what should be done about urban unrest: use all necessary force to put down riots or solve the underlying problem of poverty? Blacks clearly favor solving the problem of poverty, while the position of whites is somewhere between ending poverty and using force to put down riots. Similarly, on the question of how fast programs for blacks should go, blacks want faster progress while some whites want slower progress.

It appears, then, that there is some danger of continued racial conflict as well as some hope for cooperation between the races. Both groups have at least a general commitment to the democratic system, and today there is

Though blacks and whites have developed more favorable attitudes toward each other in recent years, some issues still produce racial antagonism.

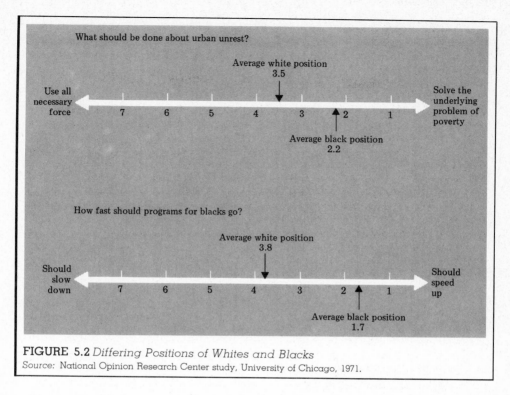

FIGURE 5.2 *Differing Positions of Whites and Blacks*
Source: National Opinion Research Center study, University of Chicago, 1971.

greater acceptance by whites of black goals. But conflict may arise from specific differences such as blacks' lack of confidence in government officials or whites' disapproval of black tactics.

RADICAL POLITICS

During the 1960s and early 1970s there was a striking increase in radical political activity in the United States. Why did some groups—blacks, Chicanos, radical students—challenge the political system itself?

A radical challenge to the democratic process—to the rules by which decisions are made—can come from either the "left" or the "right." Democratic procedures may be rejected by people who think those procedures tend to block social change. "Problems such as war, pollution, poverty, and racism are too big to be solved by 'the system,'" they may say. On the other hand, democratic rules may be rejected by people who see such rules as a cause of violence and destruction: "We have too much freedom of speech. We cannot allow freedom of speech for those who want to destroy 'the system.'"

In reality few groups take such stands. As we have seen, agreement on the rules of the democratic game is widespread even among people who are not satisfied with the way the system operates. The young are much more critical of the system than the population as a whole. A 1972 poll found that six out of ten young adults believe the country is democratic in name only and is run by powerful interest groups. But only 18 percent think it needs radical change. Similarly, 62 percent think political parties need major change, but only 12 percent think the Constitution does.[10]

Much of the radical criticism of American politics comes not from people who would prefer other rules but from people who think the rules are working poorly. They may, for instance, want more real participation by the poor in the policy-making process or greater power in the hands of local government.

DOES PUBLIC OPINION MAKE A DIFFERENCE?

Does public opinion shape government programs, or do officials pay it only lip service? In the 1930s, when the public-opinion poll was first used, some people thought it would be a great thing for democracy. Now public policy could really be based on the opinions of citizens. On the other hand, there were people who thought polls would cause trouble. They argued that the public is too poorly informed and irrational to guide government policy.

Actually, however, the public-opinion poll was never used to set government policy. Most officials—especially elected ones—do pay attention to public-opinion polls and do believe public opinion should be followed, at least up to a point. Yet policy is rarely based directly on public opinion.

Public Opinion Does Not Always Become Public Policy

Consider the following example: In 1972 the Harris poll asked a sample of Americans whether there should be a law requiring that handguns be registered. Although 70 percent said yes, no such law has been passed. You might point out that such things take time; if the public continues to feel that way, the law is likely to be passed. Back in 1940, however, a Gallup poll had asked the same question. At that time 79 percent of the people favored a gun control law.

How can a large majority of the people favor a particular policy for more than 30 years and get no response from Congress? The answer is that they do

---

[10] Daniel Yankelovich, *The New Morality: A Profile of American Youth in the 1970's* (New York: McGraw-Hill, 1973), p. 116.

not feel very strongly about the issue, while some members of the minority that oppose gun control *do* feel strongly about it and are active in trying to prevent control. Thus, as we pointed out in Chapter 1, policy is affected not only by public preferences but also by the *intensity* of those preferences. We will see in the next chapter that an intense minority is usually more effective than a less concerned majority.

Public Opinion Tends to React to Public Policy

As mentioned earlier, government officials try to keep informed about public opinion. They know that the public may react negatively if they do a bad job. Therefore they do not use public opinion as a guide in making policy, but they do use it to find out how they will do in the next election if they do not deal with a particular problem. In other words, the public will not tell political leaders what to do about inflation, but it will let them know if it is worried about high prices.

Again we can use the Vietnam War as an example. Beginning in 1964 or 1965, the percentage of the American people who were satisfied with the government's Vietnam policy went steadily downward. It hit its lowest point in 1968, when President Johnson decided not to run for a second term. Yet public opinion was not a useful guide for specific policy. When citizens were asked what the government should do about the war—try harder to win, get out of Vietnam, or continue current policy—their answers were divided across all three positions. How could the President follow public opinion in such a case? It was obvious that the public was unhappy and wanted results—political leaders had to do something or they would lose the election. But what the public wanted done was unclear.

Limits to Public Tolerance

There is another way of looking at the role of public opinion, and this is to recognize that there are some things the public just will not stand for. It is true that public tolerance sets some limits on government policy, but even those limits are unclear. One reason for this is that we do not know those limits in advance but may have to test the public to find out what they are.

American policy toward China is a good example. For many years it was assumed that the American public would not tolerate formal recognition of the People's Republic of China by the United States, and this assumption was backed up by the findings of public-opinion polls. But in 1973, when President Nixon went to China, the Harris poll found that 73 percent of the people approved. The idea that public opinion stood in the way of better relations with China had been a myth. Government policy toward China did not reflect public attitudes—public attitudes reflected government policy. Change the policy and the attitudes change.

On issues closer to home the limits set by public opinion may be less changeable than on matters of foreign policy. Attitudes on racial matters, for example, are hard to change. On such issues public attitudes may have a stronger effect on leadership. Yet even in these areas we can never be sure, as is illustrated by the fact that public support for integrated schools showed a large increase after the Supreme Court ruled that segregated schools were unconstitutional.

HOW WE FIND OUT ABOUT POLITICS: II

Public Opinion and Voting

Throughout this book we discuss the attitudes and beliefs of the American people. We look at their political beliefs, at their political behavior, at how they vote, and at how they decide to vote the way they do. How do we find out these things?

There are many ways of getting inaccurate information about the American public. To begin with, we often look at our own views and assume that other people feel the same way. This is not a safe assumption. People have a wide variety of views on political issues and react to political events in very different ways.

Sometimes we think we can learn about public opinion by talking to our friends, neighbors, or fellow workers. But most of us meet only certain kinds of people. For example, during the late 1960s some college students began to talk about a "generation gap" between their generation, which seemed to be solidly opposed to the Vietnam War, and the older generation, which seemed to be in favor of the war. However, if you looked at the entire younger generation—those who did not go to college as well as those who did—you found a much wider range of opinions and a lot of support for the war. Students who talked only to people like themselves had gotten an inaccurate view of public opinion.

Even reading newspapers or watching television can give us an inaccurate picture of the public. Do people who write letters to the editor represent the general public? Do the demonstrations and speeches reported by the evening news represent the views of the majority? It is hard to tell.

The sample survey, or public-opinion poll, was developed to get a more accurate picture of public opinion. Such surveys—the Gallup and Harris polls, for example—can be very accurate. Polls must be used with care, however. The people the pollster talks to and the questions he or she asks can greatly affect the accuracy of the findings.

If we want to find out about public opinion the best thing we could do is talk to all Americans, but obviously this would be too costly and time-consuming. Since we can talk to only some

Americans, we need to choose a number of people who represent the whole population—a sample.

What Is a Good Sample for a Public-Opinion Poll?

An Adequate Number. It is not enough to talk to one, two, or a few dozen citizens. There is too much chance that they will be very different from the rest of the public. Most good public-opinion polls interview about 1500 people.

A Wide Geographic Spread. It is not enough to talk only to people in the pollster's home town. Survey organizations interview people all over the country in order to get a wide geographic spread.

A Wide Range of Types. An important thing about a sample is that it should give all types of citizens an equal chance to be interviewed. In the past many surveys were taken in public places such as railroad stations. Such surveys were often inaccurate. They left out people who did not travel by train—homemakers, college students, the elderly, and so on. Certain groups, such as working men, were overrepresented, while other groups were underrepresented.

A Random Selection. The pollster chooses the people to be interviewed on the basis of statistics; he or she does not allow people to volunteer to be interviewed. This is what makes the sample survey different from other ways of finding out about public opinion.

The fact that the pollster talks to all kinds of people is both the greatest strength and the greatest weakness of the public-opinion poll. It is its greatest strength because it allows the survey to find out the opinions of all citizens—those who are eager to express their views as well as the "silent majority." But this can be a weakness as well, since it means that the pollster records the opinions of citizens who basically have no opinion. Often a person has not thought about a particular issue before the pollster asks about it. Rather than admitting that he or she has no opinion on the issue, such a person will usually give an offhand answer—and might give a different answer the next day.

How Do the Questions Used Affect Results?

Sometimes two different polls come up with different results on the same issue. When this happens it is usually because the two polls have asked different questions. The answers you get depend on the questions you ask. Even small changes in the wording of a question can change the results of a survey. This is because people respond to the *symbols* contained in

questions. If you ask a question about "Communist Russia," people will respond more negatively than they would if you ask about "Russia," simply because the question contains the negative symbol "communist." Similarly, if you ask about "aid to families with dependent children," you get a different set of answers than you would if you asked about "welfare" or "government giveaway programs."

To sum up, polls are quite accurate in telling us how Americans respond to a particular question, but the wording of the question always has an effect on the answer. Thus public-opinion polls give us useful information about the American public, but that information must be used carefully.

SENIORS FOR ADEQUATE
SOCIAL SECURITY

As we said in Chapter 1, politics involves conflict and competition. The government distributes benefits among various groups in society, and the government's major decisions have to do with who gets the benefits and who pays the costs. Even if everyone agreed on what the government should do —for example, that it should spend more on roads—there would still be conflict. Choices have to be made as to what kinds of roads to build and where to build them. Of course not all citizens want roads. Some think more should be spent on mass transit and less on roads. Some think the money should be spent on education or housing instead. Some think the most important thing is to cut spending in order to cut taxes.

In short, conflict arises not only over who should benefit from a particular policy but also over what policy is most desirable. In addition, conflict arises because a policy that benefits one group appears to hurt another group. A decision to build public housing in suburban communitities may be favored by blacks but opposed by suburban residents. Higher tariffs on textiles imported from Japan may be favored by American textile manufacturers but opposed by consumer groups.

This chapter is about the *groups* that compete for benefits, because most political competition is between groups, not between individuals. Those groups may be auto workers, Chicanos, Republicans, airline pilots, women, parents, fishermen, conservationists, and many more. Such groups are sometimes called *interest groups,* sometimes *pressure groups.* The members of each group have interests in common, and they work together to pressure the government to favor those interests.

But not all groups of individuals have interests in common, and not all of those that do have such interests put pressure on the government. Thus we begin with the question, What makes a group politically relevant?

WHAT MAKES A GROUP POLITICALLY RELEVANT?

Anything a set of individuals have in common can be the basis of a group— sex, occupation, political beliefs, ethnic background, and so on. But not all groups are politically relevant. Chicanos and blacks are relevant political groups. A few years ago women were not; now they are. Suburbanites may or may not be, depending on the suburb. But tea drinkers, red-haired citizens, and people who live in odd-numbered houses are unlikely ever to be a relevant political group.

Why are Chicanos politically relevant while tea drinkers are not? Why are women politically relevant now, when 15 years ago they were not? Three things make a group politically relevant: (1) a common interest, (2) awareness of that interest, and (3) organization. In addition, successful groups are able to provide incentives to get their members to give time, effort, and money to the group.

Common Interests

A group is likely to be politically relevant if the thing that defines it as a group is something that creates a common interest—especially if that interest can best be served by some action of the government. Blacks are defined by their race, which creates a common interest in housing policy, desegregation, and the like. Tea drinkers might have a common interest in the tariff on tea imports, but people who live in odd-numbered houses do not have interests in common, and it is hard to believe they ever would.

Not all common interests lead to the formation of a politically relevant group. Tea drinkers may have interests in common, but those interests are not important enough to get them to act because the change in the price of tea that might result from a change in the tariff on tea would have too little impact on them to make any difference. On the other hand, it is hard for an American black to be unconcerned about policies that affect blacks.

However, while tea drinkers may not consider the price of tea important, tea importers do. The price of tea—and, therefore, the tariff on tea—has a large impact on those who earn their living by importing and selling tea; it has a small impact on those for whom it is just one item in a shopping bag.

This is an important point. Different groups of citizens are interested in different *areas* of government policy. Tea drinkers may be interested in tea tariffs; coffee drinkers probably could not care less. Chicanos may be interested in Spanish-language teaching in the schools; citizens in states where there are no Chicanos will have no interest in this matter. Moreover, even when several groups are interested in a particular area of policy, some groups may be more concerned than others. For example, both the Chicanos and the non-Chicanos in a community may be interested in Spanish language teaching in the schools. For the Chicanos, however, it is an important issue related to their culture, while for the non-Chicanos it is probably a less important issue related to the costs of schools. Such differences in degree of concern underlie much of the political conflict that takes place in America.

Long-Term Interests vs. Short-Term Interests Citizens are more likely to be deeply concerned about interests that are *long term* in nature. Our sexual, racial, and ethnic interests are permanent, but we are students or "youth" for only a limited time. This is one reason why student or youth movements usually do not last very long. The people who are active and involved in such movements soon find that they have "graduated" from the group.

The difference between long-term and short-term interests may be illustrated by the difference between blacks and the unemployed. The blacks have become an important political force in America. One reason for this is that they have important common interests. Those interests are long term in nature—blacks share those interests all their lives. The unemployed, who have at times in recent years numbered more than 7 million, also have an important common interest—getting a job. But unemployment, except in rare cases, is not a lifelong condition, and this makes it harder for unemployment to form the basis of a political movement.

In some cases membership in a group may be long or short term, depending on the individual. A person can be a long- or short-term resident of a community or can hold a particular job for a long or short time. Those who have been a member of a particular group for a long time are more likely to consider that group's interests important.

Group Solutions vs. Individual Solutions   A number of people may have similar problems but may not have to form a group to solve those problems. If people can solve a problem through individual effort, they are less likely to form a group even if other people have similar problems. Again, blacks and the unemployed provide an example. Each group faces problems that require a combination of individual effort and group activity. The unemployed can find jobs through individual effort, or they can join forces to pressure the government for policies that would reduce unemployment. Blacks can also deal with their problems either as individuals or by joining with others. While the main problem of the unemployed person can be solved if he or she finds a job, many of the problems of blacks can be solved only by governmental action; and pressuring the government requires *group* activity.

Self-Awareness

It is not enough for a group of citizens to have interests in common; they have to be *aware* of those interests. In many cases a group has interests in common for a long time, but those interests become politically relevant only when the group becomes aware of them. In recent years, for example, women's groups have been active in trying to equalize the salaries paid to men and women for doing the same work. The problem—lower pay for women—is not a new one. Only when women became *concerned* about the problem, however, did they become politically relevant.

Organization and Leadership

Groups that are organized can pressure the government more effectively. Groups with leaders have someone who can speak for them to the government. Leaders also stimulate members to work for the group.

A relevant political group must have common interests, self-awareness, and organization. Blacks in America have all three. Many economic and professional groups, such as union members, farmers, and doctors, have all three. Other groups have the first two but not the last. Such groups are called *potential groups*. Until recently they included migrant farm workers and consumers. But these groups have become more active as they have become aware of their common interests and have organized to work for policies that favor those interests.

It is easier to organize a group if its members see each other often. If the members of a group live in the same neighborhood, go to the same church, or work in the same place, they are more likely to form an organized group. Again, we can use blacks and unemployed people as an example. Blacks can organize more easily because they tend to live in the same neighborhoods. This is not true of the unemployed. Table 6.1 shows the characteristics of blacks that encourage the formation of a politically relevant group, along with the characteristics of the unemployed that make them less likely to form such a group.

TABLE 6.1 Comparing Blacks and the Unemployed as Interest Groups

Characteristics of a Politically Relevant Group	Blacks	Unemployed
Common interests?	Yes: jobs, schools, integration, and other issues	Yes: jobs and unemployment benefits
Intense interests?	Yes: Racial issues affect the vital interests of blacks	Yes: Jobs are crucial
Long-term interests?	Yes: One's racial identity sticks for life	No: For most people unemployment is temporary
Interests that need a common solution?	Yes: Many of the problems blacks face require government intervention	Not necessarily: Getting a job solves the problem, at least for the individual
Self-awareness?	Yes: Blacks identify as blacks	No: Being unemployed is not an important self-identity
Organization?	Yes: There are many black organizations	No: The unemployed are unorganized
Leadership?	Yes: many leaders	No
Geographic concentration?	Yes: Blacks live in black neighborhoods	No

Getting Members to Contribute

Why do citizens join with others and contribute time and effort to a group? At first the answer seems obvious: Citizens work together to pressure the government to respond to their needs. Women work with other women to influence government policy on sex discrimination; blacks join with other blacks to influence housing policy. These goals are the group's *policy goals,* the things it wants the government to do.

Some people argue that it is not "rational" for people to become involved in a group in order to work toward its policy goals. To see why they make this claim, recall our discussion of collective goods in Chapter 1. A collective good is something that is available to every citizen whether that person has contributed to it or not. If I can use a new city park even if I did not work to create it, why not sit back and let others work and pay for it? Obviously, if everyone did nothing there would be no park.

As we pointed out in Chapter 1, *binding* decisions are often needed if collective goods are to be created. Thus, for example, taxes (which citizens must pay whether they want to or not) are used to create parks. But why should a woman work with other women to get Congress to pass equal-pay legislation? The effort of one more person would have little effect on the outcome, so it should not make much difference if she does nothing. She will benefit from the legislation if it is passed, even if she did not work for it. The "logic" of the situation would result in no action by women—it would be rational to wait for others to act and then get a "free ride."

Groups of citizens with common interests cannot force their members to contribute to the group's policy goals. The government can make citizens pay taxes, but the women's movement cannot force other women to join. They have to volunteer.

So why do people contribute time and effort to groups even though it is not "rational" to do so? One answer is that groups that are successful in getting people to work for them usually offer other incentives besides the chance to work toward a policy goal. One such incentive is the feeling of solidarity or "belonging" that comes from working with others to achieve some goal. Social movements like the women's movement or the civil-rights movement give their members a sense of belonging, and this helps keep them active in the movement.

There are other incentives for group members too. Members may make job contacts through the group, or the group may provide recreational opportunities. For some, joining the group is a way of meeting people.

We are not trying to say that the members of a group pay lip service to its goals but actually participate in order to make friends or get a sense of belonging. Members may be strongly committed to the group's goals. But the

One reward of group membership is a feeling of solidarity.

other rewards offered by the group reinforce that commitment, and groups that offer these additional rewards are likely to be more successful.

GROUPS IN AMERICA

The tendency to form groups is typical of American political life. A study that compared Americans with citizens of other countries asked people how they would go about trying to influence their local government. In the United States over half of the respondents said they would try to get their friends and neighbors to join them so that they could approach the government as a group. In Great Britain only 34 percent of the respondents said they would form groups, and in Germany, Italy, and Mexico the percentages were even lower.[1]

In this section we will take a look at some of the types of political groups that exist in America.

Class

Unlike the situation in most democracies, social class is *not* a major basis of political conflict in America. Many other democracies have a strong socialist party that is supported by the working class and sees itself as opposed to the "bourgeois" middle class. In the United States, however, the Socialist party has never been successful, and few Americans think of themselves as socialists.

This is not to say that class differences have no effect on American political behavior. Factory workers are much more likely to vote Democratic than business executives, who tend to support the Republican party. But each party gets support from members of all social classes.

Why is class a less important basis of political conflict than it is in many other countries? We can answer this question by returning to the three factors mentioned earlier: common interests, self-awareness, and organization.

Common Interests   Most American workers have a fairly decent standard of living. Therefore, while they do have common interests (e.g., a government policy to foster full employment), they do not feel a strong need to unite in opposition to the middle class. Also, many of the problems of workers are matters that they believe they can deal with as individuals rather than through a class movement.

Self-Awareness   Americans are more likely to think of themselves as individuals than as members of a social class. This is because the United States has never had a rigid class structure. Workers have always viewed the middle class not as "the enemy" but as a group that they may someday join. The common identification of the American working class has also been weakened by the fact that workers come from a wide variety of racial and ethnic backgrounds.

Organization   The most important organizations for class-based political conflict are political parties and unions. As mentioned earlier, however, American political parties get support from people of all classes. The parties were formed before the growth of the American working class, so there was no need for workers to form their own party; instead, they were welcomed

---

[1] Gabriel A. Almond and Sidney Verba, *The Civic Culture: Political Attitudes and Democracy in Five Nations* (Princeton, N.J.: Princeton University Press, 1963), p. 203.

into the existing parties—especially the Democratic party. Compared with European unions, American unions have focused less on political activity and more on improving the economic condition of workers.

Ethnicity and Race

More important than class as a basis of group conflict is ethnicity. When we talk about "ethnics" or "ethnic politics," we tend to think of Irish Americans, Polish Americans, Jewish Americans, or perhaps black Americans. What we mean by *ethnicity* is the sense of identity that is based on where one lives or comes from and is inherited from one's parents. It is the answer you give when someone asks, "What are you?"

America, the history books tell us, is a melting pot. People from Europe, Asia, and Africa came here, mixed, and became the American people. This is basically true. For one thing, most immigrants became American citizens. For another, they all learned English. Teachers and government officials believed that to be an American meant to speak English, and the immigrants accepted this policy. The language of the "old country" rarely survived.

Thus, we are told, the melting pot took immigrants from all over the world and made one nation. But some groups—especially members of other races—did not "melt" easily. Blacks, of course, were denied citizenship until after the Civil War. Similarly, immigrants from Asia, as well as Native Americans, were often denied the benefits of citizenship.

Even white immigrants did not "melt" completely. Today ethnic identity remains strong. Ethnic organizations have widespread support, and ethnic interests come into conflict. In fact ethnic patterns are found throughout American politics. Ethnic groups such as Irish Catholics have traditionally voted over 70 percent Democratic. They tend to support members of the same ethnic group and to show concern about political problems in the old country (e.g., in Ireland or in Eastern Europe).

There are two reasons for ethnic politics. One is the desire to keep one's ethnic identity, despite the melting pot. This used to mean living near, depending on, and marrying others of the same background. Today it means rediscovering the language, history, and customs of the old country. The other reason for ethnic politics is the fact that many ethnic groups came to America as immigrants. As each group arrived, it became the most deprived group in the society. When the Irish came in the mid- to late 1800s, they found themselves in the poorest neighborhoods, with the worst jobs, and with no political power. They had to struggle with the older Yankee residents of their communities for better jobs and housing and control of the local government. A generation later the Italian immigrants found themselves in the same situation—only their struggle was with the older *Irish* residents.

For many years American politics, especially in the large cities, was ethnic politics. Large numbers of immigrants from the same country tended to settle in particular cities. These groups—the Irish, the Poles and Slavs, the East European Jews, the Italians—soon became citizens and thus gained an important source of power: the vote. The political "machines" of New York, Boston, and Chicago were based on the ethnic vote. In return for their votes the machine offered the immigrants help in finding jobs, aid if they had trouble with the police, and a Christmas basket.

The white ethnics illustrate the three factors that make a group politically relevant. They had common interests because they were newcomers in an unfamiliar country. They were aware of those interests because they lived in ethnic neighborhoods. And they were organized by the political parties, which wanted their votes.

Today ethnic groups have fewer interests in common. They are no longer new residents holding low-level jobs. Many have moved out of ethnic neighborhoods and into suburbs that are ethnically mixed. The services that used to be provided by the political machine have been taken over by social security and other welfare programs. It appears that the basis for ethnic politics is fading.

Yet ethnicity is still a strong political factor. In many cities the candidate with the right ethnic name can count on support from people with similar backgrounds. Ethnicity also plays a role in presidential elections. Ethnic associations and ethnic neighborhoods still exist. In part, ethnic politics is a response to the challenge of the blacks. Many white ethnics have "made it": They have good jobs, a decent income, a house and car, a good school for their children. They feel threatened by the expanding black neighborhoods and the blacks' firm sense of identity.

The Blacks   As mentioned earlier, the melting pot never included blacks. The blacks have always been important in American politics—not as participants but as subjects of government policy.

Before the Civil War blacks were barred from political life. Even free blacks were usually denied the right to vote. After the war the Thirteenth, Fourteenth, and Fifteenth Amendments were passed, and it became illegal to deny blacks citizenship, the vote, or the protection of the laws. In practice, however, blacks were unable to vote in the South. Segregation was legal, and in many ways blacks were not much better off than they had been before the war.

As mentioned earlier, one of the factors that makes a group of citizens politically important and effective is a sense of identity. The blacks have developed a sense of identity as a result of the deprivations they have had to endure. But black self-awareness became especially strong in the 1950s and 1960s partly as a result of the civil-rights movement and partly because the mass media—especially television—helped communicate the new movement to blacks in many parts of the country.

Thus by the 1960s blacks had both common interests and self-awareness. They became politically important because they also had organization. The NAACP, the Southern Christian Leadership Council, CORE, the Black Muslims, the Black Panthers, and Operation Breadbasket illustrate the number and variety of black organizations. Blacks are not organized into a single group, nor are they all organized, but organizations of all kinds have made blacks a strong political force.

Other Minority Groups Other minority groups besides blacks have also become politically active. In each case common interests or needs, self-awareness, and organization have combined to make the group politically relevant. Chicanos, for example, have long had common interests. They did not speak English, could get only the lowest-paying farm jobs, and were discriminated against in housing and schools. However, they were not politically active until recent years, when they developed self-awareness and were organized by such leaders as Cesar Chavez.

Another group, the Japanese Americans, also has a long history of common problems and discrimination. Japanese Americans were long barred from American citizenship and from owning land, and in World War II they were put in concentration camps (called "relocation centers."). Japanese Americans have a fairly strong sense of group identity, but unlike Chicanos and blacks they are not politically active. They have some self-awareness and

Language is an issue in America. Twelve million Americans are Spanish speaking.

even some organization, but few common interests. They face almost no discrimination in housing and schooling and often have high-status jobs. Since they have no reason to pressure the government for a particular set of policies, they are not a relevant political force.

Other Types of Groups

Occupational Groups   Occupation is an important concern of most Americans. Yet occupational groups vary in terms of common interests, self-awareness, and organization.

Not all occupational groups have important interests in common. Take shopkeepers, for example. Members of this group do not have a common fate—one may do well while another goes bankrupt. Of course all shopkeepers may be hurt by inflation or recession, but these problems affect them as part of the general economy, not specifically as shopkeepers. On the other hand, all the shopkeepers in a particular town may be hurt by the opening of a shopping center outside the town. In this case they may form a politically relevant group in that town.

Compared with shopkeepers, such groups as teachers or auto workers are much more likely to have a common fate and common interests. Teachers have common interests because their salaries and working conditions are set by the government they work for. Auto workers have common interests because they depend on a single industry.

Another difference among occupational groups has to do with how much they are affected by government policy. The more a group is affected by the government, the more likely it is to be politically active. Doctors and lawyers illustrate this point. Government policies affect the practice of medicine much more than the practice of law. Through the American Medical Association doctors are very active in politics.

Note that we are talking about political activity in relation to the *interests* of an occupational group. Lawyers are generally more active in politics than doctors. They are more likely to run for office or be appointed to positions in the government; but they do so as individuals, not as representatives of the legal profession.

Occupational groups also differ in self-awareness and organization. These two factors are related: The better a group is organized, the more its members tend to be aware of their common interests. For example, workers who are not unionized are politically inactive both because they have no organization to speak for them and because they have no self-awareness. For a long time this was true of teachers and migrant workers. Teachers felt that professional groups should not be unionized, while migrant workers were unable to form groups because of the conditions of their work. In recent years, as both groups have become unionized, both have become more active and effective.

Regional Groups The places where people live and work—state, region, city, or suburb—is another basis for common interests. Regional differences have been important throughout the nation's history and have led to differences in political behavior. Southerners, for example, have traditionally supported the Democratic party, and the Southern Democrats in Congress have traditionally voted as a unit, often joining northern Republicans to form a strong conservative bloc. But the "solid South" has become less solid as the social and political life of the region has changed as a result of industrialization and the civil-rights movement.

In recent years the main regional division in the United States has been between the "Sunbelt" and the "Snowbelt." The southern and southwestern states—the Sunbelt—have been growing in terms of both industry and population, while the northeastern and midwestern states have been declining. Political conflict between these regions has centered on the government's energy policy (the Snowbelt is more concerned over the cost of fuel) and government aid (each region claims that it is being shortchanged).

Regional politics is important because elections have a regional structure: We elect representatives and senators from particular districts and states. This point is so obvious that it is easy to overlook. But why not elect representatives by occupational group (a certain number to represent plumbers, a certain number to represent farmers, etc.) or by race and ethnicity (a certain number to represent blacks, a certain number to represent Chicanos, etc.), instead of by region? It can be argued that people of the same race or occupation have more in common than people who happen to live in the same region. Indeed, some countries have experimented with such plans. The fact is, however, that the American system of representation is organized on the basis of place of residence, and this is unlikely to change. We will have more to say about this in Chapter 10.

Religion In the United States religious differences have rarely been a source of severe conflict. This is probably due to the fact that the Constitution bans any law affecting religious beliefs. However, the Constitution has not prevented conflict over issues *related* to religion. For example, is it unconstitutional for a city to pay for school buses that take children to Catholic schools? Are school prayers unconstitutional? On such issues religious groups are concerned and active.

Sex Women make up 51 percent of the population, but they share many of the problems of minority groups. Thus, the history of the women's movement is similar in many ways to the history of other politically relevant groups.

Women have long had interests and problems in common. They have been discriminated against in jobs, property rights, and many other areas. However, only in the past 10 to 15 years have women become aware of their common interests and recognized that they require governmental action. Today they are putting pressure on Congress to pass laws banning sex discrimination and are active in support of the proposed Equal Rights Amendment to the Constitution. The self-awareness of women has been encouraged by feminist leaders and women's organizations such as the National Organization for Women (NOW), founded in 1966.

Critics of social movements like the women's movement often accuse such groups of "inventing" the problems they complain of. "Women never knew they were discriminated against until the women's-lib types told them," they claim. But that is exactly what leaders must do if they want to start a movement. They must create self-awareness among the members of a group in order to get them to act. Feminist leaders do not "invent" problems for women any more than black leaders "invented" problems for blacks. They simply make individuals aware that others have similar problems and that collective action might help solve these problems.

Age   In the late 1960s age became a basis for political action with the development of the "youth culture." More important, however, may be the growth of the elderly as a politically relevant group. As medical care improves and people tend to retire earlier, the number of older citizens in-

Women's groups have campaigned for the Equal Rights Amendment.

creases. These citizens clearly have interests in common: social security, inflation, housing, and the like. As the government has become more involved in these problems, the self-awareness of this group has increased. The elderly have also become more organized: The National Association of Retired Persons has over 7 million members, and other groups such as the Gray Panthers have become quite effective.

Special-Interest Groups Some groups are based directly on shared interests rather than characteristics such as race, sex, age, or religion. Such groups may be based on common recreational interests (e.g. hiking or bird watching), social concerns (e.g., pollution or corruption in government), or cultural interests (e.g., literature or art). Like other groups, they become politically relevant when their interests are affected by governmental action or inaction. For example, a recreational group may begin as an organization with no particular interest in government policy—as simply a group of citizens with a common interest in hiking or bird watching. As soon as those interests are affected by government policy (e.g., policy on preservation of wilderness areas), the group may become politically active.

OVERLAPPING MEMBERSHIPS

We have seen that there is a great variety of groups and potential groups in America. More important, these groups can overlap. Every citizen is a member of many potential interest groups at once, because every citizen has an ethnic background, an occupation, a religion, and so on.

Which of these memberships will be politically important? It varies, depending on the issue. A Catholic steelworker living in a suburb of Cleveland will sometimes act as a steelworker, supporting policies or candidates favorable to steelworkers. At other times he may act as a Catholic, voting for a Catholic candidate or basing his opinion on abortion law on the teachings of the Catholic Church. Or he may act as a suburban resident, perhaps opposing a plan to tax commuters who work in the central city.

Most Americans have many potential interests. At times they act in terms of one of those interests; at other times others are more important. For some people, however, one interest may override all others. Black militants respond to all issues in terms of race; militant feminists respond in terms of sex. This is an important point because it affects the nation's political life. A citizen who has a variety of interests is likely to feel less strongly about any one of those interests than a citizen who puts all of his or her energy into one interest. The "multi-interest" citizen is more willing to compromise. The "single-interest" citizen is likely to be less compromising and more militant.

Crosscutting vs. Reinforcing Memberships

Imagine a society in which people are divided by religion (Catholics vs. Protestants), occupation (workers vs. managers), and place of residence (central-city vs. suburban residents). If these three divisions are *reinforcing,* all the citizens who are similar in one of these ways are also similar in the other two ways. The society might then be divided as follows:

Group A	Group B
Catholic workers living in the central city	Protestant managers living in the suburbs

On any issue related to these interests the society would be divided into two opposing groups. For example, it might be divided as follows:

Group A	Group B
1. Favors aid to parochial schools.	1. Opposes aid to parochial schools.
2. Favors controls on profits.	2. Opposes controls on profits.
3. Favors taxing the suburbs to pay for city services.	3. Opposes taxing the suburbs to pay for city services.

In such a situation there would be a lot of political tension. The two groups have nothing in common. If government power were in the hands of the Protestants, the Catholics would have little hope that their interests would be protected, since the group in power would differ from them in every way.

But suppose these divisions are *crosscutting* rather than reinforcing. In this case some workers would be Protestant and others Catholic; some would live in the suburbs and others in the city. Citizens who were divided on one issue would be united on others. The Catholic workers would disagree with the Protestant workers over aid to parochial schools, but they would agree on profit controls. Catholic workers living in the suburbs would share interests with Protestants living there as well as with managers living there.

In general, American politics is characterized by crosscutting rather than reinforcing group memberships. This fact, together with the wide range of groups in America and the varying intensity of citizens' concern over various issues, means that there is no single pattern of division and competition in the United States. From one issue to another and from one group to another, the ways in which different parts of American society compete with each other may differ.

PATTERNS OF DIVISION AND COMPETITION

In this section we will describe several patterns of conflict among groups and give some examples of those patterns. We can understand any issue a lot

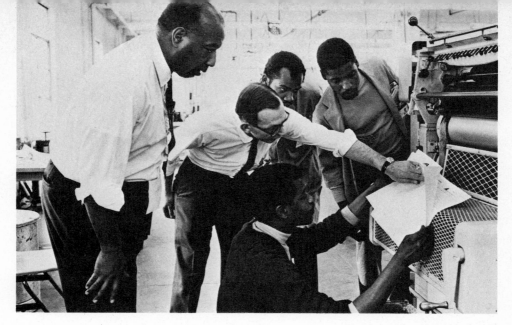

Conflict is less intense when individuals divided by one characteristic, such as race, are united by another, such as occupation.

better if it fits into one of these patterns. First, however, we have to understand the *scale of political positions.*

Political conflict begins with conflicting interests. One group of citizens favors one policy (call it A) while another group favors a different policy (call it B). Some feel strongly about the issue while others feel less strongly about it. Therefore we can put individuals and groups at various points on the scale shown in Figure 6.1. Those at point A might favor integrated housing; those at point B might oppose it. Or those at A might favor gun control while those at B might oppose it. Some citizens support position A or B strongly, some more mildly, and some not at all.

If we convert the scale of political positions into a graph, with the amount of space under the curved line showing how many people favor that policy, a variety of patterns appear.

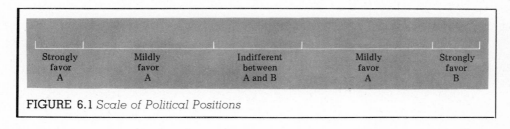

| Strongly favor A | Mildly favor A | Indifferent between A and B | Mildly favor A | Strongly favor B |

FIGURE 6.1 *Scale of Political Positions*

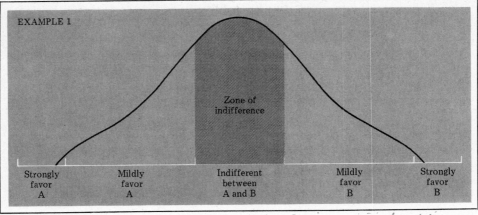

← *typical of American political societies*

Pattern 1 (See Example 1)

In this pattern the largest part of the population does not care about either A or B, and those who *do* care do not feel very strongly about the issue. Notice that this pattern is quite symmetrical—the numbers of citizens on each side are about equal. Many issues show this pattern, and on such issues there is little conflict. It makes little difference what action the government takes—if any—because there is not much concern on either side.

Pattern 2 (See Example 2)

Pattern 2, like pattern 1, is a situation in which we would not expect much competition or conflict, since all the citizens seem to support policy A. This

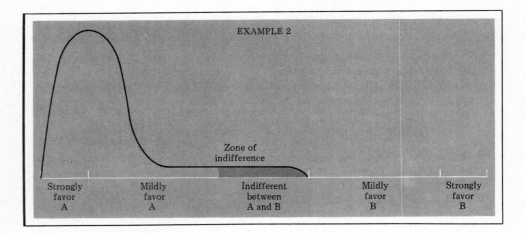

has been the case in most wars before the Vietnam War: Most Americans were strongly antagonistic toward the enemy. Such a pattern can be very helpful to government leaders if they want public support for an all-out war effort, but it can greatly limit their freedom of action if they want to take a "soft" line with the enemy.

Pattern 2 can be dangerous to democracy, however—woe to the few citizens who favor policy B! Even those who do not care may be in trouble. Freedom of speech or assembly has been severely limited in such situations, especially in wartime.

Pattern 3 (See Example 3)

Pattern 3 is very different from the first two: It shows a major division of the population. About half the citizens strongly support policy A and about half strongly support policy B. Very few are in between. Obviously, if the choice between A and B is an important one, a population divided in this way is deeply divided indeed. This pattern may describe the United States in the period just before the Civil War. Note, however, that pattern 3 is rare. Even during the Vietnam War the American population did not show this pattern. When citizens were asked whether they wanted the United States to withdraw from Vietnam immediately no matter what or they wanted the United States to do everything necessary to win the war, their answers form the pattern shown in Figure 6.2. The largest group is found in the middle, and those who took positions on one side or the other often did not feel strongly about the issue. Few were extreme "hawks" or extreme "doves."

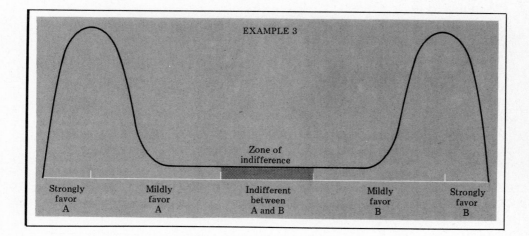

EXAMPLE 3

Zone of indifference

| Strongly favor A | Mildly favor A | Indifferent between A and B | Mildly favor B | Strongly favor B |

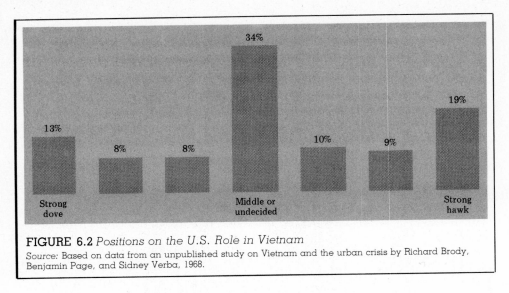

FIGURE 6.2 *Positions on the U.S. Role in Vietnam*
Source: Based on data from an unpublished study on Vietnam and the urban crisis by Richard Brody, Benjamin Page, and Sidney Verba, 1968.

The pattern shown in Figure 6.2 is a common one. Indeed, the positions of Americans on a political scale ranging from liberal to conservative is very similar. (See Figure 6.3.) Opinions tend to cluster near the center. This pattern—pattern 4—is found on a number of issues.

Pattern 4 (See Example 4)

Pattern 4 is actually a slight variation on pattern 1. Few people care much

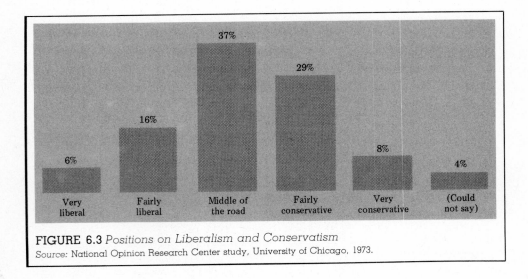

FIGURE 6.3 *Positions on Liberalism and Conservatism*
Source: National Opinion Research Center study, University of Chicago, 1973.

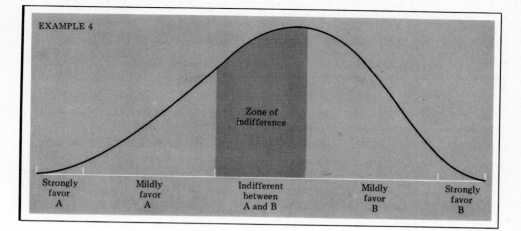

EXAMPLE 4

Zone of
indifference

| Strongly favor A | Mildly favor A | Indifferent between A and B | Mildly favor B | Strongly favor B |

about either policy A or policy B, but those who do have an opinion seem to prefer B. Policy B stands a good chance of getting favorable action, but this is by no means certain. Those who support policy B may have no organization or leadership, or they may not try hard enough to win the support of those who do not care. Even if they succeed, there will be little conflict because no one feels very strongly about the issue.

The division of Americans into Democrats and Republicans illustrates this pattern. Most Americans are either Democrats or Republicans; some are independent. But few people support their party so strongly that they would be entirely opposed to having members of the other party in leadership positions. Over the years more citizens have become Democrats than Republicans. This does not mean, however, that there is a Democrat in the White House after every election. Since citizens do not identify very strongly with their party, they can often be persuaded to vote for candidates of the other party.

Students of American politics often praise the fact that the pattern of division in the nation usually looks like Example 4. It is true that a society divided as shown in Example 3, with two groups of citizens far apart and hostile to each other, would be more likely to fly apart. But the pattern shown in Example 4 may have the opposite result: Nothing ever changes. This can lead to stagnation in government policy.

Pattern 5 (See Example 5)

In pattern 5 a small group is strongly in favor of a particular policy while the bulk of the population either does not care or mildly favors the other side. Drug manufacturers, for example, care a lot about government regulation of the manufacture or sale of drugs, since such regulation may cut into their

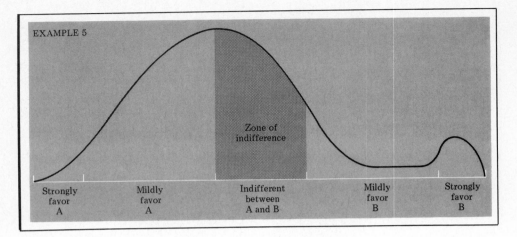

profits. People who do not use many drug products do not care. Those who use many drug products may favor such regulation but will be much less intense than the manufacturers.

Pattern 5 also applies to gun control. As mentioned earlier, about 70 percent of the American people favor gun control. The opposition is small, but it is intense. It is more likely to be vocal and to be organized, and thus is likely to have its way.

Pattern 6 (See Example 6)

Our final example shows a pattern that has become more common in recent years. Here an intense minority faces an equally intense majority. Such a situation exists when there are groups in the society that are cut off from the rest

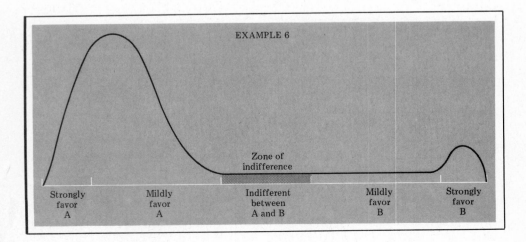

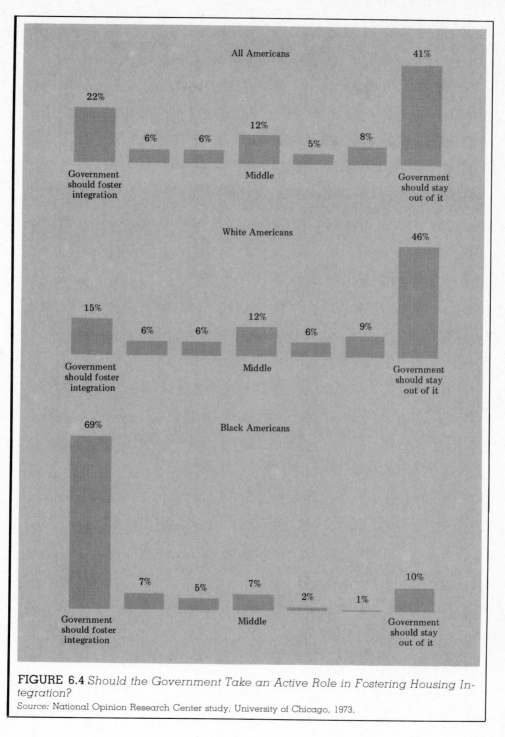

FIGURE 6.4 *Should the Government Take an Active Role in Fostering Housing Integration?*

Source: National Opinion Research Center study, University of Chicago, 1973.

of the population by a set of reinforcing divisions. An example is the situation in several large metropolitan areas. In the decaying central city lives a population that is poor and black. In the suburbs lives a population that is more affluent and white. The two groups are divided by race, economic condition, and place of residence, and therefore they have few common interests. The central-city residents want social services, and they want the costs of those services shared by those who live outside the city; they also want access to better schools and a chance to get housing outside the city. Suburban residents oppose them on all of these issues.

Figure 6.4 (on p. 117) illustrates this division of opinion. In 1973 citizens were asked about housing policy: Should the government see to it that blacks are allowed to buy houses in white neighborhoods if they want to, or should it stay out of the matter? Most people took positions at one end of the scale or the other. Those who felt that the government should stay out of the housing issue outnumbered the others by two to one.

When we look at black and white opinions separately, the degree to which American society is divided over this issue becomes even clearer. Some whites strongly favor integrated housing, but most whites are at the other end of the scale; they want the government to stay out of the matter. Most blacks want the government to do something about the problem of integration. Such a pattern leads to conflict. That, of course, is the situation on this issue.

Participation and Leadership

In this chapter we will begin by discussing the various ways in which citizens participate in politics. Then we will go on to see how our political leaders are recruited. The two topics are related because political leaders are recruited from the more active citizens.

HOW DO CITIZENS PARTICIPATE?

Participation refers to the ways in which citizens influence what the government does. Voting is the most familiar way of participating in politics, but there are many other ways as well. For example, citizens can try to influence the way other citizens vote. Thus one of the most common forms of political activity takes place at election time, when people ring doorbells, work at the polls, or talk to friends and neighbors to try to affect how they vote.

Elections have a big drawback, however: They take place at a fixed time and offer a limited choice. Citizens have many different interests, and they have those interests all the time, not just at election time. Participation in election campaigns is not enough to tell the government what citizens want. Other means of participation are needed to fill in the gaps left by elections.

Communal Activity

The activity groups of citizens working together to try to influence the government in a specific area is called *communal activity*. The group may be informal, as when neighbors join in a protest to city hall over some local issue. Or it may be a formal organization such as a union, the PTA, or a civic association. This kind of activity is important in two ways: (1) Citizens work together, and the government is more likely to be influenced by a group than by an individual. (2) Citizens are active in relation to the problems that concern them most.

Individual Activity

Political participation may also be an individual activity, as when a citizen writes to his or her representative in Congress or to a newspaper, or visits a government office to make a complaint. This activity often has to do with problems that matter only to that particular individual, such as the condition of the sidewalk in front of his or her house. But this is another way in which citizens influence what the government does.

Marches and Demonstrations

Citizens sometimes use more dramatic means of showing how they feel about an issue. They may march to protest American foreign policy or the busing of schoolchildren. Such protests have become more common in recent years. They are used by citizens who believe that "ordinary" ways of participating will not work or that the problem is too urgent to be solved by ordinary means.

HOW ACTIVE ARE AMERICANS?

Some people say there is a lot of political participation in America. Others say there is very little. This contradiction may be due to differences in what people expect. If you expect all citizens to be politically active, you will be disappointed to find that "only" 10–20 percent of the population is active. But if you expect most people to be private, home-centered citizens, you will be surprised to find that "as many as" two out of ten Americans are active in politics. Table 7.1 shows the percentages of citizens who are active in various ways. Note that a majority of the people are active only in presidential elections. The turnout for those elections is usually about 55–65 percent of the

TABLE 7.1 Political Activities of Citizens

Mode of Activity	Percent Active
A. *Voting*	
Voted in 1976 presidential election	53%
Voted in 1972 presidential election	55%
Votes regularly in local elections	47
B. *Taking Part in Campaign Activities*	
Persuade others how to vote	28
Ever worked for a party	26
Attended political rallies	19
Contributed money in a political campaign	13
Member of a political club or organization	8
C. *Cooperative Activities*	
Worked through local group	30
Helped form local group	14
Active member of organization engaged in community activities	32
D. *Contacting Officials*	
Contacted local officials on some problem	20
Contacted extralocal officials on some problem	18
Wrote a letter to a public official	17
Wrote a letter to an editor	3

SOURCE: All but the first two and last two items based on data from Sidney Verba and Norman H. Nie, *Participation in America: Political Democracy and Social Equality* (New York: Harper & Row, 1972); the last two items in D based on data from 1964 presidential election study, University of Michigan, Institute for Social Research, Survey Research Center.

voting public. By contrast, in local elections less than half the voting public votes regularly.

Campaign activity takes more time and effort than voting, and it is clear that such activity is not for everyone. Fewer than one-third of the American people try to persuade others how to vote; only about one-quarter have worked for a political party.

About one-third of all citizens participate in informal communal activity, and a similar number have worked through formal organizations. As for individual activity, citizens often say "I'm going to write to my congressman!" but only about one out of six has ever written to any public official, and only about one out of five has ever contacted a government official about a problem.

When it comes to marches and demonstrations, it is hard to get accurate figures, but it is likely that few citizens take part in such activities. For example, in the late 1960s, at the height of the Vietnam War protests, one study found that only 8 out of 1500 citizens had taken part in a demonstration about Vietnam—about one-half of one percent. Note, however, that while only a small percentage of all citizens may take part in demonstrations, larger portions of particular groups may participate in this way. In the case of Vietnam, over half of the students who were in college during the war said that they had taken part in antiwar demonstrations.

Types of Participants

We can divide the American public into six types of participants based on how active they are in politics and the kind of activity they prefer:[1]

1. *Inactives*. About one-quarter of all Americans are not active in politics. They do not even vote regularly, though they may vote from time to time.
2. *Voting Specialists*. Some citizens almost always vote—but that is all they do. They account for about 21 percent of the population.
3. *Parochial Participants*. These citizens—about 4 percent of the population[2]—contact government officials on matters that affect them or their families. They avoid any activity that is likely to affect more public issues.
4. *Communal Participants*. A fairly large part of the population—about 20 percent—is active in nonpartisan community affairs. They join civic groups, are active on school issues, help in charitable campaigns, and the like.
5. *Campaign Activists*. Another 15 percent of the population takes part in political campaigns but is less involved in nonpartisan activities.

[1] Sidney Verba and Norman H. Nie, *Participation in America: Political Democracy and Social Equality* (New York: Harper & Row, 1972), chap. 4.
[2] Note that this figure is lower than the number of people who write to government officials, just as the figure for "voting specialists" is lower than the number of voters. We are talking about people who *only* vote or *only* write to their congressman.

6. *Total Complete Activists.* A small but important part of the population—11 percent—is active in every way. These people never miss an election, are active in community affairs, and participate in campaign activities.[3]

Comparing the United States with Other Nations

As mentioned earlier, Americans are more likely than citizens elsewhere to believe that they can influence the government if they want to. Perhaps more important, they are more likely to feel that the citizen has a duty to be active in the affairs of his or her community. But when it comes to actual participation the pattern is mixed.

Voting Voter turnout is usually lower in the United States than in many European democracies. The turnout for American presidential elections tends to be between 55 and 65 percent, whereas in many European countries the turnout is 80–90 percent. In recent years the U.S. turnout has dropped

---

[3] Seven percent of the sample studied was unclassifiable because of mixed patterns or missing information.

Difficult registration laws used to keep turnout low. Laws have eased in recent years.

There is much community-oriented activity in America.

still lower, even though literacy tests, residency requirements of more than 30 days, and other barriers to voting have been removed. Political scientists are not sure why this has happened. One explanation is that there are more voters in the 18- to 20-year-old age group, which usually has a very low turnout rate. Another is that the attitudes of American voters are changing. Many are more cynical about elections. Furthermore, as we will see later, fewer citizens identify with a particular party, and those without party ties are less likely to vote.

Communal Activity Americans seem more likely than people in other nations to participate in communal activity. When asked how they would go about influencing the government, Americans tend to say they would join with others. This willingness to work with others—friends, neighbors, and the like—is found in all social groups in the United States. In other countries people are more likely to work alone or through a formal organization such as a political party.

Data on the actual behavior of citizens show that there is much more communal activity in the United States than elsewhere. For example, 32 percent of Americans belong to an organization that is active in community affairs, compared to 9 percent in Austria, 7 percent in India, 11 percent in Japan, and 15 percent in the Netherlands.[4] This is nothing new. Over 100

4 Sidney Verba, Norman Nie, and Jae-On Kim, *Participation and Political Equality: A Seven Nation Comparison* (New York: Cambridge University Press, 1978).

years ago Alexis de Tocqueville commented on the tendency of Americans to participate in group activities.

WHO PARTICIPATES?

The way American democracy works depends largely on who participates and how. By participating in politics people tell the government what they need and want. If some citizens participate more than others, the government is likely to pay attention to the active citizens and ignore the inactive ones.

The important question, however, is not whether all citizens participate but whether those who do are representative of the rest of the population. If the activists have the same problems, needs, and preferences as the nonactivists, they may speak for those who do not participate. On the other hand, if they are different from the nonactivists—if they come from a select social group or want the government to do special things—then the government will respond only to the needs of that particular group.

No group is barred from participating in American politics, but certain kinds of citizens participate more than others. Studies have shown that a person with a college education is much more likely to be politically active than a person with less education. Also, people with higher incomes are more likely to be active than the poor. Race, sex, and age affect participation too: Blacks are, on the average, somewhat less active than whites, and women are less active than men. Both young and old citizens tend to be less active than those in their middle years.

These differences in participation rates make a difference in what gets communicated to the government. Those who are inactive—the poor, for example—have different problems than those who are more active. Inactive citizens are nearly twice as likely as active ones to say that they have recently faced serious problems in paying for medical care, getting a job, or finding adequate housing. Inactive citizens also have different ideas about what the government should do. For example, while active citizens believe the poor should solve their problems by themselves, inactive citizens think the government should deal with those problems. But this view is less well communicated to the government, since these citizens participate less in politics.

Participation and Equality

This brings us to a major problem of American politics. The people who need government action most—the poor, the uneducated, those who are discriminated against—are the least active. Those who need government action least are the most active. The reason for this is that the things that make citizens better off in social and economic terms are the very things that make them more likely to participate.

Wealthy citizens can make large contributions to political candidates, and therefore are likely to have greater political influence. Well-educated citizens are more likely to "know the ropes" of politics—whom to see and what to say. In addition, better-educated citizens are more motivated to take part in politics. We pointed out earlier that Americans are more likely than citizens of other nations to believe that they can be active. These beliefs are stronger among well-educated citizens than among those who are less well educated. (See Table 7.2.)

This situation illustrates once again the contradiction between political equality and social and economic inequality. The fact that some citizens have more education and income than others means that the goal of political equality cannot be achieved. The richer and better-educated citizens have the resources and the motivation to participate in political activity. Thus, while the opportunity to participate is legally available to all, the citizens who take advantage of this opportunity are those who are already well off.

Equalizing Participation

Can anything be done to make political participation more equal? One way of equalizing participation would be to mobilize inactive citizens—to raise their level of participation so that it matches that of the more active citizens. This requires the three factors discussed in Chapter 6: common interests, self-awareness, and organization. The process of mobilizing a disadvantaged group is illustrated by the recent political activity of blacks.

Among blacks we may see the beginnings of a break in the vicious cycle that leaves the disadvantaged even worse off because they are not politically active. The break has come, we believe, through organization and self-awareness. American blacks, forced to live apart from whites, have organized

TABLE 7.2   Citizens' Beliefs About Political Participation, by Educational Group

	No High School	*Some High School*	*Some College*
Percent who say they could influence a decision of the local government	60%	82%	99%
Percent who say the ordinary person should be active in politics	35%	56%	66%

SOURCE: Based on data from Gabriel Almond and Sidney Verba, *The Civic Culture: Political Attitudes and Democracy in Five Nations* (Princeton, N.J.: Princeton University Press, 1963).

as a political group. The separation of blacks from the mainstream of American society has also caused them to develop a clear sense of group identity, which may be seen in the slogans "black power" and "black is beautiful."

Studies show that self-awareness increases black participation in politics. As mentioned earlier, black Americans tend to participate somewhat less than white Americans. This is not surprising, since blacks, on the average, have lower incomes and less education than whites. But if we look at blacks who have a sense of group identity, we find that they are as active in politics as whites. In other words, black self-awareness is a way of overcoming the tendency for blacks to be less active in politics because of their disadvantage in terms of income and education.[5]

Women in Politics

The difference in political activity between men and women is much smaller in the United States than in other nations. However, this applies mainly to "low-level" activities such as campaign work (i.e., ringing doorbells, sending out letters, and the like). When it comes to "higher-level" activities, the gap between men and women widens. While women are as likely to work in campaigns as men, they are less likely to direct those campaigns. While they are just as likely to work *for* a candidate, women are less likely to *become* candidates themselves (we will have more to say about this later in the chapter). In short, as we move up the political ladder we find fewer and fewer women.

PARTICIPATION AND PROTEST

Any description of political activities in the United States would be incomplete without a discussion of demonstrations, marches, and the like. Such direct—sometimes violent—activity has become more important in recent years. It seems likely that groups have become more willing to engage in direct action such as marching or seizing a building.

Recent protest activity has focused on two issues: the Vietnam War and racial matters. Busing of schoolchildren is another major issue. Throughout the nation's history, however, there have been protests on many issues. What these activities have in common is the belief that ordinary political processes are too slow or not responsive enough. As the Chicago Riot Study Committee put it, "There is a conviction on the part of a clear majority of our Black citizens that political representation is entirely unsatisfactory and must be improved."[6]

---

[5] Verba and Nie, chap. 10.
[6] Chicago Riot Study Committee Report (Chicago, 1969), p. 112.

Is Protest Appropriate?

Some people argue that protest activity is not appropriate in a democracy, where other means of influencing the government, like voting in elections, are available. Other channels should at least be tried first. Some say that even if those channels are ineffective the use of direct action is inappropriate.

Others answer that direct action is often used when all other channels have been tried. Besides, those channels are not equally open to all. Some groups have no choice besides direct action. The defenders of direct action argue that some issues—such as stopping a war or preventing the busing of schoolchildren—are so important that firm and direct action is necessary.

It is not clear which side is right. Part of the debate is over facts: Are ordinary political channels open to all, and were they tried first? The main question, however, is a moral one: What kind of action is appropriate?

Is Protest Effective?

The purpose of direct action is to get a response from the government. Does it succeed?

It is not clear whether protests are more effective than ordinary political participation. Many government leaders claim that they pay no attention to such activity—President Nixon once made a point of watching a football game on TV while the White House was surrounded by antiwar protesters. Other people—especially leaders of demonstrations—claim that protest is the only effective political activity.

Probably the truth is somewhere in between. The most effective political activity is often the slowest and hardest—the patient doorbell ringing that goes with campaigning. Protests sometimes arise quickly and then fade, leaving no trace. Yet sometimes a violent demonstration or a march on Washington may cause government leaders to change their course.

Protests are especially important as "signals." Because they are dramatic and get a lot of attention, they are a powerful means of signaling discontent to political leaders. They also attract participants—for example, it is no accident that the increased participation of blacks in politics came at a time when direct action was becoming more common.

On the other hand, most Americans disapprove of direct action—even when they approve of its goals. A large majority (75–85 percent) of the American people disapproved of the student protests against the Vietnam War. One study found that even citizens who thought the war was a mistake disapproved of the students' actions.[7]

Thus it is possible that direct action does more harm than good, but it is

---

[7] Milton J. Rosenberg, Sidney Verba, and Phillip E. Converse, *Vietnam and the Silent Majority* (New York: Harper & Row, 1970), pp. 44–45.

hard to tell whether this is so. The results are mixed, and any judgment on this matter depends on the values of the person doing the judging. Some people believe that violence (or the risk of violence) is wrong in almost any situation. Others feel that it is necessary if social change is to happen. Out of such differences come "ordinary" politics as well as violent politics.

LEADERSHIP

We turn now from political participation to political leadership. For our purposes, the leaders of American society are the men and women who own, manage, direct, or otherwise control the nation's major public and private institutions—banks, public agencies, corporations, newspapers, Congress, universities, labor unions, and so on. Here we are interested mainly in national leaders, people whose influence is felt across the nation, who hold positions in the dominant institutions of our society. We are interested in the officers and directors of IBM, the Secretary and assistant secretaries of the Department of Agriculture, the publisher and editors of the *New York Times,* the officers and trustees of the Chase Manhattan Bank.

The most striking fact about this group of national leaders is how few people it includes:

> In all assemblies and groups and organized bodies of men, from a nation down to a committee of a club, direction and decisions rest in the hands of a small percentage, less and less in proportion to the larger size of the body, till in a great population it becomes an infinitesimally small proportion of the whole number. This is and always has been true of all forms of government.[8]

To illustrate, there are 140 million adult citizens in the United States, but it has been estimated that fewer than 4000 of them are directly involved in making major decisions that affect the whole society.[9] This estimate may be on the low side, since it leaves out the leaders of important organizations such as consumer and civil-rights groups. Even so, it is clear that American society is led by a very small number of people.

In the rest of this chapter we will focus on *political* leaders, that is, on the top elected and appointed officials in the government.

CHOOSING NATIONAL LEADERS

How do people move into and out of top leadership positions? Do members of certain groups have an advantage over members of other groups? What are the political attitudes of the nation's leaders?

---

[8] J. Bryce, *Modern Democracies* (New York: Macmillan, 1942), p. 542.

[9] Thomas R. Dye and John W. Pickering, "Governmental and Corporate Elites: Convergence and Differentiation," *Journal of Politics* 36 (November 1974).

Until about 200 years ago there was never any question as to who would rule. Either you were born into the ruling class or you were not. The democratic revolution separated political office from birthright. Now, instead of inheriting authority one must somehow earn it. While there are still only a few people in the top positions, those positions must be won through merit, talent, and performance.

Standards for Choosing Leaders

We can compare the process of choosing national leaders to the ancient Chinese box puzzle in which a set of boxes are designed so that to find the smallest box you have to open all the boxes in the set. (See Figure 7.1.) The largest box represents the entire adult population; the smallest represents the leadership group. The other boxes represent smaller and smaller "pools" of potential leaders. Only part of the adult population is legally qualified for political office; of this group, only part has the "right" social background. Among people who are both legally qualified and socially eligible, only a few are political activists, and of the activists only a very few become candidates for leadership positions.

Legal Qualifications   The Constitution sets minimum ages for some positions. Other legal qualifications include residency requirements—for example, you must live in the state in which you want to be elected senator—and professional standards such as legal training (especially for judicial positions). These qualifications are not hard to meet, however—almost any adult citizen is legally qualified to hold public office.

Social Background   To understand what we mean by the "right" background, consider the following list of younger citizens:

The son of a corporation lawyer who heads a law firm in Washington, D.C. He has just graduated from Princeton, where he was active in student politics and

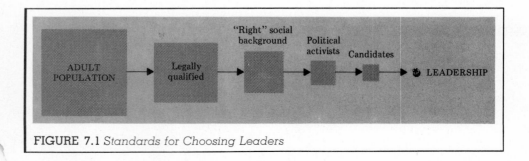

FIGURE 7.1 *Standards for Choosing Leaders*

was editor of the campus newspaper. Next year he will enter Harvard Business School.

A black longshoreman in San Francisco who is keenly interested in trade union affairs. He has already been elected secretary of his multiracial local. His formal education is limited to community college, but he is a good organizer and is popular with fellow workers. He has campaigned actively for local Democratic candidates.

A student body president of a large state university in the Midwest. She is the daughter of a small-town mayor and has served her father as an unofficial consultant on ending sex discrimination in the town's schools and hospitals. Although she is known to be very sharp politically, her academic record is average. She has been admitted to the university's graduate school of education.

A farmer's son who graduated with honors from Jerseyville High School but decided against further education. He was a football hero in the community and has recently joined the Elks, partly because some local businessmen have hinted that they would like him to serve on the town planning commission.

What are the chances that 30 years from now any one of these four people will have reached a top government position? We would rank their chances in the order in which they are listed. For every 100 people like the Princeton graduate, perhaps one will end up in a top position, while only one out of every 10,000 budding labor leaders is likely to get that far. The third person on the list is at a disadvantage because of her sex and because her training is in education rather than law or business. Finally, the high school hero is the least likely of these four individuals to reach a high position.

Clearly, leaders are chosen from a small part of the adult population. If you come from a wealthy family, are white and male, and went to a good university or college, you have a good chance of moving into the group from which leaders are selected.

Compare two people on our list: the Princeton graduate and the farmboy. The Princeton graduate has begun a career that often puts people like him in line for the top positions in our society. No one would think it odd if he announced that he was going to run for political office. The farmboy, by contrast, is unlikely to see himself as a future political leader. At most, he may aim to become mayor of his town. The point here is that most people eliminate themselves from the race for the few top positions. Only if you are born with a foot on the ladder to power are you likely to try to climb it.

Movement into leadership positions is also influenced by the judgments of people who are already in office. Those who occupy high positions will encourage people from similar backgrounds. Thus self-selection is reinforced by selection from above.

Note, however, that social background is only one of several factors that affect the selection of leaders. All four of the people on our list have a better chance than someone who has shown no leadership skill at all. Another Princeton graduate, for example, may have concentrated on chemistry for the past six years. He is now in graduate school and is avoiding any activity that might distract him from his studies. He is very unlikely to become a candidate for political office.

Political Activists   About 1 out of 20 adult Americans is a political activist, and it is from this group that candidates are chosen. Activists pay close attention to political matters. They serve on committees and work in campaigns; they know and are known by those who are already in office. Most members of this group are middle- or upper-middle-class males.

There is no clear boundary between the activists and those who are less active. People become more active or less so as their interests change, as their careers move them closer to or farther from politics, and as they respond to the chance to have a political career. To a large extent the activists are self-selected, but they often come from families with a tradition of political activity. They are exposed to politics as children and simply carry political habits into their adult life. About one-third of the officeholders in the United States can trace their interest in politics to the influence of the family.

Candidates   Within the activist group there is an even smaller number of people who become candidates for top positions—those who are nominated for elective offices and whose names are suggested for appointive offices. The process by which some activists become candidates and others do not is not well understood, but self-assertiveness is certainly a factor. President Johnson is a good example. "As long as I can remember," he said, "I've always been the kind of person who takes over in any group, who takes responsibility for calling the gathering together, setting the agenda for the meeting and carrying out the assignments."

Another factor is the attitude of people who already hold powerful positions. They can have an important effect on other people's careers. For example, when Johnson was Senate majority leader he helped John F. Kennedy obtain a seat on the Senate Foreign Relations Committee. This gave Kennedy a platform from which to launch his campaign for the Presidency.

The Test of Achievement

The example of the Chinese box puzzle shows how political leaders are chosen from a very large population. We have noted that those leaders tend to be white males from well-to-do families. Because this is so, some students of American politics say that *who you are* is more important than *what you can do*. But in reality, while the "right" social background is an important advantage, it does not guarantee a place among the nation's political leaders. Nor does it keep out members of other social groups.

America's leaders are achievers. They have shown that they can manage large enterprises or attract the loyalty of large numbers of people. Thus at any given time the President's Cabinet will include people who were formerly officers of giant corporations, heads of foundations, university presidents, members of well-known law firms, and the like.

This may sound contradictory: First we point out that most leaders are white males from high-status families. Then we go on to say that they are able and talented people. It might look as though ability and talent are found only in wealthy white males; but this is obviously untrue. The fact is that some people have more chances to develop and display their talents than others.

Display of Talent   To become a national political leader you must show your ability on a grand scale: by running Ford Motor Company or serving as president of a well-known university or as mayor of New York City. It may take more skill to sell used cars or teach grade school or serve as mayor of a smaller city, but this will not put you in line for top positions.

This being the case, it is easy to see why so many of the nation's leaders come from wealthy families: They have the education and contacts to reach positions in which they can display their talent on a grand scale. The used-car salesman may be as skilled and hardworking as the president of Ford Motor Company. However, he was born into the working class, not the upper class; he went to junior college, not Harvard Business School; and while he is sometimes active in local politics, he does not give thousands of dollars to presidential candidates. When nominations or appointments are being made, the list of possible candidates never includes the used-car salesman, but it often includes the head of the company whose worn-out products he sells.

Winning Elections   Political leadership often comes as a reward for a different kind of skill: the ability to win elections. Richard Nixon built on a series of election victories, starting with his campaign for the House of Representatives in 1946 and ending with his landslide victory in the 1972 presidential election. Johnson also went from the House to the Senate to the Vice-Presidency to the Presidency. Of course not all major election victories build on a series of lesser victories. Dwight D. Eisenhower won the Presidency without ever having been active in politics, while the former governor of California, Ronald Reagan, moved into that position directly from a career as a movie actor.

The ability to win elections makes up for the lack of family wealth or a high-status education. In fact, of the past seven Presidents, only one—Kennedy—came from a wealthy family.

AGREEMENT AND DISAGREEMENT AMONG NATIONAL LEADERS

How much agreement is there among our national leaders? On the one hand, it is claimed that leaders generally think the same way about public policy, with only small differences allowed. On the other hand, it is argued that leaders represent competing groups, have different ambitions, and therefore are always in conflict. Which view is correct?

How Leaders Disagree

Political leaders express sharply different views on such issues as tax reform, defense spending, and energy policy. This is unavoidable, since they represent many different groups: Republicans and Democrats, North and South, Protestants and Catholics, workers and management. In addition, there are conflicts between the different levels and branches of the government.

But leaders can be divided in a more general way into conservative believers in free enterprise and liberal social engineers. Conservatives believe that both individual citizens and society as a whole would benefit most from the free operation of the marketplace. Government interference may be necessary at times, but it should be kept to a minimum. Liberal social engineers, by contrast, do not believe that the free marketplace will automatically produce individual well-being and social progress. They favor the use of "social engineering"—government programs and policies—to supplement the marketplace.

The question of whether the government should try to solve the problem of poverty illustrates the difference between these two leadership groups. The liberal social engineers believe the government should take action to reduce the income gap and see to it that everyone has a job. Few conservatives favor such action. This does not mean that they favor poverty and unemployment. Rather, these leaders believe that the problem must be solved through the operation of the marketplace without governmental interference.

How Leaders Agree

The areas in which leaders disagree are only half the picture. There are also certain values and assumptions—such as the belief that the United States should remain a capitalist economy—that are shared by most of the nation's leaders. This is not surprising, since most leaders represent the political *mainstream*.

The political mainstream includes the broad policies that most Americans support or tolerate. For example, most Americans agree that military preparedness is necessary. Not all citizens take this view—some believe the United States should disarm. Such a belief is outside the mainstream of American political thought. So is the belief that the United States should make nuclear strikes against its supposed enemies.

One reason leaders tend to represent the mainstream is that voters are unlikely to support candidates whose views conflict with their own. This does not mean that every political leader is equally acceptable to every voter. Northern blacks, for example, might find the views of a representative from rural Mississippi obnoxious. But the policy views of the leadership group as a whole represent the mainstream.

Leaders reflect the political mainstream in a second way: They agree on the need to "work within the system." There is an acceptable way of doing things and an unacceptable way. Hostility toward peaceniks, black militants, hippies, and the like stems from the belief that their actions would destroy "the system." Without "the system" it would be impossible to achieve such goals as lasting peace or racial justice.

Thus agreement on *how* to bring about change cuts across sharp disagreements on *what* changes, if any, are needed. Leaders generally share a commitment to the rules of the game. This results in a common approach to governing despite different policy views.

LEADERSHIP AND CHANGE

The small group of national leaders is constantly changing. Individual members leave in a variety of ways (e.g., defeat or retirement); new social groups push aside more established groups; and new viewpoints and skills are called for to cope with a changing political agenda.

The Continuing Skill Revolution

The main job of leadership is to be prepared for the problems of society and to solve them. This requires skills that are suited to the times. Leadership skills change as the problems facing society change. The struggle to keep up is what causes a skill revolution.

A skill revolution is linked to the political agenda. On the agenda are the nation's most pressing problems. When leaders lack the skills to solve them,

Leaders are selected from among those who can adapt themselves to changing political agendas and conditions.

the problems get worse. When the right skills are provided, solutions are found. In the meantime we have a "national crisis."

An example is the depression of the 1930s. Traditional economic solutions did not solve the problem. Then President Roosevelt took over, bringing with him people whose views on economic and social matters were very different from those of the previous administration. Out of this skill revolution came the New Deal.

Today another skill revolution is in progress. Americans are dissatisfied with the policies that arose out of three decades of concern over issues of national security and international politics: World War II, the cold war, the Korean War, the Berlin crisis, the Cuban blockade, the Vietnam War. Now domestic problems are clamoring for attention—energy, pollution, crime, taxes, inflation. As a result, according to some political scientists, political power is shifting from the "military-industrial complex" to the "social-services-industrial complex," and there is a demand for leaders who can solve problems in the fields of health, education, transportation, urban life, consumer protection, and so on.

New Social Groups

Earlier we pointed out that national leadership has long been a white male club. But within this club there have been some important changes. The ministers, lawyers, and landowners who founded the nation did not expect that 100 years later it would be governed by wealthy industrialists. Nor did the bankers and industrialists of the late 1800s and early 1900s expect to be sharing power with the leaders of labor unions within a few decades.

Today new social groups are getting into the club. Each year there are more blacks and women among the nation's leaders. Table 7.3 shows how

TABLE 7.3 Black and Women Members in Congress, 1947–1978

Congress[a]	BLACK MEMBERS Senate	House	WOMEN MEMBERS Senate	House
80th		2	1	7
81st		2	1	9
82nd		2	1	10
83rd		2	3	12
84th		3	1	16
85th		4	1	15
86th		4	1	16
87th		4	2	17
88th		5	2	11
89th		6	2	10
90th	1	5	1	11
91st	1	9	1	10
92nd	1	12	2	13
93rd	1	15	0	14
94th	2	16	0	18
95th[b]	1	17	1	17
96th	0	14	1	16

SOURCE: Based on data from *Current American Government* (Washington, D.C.: *Congressional Quarterly*, Spring 1973), pp. 25–26; and *Current American Government*, Spring 1975, p. 17.

[a] Each congressional session lasts two years. There are a total of 435 members of the House and a total of 100 members of the Senate.

[b] November 1976 election. In 1978, Muriel Humphrey was appointed Senator from Minnesota to fill the remainder of the term of Hubert Humphrey, who died while in office.

Leadership in the United States is not the exclusive male club it was a few years ago.

many have won seats in Congress over the past 25 years. In addition, 2 out of 50 state governors are women, and several large cities have black mayors. Changes are taking place in business, universities, newspapers, hospitals, and law firms as well. It is a slow process, but once started, it continues to put pressure on the leadership group.

CONTROVERSY

Does the fact that the better-educated, higher-status members of society reach the top leadership positions represent the proper working of American democracy, or is it a flaw in the system?

One Side

The fact that wealthier and better-educated citizens make it to the top of the political ladder says nothing bad about American democracy. These people get to the top because they choose to do so. Lower-status citizens are less interested, and therefore they have less influence on the government. This is not the fault of the system. As long as citizens are *free to participate* and *free to run for office*, the system is working.

Besides, this situation has a good result: The best-qualified people are at the top of the political ladder. Even under the best of conditions it is hard to find skilled people. If leadership positions are filled by successful businessmen, lawyers, and civic leaders, there will be fewer mistakes. These people have shown that they can succeed where the competition is toughest.

Think about the four young citizens described in the chapter. Of the four, the corporation executive's son has the best chance of reaching high political office. Of the four he is the most likely to be able to grasp the complex problems of American society. The black labor leader will know how to develop a race relations program for the docks of San Francisco, but he may not have enough experience to create a more broad-based program. Such a program would have to apply to Alabama farms, army bases in Europe, the sales forces of Boston insurance agencies, and so on. In addition, it might have to be coordinated with a U.S.–African student exchange program planned by the Department of State or with a training program for police officers run by the Department of Justice. Our Princeton graduate—who is now an IBM executive, has served on the Civil Rights Commission, spent two years as a consultant in Nairobi, and recently advised the Ford Foundation on its grants to inner-city schools —is probably the best choice to direct a federal agency dealing with race relations.

We should choose our leaders from the small group of citizens who have proved their ability. It is unfortunate that this group is mostly white, male, wealthy, and Protestant. But the solution is to end race, sex, and class discrimination, not to put unskilled citizens into leadership positions.

The Other Side

Democracy works only when all citizens have an equal voice. Therefore the fact that the richer and better-educated citizens are more active in politics and more successful at climbing the political ladder is a major flaw in American democracy. It is not fair to say that poorer citizens do not go far politically because they choose not to. Lower-status citizens participate less because they lack the necessary resources. Those who cannot make large contributions to election campaigns are not "equally free" to influence the government, and they are even less likely to be able to run for office themselves.

Besides, it is not true that only the "best" people make it to the top leadership positions. Maybe they have more education, but they may lack important skills and attitudes. Upper-class white males do not necessarily have the skills needed to bring about racial harmony, provide decent education and health care, and so on. Leaders should be chosen from groups that have direct contact with the problems of American life.

The white corporate executive may have more education and more organizational ability than the black union leader, but does that mean he will be able to ease racial tensions in the American working class? Maybe the feminist leader could bring a fresh approach to the Department of Health, Education and Welfare. Maybe the Jerseyville town planner would be more sensitive to protecting small communities against urban blight. In short, American society may be shortchanging itself by always choosing its political leaders from the successful business and professional classes.

Interest Groups

As we saw in Chapter 6, the United States is divided into many groups with different interests. We pointed out that groups that are organized are likely to have a greater effect on government policy than those that are not organized. In this chapter we will look more closely at groups that try to influence the government. How many such groups are there in the United States? How powerful are they? What makes some more powerful than others?

THE ROLE OF INTEREST GROUPS

Some students of politics argue that you can learn all you need to know about American politics by studying the role of interest groups. They claim that Congress and the President do not initiate policy but simply respond to the demands of such groups. At best, the government acts as a "broker" among organized groups, seeing that each one gets a little something in response to its demands. Policy grows out of the conflicting pressures applied to the government by those groups.

Most writers on this subject believe that government policy is more than a response to group pressures. Yet there is some truth to the view that group pressures shape policy. Organized groups are not all-powerful, but they are better able to pressure the government than unorganized groups. And this affects who will benefit from government policy.

Critics of "pressure groups" argue that they serve the selfish interests of particular groups of citizens—especially business groups. Each group is out to "take care of its own" at the expense of society as a whole. While pressure groups compete for benefits for their members, no one works to solve the problems of society as a whole. A policy that benefits one group may actually hurt the rest of society.

Other students of politics argue that there is no conflict between the interests of particular groups and those of the general public. The public good, they say, does not exist outside of the interests of particular groups of citizens. Rather, the public good is the sum of the interests of various groups, and the competition among those groups results in the most effective policy.

Those who defend the pressure group system admit that not all groups are represented equally. But they believe the answer is more, not less, group activity. If some interests are not well represented by organized groups and others are not, then the others should organize as well.

We will return to the question of whether interest groups are helpful or harmful after we have taken a closer look at their role in American politics.

HOW MUCH ORGANIZATION?

America has often been called a society of joiners—we are quick to form organizations, and those organizations are numerous and varied. About six out of ten adult Americans belong to some organization, while in other comparable nations less than half the adult population is likely to belong to organized groups. This does not mean, however, that most Americans have some organization that takes care of their political interests. Not only is there a large minority—four out of ten—who are not organization members, but organizations do not represent all social groups equally. Upper-status citizens—the wealthy, the educated—are more likely to be organization members. Thus, not only are there many citizens who are not group members, but group membership is not spread equally across the society.

Political and Nonpolitical Groups

Note, too, that not all organizations are political. Only 8 percent of the American people belong to specifically political groups such as Democratic or Republican clubs, the League of Women Voters, or the NAACP. Most organizations are formed for other purposes besides pressuring the government. Table 8.1 lists some of the types of nonpolitical groups to which many Americans belong.

It would be a mistake, however, to think that only political groups represent citizen interests to the government. Nonpolitical groups may become politically active, and some are active all the time. The National Rifle Asso-

TABLE 8.1   Types of Organizations to Which Americans Belong

Type of Organization	Percent of Population
Political groups such as Democratic or Republican clubs: political-action groups such as voters' leagues	8
School service groups such as PTA or school alumni groups	17
Service clubs such as Lions, Rotary, Zonta, Junior Chamber of Commerce	6
Youth groups such as Boy Scouts, Girl Scouts	7
Veterans' groups such as American Legion	7
Farm organizations such as Farmer's Union, Farm Bureau, Grange	4
Nationality groups such as Sons of Norway, Hibernian Society	2
Church-related groups such as Bible Study Group, Holy Name Society	6
Fraternal groups such as Elks, Eagles, Masons, and their women's auxiliaries	15
Professional or academic societies such as American Dental Association, Phi Beta Kappa	7
Trade Unions	17
School fraternities and sororities	3
Literary, art, discussion, or study clubs such as book review clubs, theater groups	4
Hobby or garden clubs such as stamp or coin clubs, flower clubs, pet clubs	5
Sports clubs, bowling leagues, etc.	12

SOURCE: Based on data from Sidney Verba and Norman H. Nie, *Participation in America: Political Democracy and Social Equality* (New York: Harper & Row, 1972.)

ciation, for example, was organized as a recreational group, but it became an important political force when its interests were challenged by the supporters of gun control. This can happen to any type of group. Church groups do not have political goals, but they can get involved in conflicts such as abortion or school prayer. Groups with economic goals are constantly involved in such conflicts.

Lobbies

Some organizations are more active in trying to influence the government than others. They have offices, called *lobbies,* in Washington and in state capitals, and their professional representatives, or *lobbyists,* are in close contact with the government. There are hundreds of lobbies in Washington, and they cover a wide range of interests. Some represent particular industries (e.g., the American Petroleum Institute or the National Association of Insurance Agents). Some represent professional groups (e.g. the American Medical Association or the National Education Association). Groups of workers such as letter carriers or auto and aerospace workers are represented by their unions. Some organizations represent citizens who are interested in matters such as environmental protection (e.g., Common Cause) or lower taxes (e.g., Citizens for Control of Federal Spending).

These examples also illustrate the main reason why some groups are active while others are not: Groups become politically active when government policy affects them—when they want the government to stop some activity that they believe is harmful or take some action that they believe would be beneficial. Thus some of the most active groups are those that represent employees of the government and those that speak for businesses that are heavily affected by federal and state legislation.

Business Lobbies Most lobbying is done by business organizations with full-time staffs in Washington. The major defense contractors and multinational corporations are in this category. In addition, there are many trade associations (e.g., the National Association of Retail Druggists) that represent a single industry, as well as "peak" associations such as the National Association of Manufacturers (NAM).

These organizations usually focus on specific interests—lobbyists for the oil industry worry about oil imports; lobbyists for the textile industry worry about tariffs on foreign textiles. Sometimes, however, they take stands on more general issues; for example, the NAM has been active in opposing welfare legislation.

Labor Unions Traditionally, American labor unions have been less "political" than unions in other nations. They put most of their energy into collective bargaining with employers for better wages and working conditions rather than engaging in political activity. But unions are a political force because their economic goals depend on government policies. Some unions, such as the United Automobile Workers and the United Steel Workers, have been especially active in politics. The AFL-CIO has a large lobby in Washington, and its Committee on Political Education is active in political campaigns.

Professional Associations Most major professional groups—doctors, lawyers, scientists, and the like—have professional associations that lobby for their members. The American Medical Association may be the best known of these; until 1975 it actively opposed federal medical-care programs. Other organizations of this type are the National Education Association, which lobbies for more spending on education, and the American Association for the Advancement of Science, which lobbies for more spending on scientific research.

Citizen and Consumer Lobbies In recent years consumer groups and "citizens' lobbies" have become important. The largest of such groups is Common Cause, which is active in a variety of areas ranging from consumer protection to reform of political-campaign financing. Other groups—such as The Public Citizen, led by Ralph Nader, and the Sierra Club—represent the interests of citizens in matters such as environmental protection and automobile safety. With their professional attitudes and willingness to fight for their demands in Congress and in the courts, these organizations have been quite successful. For example, Nader's lobbying was a major factor in obtaining seat belt legislation for cars, and Common Cause was the main force behind the recent campaign reform laws.

Are the new organizations that represent environmental and other noneconomic interests any less "selfish" that other interest groups simply because they lobby for consumers of goods and services rather than for their producers? Groups like Common Cause claim that they are fighting for the "people's interest" against the "special interests" that have always dominated the political system. But here is what one business leader has to say about them:

> The political system is out of balance. . . . We find our fate increasingly in the hands of a few relatively small but highly vocal, selfish, interest groups. . . . These groups . . . pursue their own interests with complete disregard for the impact of their wants on the rest of the economy. . . . And while they shout about the environmental impact of almost everything, they have no concern whatever for the economic impact of their corrective legislation.[1]

---

[1] *Consumer Reports,* January 1975, p. 53.

146

(Citizen groups describe the business lobbies in almost the same words.)

It is unclear whether citizen groups represent a new type of "selfish" interest or the general public interest. In either case, it appears that such groups are here to stay.

Beneficiary Groups   Whenever the government helps a particular group, it creates a set of "beneficiaries." Members of such groups have a stake in seeing that government support for their group is continued and perhaps increased. Many of the groups that pressure the government are beneficiary groups—farmers lobby for price supports, veterans for veterans' benefits.

ORGANIZATIONS AS PRESSURE GROUPS

How does the activity of organized groups affect government policy, and who benefits from any impact it may have? Some students of pressure group activity have concluded that the government is dominated by lobbies. They believe neither the public as a whole nor the government itself plays a part in the making of policy. The government merely reacts to group pressures.

Such a description of policy making—in Washington or in state capitals —exaggerates the power of organized groups and plays down the other forces acting on the government. One study of Washington lobbyists concludes that "there is relatively little influence or power in lobbying per se. There are many forces in addition to lobbying which influence public policy; in most cases these forces clearly outweigh the impact of lobbying."[2] These other forces include public opinion and the feelings of members of Congress about the next election, as well as the influence of the executive branch on Congress. Besides, members of Congress have their own opinions. They like to hear what lobbyists have to say, but they do not always base their views on those of the lobbyist.

In short, organized interest groups are not all-powerful, nor are they weak. Groups vary in their effectiveness, depending on their resources, their areas of activity, and where they apply pressure.

Organizational Resources   *first technique was bribery and blackmail.*

Organizations are effective when they have the resources they need to influence the government. What are those resources?

Money   Lobbying is expensive. The major lobbies have full-time professional lobbyists in Washington and in state capitals. They sometimes carry out expensive campaigns to influence Congress or the public. The American

---

[2] Lester W. Milbrath, *The Washington Lobbyists* (Chicago: Rand McNally, 1963), p. 54.

Medical Association, for example, spent over $1 million in three months during its campaign against Medicaid. Organizations also make large contributions to political campaigns—in 1974 the milk producers' lobby contributed over $2 million to congressional campaigns.

People   Organizations that can get their members involved in political activity are also likely to be more effective. The number of members is not as important as their willingness to give time and effort to the organization. For example, the National Rifle Association (NRA) faces the large majority of Americans who favor gun control. As mentioned earlier, however, the NRA's members are more deeply concerned about the issue. The NRA keeps its members informed through its monthly *American Rifleman* and numerous legislative bulletins. As a result, whenever a legislative committee holds a hearing on a gun control bill it is jammed with NRA members.

Information   Lobbyists have one resource that ordinary citizens and even members of Congress do not usually have: a staff of experts who specialize in the subject in which the lobby is interested. These experts often know much more about the subject than members of Congress, who have many other things to think about. The textile industry lobby knows the number of yards of cloth imported from Hong Kong each month; the National Association of Retail Druggists can tell you how many drugstores go out of business each year. These groups know what policies they want to influence, and they often have more information than the government officials who must make those policies. Thus the officials may depend on the lobby for information.

usually involves interest groups

Access   Access to government officials is another resource that makes organizations more effective. All citizens have the right to contact their representative in Congress or make a complaint to a government official. But professional lobbyists develop close ties with particular government officials, such as the chairperson of the congressional committee that is concerned with the organization's area of interest.

Mobilizing Group Members

A group that wants to pressure the government must be able to depend on its members. For one thing, it must keep up its membership. An organization that tries to speak for a group needs to have a fairly high percentage of that group among its members. In addition, it needs membership dues to pay for its activities. If it can get its members to be active—to write to government officials or campaign for the candidates it favors—it can increase its influence.

Organizations are most effective when they offer many rewards to their members. As we saw in Chapter 6, the group's policy goals may not be enough to motivate members to contribute time and effort to the group. Most successful organizations also offer their members *selective benefits*— benefits that are available only to members. Business and professional organizations offer their members technical publications, insurance programs, and many other services. Members of the American Bar Association, for example, may benefit from the following:

> lawyer placement service
>
> retirement income plans
>
> group life insurance program
>
> dependents' life insurance program
>
> group disability insurance program
>
> in-hospital insurance program
>
> specialized information on all sections of the law
>
> legal publications and reports; the *American*
>
> *Bar Association* journal; the *American Bar News*

Citizen's lobbies also need to motivate their members. Some of these groups provide selective benefits—members of Consumers' Union receive the monthly *Consumer Reports,* which rates products for safety, durability, and the like; members of the Sierra Club are offered wilderness trips and publications. But other citizens' lobbies offer few such benefits and still have wide support. Why do citizens support such groups? The answer is that citizens *can* be motivated by policy goals. Public-interest organizations are more likely to attract college-educated citizens, and the number of such citizens has been growing. In addition, the public-interest groups have effective leaders such as Ralph Nader of The Public Citizen and John Gardner of Common Cause. These leaders argue that well-organized "special interests" have usually defeated less well-organized groups working for the "public interest." This argument seems to have persuaded many citizens to support the public-interest groups.

Areas of Activity

The narrower and more technical the issue, the more effective organized groups are likely to be. To understand why, we need to discuss the two levels of policy making.

General policy guidelines are set by Congress. These guidelines are largely symbolic, however. They indicate the general direction of government policy, but the actual policy that results depends on details worked out in congressional committees, on how government officials apply the law, or on the way the courts interpret the law. The point is that while the broad policy guidelines may appear important, it is often the way the law is applied or interpreted that really counts.

Pressure groups are active in the struggle for major legislation, but this is not their main area of activity. They have more influence at the second level of policy making—the congressional committees and executive agencies that work out the details of a bill. Here they can use their professional knowledge and access to government officials to the fullest.

Tax Legislation   Tax legislation is a good example of the two levels of policy making. The Sixteenth Amendment sets the general policy of progressive taxation: Those who can pay more are to be taxed at higher rates. Few people argue with this general principle—and there is no need to argue, because the principle is hardly ever applied.

Many attempts to reform the income tax laws have been made, and the results are almost always the same. Congress sets some broad guidelines, and then the House Ways and Means Committee or the Senate Finance Committee approves a number of exemptions such as the 22 percent depletion allowance for oil companies. At the hearings on major tax bills hundreds of interest groups ask for special treatment on issues that affect them. On each issue there is no one to oppose the group making the request since no other group is affected as much.

The result is that although the principle of progressive taxation is never challenged, tax policy turns out to be relatively nonprogressive in fact. For example, the tax law allows for a maximum rate of 70 percent, but few people pay as much as 50 percent.[3] There are so many exemptions—for municipal bonds, capital gains, real estate transactions, and the like—that the principle of progressive taxation does not take effect.

Business Regulation   Government regulation of business also illustrates the pattern in which general principles are not always carried out in practice. Congress will pass general legislation to regulate some aspect of business, such as the quality of food products or the flameproofing of fabrics. The general principle will be clear: Sell pure food; produce flameproof fabrics. But the details (How pure? What about slow-burning fabrics?) are usually worked out with representatives of the businesses involved, since they have the information on which the details of the regulation must be based. This gives businesses a special voice in policies that concern them.

To understand why this is so, think about the patterns of division described in Chapter 6. When a group with a specific interest wants something that many other citizens oppose in principle, the pattern will look something

---

[3] See William L. Cary, "Pressure Groups and the Revenue Code," *Harvard Law Review,* 68 (1955), 745–780.

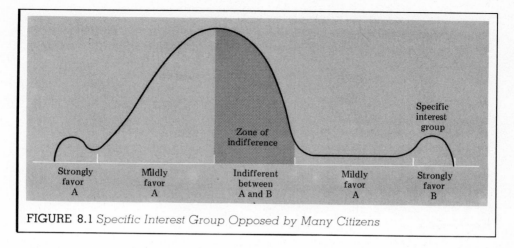

FIGURE 8.1 *Specific Interest Group Opposed by Many Citizens*

like Figure 8.1. On the right is the interest group, small in number but firm in its support of policy B. On the left are the people who are generally opposed to policy B. In such a case the group that favors B could win only after a public fight, and it would be more likely to lose, since many citizens could get involved. For example, if the U.S. Chamber of Commerce tried to get Congress to pass a law greatly reducing the tax rate for large corporations, and made public statements criticizing the principle of progressive taxation, it would face strong opposition and would probably lose. Members of Congress might listen to the interest group, but they would listen more closely to election predictions.

When it comes to technical issues, however, the pattern of division often looks like Figure 8.2. A deeply concerned and well-informed group favors

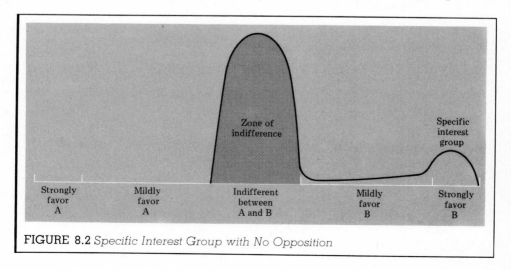

FIGURE 8.2 *Specific Interest Group with No Opposition*

Consumer advocate Ralph Nader meets with a group of Nader's Raiders who have been studying nursing home abuses.

policy B. It looks like a technical matter about which the public knows very little. As a result there is no opposition and the interest group can be quite effective. Suppose the House Ways and Means Committee approves a stock option plan in which profits from the sale of stock received under the plan can be treated as capital gains if they are sold at least two years after the grant of the option and six months after the transfer of the stock. The public is unlikely to become concerned on such a technical matter. It will not be clear that a particular group is being favored at the expense of others.

Citizens' lobbies try to convert the pattern shown in Figure 8.2 into the one shown in Figure 8.3, in which one lobby opposes another. Lawyers

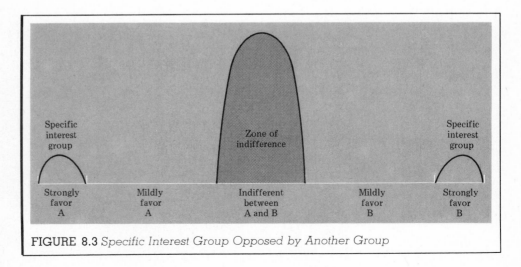

FIGURE 8.3 *Specific Interest Group Opposed by Another Group*

working for The Public Citizen watch over the process by which exemptions are written into the tax law and try to lobby against them. The battle is not always equal—there are many more special-interest lawyers than public-interest lawyers. It is likely that the pattern shown in Figure 8.2, in which an interest group is not opposed by any other group, is more common than the pattern shown in Figure 8.3.

Where Are Pressure Groups Active?

One way in which pressure groups are active is in trying to influence the public through media campaigns. They also support candidates in elections. This is the most general level of interest-group activity. But groups are more active, and probably more effective, when they deal with specific committees of Congress or agencies of the government, or with the courts.

Congressional Committees   Representatives of pressure groups often develop close ties with members of Congress and with committee staff members. They often provide the information needed for the writing of a particular bill.

Executive Agencies   Interest groups can also develop ties with the agencies of the executive branch that affect them. Farm interests become linked with the Department of Agriculture, business interests with the Department of Commerce, and so on. This is especially true of independent regulatory commissions and the industries they are supposed to regulate (e.g., the Federal Communications Commission and radio and television interests).

The Courts   The real impact of government policy often comes by way of court decisions, and interest groups are active in this area too. They provide lawyers to prepare cases and often choose the test cases themselves and file *amicus curiae* ("friend of the court") briefs. The best example of such activity is the series of cases prepared by the NAACP with the goal of ending school segregation. Groups like the NAACP and the American Civil Liberties Union—that is, groups whose primary interest is in certain rights guaranteed by the Constitution—are most active in the federal courts.

Election Campaigns   As mentioned earlier, organized groups are often very active in election campaigns. The reason for this activity was expressed by the president of the Mid-American Dairymen as follows: "I have become increasingly aware that the soft and sincere voice of the dairy farmer is no match for the jingle of hard currency put in the campaign funds of the politician."[4] Many interest groups have special committees for campaign activity,

---

[4] Quoted in "Dollar Politics," *Congressional Quarterly* 2 (1974), 13.

such as the American Medical Political Action Committee or the Committee for Thorough Agricultural Political Education.

In 1976 such groups gave more than $20 million in campaign contributions to candidates for the House and the Senate. Were these contributors trying to "buy" special treatment? They probably were. Candidates who receive such contributions—which can run as high as $10,000—are more likely to listen to the group that made the contribution when they are considering laws that would affect that group.

INTEREST GROUPS AS QUASI-GOVERNMENTS

There is another way in which private groups play a political role. Interest groups sometimes act as "quasi-governments" in that they have the power to make *binding* decisions in a particular area. For example, many groups control entry into the professions they represent. Medical and bar associations control examinations; craft unions control apprentice programs; educational associations control accredition. Their decisions are binding on the citizens concerned—those who want to practice law or medicine or join the plumbers' union or operate a private school. In this way such organizations act like governments.

Of course everyone wants a way of judging doctors or lawyers as professionals so that people who need medical care or legal advice can trust them. Yet only other doctors or lawyers can make such judgments. But control of this kind can also be used to keep the members of a profession in line. The American Medical Association has used its powers to get doctors to support its policy on national medical care. State bar examinations, which include a section on "character," have been used to keep out people with radical views. Craft unions have used their power to prevent blacks from becoming plumbers, electricians, and the like.

Another area in which organizations act as quasi-governments is in setting standards for a particular industry. The movie industry's organization gives films the familiar G to X-ratings. This gives control to those who are supposed to be controlled. A similar situation arises in the distribution of public funds. Many government programs are carried out by private groups. The government sets broad guidelines for those programs, but control is basically in the hands of the private group; besides, the guidelines are often so vague that the private organization is free to do almost anything it wants with government funds.

There are many examples of this setup: Urban-renewal funds are often controlled by private developers; funds for hospitals are often controlled by private charitable groups; funds for the antipoverty program were controlled

Men supporting the farmers' strike stand near the Capitol building in Washington D.C.

largely by local groups. One result is that many more citizens participate in such programs—people who are familiar with local conditions. But this system also gives power over public funds to private groups that are not accountable to the public the way government officials are and that may not really represent the people they are supposed to represent.

WHO IS REPRESENTED BY INTEREST GROUPS?

Do Interest Groups Favor the Rich?

Whose interests are really served by interest groups? Do they serve the rich more than the poor? Critics of the interest group system claim that it does. As we have seen, wealthier and better-educated citizens are more likely to belong to organizations than the disadvantaged—slum dwellers, migrant workers, the unemployed. A recent study found that 43 percent of employed workers were members of organizations, compared to only 25 percent of unemployed workers.[5] Clearly, many people who need help from the government have no organization to speak for them.

On the other hand, business and professional organizations have been very successful in representing their members. Labor unions and citizens' lobbies offset this bias somewhat, but even these groups tend to represent better-paid workers and better-educated citizens.

[5] Kay Lehman Schlozman and Sidney Verba, *Injury to Insult: Unemployment, Class, and Political Response* (Cambridge: Harvard University Press, 1979).

Even when well-organized business interests are "balanced" by citizens' groups, the two sides are often unequal in the resources available to them. Business lobbies can usually outspend their opponents. In 1976, for example, an environmental-protection group collected enough signatures to place on the Massachusetts ballot a referendum to ban nonreturnable bottles and cans. It spent $32,000 during the campaign, and the referendum came within 12,000 votes of passing. However, a lobby of container manufacturers and bottlers spent $2.25 million, or 70 times as much as the environmental-protection group, on a massive advertising campaign against it. The difference in resources was responsible for the defeat of the referendum.

Do Interest Groups Speak for Their Members?

When an interest group takes a stand on an issue, it claims to speak for its members. But does it? It is hard to tell. There is a tendency for any organization to be run by a small group of members who give a lot of time and effort to its activities. These members tend to become professional leaders. In fact many organizations are controlled by professional officials who do not necessarily speak for their members.

The American Medical Association is an example. Its leaders are executives, not practicing physicians. Its members meet rarely, if ever, and control over the activities of the organization is in the hands of its professional staff. One may question whether such an organization really speaks for its members.

On the other hand, central control allows an organization to plan more effectively so that when it *does* speak for its members it can have a greater impact. Besides, central control often develops because the members are not interested enough. Members are, however, free to challenge the actions of the organization's leaders, and they sometimes do. In recent years, for example, the conservative leaders of the American Medical Association have been challenged by younger, more liberal members, and this has had an impact on the organization's policies.

HOW POWERFUL ARE INTEREST GROUPS?

We said earlier that interest groups are neither powerless nor all-powerful. They are most effective when they operate quietly on issues that do not arouse much public concern. In major conflicts over public policy, however, they become only one voice among many.

Interest groups cannot act alone. They need cooperation from government officials. The groups that are most effective often have close ties with the congressional committees or executive agencies that are concerned with their interests. Sometimes these ties develop into a strong alliance, with the result that the interest group has an important voice in the policies that affect it.

There is some evidence that this situation is changing. For one thing, the federal bureaucracy has grown not only in size but also in the extent to which it takes the initiative in making policy. Many executive agencies have become "interest groups" themselves. In addition, the rise of citizens' lobbies means that special interests are more often opposed by groups representing "the public interest." However, such groups do not necessarily speak for the whole public, and it is not always clear which side represents the true public interest. For example, citizens' lobbies have succeeded in delaying, if not blocking, the construction of nuclear power plants. They claim to speak for the public's interest in environmental protection. On the other hand, those who favor nuclear power claim to speak for the public's interest in increased energy supplies.

There is no easy answer to the question of which side is acting in the public's best interest, but it is probably true that the public benefits more when interest groups compete with each other than when special interests face no opposition.

CONTROVERSY

How much, if anything, do interest groups contribute to the public good?

One Side

The interest group system communicates citizens' needs and preferences to the government. Without such groups policy makers would not get the information they need. Interest group activity allows government policy to be "fine tuned" to specific citizen needs.

Interest groups do not discriminate against other citizens. All groups have the right to organize and to pressure the government. The fact that a group is organized and active shows that it is serious about its concerns. If other groups do not organize, they must not really care about their interests.

The close ties between interest groups and the government are a way of using the knowledge and skills of professionals in making public policy. The result is better policies. Moreover, when citizens voluntarily work with the government in making policy, it follows that they will voluntarily comply with that policy. This also benefits society—the less force is used, the better off everyone is.

Finally, the policy that results from the competition among specific groups does not hurt the general public—for the public interest is the sum of the interests of all the various groups in society. Thus the interest group system not only represents the interests of specific groups but also serves the needs of the country as a whole.

The Other Side

The interest group system does not always communicate the most important interests of citizens. Many groups with serious problems are unorganized. They are inactive not because they do not care but because they lack resources. As a result, the interests that get communicated are those of upper-status groups, especially business groups. The interests of other groups are represented to varying degrees— unionized workers, for example, do better than nonunionized, though the nonunion workers may need more help from the government. The result is that government policy tends to benefit the privileged members of society more than the disadvantaged ones. The situation is made worse when power is given to groups that the government is supposed to regulate.

Interest group activity may be voluntary, but social change sometimes requires force. Citizens may have to be forced to accept changes that they do not want—to accept income redistribution or housing desegregation—if change is to take place. A major change in American society requires strong action by the government. It is in this area that the interest group system is an obstacle: No one is concerned with the general public interest. To solve the serious problems facing American society the government will have to listen to other voices besides those of narrow, selfish interests.

Which side is right? This is a basic question of American politics. Whether you believe that the interest group system benefits the public or not, this system is a fact of American political life that is unlikely to change very much.

HOW WE FIND OUT
ABOUT POLITICS: III

Policies and Leaders

In studying public policy many political scientists do *documentary research,* research that makes use of the records kept by the government about its own activities as well as the records of groups outside the government. In our technological society people who make important decisions need a lot of information, and therefore large amounts of information are gathered and stored. As a result, the researcher can work with a wide variety of documents.

The government describes its employees, activities, and policies in hundreds of reports. In addition, it describes many other areas of American life. You can find out from government documents the number of scientists being trained in American universities, the number of private airplanes sold each year, the number of American businessmen living in Mexico, and so on. Moreover, because the government is involved in such a wide range of activities, many agencies outside the government keep records about the government. For example, the AFL-CIO publishes the voting records of all members of Congress on all bills that concern labor unions.

All of these reports and documents must be used carefully. The following points should be kept in mind.

1. *Institutional bias.* Many government records are *self*-reports: Crime statistics are published by the FBI and the police; records of campaign contributions are kept by the political parties; and so on. Such reports are often biased. A police department that wants a budget increase might report every loss of property as "suspected theft" in order to show an increase in crime. A police department that has just received a large budget increase might report only cases in which theft actually took place in order to show a decrease in crime. The careful researcher tries to recognize possible bias in such reports.

2. *Durability.* Some records last longer than others. The researcher may find that the records he or she needs were destroyed in a fire or were

never kept in the first place. For example, suppose you wanted to compare voter turnout in local and national elections for the past 100 years. You would have no trouble finding the information for national elections, but for some localities you might be able to find records of voter turnout only for the past 10 or 20 years.

3. *Secrecy.* In a democracy the business of government is supposed to be public. Yet even so, much government business is kept secret. This is understandable in matters involving national security, but governmental secrecy goes much further. Nearly everything that goes on inside the White House has traditionally been kept secret. In Congress, floor debate is public but committees sometimes meet in private (although the recently passed "sunshine laws" requiring open meetings have reduced congressional privacy). While Supreme Court decisions are announced publicly, the meetings of the justices are private.

In short, it is much easier to get information on the final decisions of a legislative, executive, or judicial agency than information on the process by which those decisions were made. Thus, the study of public documents is the study of what the government chooses to let the outsider know.

Under such conditions, what can be learned from documentary research? Here are some examples:

1. *Representation.* Several kinds of information can be combined to give the researcher an overall picture of political representation. Census data can tell you whether the citizens of a particular district are rich or poor, black or white, urban or rural. This would give you some idea of whether a representative of that district would favor, say, farm subsidies or mass transit subsidies. Since there are records of the actual votes, you would be able to check your hunch.

2. *Legislation.* A useful source of information about Congress is the weekly *Congressional Quarterly,* which reports the roll call votes of

members of Congress and contains information about major bills—their subject matter, their sponsors, and so on—and the committees involved. This kind of information is useful in studying a variety of questions about the legislative process: Is a committee headed by a southern Democrat likely to handle a civil-rights bill differently than a committee headed by a northern Democrat? Are unified subcommittees more successful in getting their bills passed than divided subcommittees? From studies of this sort—in state legislatures and city councils, as well as at the national level—political scientists have gained a detailed understanding of the legislative process.

3. *The "power elite."* Information about top government officials is contained in a variety of publications, including the *Congressional Directory*, the State Department's *Biographical Register, Who's Who in America*, and biographical directories of special groups such as blacks or lawyers. This information can be used to determine how much various power groups overlap. For example, do the same people who serve

on the boards of trustees of large universities also serve on the boards of major corporations? Are these the same people who serve as advisers to important political leaders? This information can also be used to find out about the social backgrounds of political leaders. It could tell us what percentage of the members of Congress graduated from Ivy League colleges, or whether there are more blacks in the government today than there were ten years ago, or whether the percentage of lawyers in the Senate has changed in the past 100 years.

These are only a few of the ways in which political scientists use documentary research to find out about politics and government in the United States. They show how much information is available and how useful it can be. The sample survey is used mainly for studies of the population as a whole because it is the only way we can get data on public opinion. When it comes to specific groups or institutions, however, data are often available in documents, records, budgets, and the like.

Political Parties
and Elections

It is often said that political parties "organize the weak against the strong." The individual citizen acting alone cannot easily challenge established policies or force unsatisfactory leaders out of office. This requires organization, which is provided by the political parties.

The Constitution does not mention parties. Yet political parties arose soon after the nation's founding and became crucial institutions in American democracy. It would be hard to imagine democratic politics without political parties. In a democracy the people control their government, and in representative governments such as the United States this is done through elections. Political parties "organize" citizens by giving them choices at election time. They also control the legislative and elective branches once their candidates have been elected. In this way the preferences of the people, expressed through elections, are converted into control over the government—at least in theory.

THE HISTORY OF AMERICAN PARTIES

The political parties that are so familiar to us today—the Democrats and the Republicans—have evolved over the past 190 years. Political scientists divide this period into five eras, each of which is characterized by changes in the structure of the parties and the groups supporting them.

The Early Period

The first of these five eras extends from the nation's founding to around 1824. There were two parties at this time—the Federalists and the Democratic-Republicans. But these parties were formed to organize political support for leaders *within* the government. They were not very useful in elections. (Remember, only white male property holders over the age of 21 could vote.)

The Jacksonian Period

Beginning in the mid-1820s, and especially after Andrew Jackson was elected President in 1828, political parties ceased to be small, elite groups and became mass-based organizations. The right to vote was extended to all adult white males, and voter participation increased dramatically. In addition, presidential candidates were nominated by party conventions rather than by congressional caucuses.

Jackson was the first President to be nominated by a party convention. His followers became known as the Democratic party. To oppose the Democrats a new party, the Whigs, was formed. It was supported by manufacturing interests and by New Englanders who wanted to end slavery.

The Civil War and the Postwar Period

The party system of the 1830s and 1840s could not handle the severe conflict over the slavery question that developed during those years. A new system arose in the mid-1850s and lasted almost until 1900. Today's major parties were first organized during that period. The Republicans were the party of the North. They represented commercial interests and opposed slavery. The Democrats, by contrast, got most of their support from the South. As a result, after the Civil War it was hard for Democrats to win national elections, so the postwar period was dominated by the Republicans.

The Progressive Period

From the mid-1890s to the early 1930s the party system was strongly influenced by a minor party, the Progressives. Several reforms in party politics were made during this period. The reformers were bothered by the "buying" of votes and the "spoils systems," in which loyal party members were rewarded with jobs in the government. They pressured for such reforms as voter registration and nonpartisan ballots. Unfortunately, this made it harder for citizens to vote and for parties to organize.

During this period the Republicans established themselves as the party that favored business interests, while the Democrats represented farm interests and were opposed to industrialization and urbanization. Neither party paid much attention to the growing immigrant population in the cities because the immigrants did not vote in large numbers.

The Parties Today

In the late 1920s the Democratic party began to tap the huge block of voters in the cities. The Democrats were still supported by the "Solid South," but now it also drew heavily on the votes of industrial workers in the northern cities. The party began to push for social welfare, government intervention, and civil rights. The Republicans continued to favor business interests, but they also gained the support of the farm regions in the Midwest.

Today some students of politics are wondering whether this system still exists. There have been many changes in the past 40 years; for example, the South is no longer solidly Democratic. We will discuss these changes later in the chapter.

Roosevelt built a strong Democratic Party with the support of the working class and trade unions.

THIRD PARTIES

Major parties are often affected by the rise of *third* (or *minor*) *parties*. Third parties are similar to the major parties in structure and purpose. They usually run candidates in state and local elections; sometimes they have enough support to challenge the major parties in a presidential election, as George Wallace's American Independent party did in 1968.

Third Parties and Social Change

Third parties are often created for the purpose of bringing new issues—or new ways of looking at old issues—to the political agenda. The most successful parties of this kind have been the Populists, who were active in the 1880s and 1890s, and the Progressives of the early 1900s. The Populist party was founded by western and midwestern farmers who were upset by the growth of corporate monopolies and trusts in the late 1800s. Both the Populists and the Progressives favored direct election of senators, the use of primary elections to nominate candidates, women's suffrage, and similar reforms.

Breakaway Parties

A second type of minor party is formed when a particular group breaks away from a major party because it disagrees with the major party's policy. In

1912, for example, Theodore Roosevelt's Bull Moose party was formed as a result of a split in the leadership of the Republican party. More recently, the American Independent party broke away from the Democratic party after it nominated Hubert Humphrey to run against Richard Nixon.

Third-party presidential candidates have little chance of being elected, but they can affect the outcome of an election. A third-party candidate with a strong regional base can win some electoral votes by gaining the largest share of the popular vote in a few states.[1] Wallace did this in the South in 1968. If such a candidate wins enough electoral votes so that neither of the major-party candidates has a majority, the election must be decided by the House of Representatives. This is very rare, however: The last time an election went to the House was in 1824.

Eventually most third parties are absorbed by the major parties. As they succeed in getting the major parties to support their policies, their reason for existing disappears. Socialist party candidate Norman Thomas said that he stopped running for office because the New Deal included most of the policies for which his party had been fighting for years.

PARTIES AND THE GOVERNMENT

Political parties do not play an important role within the government: They do not propose policies, see that certain laws are passed, or punish members of Congress who do not vote the way the parties want them to. This is because the parties themselves represent a variety of viewpoints and are highly decentralized in structure.

Variety Within the Parties

The wide range of political viewpoints represented by each party is partly a result of historical developments. As we have seen, for many years the Democrats included both northerners who favored more civil rights for black citizens and southerners who opposed civil rights. While the South is less conservative on civil rights and social welfare than it used to be, the Democratic party still includes a variety of viewpoints.

The Republican party has also been shaped by history. After the Civil War it became the party of the commercial and industrial class in the Northeast. It also won the support of the farmers in the West and Midwest. Today it has a "liberal" northeastern wing which favors an activist government and a "conservative" southwestern wing which favors reduced government activity.

---

[1] "Electoral votes" refers to votes in the Electoral College, which actually chooses the President (see pages 176–177).

The variety within each party makes it hard for them to come up with unified programs. Republicans are united in the desire to defeat Democrats, and vice versa. On other issues the parties tolerate many different viewpoints. One result is that conflict *within* the parties is sometimes as intense as the struggle *between* the parties.

Party Structure

In the United States, political parties are organized at the local, state, and national levels. However, there are few ties between those levels. This decentralized party structure is due mainly to the structure of the U.S. government. Power is shared between the national government and the states, and there is a tradition of strong local government as well. As a result the American parties developed as state and local organizations. There are actually 50 separate Republican parties and 50 separate Democratic parties—more if we include some of the stronger county and city organizations. The state and local parties are loosely linked by a national committee, but for all practical purposes they are independent organizations.

At the local level the parties have city or county committees based on townships, precincts, or wards. The famous political "machines" in cities like Chicago and New York were committees of this type. Through their ability to "deliver the vote" for candidates for national and state office these committees gained considerable power.

At the state level each party has a central committee whose members are chosen by each county or election district. This committee organizes state party conventions, coordinates campaigns, and raises money. State committees tend to be fairly weak unless they have a strong leader, such as the state governor or a big-city mayor, who can attract support for the party.

At the national level is the party's national committee, which has little control over the state and local committees. The active units of the party are at the local level. This adds to the variety within the parties—the Democratic party of Biloxi, Mississippi, is a different political animal from the Democratic party of Palo Alto, California. Within each party, decisions that affect the party as a whole, such as the nomination of a presidential candidate, are made through a process of negotiation and compromise. On other matters each unit goes its own way without worrying about what another country or state party might be doing. There is no chain of command with policies decided at the national level and passed down the line to the local level.

This point is important because it affects the role the parties play within the government. In countries where nominations and campaigns are controlled by a central party organization, elected officials are dependent on that organization. The party thus has the power to discipline its members and can see that they vote as it wishes. In the United States, members of Congress do not depend on the national committee for nomination or election and therefore are free to vote as they choose.

HOW DIFFERENT ARE THE MAJOR PARTIES?

During his 1968 third-party campaign for the Presidency George Wallace claimed that there is "not a dime's worth of difference" between the two major parties. Many people agree with him. They believe the two-party system actually reduces the voters' freedom to choose between competing viewpoints. Since each party has to attract and hold the support of a wide variety of groups and individuals, it will tend toward the middle of the road, where most of the voters are. As a result the candidates chosen by the two parties will be quite similar.

Other people disagree. They believe the parties reflect the basic division of the population into haves and have-nots, businesspeople and workers, producers and consumers. The competition for public office, in their view, is actually a democratic class struggle.

Which of these views is closer to the truth? Let's take a look at the evidence.

1. *Different Social Groups Support the Two Major Parties*. The Democrats and the Republicans tend to get their support from different social and religious groups. In general, Republicans have higher-status jobs, higher incomes, and more education than Democrats. Catholics are more likely to be Democrats, while northern white Protestants are more likely to be Republicans. The Democratic party has long been the party of blacks, workers, the poor, and the unemployed.

   However, important changes are taking place in the makeup of the two major parties. Workers are still likely to be Democrats, but they are more willing to listen to Republican candidates. The Republicans, meanwhile, are getting less support from northern white Protestants. As we will see later in the chapter, the number of "independents"—voters who do not identify with either party—is growing.

2. *The Major Parties Differ in Political Philosophy*. Studies have shown that there are differences between the political beliefs of Democrats and Republicans, especially among party activists. A study of the delegates to the presidential nominating conventions in 1956 concluded that the Democratic party "is marked by a strong belief in the power of collective action to promote social justice, equality, humanitarianism, and economic planning, while preserving freedom," while the Republican party "is distinguished by faith in the wisdom of the natural competitive process and in the supreme virtue of individuals, 'character,' self-reliance, frugality, and independence from government."[2] A 1976 study found a similar pattern.

---

[2] These findings are taken from a study of the delegates to the 1956 presidential nominating conventions of both parties. The delegates come from every part of the country and from every level of party and government. For a full report see Herbert McClosky, Paul J. Hoffmann, and Rosemary O'Hara, "Issue Conflict and Consensus Among Party Leaders and Followers," *American Political Science Review*, June 1960, p. 420.

Party committee members at the national, state, and local levels were asked, "Who is to blame for poverty in America? Is it that the system does not give everyone an equal break or are the poor themselves largely to blame?" Democratic party leaders blamed the system by five to one; Republican leaders blamed the poor by four to one. "Should the government guarantee a job for all Americans who are able to work?" By six to one, Democratic leaders said yes; by ten to one, Republican leaders said no.[3]

3. *Congressional Voting Indicates Differences Between the Major Parties.* Political scientists have studied the voting records of members of Congress and reached two conclusions: (1) Party members tend to vote the same way, and their votes reveal major policy differences between the two parties. (2) When a member of Congress does not vote with his or her party, it is almost always because of pressure from the voters back home or, more likely, from an important interest group.

Table 9.1 illustrates the differences in voting records between the two parties. On economic matters, for example, the Republicans have been "protectionists" and the Democrats "protestors." The Republicans oppose government regulation of the economy and social-welfare programs and favor policies that would create jobs and stimulate economic growth through free enterprise. The Democrats favor greater governmental intervention in the economy, social-welfare programs, and tax reform, and are more concerned about unemployment.

---

[3] Data from an unpublished study of American leaders conducted by the *Washington Post* and the Center for International Affairs of Harvard University, April 1976. Questions are paraphrased.

TABLE 9.1   Party Differences in the House of Representatives, 1945–1978

Year	Selected Legislation	Democrats in Favor	Republicans in Favor
1945	Full Employment Act	90%	36%
1947	Maintain Individual Income Tax Rates	62	1
1954	Increase Unemployment Compensation	54	9
1961	Emergency Educational Act	67	4
1964	Antipoverty Program	84	13
1969	Tax Reform	86	22
1971	Hospital Construction	99	41
1973	Increase Minimum Wage	88	27
1974	Federal Aid to City Transit Systems	81	23
1975	Emergency Jobs for the Unemployed	92	13
1976	Block Deregulation of Natural Gas	70	10
1978	Full Employment and Balanced Growth	85	18

SOURCE: Based on data from Robert A. Dahl, "Key Votes, 1945–1964," *Pluralist Democracy in the United States* (Chicago: Rand McNally, 1967), pp. 238–242; *Labor Looks at the 91st Congress,* an AFL-CIO Legislative Report, 1971; *Labor Looks at Congress 1973,* an AFL-CIO Legislative Report, 1974; *Labor Looks at the 93rd Congress,* an AFL-CIO Legislative Report, 1975; *Labor Looks at the 94th Congress,* an AFL-CIO Legislative Report, 1977.

PARTIES AND ELECTIONS

The political parties play a crucial role in the electoral process. They choose the candidates who run for office; they organize the campaign; they offer the American people a choice among candidates and policies. At least this is what they used to do.

In recent years the parties' role in the electoral process has become less important. Candidates often act independently of the political parties, and voters often vote independently of the parties. In the rest of this chapter we will describe the electoral process and examine the changing role of political parties in that process. We will pay special attention to the presidential election.

NOMINATING THE PRESIDENT

In a strong, centralized party system the national party would control all nominations for public office, national, state, or local. However, this has never been the case in the United States. Even nomination for the Presidency has always involved some bargaining with state and local party organizations. The national party conventions have often been dominated by powerful state or local organizations, especially those with large blocks of convention delegates.

In recent years the influence of such organizations has decreased. The Cook County Democratic machine, with its "boss," Mayor Richard Daley, was one of the last of this breed. Before 1976 it controlled the political life of Chicago, determining who got nominated and elected, "delivering" delegate votes at the national convention and citizen votes in the general election. However, the death of Mayor Daley weakened the machine control. And in 1979 Daley's successor, who had strong support from the regular Democrats of Chicago, was upset by Jane Byrne. She promised a more open political process in Chicago.

Although the two major parties are weaker than they used to be, they are still central to the nomination of the presidential and vice-presidential candidates. In fact, the parties come together as national institutions only when the time to nominate those candidates draws near.

Over the years the nomination process has changed greatly. We will describe those changes briefly before discussing how candidates are nominated today.

Party Caucuses

The earliest political parties were small groups of men meeting in "caucuses" to decide on their party's candidates. Candidates for governor and other state offices were nominated by party caucuses in the state legislatures, while presidential candidates were nominated by congressional caucuses.

This system did not last long. "Jacksonian popular democracy," a social movement of the 1820s named after President Jackson, tried to increase the opportunities for ordinary citizens to participate in American politics. It succeeded in replacing caucuses with conventions. Since conventions were made up of delegates chosen by state and local party organizations, they were thought to be more representative than caucuses.

Primary Elections

During the 1800s, nearly all candidates for public office were nominated by party conventions. Today, conventions are used mainly to nominate presidential candidates. Candidates for most other offices are nominated in *primary elections*—party elections held shortly before the general election.

Primaries were intended to reform "undemocratic" politics. Around the turn of the century various reform groups claimed that party conventions were controlled by political bosses and that candidates were controlled by special interests. The reformers believed primaries would change all this.

Primary elections are a way of getting party members involved in the nomination process. In theory they allow party supporters to choose the candidates they think are best qualified to run in the general elections. In practice, however, they have many flaws. Voter turnout is always low; the choices presented are often confusing; and the cost in terms of both money and effort can be very high, using up resources that are needed for the general election.

Primary elections, as well as general elections, are based on the "winner-take-all" principle, as both Jimmy Carter and Henry Jackson knew when they campaigned for the Democratic Party nomination in 1976.

In short, primaries have not led to mass participation in the nomination process. They have, however, reduced the control of a small group of people over that process, and they provide a way for an opposing group to put forward its own candidates.

Presidential Primaries

One of the biggest changes in the process of choosing the President that has occurred in recent years is the growth in the importance of presidential primaries. In 1968 Hubert Humphrey won his party's nomination without entering a single primary, but by 1976 it was clear that primaries had become *the* route to nomination. Thirty states held primaries in that year, compared to 23 in 1972 and 17 in 1968. On the Democratic side, Jimmy Carter was so successful in the primaries that those victories alone gave him nearly enough convention votes to win the nomination. On the Republican side, the primaries gave Ronald Reagan a chance to mount a serious challenge to President Ford.

No longer are presidential primaries merely a series of test cases allowing the party leaders to measure the appeal of various candidates to different groups of voters. Instead, the primaries have begun to replace the nominating convention—and party leaders—as the means by which the party's presidential nominee is chosen. Primaries reduce the control of party organizations over the nomination process and allow candidates who are not tied to such organizations to win the support of the people—as Carter did in 1976.

Presidential Nominating Conventions

Every four years the two major parties, as well as several minor parties, hold conventions for the purpose of nominating their presidential and vice-presidential candidates. Several hundred party members meet in a city chosen by the national party committee to draft a "party platform" and choose a presidential "ticket." When the Democratic and Republican conventions have finished their business, two people out of an adult population of more than 100 million have a realistic chance to become President of the United States.

Who Are the Delegates? Convention delegates are a cross-section of the political party. They include members of Congress, governors, mayors, state legislators, and other office-holders, as well as party activists and contributors. Until recently most delegates to the major-party conventions were high-status white males. But both parties have reformed their delegate selection practices to include more delegates from minority groups. The number of minority delegates to the 1972 Democratic national convention showed a marked increase from 1968 levels. In 1976, however, the percentage of minority delegates had dropped somewhat. Minority groups, especially were unwilling to let their earlier gains slip away. Blacks put pressure on the party's Rules Committee to make a greater effort to increase minority representation at future conventions, and women persuaded the convention to pass a resolution calling on the state parties to move toward equal representation of the sexes in state delegations.

The Convention's Role　Do the delegates to the national conventions actually decide anything, or do they simply approve a decision that has already been made? In 1976 the Democratic and Republican conventions showed a striking contrast between an easy victory and a close-fought contest, but in both cases most of the delegates had made up their minds before the convention began (or were obliged to vote for a particular candidate under the rules by which they were chosen).

In the past there was more doubt about the outcome of the conventions. Often negotiations, compromises, and "deals" have resulted in an unexpected choice. Or there have been intense battles between different factions, with the outcome depending on how the undecided delegates finally voted. Today, however, the struggle has shifted to the presidential primaries and the state and local meetings in which delegates are selected.

Even so, it is still possible that the primaries may fail to produce a clear front runner. If the party is divided into several factions and there are many candidates fighting it out in the primaries, the delegates may really have to choose a candidate.

THE PRESIDENTIAL CAMPAIGN

If anything political gets the attention of the American public it is the presidential campaign. The faces and voices of the candidates appear on billboards, bumper stickers, newspaper advertisements, radio spots, and, most of all, television. You may not care about the results, but it is not easy to avoid the campaign. Walk past a newsstand, and a half-dozen different pictures of one or both of the candidates smile at you from magazine covers. Turn the television on, and sooner or later there is an announcement telling you how much *this* election means and how *this* candidate can solve the country's problems.

Candidates have to make a lot of decisions at the beginning of the campaign. Some of these have to do with the organization and financing of the campaign: How much should be spent on television announcements? How much effort should go into travel and personal appearances? Candidates must also decide where to do most of their campaigning. They spend less time in areas where they have little chance of winning or where they cannot

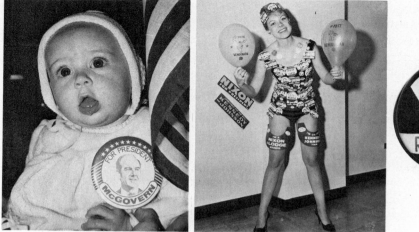

lose. Most of their effort is concentrated on large states where the outcome is uncertain. The reason for this will become clear later in the chapter, when we discuss the Electoral College.

Appealing to the Voters

Candidates also have to decide how to appeal to the voters. They can base their appeal on party loyalty, personality, or their positions on current issues.

Party Loyalty   Many citizens think of themselves as Democrats or Republicans and have done so for most of their lives. Candidates can appeal to the voters on this basis—especially Democratic candidates, since there are more Democrats than Republicans. Indeed, in many countries this is the only basis of voter appeal. Candidates do not try to win the votes of people who identify with other parties. In the United States, however, about 40 percent of the public does not identify with either party. This is a large block of voters, and most candidates try to win their votes. In addition, they often lure members of the other party over to their side. For example, millions of Democrats crossed party lines to vote for Eisenhower in 1952 and 1956 and for Nixon in 1968 and 1972.

Personality   Candidates may also try to convince the voters that they are honest, qualified, and able to run the government. For example, after the Watergate scandal both Ford and Carter emphasized their personal honesty. The candidate who appeals to the voters on the basis of personality does not ask them to support him because he is a Democrat or a Republican or because of the things he promises to do. He asks them to vote for him because of the kind of person he is.

Appealing to the voters on the basis of personality often means calling one's opponent irresponsible or incompetent. In 1964 Johnson claimed that Goldwater was irresponsible on nuclear matters, while in 1972 Nixon accused McGovern of being incompetent. In each case the candidate who made the accusation won the election.

Issues Candidates take positions on a variety of issues. On some of those issues there is little disagreement among the voters over what needs to be done (e.g., end corruption in government). All the candidate can do is claim that he will do a better job than his opponent. On other issues, however, the public is divided. These issues are of two types:

1. On some issues a small group of citizens is deeply concerned while the rest of the public does not care much. (See Example 5, page 116.) Gun control and abortion are issues of this type. Candidates often try to avoid taking stands on such issues. If they take a stand against the minority that feels strongly about the issue, they will lose votes. Indeed, if the group is large enough and is located in the right states, it can be an important voting block.

2. On other issues the public is divided more or less equally. (See Examples 1, 3, and 4, pages 112, 113, and 114.) There are many such issues; welfare spending and busing are examples. On these issues candidates are expected to take clear positions and offer the voters a real choice, but this does not often happen. A look at campaign strategy will explain why.

Campaign Strategy

Imagine a scale like the one we used in Chapter 6. A citizen can take a position on the left, on the right, or in the middle. Assume that citizens vote for the candidate whose position is closest to their own. Where will the candidate who wants to win the most votes take a stand? As close to the middle as possible. The reason for this is found in the way our electoral system works.

The American electoral system has an enormous effect on the way candidates campaign. This is because we have a *winner-take-all* system. In presidential races the candidate with the most votes wins.[4] The same is true in congressional races: The candidate with the most votes wins a seat in Congress. Those who come in second get nothing. This situation is very different from the system of *proportional representation* used in many other nations. In that system the number of seats in parliament won by each party is proportional to that party's share of the vote.

If a party that wins, say, 20 percent of the vote can get that percentage of the seats in parliament, it can afford to appeal to a small portion of the public. It can take a position on the left or the right, win the votes of the minority

---

[4] Subject to some strange things that can happen in the Electoral College, to be discussed shortly.

that shares its views, and elect some of the members of parliament. But if only one candidate can win, the winning strategy is to attract the largest number of voters. And those voters are at or near the middle position on the political scale.

Most candidates stick close to the middle of the road. But sometimes a party nominates a candidate who is left or right of center. In 1964 the Republicans nominated conservative Barry Goldwater. He was opposed by Lyndon Johnson, who took a position closer to the center. Goldwater was soundly defeated as many Republicans chose the candidate who was closer to the middle of the road. Similarly, in 1972 the Democrats nominated George McGovern, who took a position toward the left of the political scale. He too was defeated as Democrats crossed over to vote for Nixon.

The Parties' Role

A candidate for office has to convince thousands or even millions of voters that he is the best person for the job. Either the candidate himself or his campaign workers must see that speeches are planned, leaflets distributed, advertisements put in newspapers, radio and TV announcements made, and so on. Political campaigning is both complicated and expensive.

Political parties used to play a major role in organizing campaigns. The party provided a skeleton organization that came to life around election time. Party officials opened temporary campaign headquarters; volunteers licked stamps; contributors were asked to write checks. In recent years, however, party control over campaigning has decreased. The presidential campaign is now controlled by the candidate's personal advisers. Richard Nixon's 1972 campaign was managed by the Committee to Re-elect the President (CREEP), an organization that was independent of the Republican National Committee, while Jimmy Carter's 1976 campaign was managed by a group of political advisers from Georgia and not by any Democratic party organization.

Campaign Finance

Before 1976 political campaigns were extremely expensive—the 1972 presidential campaign alone cost more than $100 million. Naturally, the candidates needed all the money they could get, and sometimes they got it any way they could. The Watergate scandal revealed widespread violations of campaign finance law. For example, corporate executives had been pressured by the Nixon administration to make illegal contributions to Nixon's campaign.

In 1974 and 1976 major legislation was passed in an effort to not only end illegal contributions but also reduce the total amount spent on political campaigns. The new law has three main parts: (1) limits on the amounts that may be contributed by individuals or organizations, (2) limits on the amounts that candidates for national office may spend, and (3) a system providing for public funding of presidential campaigns. Individuals now may contribute no more than $1000 per candidate per election, organizations no more than $5000. Candidates for the Presidency may spend no more than $10 million for all primaries and no more than $20 million for the general election.

The reform of campaign finance weakens the parties somewhat. The law provides matching funds for candidates who can raise $5000 in contributions in each of 20 states. Once they have qualified, the candidates may not need the parties. It is generally agreed that public funding helped Carter, an outsider with little party support, win the 1976 Democratic nomination.

In addition, the limits on campaign spending result in a cutback in the traditional activities of political parties. In 1976, for example, there were fewer buttons, bumper stickers, posters, and storefront campaign headquarters. Because the money to finance the campaign came from the public treasury, there was less need for fund-raising dinners and picnics organized by the parties.

On the other hand, public funding aids the two major parties at election time. For one thing, it gives them an advantage over third parties. They qualify for public funding because they won a large percentage of the vote in the previous election. A minor party is entitled to funds if it won five percent of the vote in the previous election. If it did not, or if it is just starting up, it gets no support during the campaign, though it will be reimbursed for its expenses if it manages to win five percent of the vote.

The Electoral College

The Electoral College has a major effect on campaign strategy. The writers of the Constitution saw it as a means of using a small group of respected citizens to choose the President. Today it plays a far different role. It has made large states much more important than small ones.

In the Electoral College each state has a number of electoral votes equal to the number of senators and representatives it sends to Congress. This number ranges from 3 to 45 (California has the most electoral votes). Under the *unit rule* all of a state's electoral votes go to the candidate who wins a plurality of the votes in that state. This means that the largest states are the most important ones—California and New York alone can give a candidate nearly one-third of the electoral votes he or she needs to win the Presidency (86 out of 270). The effect of the Electoral College on campaign strategy is obvious: Both parties concentrate on winning the large states.

The Electoral College makes it possible for the candidate with the most votes to lose the election. This has happened three times: in 1824, 1876, and 1888. In 1976 Carter won 50.1 percent of the vote and Ford won 48.0 percent. However, if Ford had won the state of New York (which he came close to doing) he would have won a majority of the electoral votes and would have remained President, even though Carter won a larger percentage of the popular vote.

The Electoral College system has been criticized on several counts. The most serious criticism, of course, is the possibility that the candidate with the largest popular vote will lose the election. Critics also object to the winner-take-all system, in which a candidate can win in a state by the narrowest of margins yet still get all of that state's electoral votes. Moreover, the electors are legally free to vote for a candidate other than the one to whom they are pledged. This means they can ignore the will of the people.

Critics also complain about the rule that if no candidate wins a majority of the electoral votes the House of Representatives chooses among the three top candidates, with each state having one vote. In such a case the party that controls the House can vote its candidate into office. Or a third-party candidate can affect the outcome by giving his support to one of the two major candidates.

There have been many attempts to reform the Electoral College, none yet successful. Most recently, in 1977, Senator Birch Bayh proposed a constitutional amendment that would provide for direct election of the President. Under the amendment the candidate with the largest percentage of the popular vote would be elected. If no candidate won 40 percent of the vote, the decision would be made by a joint session of Congress, with each member having one vote.

THE AMERICAN VOTER

We have discussed how candidates appeal to the voters. How do the voters respond? Political scientists began studying the voting behavior of the American public in the 1950s. They found that citizens often lacked the information they needed to decide which candidate to support. Moreover, they did not have well-formed opinions on public issues. They might answer researchers' questions about a variety of issues, but their answers usually were not carefully formed opinions. (In one study citizens were asked how they felt about the "Metallic Metals Act." The act did not exist, but 70 percent of the respondents had an opinion for or against it.[5])

---

[5] Stanley J. Payne, *The Art of Asking Questions* (Princeton, N.J.: Princeton University Press, 1951), p. 18.

Studies conducted in the 1950s and early 1960s found that most Americans did not have clear political views. They could not be called "liberal" or "conservative" or "radical." In fact there was almost no connection between a citizen's position on one issue and his or her position on other issues. Citizens who were conservative on racial matters could easily be liberal on welfare or foreign-policy issues.

These findings meant that the results of elections did not depend on the issues. The public was uninformed about where the candidates stood on the issues, did not have clear opinions on the issues, and were not consistent when they did have opinions. So why did they vote the way they did?

Factors Influencing Voting

Voters can decide how to vote on the basis of three factors: party, issue positions, or personality. A "party" voter might say, "I am a loyal Democrat like my parents. The Democrats have always done more for working people like me. I don't know much about Jimmy Carter, but he's a Democrat, so he'll get my vote." An "issue" voter might say, "The nation is going to have to do something about inflation. Carter talks about it, but the Republicans are more likely to do something about it. If prices keep going up, my paycheck won't be worth anything. So I'll vote Republican." A voter who focuses on personality or character might say, "We need someone we can trust in the White House. He's got to be fair and honest. I'm not sure about Carter, but Ford is an honest person. I'll vote for him."

In the 1950s, 77 percent of the public identified with one party or the other. Most citizens inherited their party identification from their parents and kept it throughout their lives. Party identification was the best predictor of how an individual would vote. Most citizens voted for the candidate of the party they identified with. This was especially true in congressional races— in 1956, 91 percent of the voters stuck to their party in the congressional election. Voters might cross party lines to vote for a popular presidential candidate—millions of Democrats voted for Eisenhower in 1952 and 1956. They did so because of his personality, not because of his positions on the issues. Yet they continued to think of themselves as Democrats.

The Changing Voter

In the years since the 1950s citizens seem to have developed more consistent political attitudes. Today, if people are conservative on one issue they are likely to be conservative on others; if they are liberal on one, they are likely to be liberal on others. Moreover, they are more likely to judge candidates on the basis of their positions on the issues. In each presidential election since

1952 the University of Michigan's Survey Research Center has asked citizens what they liked and disliked about the candidates. Figure 9.1 shows the percentage of the public that mentioned the personality of the candidate, his party, and his issue positions. Note that citizens still pay a lot of attention to the candidate's personality. About 80 percent mention it in each election year. However, there has been a drop in the percent who mention party and a rise in the percent who mention issue positions.

There are indications that the political parties are no longer as important as they used to be. In 1974 a majority of Americans—60 percent—still identified with one of the major parties, but the percentage had fallen quite a bit. Perhaps more important, young voters were as likely to call themselves independents as to identify with one of the major parties—a big change from earlier times. Even those who continue to identify with one of the parties are more likely to vote for the other party's candidate.

As the importance of the party has decreased, the importance of issues has increased. But this does not mean that the average voter makes a careful study of the candidates' positions on the issues before deciding how to vote. The public still lacks basic political information. In 1972, for example, only

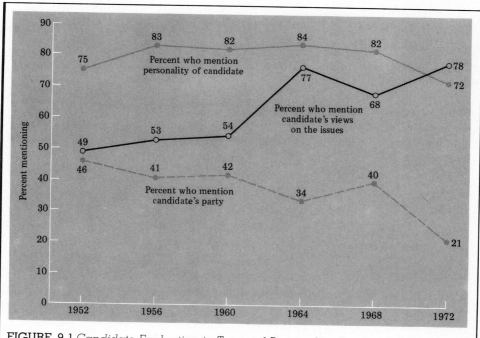

FIGURE 9.1 *Candidate Evaluation in Terms of Personality, Issues, and Party Ties*
Source: Based on data from the Center for Political Studies, Institute for Social Research, University of Michigan.

53 percent of the citizens knew the name and party of *one* of their senators. Even when issues become more important, as they have in recent elections, the connection between issue position and the vote is still weaker then the connection between party identification and the vote. Candidates can still count on a high percentage of the votes of people who identify with a particular party. (See Figure 9.2.)

Party identification is especially important when there are no other forces —such as an especially popular or unpopular candidate or an important set of issues—that might lead a voter to cross party lines. In the 1972 election only 67 percent of those who called themselves Democrats voted for McGovern, largely because they were dissatisfied with him as a person and disagreed with his issue positions. But in 1976, when there was little negative reaction to Carter as a person and less reason to reject him because of his issue positions, Carter won about eight out of ten Democratic votes.

To sum up, changes in the American voter have reduced the importance of parties. More voters are independent, and more voters base their vote on

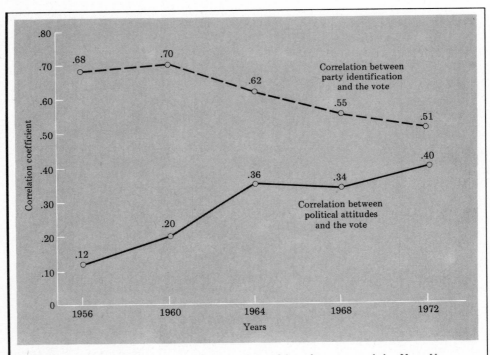

FIGURE 9.2 *As the Correlation Between Party Identification and the Vote Has Gone Down, the Correlation Between Issue Position and the Vote Has Gone Up*
Source: Based on data from the Center for Political Studies, Institute for Social Research, University of Michigan.

reasons other than party. Parties still supply labels for the candidates, but those labels mean less. Voters are now more likely to vote for the candidate rather than the label. Yet the labels are still important in that, while Republicans are more willing to vote for Democrats and Democrats to vote for Republicans, most voters still reserve their vote for a candidate who runs under one of the two major party labels.

PARTY REALIGNMENT

Many people describe the American party system in gloomy terms. It is easy to see why. Party loyalty has decreased; party supporters can no longer be counted on; party organizations have weakened. At the same time, the nation faces a new and complex set of issues: equality between the races and the sexes; the environment; energy. Can the parties deal with these issues?

One way the party system has adjusted to social change in the past is through *realignment*. From time to time an election or a series of elections results in a major, permanent change in the makeup of the political parties, as well as a shift in which party is dominant. The last party realignment took place during the Great Depression. Herbert Hoover was defeated in 1932, ending a long period of Republican dominance, and a new Democratic coalition formed around the New Deal. It was based on the urban workers in the North, many from immigrant backgrounds. At the same time, the Democrats kept control of the Solid South.

The New Deal realignment depended on two factors: new issues and new voters.[6] The new issues were related to economic reform. The Democrats called for more government regulation of the economy and for major social-welfare programs. But new issues were not enough to create a Democratic majority. A large group of new voters was also needed. These voters were found among the many young voters—often the children of immigrants—who became eligible to vote in the 1930s, as well as many who had become eligible in the 1920s but had never bothered to vote.

Is Realignment Possible Today?

Could the current problems of the party system be solved by a new party alignment? If a realignment depends on new issues and new voters, we appear to be ready for one. As mentioned earlier, new issues have come onto the political agenda in recent years, joining traditional economic issues like

---

[6] Norman H. Nie, Sidney Verba, and John Petrocik, *The Changing American Voter* (Cambridge, Mass.: Harvard University Press, 1976). See chap. 5 by Kristi Andersen.

unemployment and inflation. In addition, there are many voters, mostly young people, without party ties. Can they be molded into a new coalition?

The 1976 Election

In many ways the 1976 election looked like a rebirth of the New Deal coalition. Carter won the votes of blue-collar workers, blacks and other minorities, Jews and Catholics, the poor. He also won in almost every southern state. Ford, by contrast, won the votes of traditionally Republican groups: farmers, professional and business groups, wealthier citizens, Protestants, and a majority of whites. He won largely in the western and midwestern states.

Yet there is little reason to believe the coalition that supported Carter is evidence for the beginning of a new, stronger party system. Why not? For three reasons: (1) the complexity of the issues, (2) changes in party support, and (3) greater emphasis on the candidate as a person.

The New Issues   In the 1930s the two major parties offered a clear choice: The Democrats favored the New Deal reforms and the Republicans opposed them. But the new issues of the 1960s and 1970s did not permit such clear choices. The Vietnam War, for example, was conducted first by a Democratic administration and then by a Republican one. Many new voters were concerned about Vietnam, but the parties did not offer a clear choice between different policies on the war. As a result they rejected both parties.

The new issues also tended to crosscut each other. The Democrats can unite working-class voters on the issue of unemployment, but this group splits into blacks versus whites on such issues as busing or affirmative action. A candidate like Carter can put together a temporary coalition—especially when the issues are vague ones such as honesty in government or the need to cut down the size of the bureaucracy—but it is unlikely to be permanent.

The Party Supporters   In the 1976 election the groups that supported the Democratic and Republican parties were the same ones that had supported them in the 1930s. However, that support is a lot weaker today. Carter's victory in the South was based on heavy black support; he did not have the support of a majority of the white voters. Aside from the blacks, most of the social groups that formerly supported one or the other of the major parties are more divided and less reliable than they used to be.

The Candidate, Not the Party   Today, people may be voting more for the person than for the party. The main way voters find out about candidates is through the media rather than the party. The candidates also run their campaigns through their personal organizations rather than the party organizations. All this means that a presidential victory is a victory for the candidate, not the party. The coalition that voted him in is not likely to last until the next election.

PARTIES AND THE FUTURE

We may be in for a long period of weak parties. Voters will vote—and candidates will run—as individuals, not as party members. What does this mean for American politics?

For one thing, political affairs will be less predictable. We may see more candidates who are outsiders, as Carter was, and the voters will judge them as individuals. The image they present through the mass media will play a more important role than their party labels.

For another thing, the public's control over political leaders may be weakened. As V. O. Key has pointed out, voters hold officials accountable for what they have already done; they do not vote for policies they hope to see in the future. If they like what has happened so far, they will vote for those who are in power; if not, they will vote against them. This is a good way of keeping elected officials on their toes—they have to "perform" or lose the next election. But it depends on who is running. If one of the candidates is the incumbent, as Ford was in the 1976 election, he can be held

accountable for past actions. But when candidates run as "outsiders" more than as office-holders or representatives of their party, it is hard for democratic accountability to work the way it is supposed to.

Political parties have never played an effective role in offering the public a choice. They have not offered programs that would be carried out if their candidates were elected, but they have given the public a basis for choice that was the same from one election to the next. In the future the ability of the public to hold leaders accountable may be much weaker if the party system continues its decline.

In the years ahead the parties will try to win the support of new social groups. They will try to deal with the political agenda of inflation, unemployment, consumer protection, tax reform, social welfare, and street crime. And they will not remain unchanged. If they cannot absorb the new groups and deal with the issues, the two-party system as we know it will fade. More than once in the past, however, the party system has shown that it is flexible enough to change with the times.

CONTROVERSY

In choosing its presidential ticket, should a political party concern itself only with winning—that is, nominate middle-of-the-road candidates—or should it stress the differences between the two parties?

One Side

The American voter prefers presidential candidates who stand somewhere between a conservative outlook and a liberal one. Since the job of political parties is to win elections, they should give the voters what they want. When "extreme" candidates—such as Goldwater in 1964 and McGovern in 1972—are nominated, they will be defeated. A candidate whose views are well to the left or right of center causes many voters to switch to the other party.

Besides, losses like those suffered by Goldwater and McGovern can have bad effects other than the defeat of the party. They can give the winning party the impression that it has the right to do whatever it wants.

The Other Side

The major parties have other responsibilities besides winning. They should give the voters a clear choice and use the presidential campaign to express different goals and policies.

Most citizens pay attention to politics only in election years. If the average citizen is going to think seriously about the problems facing society, it will be while listening to debates between presidential candidates. When the campaign smooths over major differences about how to solve the nation's problems, the democratic process is not working.

A candidate who clearly differs from his opponent plays an important role even if he loses. He reminds the nation that other policies are possible. In 1972, for example, McGovern's strong stand against the Vietnam War may have led to his defeat, but perhaps it also contributed to the efforts of the Nixon administration to find a way of ending the war. McGovern himself saw it this way: "There can be no question at all that we have pushed this country in the direction of peace," he said, "and I think each one of us loves the title of peacemaker more than any office in the land."

10

Article 1, Section 1 of the Constitution states that "all legislative Powers herein granted shall be vested in a Congress of the United States, which shall consist of a Senate and a House of Representatives." In the rest of Article 1 the duties, powers, and responsibilities of Congress are set forth in detail. Congress is much more than a legislative body, however. The task of protecting the basic principles of democracy falls mainly on Congress.

The sheer size and complexity of a modern industrial society and the complicated issues and problems facing the government make nonsense of the claim that people can govern themselves. Democratic principles have been weakened by the growth of huge bureaucracies and the growing role of the government in the nation's economic and social life, and the growth of the "military-industrial complex" has caused many people to wonder whether the American political system can keep power from shifting to the small group of people who run giant corporations and huge government agencies. But as long as the government includes a representative assembly, or Congress, the concentration of power in the hands of a few individuals can be checked.

In this chapter we will begin with a discussion of the role of Congress as the branch of government that represents the people. We will then turn to the legislative functions of Congress and to the ways in which Congress has changed in recent years.

CONGRESS: THE REPRESENTATIVE BRANCH

We begin with a question: Are representatives supposed to carry out the wishes of those who elected them, or are they supposed to use their own judgment? According to one view, a representative who does not follow the instructions of the voters back home is not a representative at all. According to the opposing view, if every representative is bound by the wishes of his or her constituents there is no point in having a legislature—public policy could be decided by public vote.

Most members of Congress steer somewhere between these two views. They either mix them or lean toward the independent position, depending on the issue involved. This will become clear as we take a look at how members represent individual citizens, the voters, and organized groups.

Representing the Individual

The federal government affects the life of the individual citizen in dozens of ways: income tax laws, social-security payments, medicare, consumer protection, small-business loans, and many more. When citizens feel that they have been mistreated by a government agency or need some government service, they turn to their representative in Congress for help. As a result the job of a member of Congress includes helping the individual deal with the government. According to some estimates, senators or representatives spend up to half their time representing the individual citizen. And it is certainly true that their staffs spend much of their time on the problems of individuals. As a result of this "errand running" some people worry that Congress may become swamped and unable to perform well as a legislative assembly. Yet few members of Congress ignore the requests of individuals. Reelection can depend on being available and helpful to citizens.

Even so, there is a gap between citizen requests and public policy. A request for help in dealing with the Internal Revenue Service may have no effect on tax reform, nor does a request for help in getting a small-business loan have anything to do with economic policy. What this means is that if members of Congress solve individual citizens' problems they can be reelected regardless of how they vote on tax reform or economic policy. While senators and representatives are paying close attention to citizens' specific *problems,* they are paying less attention to citizens' general *viewpoints.*

Representing the Voters

It is often hard for a member of Congress to get an accurate picture of how voters feel about an issue. Partly this is because many voters are not very well informed and do not participate much in politics. On the average, fewer than half of the eligible voters bother to vote in congressional elections, especially "off-year" elections. Moreover, the average voter knows very little about *either* candidate, even in the most competitive congressional race.

The problem of representing the voter is complicated by the fact that a candidate takes stands on a lot of different issues. She may support a negative income tax, oppose continued space exploration, and have little to say about foreign policy. If she wins, is it because of her stand on the negative income tax or because of her stand on space exploration? Or is it because she steered clear of foreign-policy issues or because her opponent lost votes as a result of his foreign-policy statements? Maybe personal qualities such as religion or race were more important than the issues.

Still, it would be a mistake to conclude that the opinions of voters have no effect on the actions of a member of Congress. Citizens may not know much about the bills that are pending in Congress or about what their representative is doing, but they are not neutral on major issues of war, inflation and unemployment, civil rights, and so on. Members of Congress know how the voters in their district or state feel about such matters.

Unfortunately, there have been very few studies of the relationship between the policy views of members of Congress and those of the voters they represent. One such study, however, found that congressional districts that are generally liberal on civil-rights issues are represented by members who vote in favor of civil-rights legislation, whereas more conservative districts are represented by members who oppose such legislation.[1]

There are two ways of explaining this pattern. The member's views may be the same as those of the voters, in which case he or she does not have to worry about voter preferences. On the other hand, the member may not always see eye to eye with the voters but may be afraid to differ with them, at least on a major issue like civil rights. The evidence shows that the second explanation is probably closer to the truth: Members of Congress seem to change their own views on racial issues to match those of the voters. This is not true for certain other issues, however. On foreign policy in particular, senators and representatives do not seem to be affected by voter opinions, perhaps because the voters themselves do not always have firm opinions in this area.

Representing Interest Groups

Members of Congress may not be sure how voters feel about a particular issue, but this does not apply to the major groups in their district or state, especially when proposed bills affect the interests of those groups.

A member of Congress who wants to be reelected must keep in mind the policy preferences of the groups that represent large numbers of voters. It is not hard to learn those preferences. As we have seen, such organizations spend a lot of time and money lobbying for favorable treatment. In exchange for such treatment they offer either campaign contributions or votes.

Two Forms of Group Politics   It is important to keep in mind the fact that organizations are active in two ways. First, they act as local pressure groups trying to persuade a member of Congress to support legislation that will benefit his or her local area—to control the route of a federal highway, to get contracts for local industries, and the like. They usually have little trouble getting their representative to support their preferences, and whatever conflict there may be takes place *within* Congress as different parts of the country compete for the same highway or defense contract or what have you.

On the other hand, groups can also compete with each other in trying to influence legislation that may affect their members. Powerful national organizations such as the AFL–CIO, the American Farm Bureau Federation, and

---

[1] The study cited here is from Warren E. Miller and Donald E. Stokes, "Constituency Influence in Congress," *American Political Science Review* 57 (1963), 45–57.

the American Legion put a lot of effort into such activity. The results of those efforts are quite different from the results of local pressure group activity. The issues on which national organizations are active lead to battles between business and labor, between farmers and consumers, or between land developers and environmentalists. Congress itself is the battlefield, and its members are pressured from both sides.

Group Politics and Geography Our representational system is based on geography; that is, the constitution makes place of residence the basis for electing members of Congress. But does a doctor in St. Louis really have more in common with the grocery store owner who lives next door than with another doctor who lives in Dallas? The answer is that it depends on the issue.

Consider the following example:

	Citizen A	Citizen B	Citizen C
Residence	Chicago suburb	Chicago suburb	Small town in Kansas
Occupation	Retired military	Public-school teacher	Shop owner
Race	White	Black	White

On an issue that is directly related to place of residence, citizens A and B might be aligned against citizen C. But on other issues the alignment might shift as follows:

Issue	Alignment of Citizens
Federal support for mass transit	A and B vs. C
Increased veterans' benefits	B and C vs. A
Compensatory hiring of blacks	A and C vs. B

This is where national organizations come in. On many issues they cross geographic boundaries and provide an umbrella under which citizens can gather on issues that affect them regardless of their place of residence—issues that affect them because of their job or their race or their sex or anything else they may have in common. The American Medical Association represents doctors from Honolulu to Huzzah, from Mississippi to Maine. The National Council of Senior Citizens does the same for older people, no matter where they live. To the extent that Congress responds to national organizations on national issues, it is less "parochial" in its outlook than some critics claim.

The Members of Congress

According to former Representative Bella S. Abzug, in a truly representative Congress half of the members would be women and 11 percent would be black. There would be more younger people, more members of the working class, more teachers, more artists, and so on. She was correct in pointing out that Congress is dominated by men (mostly white men) who are better educated than the general population and are either professional people (mostly lawyers) or businessmen. (See Table 10.1.)

The fact that the membership of Congress does not mirror the general population has long bothered its critics. Reformers believe that changing the makeup of Congress would change its policies. For example, civil-rights groups support black candidates because they think blacks can best represent black views, and the Women's Caucus supports women candidates because it

TABLE 10.1 Membership of the 95th Congress, 1978

House		Senate
	Party	
292	Democrats	61
143	Republicans	38
		1
	Sex	
418	Men	99
17	Women	1
	Age	
27	Youngest	34
77	Oldest	80
49	Average	54
	Religion	
255	Protestants	69
107	Catholics	12
18	Jewish	5
4	Mormons	3
51	Others	11
	Profession	
215	Lawyers	65
81	Businessmen and bankers	13
45	Educators	6
14	Farmers and ranchers	6
22	Career government officials	0
24	Journalists, communications executives	4
2	Physicians	0
1	Veterinarians	1
0	Geologists	2
6	Workers and skilled tradesmen	0
25	Others	3
	Ethnic Minorities	
17	Blacks	1
2	Orientals	3
4	Spanish	0

SOURCES: "Congressional Directory," National Democratic and Republican Congressional Committees, Associated Press. Reprinted from *U.S. News & World Report*, 10 January, 1977, p. 29. Copyright 1977 U.S. News & World Report, Inc.

assumes that they can present the case for women's rights more forcefully than men. Yet not all women support the women's movement, and black skin can cover an Uncle Tom as well as a black militant. On the other hand, if you are a middle-class white male you are not necessarily hostile to the interests of blacks, women, or the working class. The important qualities in a member of Congress are political viewpoint, ability, experience, and character, not race, sex, or occupation.

CONGRESS: THE LEGISLATIVE BRANCH

In this section we will take a look at how Congress is organized and how it operates. First, however, it is necessary to note some differences between the two houses of Congress.

Differences Between the Senate and the House

The Constitution divides Congress into two houses, the Senate and the House of Representatives. But it says nothing about how the two houses should organize themselves, and this fact, together with differences in number of members and term of office, has led to some important differences between the two houses.

Number of Members With only 100 members (2 from each of the 50 states), the Senate is smaller and less formal than the House. "The Senate . . . is a small and special world," writes one student of Congress.

> The chamber is quiet. It must be, because there is no public address system and business is conducted in conversational tones. It is dignified: somber-suited men, a few quite old, move in the perpetual twilight of its high ceiling lights. . . . Yet its nerve ends are in the great world outside, and its reaction to events can be instantaneous.[2]

The House, by contrast, has 435 members. The number from each state depends on its population—California sends 43, while some small states send only one representative apiece. House business is regulated by a complex set of formal procedures. While power is more widely distributed in the House now than it was ten years ago, it is still largely in the hands of a smaller percentage of its members than is the case in the Senate.

Prestige Since a senator's term of office is six years while a representative's is only two, even a new senator will be in Washington long enough to be noticed. A House member must be reelected several times before he or she begins to be known. Many senators are as well known as state governors— some are nearly as well known as the President himself—but it is unusual for a member of the House to gain a national reputation.

The Senate is generally more visible to the public than the House; for example, Senate debate gets more attention from the mass media than House debate. This is partly because Senate debate is unlimited unless it is closed by the members themselves, and a "filibuster"—in which a group of senators tries to "talk a bill to death"—can sometimes last for days or even weeks.

---

[2] Ralph K. Huitt, "The Internal Distribution of Influence: The Senate," in David B. Truman, ed., *The Congress and America's Future* (Englewood Cliffs, N.J.: Prentice-Hall, 1965), p. 15.

Senator Kennedy has been an active promotor of health legislation.

House debates are much less dramatic: Speakers are usually limited to five minutes, and only a certain number of speakers will debate a particular issue.

Powers Although senators tend to have more prestige than representatives, this does not mean that the House is less powerful than the Senate. Both houses share the power to legislate, and a bill must be passed by both the House and the Senate before it can become law. However, certain powers are assigned to only one house of Congress. The Senate, for example, has the power to confirm the President's appointments of Supreme Court justices, ambassadors, and heads of executive departments, while the House has the power to initiate all money bills—not only tax and tariff bills but also the bills that appropriate money to run the federal government.

Congessional Leadership

Leadership in the House Generally the most powerful member of the House is the *Speaker*. The Speaker presides over floor debate and nominates his party's Rules Committee members. (Before 1910 he appointed the members of other standing committees as well.)

Before the opening of a new session of Congress, the members of the party with the most members in the House of Representatives—the majority party—meet to nominate a Speaker and other leaders. The Speaker is then formally elected by the entire membership of the House. Other important majority party leaders include the *floor leader* and the *whip*, who work closely with the Speaker in planning party strategy in the House. The floor leader negotiates with committee chairpersons and with members of the House

Rules Committee that controls which bills will come before the House. The party whip, along with deputy whips, is responsible for knowing how many party members are likely to support a particular bill. The whips try to round up members in time for important votes.[3]

Leadership in the Senate According to the Constitution, the Vice-President is supposed to preside over the Senate, but this rarely happens. In the absence of the Vice-President, another Senator will preside (known as the *president pro tempore*). However, the recognized leader of the Senate is the *Senate majority leader,* who is elected by the majority party.

The powers of the majority leader are derived not only from his position as head of the party but also from his leadership skills. Montana Democrat Mike Mansfield, majority leader from 1961 to 1976, said, "I am neither a circus ring master, a master of ceremonies of a Senate night club, a tamer of Senate lions, nor a wheeler and dealer." By contrast, Lyndon Johnson, who was majority leader before Mansfield, was all of those things. He persuaded and threatened, traded and compromised, and most of all, counted votes. He knew who might support what version of which bill, and he used his knowledge to shape legislation.

The contrast between Mansfield and Johnson illustrates an important point: Often it is not the position itself but the personality and drive of the person in that position that determines how effective a leader is.

Minority Party Leaders In both the House and the Senate the leadership of the minority party matches that of the majority party. A major role of minority party leaders is to serve as a link between Congress and the White House when the President is a member of the minority party.

The Committee System

It is impossible for 535 people to come together, debate dozens of complicated issues, and reach collective decisions on those issues. Even separating those people into two groups does not solve the problem. Therefore both houses of Congress have chosen the *committee system* of organization.

Standing Committees Complicated legislation must be drafted by a small group of experts. This is the reason for the *standing committees* of Congress. (See Table 10.2.) Each standing committee has a specific area of responsibility. It considers each bill referred to it, writes and rewrites the actual legislation (holding public hearings if necessary), and then sends the bill to the House or the Senate with its recommendations.

---

[3] The term *whip* is derived from English fox hunts, in which the man who is supposed to keep the hunting dogs from straying is called a "whipper-in."

    The responsibilities of a standing committee can cover a wide range of topics, and the membership of some committees is quite large (the House Appropriations Committee has 50 members). Therefore there is a need for subcommittees as well as committees. Subcommittees have become more important in recent years; today there are nearly 250 of them. The Appropriations Committee alone has 13 subcommittees, ranging from Agriculture and Related Agencies to Treasury—Postal Service—General Government.

TABLE 10.2　Standing Committees of Congress (in Groups, in Order of Importance)

Senate (18)	House (22)
I　Appropriations 　　Finance 　　Foreign Relations	Appropriations Rules Ways and Means
II　Agriculture and Forestry 　　Armed Services 　　Budget*a* 　　Commerce 　　Judiciary	Agriculture Armed Services Budget*a* Government Operations International Relations Interstate and Foreign Commerce Judiciary
III　Aeronautical and Space Science 　　Banking, Housing and Urban Affairs 　　Interior and Insular Affairs 　　Human Resources 　　Public Works	Banking, Currency, and Housing Education and Labor Interior and Insular Affairs Public Works and Transportation Science and Technology Small Business
IV　Government Operations 　　Post Office and Civil Service 　　Veterans Affairs	Merchant Marine and Fisheries Post Office and Civil Service Standards of Official Conduct Veterans Affairs
V　District of Columbia 　　Rules and Administration	District of Columbia House Administration

a New committees with important formal powers but not yet clearly established policy influence.

Committee Assignments　Each member of the House is normally assigned to only one or two standing committees but may serve on several subcommittees. Senators, by contrast, usually serve on three or four committees and about ten subcommittees. As a result of this difference House members are able to specialize more than senators can, and they sometimes become experts in subjects such as fiscal policy or farm price supports. This increases the influence of the House.

Committee assignments in both the House and the Senate are made by special party committees, with party leaders having a major voice in those decisions. Committee seats are divided between the parties on the basis of party representation in each house; that is, if two-thirds of the senators are Democrats and one-third are Republicans, each Senate committee will be about two-thirds Democrats and one-third Republicans.

Seats on the more powerful committees are highly prized, and this is one of the main sources of the power of party leaders. It gives them a chance to reward party members who "play by the rules" and to punish those who do not. Reelection to Congress often depends on the member's committee assignment, and a position on a particular committee can give a member a lot of power within Congress. An example is the career of the late Senator Robert S. Kerr of Oklahoma:

> The base of Kerr's power was never his major committees. Rather, it was his chairmanship of the Rivers and Harbors Subcommittee of the Public Works Committee, an obscure post that makes few national headlines, but much political hay. Kerr not only used it to consolidate his position in Oklahoma by festooning the state with public works but placed practically all Senators under obligation to him by promoting their pet home projects. He never hesitated to collect on these obligations later, when the votes were needed.[4]

Newcomers to the House are rarely appointed to important committees. One who was lucky enough to get a seat on the Appropriations Committee explains why:

> The Chairman . . . did some checking around in my area. After all, I was new and he didn't know me. People told me that they were called to see if I was—well, unstable or apt to go off on tangents . . . to see whether or not I had any preconceived notions about things and would not be flexible— whether I would oppose things even though it was obvious.[5]

Party leaders can also use their power to assign "unwanteds" to committees that have little meaning to the people in their districts. When Representative Herman Badillo of the Bronx was assigned to the Agriculture Committee he objected, saying that "there isn't any crop in my district except marijuana." Shirley Chisholm of Brooklyn, also assigned to Agriculture, complained that "apparently all they know here in Washington about Brooklyn is that a tree grew there." Both committee assignments were changed in response to pressure by New York's more powerful members of Congress.

It is reasonable for a senator or representative to want to serve on a committee that is related to the interests of his or her area—for a representative from a rural district to try to get a seat on Agriculture, for example, or for a senator from a western state to request a seat on Interior and Insular Affairs. The disadvantage of such assignments is that a committee may become dominated by special interests. Public policy then becomes a result of compromises among small groups that worry more about satisfying the voters back home than about dealing with national issues.

Again we can take the Agriculture Committee as an example. For a long time this committee was dominated by representatives from the farm belt

---

[4] Nelson W. Polsby, *Congress and the Presidency* (Englewood Cliffs, N.J.: Prentice-Hall, 1964), p. 38.

[5] Cited in Richard F. Fenno, Jr., "The House Appropriations Committee as a Political System: The Problem of Integration," in Leroy N. Riselbach, ed., *The Congressional System* (Belmont, Calif.: Wadsworth, 1970), p. 194.

while representatives like Badillo and Chisholm tried to get seats on committees dealing with urban concerns. But bills assigned to the Agriculture Committee affect other people besides farmers. For example, the committee has an important influence on federal school lunch and food stamp programs. It finally became clear to liberal, urban representatives that changes were needed if food and farm programs were to benefit consumers as well as producers. In 1975 the Democrats in the House removed conservative Texan W. R. Poage from the committee chairmanship and assigned 20 new members, many of them liberal and consumer oriented, to the committee; the committee then began to promote different policies.

Sources of Committee Power Not only congressional leaders but the committees themselves have a great deal of power. Four factors contribute to this power:

1. *Control Over the Flow of Legislation.* Ninety years ago Woodrow Wilson wrote that

> the practical effect of this Committee organization of the House is to consign to each of the Standing Committees the entire direction of legislation upon those subjects which properly come to its consideration. As to those subjects it is entitled to the initiative, and all legislative action with regard to them is under its overruling guidances.[6]

Today the legislative agenda is often set by the executive branch, but Wilson's description is still accurate.

2. *Expertise.* If an organization subdivides itself into working committees, and if those committees are permanent and the same people remain on them for a long time, it is natural for each committee (and subcommittee) to develop a great deal of expertise in its area. On many issues a sort of division of labor occurs. "They are the experts in this field, and usually know what they are doing," a member of Congress may say as he or she goes along with a committee recommendation. Most of the time a subcommittee's recommendation is accepted by the full committee and the full committee's recommendation is accepted by the full House or Senate. It is *within* the committee or subcommittee that we are likely to find lobbying, negotiation, sharp debate, and the final shaping of legislation.

3. *Relationships with Other Groups.* Another source of a committee's power is its ties with interest groups and executive agencies. The committee, the interest group, and the agency may form an alliance against "enemies" who threaten their power. Such alliances are common in agriculture, labor, commerce, welfare, education, defense, and many other areas. For example, the chairpersons of the two Agriculture Committees probably receive campaign support from the American Farm Bureau Federation and also have a close relationship with officials of the Department of Agriculture. This three-way partnership strengthens the committee's control over legislation in its area.

---

[6] From Woodrow Wilson, *Congressional Government* (first published in 1884).

4. *Public Hearings.* A committee or subcommittee can hold public hearings on legislation that it is considering. Such hearings help members of Congress gather information and opinions from interested groups; they also give those groups a chance to influence public policy. A public hearing on something like price controls will call a large number of "expert" witnesses representing executive agencies and major interest groups. If a committee wants to hear the views of an individual who refuses to appear, it can issue a subpoena.

How a Bill Becomes Law

We have seen how Congress is organized. Now, how does this organization produce legislation?

As Figure 10.1 shows, a bill must be introduced in both houses of Congress. It is then referred to a committee. The committee or one of its subcommittees holds hearings and drafts the bill. If it "reports out" the bill, that bill is placed on the legislative *agenda,* or calendar. It is then debated, perhaps amended, and either passed or defeated.

If the House and the Senate pass different versions of a bill, a *conference committee* made up of members of both houses works out a compromise bill. If this bill is passed by both the House and the Senate, it is sent to the President. If he signs the bill, it becomes law. If he vetoes it, it can still become law if it is passed again by a two-thirds majority of both houses of Congress.

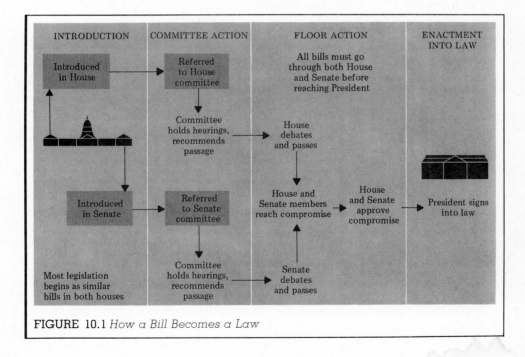

FIGURE 10.1 *How a Bill Becomes a Law*

If the President does not act within ten days, the bill automatically becomes law if Congress is still in session. However, if Congress has adjourned, the bill becomes the victim of a "pocket veto." This may appear to be a minor detail, but since many bills are passed just before the end of a session the pocket veto is important.

It is easy to see that a bill must overcome many obstacles to become a law. It might be tabled by an unfriendly committee; it might get bottled up in the House Rules Committee, which sets the agenda for the House; or it might be killed by a Senate filibuster. The moment of truth, however, comes when the bill is put to a vote. Therefore to understand how Congress works we need to know something about the factors that influence congressional voting.

Congressional Voting

Members of Congress have to consider dozens of major bills and hundreds of minor ones. They do not have the time to study each one thoroughly. As a result their votes are influenced by many other factors besides floor debate — bargaining, friendship, economic interests, committee recommendations, party ties, the voters back home, and many more.

Bargaining   Outright bargaining for votes is not uncommon. Here is an example from a 1956 debate on federal support for tobacco:

MR. LANGER (North Dakota): We do not raise any tobacco in North Dakota, but we are interested in the tobacco situation in Kentucky, and I hope the Senator will support us in securing assistance for the wheat growers in our state.

MR. CLEMENTS (Kentucky): I think the Senator will find that my support will be 100 percent.

MR. BARKLEY (Kentucky): Mr. President, will my colleague from Kentucky yield?

MR. CLEMENTS: I yield.

MR. BARKLEY: The colloquy just heard confirms and justifies the Woodrow Wilsonian doctrine of open convenants openly arrived at. [Laughter.][7]

Friendship   The role of friendship in congressional voting may be illustrated by the following incident, which occurred when the Senate was about to vote on a bill to "bail out" Lockheed Aircraft Corporation by means of a federal loan guarantee. Senator Lee Metcalf of Montana planned to vote against the bill because he was opposed to "big-business slush funds." However,

as he approached the floor he was cornered by his friend Alan Cranston of California, home of potentially unemployed Lockheed workers. Senator Cranston beseeched his Democratic colleague not to throw thirty thousand

[7] *Congressional Record,* 16 February 1956, pp. 2300–2301.

people out of work. Metcalf, weakened, finally chose employment over ideology and voted for the Lockheed loan, which slipped by the Senate 49–48.[8]

Economic Interests Some members of Congress are interested in particular bills for economic reasons. For example, James Eastland of Mississippi, a member of the House Agriculture Committee, can be counted on to vote against ceilings on farm subsidies. In 1971 his wife received $159,000 in subsidies for farmland held in her name. Russell Long of Louisiana, for many years chairman of the Senate Finance Committee, opposed any change in the oil depletion allowance. Between 1964 and 1969 his income from oil was $1,196,915, of which more than $300,000 was tax free.[9]

Committee Recommendations As mentioned earlier, committee recommendations are a very important influence on congressional voting. One study found that if a large majority of the members of the committee in charge of a Senate bill support that bill, the chances that it will be passed are nearly perfect. On the other hand, there is only a 50–50 chance that a bill coming from a divided committee will be passed.[10]

Party Ties Members of Congress are free to vote against the wishes of party leaders. But this does not mean that there is no connection between party ties and congressional voting. In general, members of Congress prefer to vote with their party rather than against it. Usually this means that members who belong to the same party as the President try to support his programs while the "opposition" party tries to block them. Indeed, students of Congress have concluded that party pressure, direct or indirect, is the strongest influence on congressional voting.

The Voters When members of Congress vote against their party, it is usually because of the preferences of the people who elected them. There are times when the voters back home take a strong interest in the actions of their representative in Congress. For example, a representative from Seattle, where many people work for the Boeing Aircraft Company, would be unlikely to vote against federal funding for a supersonic transport plane. Similarly, no senator who depends on the labor unions in his or her state for campaign funds would vote for a bill that outlaws strikes. In short, voter opinion *does* matter on questions that matter to the people back home.

Caucuses In the past ten years there has been a spurt in the formation of special congressional caucuses. One of the best known of these is the Black Caucus in the House, whose 16 members often vote together on bills that

[8] Mark J. Green, James M. Fallows, and David R. Zwick, *Who Runs Congress?* A Ralph Nader Congress Project Report (New York: Bantam, 1972), p. 211.

[9] Evidence for this paragraph comes from ibid., p. 140.

[10] Donald R. Matthews, *U.S. Senators and Their World* (New York: Vintage, 1969). p. 170.

would affect black citizens. Other caucuses include the Women's Caucus, the Rural Caucus, and several regional caucuses. Recently, 13 House members with working-class backgrounds formed the Blue Collar Caucus. Its founder, Edward P. Beard of Rhode Island, admits that the members of the caucus do not always agree. "But when the little guy stands to get the short end, that's when the blue collar caucus speaks as one."[11]

Membership in a caucus, thus, is another factor influencing how members of Congress vote. Since the caucus often includes members of both parties, it tends to weaken the power of party leaders over congressional voting.

Pressure from the White House A final factor influencing congressional voting is pressure from the White House, especially on bills that have been proposed by the President. We will have more to say on this subject in the next chapter.

OUR CHANGING CONGRESS

Congress has changed greatly since the nation's founding—it now has 535 members instead of 81, for example; it is in session year-round instead of for a few months; and important legislative work is done by committees instead of by the full House or Senate. But in the past ten years Congress has changed even more: The 1970s have seen a number of important congressional reforms in response to a widespread belief that Congress is failing to do its job.

Congress Under Attack

No institution of the U.S. government has attracted as much criticism in the past 30 or 40 years as Congress. Much of the criticism centers on the belief that the *institution* has not kept up with the *issues*. The issues are national in scope, but Congress is basically a local institution. This is illustrated by the career of a typical member of Congress.

The Career of a Member of Congress Although they serve in the national government, members of Congress are closely tied to a particular part of the country. Most members have always lived in the district or state they represent—they have been educated there, practiced law there, or worked for companies located there. The typical member of Congress has also held state or local office.

---

[11] *New York Times*, 23 June 1977.

These local ties are strengthened by the fact that representatives must stand for reelection every two years. This keeps them from forgetting their campaign promises after they have been elected. It also keeps them in touch with local organizations.

Many members of Congress have rather long careers. Nine out of every ten who stand for reelection win. Being a representative or a senator is a career in itself—indeed, some members serve for their entire adult lives. Critics claim that this pattern isolates Congress from a changing society. Congress is controlled by people who first came to office more than 20 years ago. As long as they continue to satisfy the narrow interests of a few key groups back home, they can remain in office. The longer they stay, the easier it is to take care of those interests, since it is the old-timers who chair the most powerful committees in Congress.

The Committee System   Critics of Congress often complain about the committee system. They claim that it gives a small group of members almost total control over legislation in a certain area. Though they are supposed to make laws for the nation as a whole, they are accountable only to the voters who elected them. As a result a committee's policy decisions may not match the preferences of a majority of the American people, and for this reason the committee system is accused of being undemocratic.

The major target of many attacks on Congress is the *seniority rule,* an informal rule that when a committee chairmanship becomes vacant the new chairperson will be the committee member from the majority party who has served longest on that committee. A member of Congress thus becomes a committee chairperson simply by outlasting his or her fellow members— not by having greater ability.

Seniority rewards age as well as long service, for the two cannot be separated. Congressional power is held by people in their 60s and 70s, some of whom first came to office in the 1930s and 1940s. Many of these individuals fail to change with the times.

Secrecy   Congress is also criticized for doing much of its business in secret. Such secrecy makes members of Congress less accountable for their actions, since it allows them to take a stand in public and act differently in private.

Understaffing   Many critics feel that Congress performs poorly because it is understaffed. They argue that if Congress is to deal with serious national problems it needs the help of experts in housing, transportation, health care, and so on. Congress has always been reluctant to increase its staff, fearing that the voters would disapprove, and has depended instead on experts in the executive branch.

Presidential Domination   Concern about presidential domination of Congress arose as a result of the events of the late 1960s and early 1970s: the Vietnam War, in which the Presidency dominated Congress; conflicts over government policy during the Nixon years; the Watergate scandal; and revelations of illegal actions by the FBI and the CIA. The critics accuse Congress of merely responding to the President's initiative and failing to fulfill its duty of overseeing the operations of the government.

Congressional Ethics   Members of Congress are continually accused of using their position to satisfy personal desires. A major target of reformers is the "fact-finding trip," which is actually a vacation paid for by the taxpayer. Other abuses were brought into sharp focus in 1976 when Elizabeth Ray, supposedly a secretary to Congressman Wayne Hays, revealed that she was being paid a government salary to perform sexual duties rather than secretarial ones. Within a few days several similar abuses were revealed, including some that appeared to violate criminal laws.

In the past Congress punished its members only for very serious offenses, but in the 1970s, with Watergate fresh in everyone's memory, congressional ethics were a matter of concern to the public. The House of Representatives responded to public pressure by forming an Ethics Committee to investigate charges of improper conduct.

Output   Finally, Congress is accused of being unproductive. In recent years the number of laws passed by Congress has decreased sharply. On the other hand, the laws that are passed are longer than they used to be. Twenty years ago the typical bill was only two pages long; today it is more than five pages long. This suggests that Congress may be spending more time on complex policy matters than on routine business. The more complex the bill, the more parts it has and the longer it will be when it is finally passed. The more time Congress spends on such bills, the less time it has for routine bills, so that its total output decreases.

Congressional Reform

Beginning in the 1970s Congress responded to these criticisms with a series of reforms. These reforms have resulted in some fundamental changes in the way Congress legislates.

Reform of the Seniority System   The seniority rule made the choice of a committee chairperson automatic, and as a result the chairperson was not controlled by party leaders and did not have to go along with party policies. But this came to an end in January 1975, when the Democrats in the House deposed three powerful committee chairmen.

Not since 1925 had anything like this happened. The Republicans took the first step in 1970, when they decided to use secret ballots to determine the highest-ranking Republican on each House committee. The Republicans do not control the House, however, so this did not affect committee chairmanships.

In January 1973 the Democrats used a similar method, but no committee chairmen lost their positions. But the 1974 election—the first after Watergate—brought 92 new representatives to the House, 75 of them Democrats. Their votes led to the removal of several old-timers from committee chairmanships.

Despite this reform, the seniority rule will probably continue to be followed in both the House and the Senate. However, the threat of removal forces committee chairpersons to pay more attention to party policy.

The House Democratic Caucus　The House Democratic Caucus—that is, the Democratic members of the House—is playing a new role in the legislative process. For the first time in nearly 50 years it is taking a stand on every major issue that comes before the House. While it does not bind its members to vote in a particular way, it sometimes tells a committee how to act on a bill. (The Democratic members of the committee will feel an obligation to support the party's policy; if they do not, they may lose their seats on the committee.)

This point is important because it means that the party can offset the major committees as an influence on legislation. It is true that a number of powerful, independent committees can develop detailed knowledge in a variety of policy areas. However, such a system makes it almost impossible to create a unified legislative program. Many people think the majority party caucus offers a way of overcoming this problem. The majority party, operating through the caucus, can propose a unified program, and the minority party can propose an "opposition" program. This would give the voters a clear choice every two years.

The Role of Subcommittees　Another change that has decreased the power of committee chairpersons in both the House and the Senate is the increasing independence of subcommittees. In the past, a subcommittee's membership, resources, and area of activity were completely in the hands of the chairperson of the full committee. Recently, however, both houses of Congress have reduced the committee chairperson's authority over subcommittees. The structure and membership of subcommittees are now determined by the majority party caucus of the full committee, and each subcommittee chairperson has the authority to hire staff members. As a result the power of congressional committees has been decentralized.

"Government in the Sunshine"   A major reform of the past few years is the almost complete elimination of secret committee meetings. In the 1950s and 1960s about 40 percent of all House and Senate committee meetings were held in secret. By 1975 the number of secret meetings had fallen to only 7 percent of the total. Moreover, House committees now allow radio and television coverage of their hearings (this was already true of the Senate). At present both houses are also experimenting with similar coverage of floor debates. In addition, House voting rules have been changed. Now, instead of simply recording the total of votes "for" and "against" important bills, the House records the vote of each representative.

Weakening the Filibuster   A much-criticized rule of Congress is the one that allows unlimited floor debate in the Senate. This is one of the Senate's oldest traditions, going back to 1789. Its purpose is to allow for thorough debate of important issues. In the twentieth century, however, this rule has often been used by a minority of senators to prevent passage of a bill they opposed. Critics claimed that this tactic—the filibuster—was undemocratic.

   In 1917 a change in Senate rules made it possible for two-thirds of the senators present and voting to end debate. Under this rule it was still very hard to end a filibuster, but in 1975 the Senate reduced the number of votes needed to three-fifths of the full Senate (i.e., 60). This compromise was intended to allow a sizable minority to force the Senate to debate an issue thoroughly while at the same time allowing a majority of three-fifths to end a filibuster. The filibuster has been less effective as a result.

Expanding the Congressional Staff   Congress has also responded to the claim that it is understaffed. Table 10.3 shows the growth of the congressional staff since 1955. Equally important has been the expansion of the agencies that work for and answer to Congress. The Congressional Research Service has grown from 219 employees in 1965 to 703 in 1975, and in 1972 Congress

**TABLE 10.3   Growth of Senate and House
Staffs, 1955–1975**

	Senate	House
1955	1962	3623
1960	2643	4148
1965	3219	5672
1970	4140	7134
1975	5543	9951

SOURCE: U.S. Civil Service Commission, as cited in "Inside Congress" (Washington, D.C.: *Congressional Quarterly*, January 1976), p. 19.

Expansion of congressional staffs has led to overcrowding in the halls of the congressional office buildings.

created the office of Technology Assessment and the Congressional Budget Office.

There are two main reasons for this expansion. One is the fact that the process of making government policy has become very complex. A member of Congress may need the help of up to 18 staff aides, many of whom have advanced training in particular policy areas, as well as the assistance of the Research Service or the Budget Office. The other reason for expanding the congressional staff is Congress's desire to match the policy-making skill of the executive branch. At least it can try to consider policy choices as carefully as the Executive Office does. The congressional staff can also be a source of policy proposals, making Congress less dependent on proposals by the executive branch.

CONCLUSION

Partly as a result of these various reforms Congress has become much more assertive in recent years. Presidents Ford and Carter both complained that it was difficult to get cooperation from Congress on such broad issues as an energy policy or the fight to control inflation. Congress has also undergone changes as the old leadership has retired or been defeated in elections, and many newcomers have arrived in Washington. This has made it difficult for the party leadership to impose its own programs and policies. Individual members of Congress are more independent of either party or presidential leadership than was the case in previous decades.

CONTROVERSY

Should members of Congress represent the interests of those who send them to Washington or the broader public interest?

One Side

Members of Congress should support the interests of the people who elected them if they know what those interests are. They should also try to represent the organizations that supply them with campaign funds. A member from a wealthy area should try to whittle away at the progressive income tax, just as a member from a poor district should try to make taxes more progressive. No one expects a black member from a northern city to prefer farm subsidies over an educational head start program, and no one should expect a member from Montana to prefer the head start program over farm subsidies.

Take the case of Representative Jamie Whitten of Mississippi. As chairman of the House Appropriations Subcommittee on Agriculture he has delayed and blocked various programs that would provide food for schoolchildren and other hungry citizens. He opposes any attempt to study how new farming methods might affect the lives of farm workers or sharecroppers. Yet he has been reelected every two years since 1941.

Reelection is the true test of democracy, because this is the main way in which the people control their representatives. Those who want to be reelected must support policies that benefit the voters or the groups that provide campaign funds. That is what members of Congress are paid to do.

The Other Side

Two hundred years ago Edmund Burke argued against representing narrow interests in his famous speech to the Electors of Bristol:

> Parliament is not a [collection] of ambassadors from different and hostile interests, which interests each must maintain, as an agent and advocate, against other agents and advocates; Parliament is a deliberative assembly of one nation, with one interest—that of the whole—where not local purposes, not local prejudices, ought to guide, but the general good, resulting from the general reason of the whole. You choose a member, indeed; but when you have chosen him, he is not a member of Bristol, but he is a member of Parliament.[12]

Burke believed that there is more to representation than satisfying your supporters. Someone has to think about the whole picture and try to figure out what is best for the entire nation.

Again we may take Jamie Whitten as an example. During World War II a study was proposed that would help the government prepare for the variety of social and economic problems that would be faced by black GIs returning to the South. Whitten killed this proposal. As he saw it, the Department of Agriculture's job was to help cotton planters, not the rural poor. But in killing this study and similar proposals Whitten may have contributed to the postwar migration of southern blacks and poor people to northern cities. The cities, unprepared for this huge inflow of people, have been unable to handle the problems it created.

---

[12] Edmund Burke, "Speech to the Electors of Bristol" (1774), *Works, II,* 11.

It would be foolish to say that Whitten somehow "caused" the urban crisis of the 1960s. It is not foolish to say that creative programs begun in the 1940s but looking toward the 1960s might have reduced the problems caused by the postwar migration to the cities. A Congress full of representatives concerned only with narrow interests is unlikely to come up with such programs, but that is what a truly representative legislature would do.

HOW INSTITUTIONS WORK: II

How a Bill Becomes a Law

Where Do Bills Start?

Any member of the House or Senate may introduce a bill, except that all money bills must be introduced in the House. Since a bill cannot become law unless it is passed by both the House and the Senate, the usual procedure is to introduce identical bills in both houses of Congress.

What Is the Difference Between "Public" and "Private" Bills?

A private bill deals with individual citizens, a public bill with general classes of citizens.

What Happens After a Bill Has Been Introduced?

It is referred to the appropriate committee. Private bills are referred to the committee indicated by their sponsors.

Why Do Many Bills "Die" in Committee?

Congress is asked to deal with many more bills than it can possibly handle; so are most committees. The committee chairperson decides which bills the committee will consider. It is at this point that the majority of bills are "pigeonholed"; that is, no action is taken on them. Such bills can be rescued by a discharge petition signed by a majority of the House, or by a special resolution of the Senate, but this is rare.

If a Committee Takes Up a Bill, What Happens Next?

First the bill is scheduled for consideration by the committee or subcommittee. If it is important enough, hearings, either public or private, are held. The bill is then amended, rewritten, or "marked up." The committee then votes on whether to report the bill to the House

or the Senate. Here, too, many bills die because the committee votes against them or simply takes no action at all.

If a Bill Is Reported Out by a House Committee, How Is It Brought to the Floor for a Vote?

Bills coming from certain committees (e.g., Appropriations) can be reported to the full House at any time for action. Any other bill will be placed on one of several legislative calendars. Important bills are assigned to the House calendar and need a "special rule" from the House Rules Committee to be sent to the floor for debate.

What Is the Role of the House Rules Committee?

The Rules Committee has been compared to a traffic cop directing the flow of legislation. It determines the order in which bills get to the House floor and sets the conditions for debate. When a bill is reported out by a committee and entered on the calendar, the committee chairperson asks the Rules Committee for a special rule taking the bill off the calendar and putting it before the House. The Rules Committee holds hearings at which the bill's managers and its opponents argue for or against the granting of a special rule. Any bill that does not get through the Rules Committee has probably been derailed for good.

Is There Any Way a Bill Can Be Rescued If It Has Been Blocked by the Rules Committee?

There are several means by which the Rules Committee can be forced to send a bill to the floor, but they are rarely used. Most of the bills killed by the Rules Committee are not very important. Besides, the Rules Committee does not have control over all bills reported out of committee. Most of the bills that are brought to the floor are more or less routine and are handled via the "consent" and "private" calendars. In each session of Congress only about 100 bills are controversial enough to require debate.

How Is a Bill Brought to the Senate Floor for a Vote?

There is only one legislative calendar in the Senate, so all bills reported out of Senate committees are placed on that calendar. Floor action on those bills is scheduled by the majority party's Policy Committee.

What Are the Rules of Debate in Congress?

The rules for House debate are usually contained in the special rule issued by the Rules Committee. The rule states how long a bill may be debated and whether it may be amended on the floor. If such amendments are not allowed,

the rule is a "closed rule"; only members of the committee that reported on the bill may make any changes in it. An "open rule" allows amendments from anyone on the floor.

Senate debate, by contrast, is unlimited, and as a result senators who are opposed to a bill may engage in a filibuster that can tie up the Senate for days or even weeks. The purpose of a filibuster is to force changes in the bill or to get it set aside. It can be broken only by a three-fifths vote of the full Senate.

What Happens If the House and Senate Pass Different Versions of a Bill?

If the differences are minor, one house may simply agree to the other's version. If there are major differences, a conference committee is appointed. This committee, made up of members of the House and Senate committees that sponsored the bill, irons out the differences between the two versions. The final version must then be approved by both houses of Congress.

Carter promised an informal Presidency.

No institution of American government is harder to describe than the Presidency. We can tell stories about individual Presidents—about Jimmy Carter's surprising election victory, about Richard Nixon's abuse of power, about John Kennedy's violent death, and so on all the way back to Presidents who are more myth than men: Lincoln, Jefferson, Washington. But while Presidents are interesting because of the powers they have, those powers mean little unless they are transformed into policies. So we need to go beyond the individual to the institution, beyond the President to the Presidency.

We will start with the major powers granted to the President by the Constitution. Then we will turn to the growth and organization of the Presidency.

THE POWERS OF THE PRESIDENCY

More than anyone else, the President of the United States can affect—though not control—history. Here is how John Kennedy described the job of the President:

> He must above all be the Chief Executive in every sense of that word. He must be prepared to exercise the fullest powers of his office—all that are specified and some that are not. He must master complex problems. . . . He

must originate action. . . . It is the President alone who must make the major decisions of our foreign policy. That is what the Constitution wisely commands. And even domestically, the President must initiate policies and devise laws to meet the needs of the nation. And he must be prepared to use all the resources of his office to insure the enactment of that legislation. . . .

But the White House is not only the center of political leadership. It must be the center of moral leadership—a "bully pulpit," as Theodore Roosevelt described it. For only the President represents the national interest. And upon him alone converge all the needs and aspirations of all parts of the country, all departments of the Government, all nations of the world.

Kennedy probably claimed more powers for the Presidency than the Constitution intended, but he was not alone. "Strong" Presidents like Jefferson, Jackson, and Lincoln in the 1800s and Wilson, both Roosevelts, Truman, Johnson, and Nixon in this century have poured a lot of meaning into the simple statement "The executive power shall be vested in a President of the United States of America" (Article 2).

The Constitution does not say very much about the Presidency. Section 2 of Article 2 states that the President shall be Commander-in-Chief of the armed forces, and Section 3 instructs him to inform Congress on the State of the Union and to recommend legislation. Yet these duties have been the basis for the huge growth of the executive branch of the government. At the center stands the President, who, with his close advisers and department heads, controls the vast military, economic, and personnel resources of the executive branch.

The President as Commander-in-Chief

In 1957 a federal court order directed the school system of Little Rock, Arkansas to desegregate its public schools. The school officials, with the support of the white citizens of Little Rock and the governor of Arkansas, refused to obey the court order. President Eisenhower, acting as Commander-in-Chief, sent federal troops to Little Rock to enforce the order. Speaking to the nation on radio and television, he explained his action as follows:

> For a few minutes this evening I want to speak to you about the serious situation that has arisen in Little Rock. . . . In that city, under the leadership of demagogic extremists, disorderly mobs have deliberately prevented the carrying out of proper orders from a federal court. . . . I have today issued an executive order directing the use of troops under Federal authority to aid in the execution of Federal law at Little Rock, Arkansas. . . . Unless the President did so, anarchy would result.

The President's War Powers

No one questioned Eisenhower's authority to act as he did, nor did anyone question President Kennedy's authority to order the military blockade of

Cuba during the missile crisis of 1962. The Constitution clearly states that the President is Commander-in-Chief.

And yet the Constitution gives *Congress* the right to declare war. We might expect, therefore, that the President's authority as Commander-in-Chief would come into play only when war has been declared. But this is not the case. There was no war in Little Rock in 1957, and we were not at war with either Cuba or the Soviet Union in 1962.

Thus the President's power as Commander-in-Chief is much greater than it may seem at first glance. He can order military action whether there is a declared war or not. In fact Congress has declared war only five times since 1789,[1] but in the same period U.S. forces have been involved in military action more than 150 times.

In 1970 William Rehnquist, now a Supreme Court justice, wrote that "the United States may lawfully engage in armed hostilities with a foreign power without a congressional declaration of war." This view has been challenged by members of Congress, and congressional resolutions have limited the kinds of military action the President can take. But the fact remains that military action and war are not the same thing.

The distinction between military action and war has played a major role in the growth of presidential power in the twentieth century. It permitted Roosevelt to give military protection and supplies to Britain in the months before Pearl Harbor; it allowed Truman to take military action in Korea in 1950. More recently, it was the basis for U.S. attacks on North Vietnam (under Johnson) and Cambodia and Laos (under Nixon), as well as the attack on Cambodian forces to free the crew of the *Mayaguez* (under Ford). Clearly the President's power as Commander-in-Chief amounts to the power to make war, and this has greatly increased the role of the President in both domestic and foreign affairs.

Most of the military actions ordered by Presidents throughout our history have been supported by the people and approved of by Congress. However, the Vietnam War convinced many people that this presidential power must be limited. As a result, in 1973 Congress passed the War Powers Act over President Nixon's veto. This law requires that the President report any military action to Congress within 48 hours and that U.S. forces be withdrawn after 60 days unless Congress authorizes further action. In effect, Congress has been given the power to "declare peace" if it believes the President's action is misguided. When Nixon vetoed the act he claimed that it would "seriously undermine this nation's ability to act decisively and convincingly in times of international crisis." We do not yet know whether the act will have any such effect, but there is no doubt that Presidents no longer have unlimited power to engage in armed conflict.

---

[1] The War of 1812, the Mexican War, the Spanish-American War, World War I, and World War II.

The President's Foreign-Policy Powers

It is often said that the world has shrunk during the past 50 years. Things happen quickly, and what happens in one part of the world affects what happens in other parts. The United States has business, military, and diplomatic interests throughout the world. A language riot in India, a change of government in Iran, a border incident in Latin America, a monetary crisis in Europe, a new security pact among the Arab nations—these and thousands of other events affect American programs and people and require immediate attention and action.

The President is in a position to act. He has authority over the nation's military forces and its diplomatic representatives; he has access to the information on which foreign policy is based. And he cannot avoid making policy. Nixon's dramatic visit to China in 1972 is a good example. The trip, which did not need congressional approval, was kept secret until all the arrangements had been made. Yet it was probably the most important thing Nixon did in his first term. It affected China's entry into the United Nations, U.S. policy toward India and Japan, and summit talks with the Soviet

Formal recognition of China took place in 1979.

Union. It affected our trade and tariff policies and our nuclear strategy. It also led to formal recognition of China during the administration of President Carter.

The President does not have complete control over U.S. foreign policy, however. From time to time Congress threatens to shut off funds for foreign programs it disapproves of. It can also refuse to ratify treaties. But the President can get around Congress by using *executive agreements,* agreements between the United States and another nation that do not need congressional approval. Such agreements can deal with important matters such as the location of military bases and the types of aid given by the United States to other nations.

The President's Program

The Constitution says the President "shall from time to time give to the Congress information of the State of the Union, and recommend to their consideration such measures as he shall judge necessary and expedient." This brief statement has been the basis for major presidential programs such as Roosevelt's "New Deal," Kennedy's "New Frontier," and Johnson's "Great Society." These programs are proposed in the President's annual State of the Union Address, Budget Message, and Economic Report. In addition to these formal speeches, the President can send special messages to Congress at any time, as President Carter has done in the case of energy and economic policy.

The State of the Union Address is often used to announce a presidential program. An example is Nixon's 1972 address in which he proposed legislation in 18 different areas, including welfare reform, environmental protection, health care, hunger and nutrition, the needs of older people, civil rights, women's rights, veterans' benefits, crime, and consumer protection. These proposals became part of the legislative agenda. In one year, for example, President Johnson asked Congress to act on 469 separate proposals.

THE ROOTS OF THE PRESIDENCY

The modern Presidency has roots that go back to the founding of the nation. The Constitution states that the President "may require the Opinion, in writing, of the Principal Officer in each of the executive Departments." During George Washington's Presidency these officers consisted of the Attorney General and the Secretaries of State, War, and the Treasury. In Washington's time a small staff was all that was required to advise the President and provide the information he needed.

Over the years, as the activities of the government became more complex, the number of advisers and departments grew. We will outline the history of the Presidency in terms of three institutions: the Cabinet, the White House Staff, and the Executive Office of the President.

The Cabinet

The Cabinet is made up of the Secretaries of the major executive departments. In 1789 there were only three such departments; today there are 12. Each department was formed in response to the development of new governmental functions and the rise of new groups whose needs had to be met. In the nineteenth century, for example, the Department of the Interior was formed to manage the nation's western lands. The Agriculture Department was formed to meet the needs of farmers. Early in the twentieth century the Departments of Commerce and Labor were formed to deal with the problems created by industrialization. New social problems led to the formation of new departments—Health, Education and Welfare (HEW), Housing and Urban Development (HUD), Transportation, and most recently, Energy.

Many of these departments were formed in response to the needs of social groups for government services, and as a result they often have close ties with those groups and represent their interests. The Agriculture Department works closely with farm groups, the Labor Department with unions, the Commerce Department with business. This sometimes makes it hard for the President to control the departments, which are often more responsive to the interests of the groups they serve than to presidential directives.

The heads of the departments—that is, the members of the Cabinet—are appointed by the President. They and their departments are responsible for giving the President information and advice, developing policy proposals, dealing with Congress, and carrying out the laws and programs authorized by Congress.

In the past the Cabinet actually met with the President to discuss various policy proposals and vote on them. But over time the President became more powerful. (Once, when he had been outvoted by his Cabinet, President Lincoln announced the vote as "seven nays and one aye—the ayes have it.") In addition, the President turned more and more to his personal staff for advice. A close adviser to President Johnson explains why:

> Power, in the Presidential sense, is a very personal thing. It is invested in one man in the White House. Since power is his greatest resource, it is the instrument by which he works his will. It is not something he is likely to invest in people whose first allegiance is not to him. He is not likely to share what is his most precious resource with people whom he does not know well. Many Cabinet officers are men who are not well known to the President personally prior to his inauguration. They also become men with ties to their own de-

partments, to the bureaucracy, to congressional committees, rather than exclusively to the President, as is the case with White House assistants.[2]

Some people think the Cabinet should meet periodically to coordinate their activities and advise the President on policy matters. But few Cabinets have done this. Most department heads are constantly trying to expand their own departments and have no experience and little interest in other areas. This is understandable, but it keeps the Cabinet from becoming a useful advisory group. Most Presidents use Cabinet meetings to inform one executive department of what other departments are doing. For advice on policy matters they turn to their personal advisers.

The White House

By the late 1930s the President was surrounded by so many executive departments and agencies that he was unable to coordinate their activities. As a result, in 1939 two new units were added to the executive branch: the White House Staff and the Executive Office of the President.

The White House Staff   The members of the White House Staff—the group of advisers who are closest to the President—generally have access to the President and supply him with much of the information he needs. They work in the White House, and their main job is to communicate the President's directives to other parts of the executive branch and to summarize the information that comes to the White House from the executive departments and agencies as well as from Congress, the public, and interest groups.

The White House Staff consists of about 550 people. Some have titles such as "special adviser" or "assistant to the President." Their areas of activity range from national security to social security; they also deal with problems that come up unexpectedly or cannot be handled by other agencies.

Every President brings a somewhat different style to his relationship with the White House Staff. For example, Kennedy had a habit of calling together small, informal groups to work on a particular issue until a decision had been reached as to what action should be taken. Nixon, by contrast, depended on a few key advisers, as we will see later when we discuss Watergate.

Despite such differences in style, there are common problems in the relationship between the President and his staff. The President needs information and advice, and therefore he surrounds himself with experienced advisers. It is natural for those people to have opinions of their own, but there is a strong tendency to say what "the Chief" wants to hear. For while the President expects his staff to come up with new ideas, he also expects them to be loyal

---

[2] Bill Moyers, taken from an interview conducted by Hugh Sidney, reprinted in Charles Peters and Timothy J. Adams, eds., *Inside the System* (New York: Praeger, 1970), p. 24.

to him and to his program. Thus, when Secretary of the Interior Walter Hickel wrote a letter complaining that the Nixon administration was not sensitive to the demands of college students, Nixon fired him. As far as Nixon was concerned, Hickel had crossed the line between loyal disagreement and disloyal opposition. In the summer of 1979, President Carter removed five cabinet secretaries in one forty-eight hour period. In at least two of these replacements, Carter was ridding his administration of persons who had not shown as much loyalty to him and his programs as he wanted.

The Executive Office of the President The Executive Office employs about 600 people and is located in a building across the street from the White House. The Executive Office does not work as closely with the President as the White House Staff, but it has an important influence on the President. Its agencies collect information, draft policy proposals, and carry out policy — responsibilities that used to be assigned to the Cabinet.

The major agencies in the Executive Office are the National Security Council, the Council of Economic Advisers, and the Office of Management and Budget (OMB). The National Security Council is heavily involved in foreign-policy and national-security affairs. It includes the Central Intelligence Agency (CIA), which provides intelligence on the activities of other nations and until recently carried out secret U.S. actions overseas (such as the unsuccessful attempt to invade Cuba during Kennedy's Presidency). The Council of Economic Advisers supplies the President with information about economic matters and advice on what to do about economic problems. Its policy proposals affect employment, inflation, and business investment. The OMB (formerly the Bureau of the Budget) coordinates all the various parts of the executive branch. It prepares the budget that the President sends to Congress each year, and it is supposed to oversee the carrying out of government policy.

THE PRESIDENT IN ACTION

It is hard for a President to resist the temptation to create new programs and expand the government. After all, this is what it takes to get elected—Carter won the Presidency by promising to do more, not less. Besides, there is a lot of pressure on the President to find new solutions to old problems. In this section we will take a look at this process.

Where Do Proposals Come From?

Many proposals come directly from the President's close advisers. This is illustrated by the role of Henry Kissinger, national-security adviser to Presidents Nixon and Ford. Kissinger was brought to the White House to study long-term security and foreign-policy questions. He was authorized to hire about 50 staff members who were experienced in security, military, and diplomatic affairs. Kissinger and his staff were soon involved in the day-to-day decisions of foreign policy. They set up Nixon's summit meetings with Chinese and Russian leaders, negotiated the end of U.S. involvement in the Vietnam War, and took part in Middle East peace talks.

Policy proposals can come from a variety of sources besides the White House Staff—and they can be greatly changed or even blocked long before they reach the President. Typically, an executive department or agency begins to plan a new program or revise an existing one. Even at this early stage it may consult with the appropriate congressional committee or with interest groups that might be affected. For example, if HEW is planning a program of federally financed university scholarships, it will probably get in touch with the congressional committee that usually handles education bills. It will also contact organizations like the American Association for the Advancement of Science. The plan will begin to take shape, adding some provisions and dropping others, depending on the reactions that may be expected. The proposal is then sent to the OMB.

The OMB acts as a clearinghouse for the hundreds of programs proposed by executive agencies. It can tell the President or his advisers that a particular program cannot be included in the budget this year. Or it may advise an agency to shelve its program because a similar proposal is being developed in a congressional committee. A proposal that does not get through the OMB has little chance of reaching the President's desk, let alone becoming law.

Even when an agency proposal gets through the OMB, it does not always become part of the President's program. The agency may be given the green light to try to get congressional action on its own. The President's program consists of legislation that he considers especially important.

It would be a mistake to believe that all the elements of the President's program are based on his own policy views. The President does not have time to think through all the details of every legislative proposal. However, his advisers, party leaders, and department heads have a strong interest in particular policies. Most of the proposals the President sends to Congress come from these sources.

Getting Proposals Through Congress

The President has many resources that can be used to get his proposals through Congress. The main one, however, is the prestige of the Presidency. This enables him to put pressure on members of Congress. President Johnson, who had served in both the House and the Senate, relied heavily on this tactic when legislation he favored was pending in Congress. This is what one

Roosevelt was the first President to use the airwaves to go directly to the people, and his lead has been followed by every President since.

member of the House Rules Committee had to say about a phone call from the President:

> What do you say to the President of the United States? I told him I'd sleep on it. Then the next day I said to myself, "I've always been a party man, and if he really wanted me of course I'd go along even if the bill wasn't set up exactly the way I wanted it." Probably I took half a dozen guys with me. We won in the crunch by six votes. Now, I wouldn't have voted for it except for this telephone call.[3]

The President can also go on national radio or television to get the public to put pressure on Congress in support of the President's policies. Franklin Roosevelt did this in his famous fireside chats. In the following example he is asking for price controls during World War II:

> Today I sent a message to the Congress, pointing out the overwhelming urgency of the serious domestic economic crisis with which we are threatened. . . . I have asked the Congress to pass legislation under which the President would be specifically authorized to stabilize the cost of living; including the price of all farm commodities.

Roosevelt said that if Congress did not act within three weeks he would act anyway. He claimed that he had the power to take whatever actions were necessary to win the war. Whether he had that power or not was never tested, because Congress acted.

---

[3] *Newsweek,* 2 August 1965, p. 22. Copyright 1965 by Newsweek, Inc. All rights reserved. Reprinted by permission.

Restraints on the President

What the President wants is not always what the President gets. A presidential proposal is rarely passed without being changed. The final bill is usually a compromise between the President and Congress.

When Congress does not like the President's program, not much of it will become law. When Kennedy was running for the Presidency in 1960 he announced his New Frontier program in speech after speech. When it came time to get that program through Congress, however, Kennedy was opposed by several conservative southern senators who headed major committees. These senators had strong positions in Congress and voter support back home, and they made it impossible for the President to push through legislation on such issues as civil rights.

Congress also has specific legal powers over the executive branch. They include the following:

1. *Organization*. Executive departments and agencies are created by acts of Congress.
2. *Limits*. Executive agencies must operate within limits set by Congress.
3. *Financing*. Congress holds the purse strings, and programs that are not funded cannot be carried out.
4. *Review*. Executive agencies are subject to review by Congress.

In recent years Congress has not used its powers to the fullest. This has led some students of politics to conclude the Congress no longer acts as a check on the President. According to the Ralph Nader Congress Project, "No matter how hard the Congress may struggle on one issue, it is overwhelmed by the vastly greater forces of the Presidency. Whether Congress wins or loses, the President ends up on top."[4]

There is evidence to support this conclusion. For example, even when Congress passes legislation that the President does not like, the battle is not over: The President can veto the bill. The veto power was included in the Constitution to guard against undesirable legislation, but it has become an important presidential weapon. This is illustrated by a special message sent to Congress by President Nixon when it was about to vote on major health and education bills:

> I will simply not let reckless spending of this kind destroy the tax reduction we have secured and the hard-earned success we have earned in the battle against inflation. . . . With or without the cooperation of the Congress, I am going to do everything within my power to prevent such a fiscal crisis for millions of our people. . . . Let there be no misunderstanding, if bills come to my desk calling for excessive spending which threatens the federal budget, I will veto them.

---

[4] Mark J. Green, James M. Fallows, and David R. Zwick, *Who Rules Congress?* (New York: Bantam Books, 1972), p. 94.

Congress can override a presidential veto with a two-thirds vote, but such a majority is hard to get. For example, Franklin Roosevelt vetoed 631 bills; only 9 were overridden by Congress. Eisenhower vetoed 181; only 2 were overridden. (Recent Presidents have had more effective opposition in Congress, however.)

The Difficulty of Starting New Programs When Gerald Ford became President the nation faced serious economic problems: unemployment, recession, and inflation. A major factor in these problems was the rising cost of energy, due mainly to large increases in the price of imported oil.

With such big problems to be solved, we might expect a number of new policies and programs. But during Ford's two-year Presidency nothing of the sort happened. Why not? Because new policies are not easy to think up. Even the powers and prestige of the Presidency cannot always attract people with the right talents, let alone get them to cooperate. And if a policy is thought up, it is not easy to put it into effect. A new energy program would affect millions of people, thousands of businesses, and dozens of other government programs. In the last chapter we will devote more attention to how policy is made and carried out. Here we will simply note that while the President's powers are great, they are not so great that he can easily cut through the barriers between a major problem and a workable solution.

The Difficulty of Stopping Old Programs If government programs are hard to start, they are even harder to stop. People's careers and interests are linked to any ongoing program. Just because a new President comes to town does not mean that old programs will be replaced with new ones. Most policy is made by adding to or subtracting from programs that already exist. Thus Eisenhower, a Republican, did not end the New Deal programs begun by Democrats between 1932 and 1952. Nor was there a major change in policy during the eight years of Democratic control of the White House that followed Eisenhower's Presidency—though many new programs were added. Nixon tried to cut back on government spending but found it nearly impossible to do so. As one writer notes,

> Where can the Administration cut . . . ? Roughly 40 percent of the projected budgets are allocated to defense, space and related activities—and it is clear the Administration does not want to cut here.
> Of the domestic budget, well more than half goes directly to people, either in cash benefits (Social Security, unemployment insurance, veterans' pensions, welfare, civil-service retirement, etc.) or in kind (Medicare, Medicaid, public housing). These people have real needs, real votes and real representatives on Capitol Hill. It is inconceivable that the President would propose legislation to cut these benefits back or that the Congress would pass it.
> Contractual obligations of the Government, such as interest on the debt,

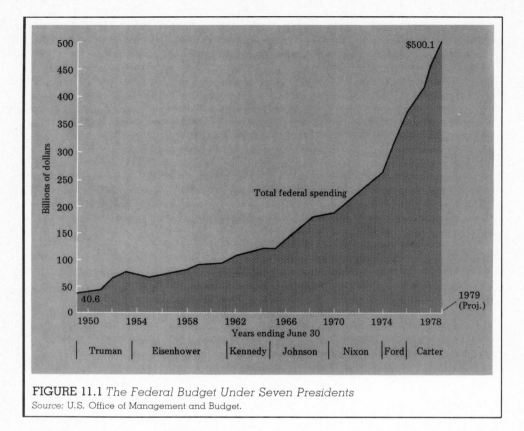

FIGURE 11.1 *The Federal Budget Under Seven Presidents*
Source: U.S. Office of Management and Budget.

cannot be tampered with, and no one really wants to cut out such services as national parks or fish and wildlife preservation.[5]

Nixon did reduce federal spending on some social-welfare programs, but he did not stop the trend toward more government spending. (See Figure 11.1.) The federal budget continues to grow whether the President is a Democrat or a Republican.

THE PRESIDENT AS A SYMBOL

America is a political community whose members share a "we feeling," as in "We are all Americans." This sense of community cuts across disagreements over particular policies or personalities. If you see yourself as an American, you are psychologically separate from citizens of other nations.

---

[5] Alice M. Rivlin, "Dear Voter: Your Taxes Are Going Up," *New York Times Magazine,* 5 November 1972, pp. 113–114. © 1972 by The New York Times Company. Reprinted by permission.

The nation's sense of political community is expressed through symbols and ceremonies, public holidays and monuments, and a shared history. The 1976 bicentennial celebration was a way of expressing the "we feeling" of Americans.

The President is the main symbol of the American political community. It is the President who proclaims National Codfish Day, dedicates a new arts center, informs Congress of the State of the Union, and greets foreign diplomats in the name of the United States. In these ways the President speaks for the entire nation.

The President is also expected to provide moral leadership. For example, in the early 1970s columnist James Reston described America as "a divided and selfish nation" and called on the President to take the lead in reuniting it:

> In such a situation, the role of the Federal Government, and particularly of the President, is critical, for in a secular society that is full of doubt about the church, the university and the press, the White House is still the pinnacle of

The important symbolic role of the President was dramatically revealed in the public response to Kennedy's sudden death.

our civil life and the hope of some moral order and presiding national purpose. . . . More than anybody else, the President has the power to establish the standard and set the model, to direct or manipulate the powerful forces of the nation, to encourage the best in us.

The issue of moral leadership was central to the Watergate scandal. The President had clearly let the country down—not because his policies were failures but because he had failed as a moral leader. Nixon's popularity dropped sharply during this period, and so did trust in the government as a whole. The Watergate affair showed that, for better or worse, the President is at the center of the nation's hopes and fears.

THE PRESIDENT AS A PERSON

The President as a person—how he copes with pressure, how he works with advisers, how he speaks to the public—has a major impact on life in this and other countries. Only 38 people in American history have had the chance to make such an impact, and each has approached the task differently, depending on his political habits and his outlook toward life. One student of presidential character has classifed Presidents along these lines, using the term *style* to refer to political habits and the term *character* to refer to outlook on life.[6]

Presidential *style* may be active or passive. President Taft, for example, had a very limited view of his duties. "The President," he said, "can exercise no power which cannot be fairly and reasonably traced to some specific grant of authority." President Eisenhower's style was similar. Eisenhower disliked the nitty-gritty of politics. He refused to pressure Congress, did not like speechmaking, tried to ignore the press, and avoided summit meetings. ("This idea of the President of the United States going personally abroad to negotiate—it's just damn stupid," was what he had to say about summits.) Other Presidents have favored a more active role. As mentioned earlier, President Kennedy viewed the Presidency as the "vital center of action in our whole scheme of government" and said the President must "place himself in the very thick of the fight."

Presidential *character* also has two aspects, positive and negative. A positive President is generally happy and optimistic, a negative one moody and irritable. President Johnson became more and more negative as opposition to his Vietnam policies increased. Toward the end of his first term he was complaining that "everybody is trying to cut me down, destroy me," and asking,

---

[6] James David Barber, *The Presidential Character: Predicting Performance in the White House* (Englewood Cliffs, N.J.: Prentice-Hall, 1972).

"Why don't people like me?" President Nixon was even more negative: He became moody, withdrawn, and irritable as it became obvious that he would be impeached if he did not resign.

Does personality make a difference? Many students of American politics think not. Decisions, they claim, are made in the context of particular situations—no matter who is in the White House, the same decision will be made. They argue, for example, that Johnson was under such pressure to escalate the Vietnam War that he really had no choice. In 1965 it was generally believed that saving South Vietnam from a communist takeover was important to America's national security. This view was shared by almost all of Johnson's advisers, by experts on foreign policy, and by leading scholars and commentators. Johnson escalated the war because it was the logical thing to do.

In this view the President simply responds to the situations facing him. But there is still room for variation. Johnson could have handled the war differently—he could have chosen different bombing targets, responded to his critics differently, been less secretive. Even small differences can be very important, and this is where personality enters the picture.

Watergate is a good example. If Nixon had simply confessed, early in the affair, that his advisers had shown poor judgment and that he had not told the truth in his earlier statements about the matter, it is likely that he would have been forgiven. Instead, he chose to fight.

WATERGATE AND THE PRESIDENCY

Since the Watergate scandal tells us many things about the President's role in American politics, let's take a closer look at it. We have already mentioned the growth of the Presidency in the twentieth century. President Nixon added still further to presidential powers, but he went too far. He came into conflict with the other branches of the government over matters such as his refusal to spend money appropriated by Congress for specific programs. But what led to his final downfall was the abuse of power. For one thing, his re-election committee tried to wiretap the offices of the Democratic National Committee and had planned to carry out some "dirty tricks" during the campaign. Also, there was evidence that money had been contributed to the campaign in return for favors such as higher price supports for milk.

The Nixon administration had also tried to harass its "enemies." The Internal Revenue Service had been told to audit the tax returns of people who were opposed to the administration. In addition, the President and his aides had covered up the Watergate break-in. This included trying to get the CIA and the FBI to limit their investigations of the matter.

Finally, the President claimed that the doctrine of *executive privilege* permitted him to keep his documents and tape recordings secret, even though they were connected with the case. According to Nixon, only the President can decide what information about the activities of the executive branch should be revealed to the public or to other branches of the government.

These abuses of presidential power were the basis of the attempt to impeach Nixon. It is important to note that this movement was not based on *policy* disagreements between a Republican President and a Democratic Congress. There were a number of conflicts over policy, of course, and in some governments such conflicts could lead to the overthrow of the prime minister by a "vote of no confidence." In the American system, however, Congress cannot vote the President out of office because it disagrees with his policies. Instead, the House Judiciary Committee voted articles of impeachment naming *illegal actions* of the President.

Removing the President from Office

Nixon was reelected by the largest majority in U.S. history. He held the most powerful office in the world. He was at the head of a huge bureaucracy whose activities affected every aspect of American life. And he was determined to use his powers to the fullest in order to achieve his goals.

Less than two years later he resigned from office.

How did Nixon's downfall come about? To find the answer we turn to the Constitution. *The Federalist* remarked that we would need no controls on government "if angels were to govern men." The writers of the Constitution knew that public officials are not likely to be angels. The Watergate scandal shows how right they were. The Nixon administration was not a band of angels, and the controls included in the Constitution were used to end its abuse of power.

The Role of Congress   Article 1 of the Constitution gives Congress the power to remove the President from office. The House of Representatives may impeach the President; that is, it may formally charge him with failure to carry out the constitutional duties of the office, or with violating constitutional principles. The Senate conducts the trial after impeachment has taken place, with the Chief Justice of the Supreme Court presiding and a two-thirds vote needed for conviction. The Constitution states that the President can be removed from office only if he is convicted of "Treason, Bribery, or other high Crimes or Misdemeanors" (Article 2, Section 4).

Much of the debate over whether Nixon should be impeached centered on this point. Some people argued that the President could be impeached only if he had committed a crime for which an ordinary citizen would be convicted in court. Others argued that he could be impeached for serious misconduct in office, even if the misconduct was not criminal in nature. Their argument prevailed: The articles of impeachment that were voted against Nixon included not only criminal actions such as interfering with investigations but also other misconduct—such as failure to supervise the activities of subordinates—that was not criminal.

The impeachment process was not completed in 1974 because Nixon resigned after the House Judiciary Committee had voted three articles of impeachment against him. The next step would have been a vote by the full House on those articles. If a majority had voted for impeachment, the case would have gone to the Senate for trial. But even though the process was not completed, it is clear that it was the threat of impeachment that led to Nixon's resignation.

The Role of the Courts   In a constitutional crisis the Supreme Court often plays a key role. This was true in the case of Watergate. A conflict arose over the tape recordings of presidential conversations that had been subpoenaed for the trial of some of Nixon's aides. Nixon claimed that only he could decide whether the tapes would be released to the courts. He argued that the doctrine of executive privilege permitted the President to keep his records secret.

The case went to the Supreme Court. It ruled that the President could keep secret records if they were needed to carry out his work. But there were limits on executive privilege. If the President's records were needed in a criminal case, he must turn them over to the courts. What the Court was saying was that no branch of the government is above the law or has unlimited powers.

This decision was an important step leading to Nixon's resignation. He could not ignore the Supreme Court. It was clear that he would be impeached if he did not release the tapes. When the tape transcripts revealed that Nixon had known about the Watergate cover-up for a much longer time than he had admitted, he lost whatever support he had in Congress.

"The Fourth Branch"   We have seen how the power of the President is checked by the other two branches of the government. But outside forces are also important in controlling the government. Full disclosure of the Watergate scandal would not have been possible without the efforts of a few journalists, especially reporters for the *Washington Post* and the *New York Times*. They were able to play this role because of the First Amendment's protection of freedom of the press. Only in a few nations can the press be so aggressive. Even in Great Britain the media would have been legally barred from revealing the details of a scandal like Watergate.

Watergate and the Constitution

The Watergate affair illustrates how constitutional principles such as separation of powers meet the demands of a changing society. This process is not an automatic one in which members of Congress or Supreme Court justices read the Constitution and apply it to a particular case. The language of the Constitution must be interpreted. The meaning of words like *impeachment* is not clear, and executive privilege is not even mentioned in the Constitution.

How do members of Congress or Supreme Court justices determine what is meant by impeachment or executive privilege? First, of course, they look at the Constitution itself. If the Constitution is unclear, they look further—at other writings by the nation's founders, at the debates that took place at the Constitutional Convention, at earlier legal practice. Perhaps most important, they consider how others have interpreted the Constitution in the past. In the case of impeachment, the members of Congress spent a lot of time considering the impeachment of President Andrew Johnson after the Civil War. (Johnson was impeached, but he escaped conviction by one vote.)

Finally, there is no doubt that political factors play a role. The fact that Nixon was a Republican whose policies angered many Democrats cannot be ignored. It is not an accident that the members of Congress who favored impeachment were likely to be Democrats while those who opposed it were likely to be Republicans. The fact that Nixon's popularity faded during the summer of 1974 probably affected their positions on the issue.

Some critics claim that the impeachment proceedings were a purely political affair—Nixon's press secretary called the House Judiciary Committee a "kangaroo court." Members of Congress, on the other hand, sometimes talked as if the matter was a strictly legal one. Probably both views are partly true. However, the seriousness of the debate over the meaning of impeachment—and the fact that in the end the call for Nixon's resignation came from conservative members of his own party—suggest that the Judiciary Committee was not a kangaroo court.

After Watergate

Some students of politics believed that the Watergate scandal would lead to major changes in the structure of the government. Some even thought it would severely weaken the Presidency. But the results were not so dramatic. No sooner had President Nixon left office than President Ford and his staff were running U.S. foreign policy and trying to cope with the economic crisis at home. Those problems required presidential action, and the President acted.

On the other hand, Watergate seems to have affected the balance of power among the three branches of the government. Most important, it demonstrated the independence of each branch from the others. Congress called on its power of impeachment, and the President resigned. The Supreme Court ruled that the President must release the Watergate tapes, and he obeyed.

Moveover, Watergate led to greater demands for integrity and honesty in politics; demands which Jimmy Carter, among others, responded to in his successful attempt to become President. Some feel that Watergate dismantled the "imperial presidency"—the concentration of power in the executive branch—but history has yet to vote on how much really changed because of Watergate. Certainly the abuses of the Nixon presidency are not likely to be repeated, at least in the near future. But the pressure of events and the complexities of governing still seem to call for strong leadership from the White House. The United States has not seen the last of strong presidents.

HOW INSTITUTIONS WORK: III

The Federal Budget

What Is the "Budgetary Process"?

The budgetary process is the ongoing planning, implementation, and auditing of all federal spending. Both the executive branch and Congress are involved in this process.

Who Draws Up the Annual Budget?

The federal government operates on a fiscal year that begins on October 1 and ends on the following September 30. Each spring the departments and agencies of the government begin writing up their budget requests for the fiscal year beginning in October of the following year. These requests are sent to the Office of Management and Budget (OMB). The OMB reviews the budget requests and sends them to the President, who by now has also been given economic forecasts and revenue estimates for the coming year. The President uses this information to set budget guidelines. The agencies then submit detailed budget requests based on these guidelines. The detailed requests are analyzed by the OMB and sent to the President, and the final budget proposal is submitted to Congress in January or February.

What Is Congress's Role in the Budgetary Process?

Congress's budgetary activity has two parts. First it enacts *authorizations*, or bills authorizing specific programs and setting limits on funds to finance them. Then it passes *appropriations*, or bills granting the actual funds. An authorization without an appropriation is meaningless. Note, however, that close to 70 percent of the amount spent in any fiscal year is locked into the budget by previous congressional decisions.

What Happens to the Budget in Congress?

The President's budget requests are first considered by the House Appropriations Committee. An appropriation that has been passed by the House is sent to the Senate Appropriations Committee. The Senate has traditionally been a court of appeals for agencies trying to restore cuts made in the House. As a result Congress has typically spent several billion dollars more each year than the President requested. Moreover, Congress has considered the budget piece by piece instead of as a whole. To correct these problems Congress passed budget reform legislation in 1974.

What Changes Does the New Law Call For?

It created new House and Senate budget committees and a Congressional Budget Office staffed by experts. It also set up new procedures: (1) Early in each session Congress passes a joint resolution setting an overall target for governmental spending. (2) After the appropriations process has been completed, Congress reconciles any differences between the target total and the sum of the appropriations.

Is There Any Way of Making Sure Funds Are Spent as Congress Directs?

Each agency is responsible for making sure its spending is within the amount budgeted. The OMB oversees agency spending, and the General Accounting Office provides Congress with an independent audit of all expenditures.

Does the President Have to Spend the Full Amount Appropriated by Congress?

This became a subject of debate during the Nixon years, when the President "impounded" funds for certain programs and refused to spend the full amount appropriated by Congress for those programs. The budget reform law requires congressional approval of all impoundments.

Can the Executive Branch Ever Get More Funds for Special Purposes?

Yes, it can request supplemental appropriations.

We think of the government as having three branches: legislative, executive, and judicial. We see the President on the evening news or read about him in the newspaper. We read about senators and representatives, and sometimes even meet them. But the real contacts that most of us have with the government are with *bureaucrats*—the post office clerk, the government safety inspector, the tax examiner at the Internal Revenue Service.

When we think of bureaucracy we think of red tape, inefficiency, waste, and lack of concern for human needs. Everyone criticizes bureaucracy, but no one believes we could do without it. A complex modern nation needs a large administrative system. When Carter was running for office he complained about the size of the federal bureaucracy. But after he took office he did not cut down the presidential staff—he may even have increased it.

WHAT IS A BUREAUCRACY?

Modern industrial societies contain many big, complex organizations. Some are private—businesses, universities, and labor unions, for example. But the biggest and most complex organizations are found within the government—the army, the post office, the school system, and so on. These bureaucracies can be thought of as organizational machines that perform social tasks the way other machines perform mechanical tasks. Just as it takes a computer, heavy construction equipment, and the like to do certain mechanical jobs that individuals or groups could not do otherwise, it takes a bureaucracy to do social jobs; to deliver the mail, issue welfare checks, conduct foreign policy, or design and produce weapons.

Every bureaucracy has a chain of command, or *hierarchy*. The advantage of a hierarchy is that top officials can control subordinates and make sure the organization's goals are carried out. In government agencies the top officials are appointed by the President, who is elected by the people and is accountable to them. The problem with chains of command is that they can be long and inefficient. Moreover, higher officials may not really control lower ones —in the government, subordinate agencies often have a lot of freedom. (We will discuss the reasons for this shortly.)

Another feature of bureaucracies is that they bring together a large number of experts. Each of these experts understands some aspects of the complicated problems the government is trying to deal with. For example, the Food and Drug Administration employs specialists who test new drugs, inspect manufacturing plants, and the like. Specialization is necessary because no single person has all the knowledge needed to solve most problems. A number of specialists must work together on the same problem. But experts sometimes take a narrow view of things; they may not see the forest for the trees. Moreover, elected officials have trouble controlling technical experts.

Bureaucrats are supposed to carry out decisions made by others; they are not supposed to make policy themselves. They are supposed to treat each person or group equally according to rules provided by Congress or the President. It does not always work this way. In the first place, bureaucracies often make policy. (We will have more to say about this later in the chapter.) In the second place, they are not always impartial when they deal with individual cases.

In short, bureaucracies are supposed to be efficient, impartial organizations that carry out policies made by elected officials; but they are hard to control, and sometimes they themselves make policy. This leads to a major problem: Bureaucrats are not elected, yet they can make policy decisions. How can this be tolerated in a democracy, where the people are supposed to control the government through their elected representatives? There is no easy answer to this question.

THE GROWTH OF THE FEDERAL BUREAUCRACY

We have mentioned several times that the federal government has grown enormously since the nation's founding. Most of this growth has taken place in the twentieth century. Beginning in the 1930s, the government took on important new functions such as providing social services for citizens and regulating the economy. Before that time the federal government's expenditures were equal to about one-fourth of state and local government expenditures. But by 1949 the federal government accounted for 70 percent of all government spending.

The biggest and most complex bureaucracies are found in modern government.

The number of federal employees illustrates the great increase in the size of the federal bureaucracy. In 1802 the federal government had 2875 civilian employees; in 1977 it had 2,862,000. (See Figure 12.1.) Another indicator of growth is the number of departments and agencies in the government today. Not only are there 12 major executive departments, but each of those departments has many subdivisions. The Department of Health, Education and Welfare, for example, contains 11 main divisions and 76 separate agencies. The Executive Office of the President contains 18 separate units. In addition, there are 121 non–Cabinet executive agencies and 61 advisory agencies. The number of agencies is so large that according to the presidential assistant in charge of reorganizing the government, "We were unable to obtain any single document containing a complete and current listing of government units which are part of the federal government."[1]

The many agencies and departments in the government must be coordinated somehow. This leads to the creation of new agencies to coordinate the existing ones. In 1970 there were 850 interagency coordinating committees. One of the main reasons for the increase in the size of the Executive Office of the President is the President's desire to coordinate the government. The major units in the Executive Office such as the National Security Council were created specifically to coordinate policy in particular areas.

THE "BUREAUCRATIC PROBLEM"

The size of the federal budget or the number of government employees is not the cause of the "bureaucratic problem." After all, our nation is much larger

---

[1] W. Harrison Wellford, quoted in the *Washington Post*, 8 May 1977.

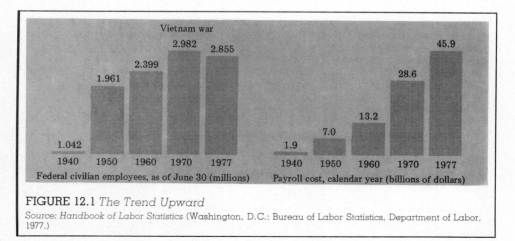

FIGURE 12.1 *The Trend Upward*

Source: *Handbook of Labor Statistics* (Washington, D.C.: Bureau of Labor Statistics, Department of Labor, 1977.)

than it was in the 1800s. Government services require more money and more personnel. Today, for example, people write more letters and pay more bills by mail. This requires more letter carriers and post office clerks. This in turn may lead to inefficiency, but it does not create a "bureaucratic problem." As long as the services the government provides—such as delivering the mail—are simply a matter of carrying out the policy decisions of elected officials, there is little chance that the bureaucracy will get out of control. A "bureaucratic problem" arises when bureaucrats are free to make policy themselves. This is called *bureaucratic discretion*.

Bureaucratic Discretion

Bureaucrats can play a policy-making role in a number of ways. For example, they often participate in the writing of legislation. Although laws are passed by Congress, the drafting of those laws is often done with the advice and cooperation of the agencies that will be affected. Since the agencies are likely to favor some aspects of the legislation and not others, their advice will not be entirely objective.

After a law has been passed, the bureaucracy is often given the task of writing guidelines for applying the law. Congress may pass an act requiring businesses to pay more attention to job safety, but the agency in charge of carrying out the law—the Occupational Safety and Health Administration —writes the actual safety regulations.

In addition, when it comes to actually carrying out federal laws and regulations, government officials often have a lot of discretion. They have to decide how a law or regulation applies to a particular case. A police officer, for instance, must decide whether a person looks suspicious, how carefully to check on activities that might be illegal, whether to interfere in a family fight,

Officers on the beat have discretion on how they apply the law.

and the like. Studies have shown that police officers vary greatly in their interpretation of the rules under which they operate. In this sense they shape policy on law enforcement.

Discretion Through Regulation

In recent years the government has taken a more active role in regulating the activities of Americans, especially American businesses. Federal regulations deal with product safety, environmental protection, and the rights of consumers. The government also regulates the lives of citizens. For example, it determines whether they are eligible for benefits such as welfare payments or unemployment compensation.

Such regulation is not new. It began in the late 1800s with the creation of the Interstate Commerce Commission to regulate railroad rates. In the 1930s the volume of government regulation increased greatly. The Securities and Exchange Commission was created to regulate the securities market; stricter banking laws were passed; the Federal Power Commission, the Civil Aeronautics Board, and other regulatory agencies were formed.

Beginning in the 1960s the federal government has intervened when business has failed to respond to demands for equal employment opportunity, pollution control, job safety, and the like. This involves regulating the day-to-day operation of businesses and has led to the formation of new agencies such as the Environmental Protection Agency, the Consumer Product Safety Commission, and the Equal Employment Opportunity Commission. Table 12.1 lists some of the major regulatory agencies and their functions.

The increase in regulation has been dramatic, and it has not escaped criticism. Many people complain of the costs of regulation. Businesses claim that they spend an enormous amount of time and money trying to comply with government regulations. On the other hand, those who support regulation

Bureaucrats often write legislation and guidelines for carrying out laws.

can point to successes such as a cleaner environment and safer products. It is clear that the debate over how much regulation there should be, and at what cost, will continue for some time.

A major source of the discretionary power of regulatory agencies is the vagueness of regulatory laws. Congress often lacks the technical knowledge needed to write detailed regulations. But the bureaucracy has this knowledge, so it is given the job of filling in the details. Moreover, Congress often writes vague laws because its members cannot agree on more precise regulations. It therefore passes the buck to the bureaucracy.

BUREAUCRATIC BEHAVIOR

Bureaucracies are organizational machines, but they are machines run by humans. They are not as rigid as we might expect. Bureaucracies do not simply carry out the law. As we have seen, they often play a major role in setting policy. In addition, they have goals over and above the policies they are supposed to carry out. One such goal is to maintain and enlarge the organization itself. Another is to continue to do things the way they have always been done.

Maintaining and Enlarging the Organization

Bureaucratic organizations compete with other bureaucratic organizations. Each agency tries to hold on to whatever power it has and, if possible, to expand. It tries to increase its budget, the number of people it employs, and the scope of the programs under its control. If it cannot expand in these areas, it will at least resist any attempt to reduce its power.

There are many reasons for this bureaucratic behavior. For one thing, bureaucrats' jobs depend on it. If the organization's budget is cut, they may be out of work. For another, the *importance* of their jobs depends on the size of the programs they control. Bureaucrats try to expand their programs in order to increase their own status within the organization.

Bureaucrats in one agency often come into conflict with bureaucrats in other agencies. The Environmental Protection Agency comes into conflict with other government agencies when it tries to get them to comply with its regulations. Or it may come into conflict with agencies of the Department of Energy that are more concerned with maintaining energy supplies than with protecting the environment.

However, bureaucrats should not be thought of as power-hungry officials interested only in their own jobs. They are usually strongly committed to their agency's programs. For example, the officials in charge of the high-

TABLE 12.1 Major Regulatory Agencies

Agency	Vital Statistics	Major Functions
	Older Agencies	
Interstate Commerce Commission	Created in 1887, it has 2100 employees, 79 field offices, and a $57 million budget.	It regulates rates and routes of railroads, most truckers, and some waterway carriers.
Antitrust Division (Justice Department)	Since 1890 it has grown to 900 employees, 8 field offices, and a budget of $27 million.	It regulates all activity that could affect interstate commerce, from trade restraints and illegal agreements to mergers.
Federal Trade Commission	Created in 1914, it has 1700 employees, 11 field offices, and a budget of $55 million.	It has very broad discretion to curb unfair trade practices, protect consumers, and maintain competition.
Food and Drug Administration	Founded in 1931, it fields a staff of 7000 with a budget of $240 million.	It is responsible for the safety and efficacy of drugs and medical devices and the safety and purity of food. It also regulates labeling; oversees about $200 billion worth of industrial output.
Federal Communications Commission	Created in 1934, it has 2100 employees, 24 field offices, and a budget of $60 million.	It regulates broadcasting and other communications through licensing and frequency allocation. It also regulates interstate telephone and telegraph rates and levels of service.
Securities and Exchange Commission	Created in 1934, it has 2000 employees, 18 field offices, and a budget of $56 million.	It regulates all publicly traded securities and the markets on which they are traded. It also administers public-disclosure laws and polices securities fraud.
Civil Aeronautics Board	Created in 1938, it has 800 employees, 8 field offices, and a $22 million budget; also administers $80 million in subsidies to airlines.	It regulates airline fares and routes.

Agency	Vital Statistics	Major Functions
Federal Aviation Administration	Created in 1958, it has 5000 employees operating on a budget of $228 million; the bulk of its money—$1.3 billion—goes to operate the nation's air traffic control system.	It regulates aircraft manufacturing through certification of airplane airworthiness. It also licenses pilots.
	Newer Agencies	
Equal Employment Opportunity Commission	Created in 1964, it employs 2500, maintains 39 field offices, and has a budget of $70 million.	It investigates and conciliates complaints of employment discrimination based on race, religion, or sex.
National Highway Traffic Safety Administration	Created in 1970, it has 800 employees, 10 field offices, and a $100 million budget. It also administers $129 million in grants to states.	It regulates manufacturers of autos, trucks, buses, motorcycles, trailers, and tires in an effort to reduce the number and severity of traffic accidents.
Environmental Protection Agency	Founded in 1970, it employs 10,000, maintains 10 regional offices, and operates more than 20 laboratories, spending $865 million. It also administers more than $4 billion in sewage treatment construction grants.	It develops and enforces standards for clean air and water, controls pollution from pesticides, toxic substances, and noise. It also approves state pollution abatement plans and rules on environmental-impact statements.
Occupational Safety and Health Administration	Created in 1971, it employs 2400, runs 125 field offices, and spends $128 million.	It is responsible for regulating safety and health conditions in all work places—except those run by governments.
Consumer Product Safety Commission	Established in 1972, it employs 890 on a budget of $39 million and maintains 13 field field offices	Its mission is to reduce product-related injuries to consumers by mandating better design, labeling, and instruction sheets.

SOURCE: Adapted from *Business Week*, 4 April 1977, pp. 52, 53, 56.

way safety program are engineers who are committed to the goal of preventing accidents on the nation's highways. The problem is that this commitment can lead to a power struggle with other organizations.

Standard Operating Procedures

Bureaucracies are often criticized for requiring too many forms, too much red tape. To some extent this criticism is unfair. An impartial, responsible agency needs red tape—that is, specific procedures to be followed in carrying out a governmental function—if it is to avoid acting arbitrarily. But standard operating procedures can lead to lack of flexibility. During the Cuban missile crisis, for example, President Kennedy wanted to block Russian ships from delivering missiles to Cuba. The blockade had to be close enough to Cuba so that the Russian ships would have time to turn back before confronting the American ships. The Navy's standard operating procedure, however, was to set a blockade several hundred miles offshore. Kennedy had a hard time persuading the Navy to change its usual way of doing things.

Bureaucrats and Their "Clientele"

Government agencies are often created to regulate a particular part of the economy: drug manufacturers, say, or airlines or railroads. Over time these agencies often develop close, cooperative relationships with the industries they are supposed to regulate. They then begin to represent the interests of those industries rather than the public interest. This is sometimes called the "capture" of the agency by the industry.

The extent of such "captures" is sometimes exaggerated, but it is clear that certain agencies work closely with their "clients." The relationship between agency and clientele is strengthened by the so-called revolving-door system, in which top industry officials are appointed to the agency that regulates their industry while agency employees move on to high positions in the industry they have been regulating. For example, weapons manufacturers and other defense-related industries often hire former military officers and Defense Department officials.

Cooperation between agencies and industries also grows out of the fact that many industries benefit from government regulation. Regulation often protects the companies in a particular industry from the competition of new companies by setting tough standards for entering the industry. It also limits competition by setting prices. Thus when the Ford administration suggested ending government regulation of the trucking industry, the industry itself protested. According to the chairman of the American Trucking Association, "We have adequate trucking primarily because of legislation for federal regulation of interstate motor transportation wisely enacted by Congress in 1935."[2]

In recent years there has been a movement away from such cozy relationships between bureaucrats and their clientele. Regulatory agencies are getting tougher and becoming more independent from the industries they regulate. Many of the new agencies, notably the Environmental Protection Agency, the Consumer Product Safety Commission, and the National Highway Safety Administration, have been quite active in performing their regulatory duties. Some older agencies, including the Federal Trade Commission and the Food and Drug Administration, have loosened their ties to the industries they regulate.

BUREAUCRACY AND ACCOUNTABILITY

In a democracy, those who govern are supposed to be accountable to those who are governed. This is accomplished mainly through periodic elections. If elected officers are not responsive to the people, they are likely to be voted out of office. Bureaucrats, however, are not elected. They do not have a limited term of office. Many remain in their positions for life. Yet these officials carry out many of the functions of government. How does this square with the principles of democracy?

One way of solving this dilemma would be to keep the bureaucracy firmly under the control of elected officials—Congress or the President. If the performance of government agencies were closely controlled by officials elected by the people, the existence of a powerful bureaucracy would not be inconsistent with the basic democratic principle of popular control over the government. But this is not the case: Elected officials do not have full control of the bureaucracy. There are several reasons for this situation, including the size and complexity of the bureaucracy, the separation of powers, and institutional loyalty.

Size   The sheer size of the bureaucracy makes it impossible for elected officials to control it closely. Under the Constitution the President is the head of the executive branch and is supposed to see that the laws are carried out. But he (or, someday, she) is only one person. He cannot single-handedly supervise all the departments and agencies in the executive branch. He might increase the number of assistants who help him perform this task, but even the large White House Staff cannot keep track of everything that goes on in

---

[2] Lee R. Sollenberger, in the *National Journal,* 24 July 1976, p. 1052.

the executive branch. Besides, the White House Staff itself has become another bureaucracy—part of the problem, not the solution.

Complexity   Another reason it is hard for elected officials to control the bureaucracy is that they do not have the technical knowledge that bureaucrats have. Few members of Congress understand the technical aspects of nuclear-weapons production, drug testing, water pollution control, and so on. Even when they do have such knowledge, they depend on the bureaucracy for information on these subjects. The FBI provides crime statistics; the Bureau of Labor Statistics has data on unemployment; the Federal Aviation Administration supplies information about new safety devices for airplanes. They can limit congressional control by limiting the information available to Congress.

Separation of Powers   The nation's founders created a government with three independent branches. They did not intend to set up a separate bureaucracy. This is, in effect, what has happened. The bureaucracy plays one branch against another and in that way gains a certain amount of freedom.

There are many examples of this process. The armed forces are supposed to be under the control of the President as Commander-in-Chief. But they also have close ties with the Senate and House Armed Forces Committees. Often they can get what they want from those committees even if the President opposes them. Similarly, the FBI was for many years almost entirely independent of the Attorney General, who is legally in charge of it, because it had strong support in Congress.

Institutional Loyalty   Still another reason bureaucracies are hard to control is that bureaucrats often develop strong loyalty to their agency and to their fellow workers. They will do anything they can to protect the agency and each other, including suppressing information about mismanagement within the agency. The penalty for breaking this unwritten rule can be severe, as is illustrated by the case of Dr. Stanley Mazaleski, a government scientist:

> In the Spring of 1974, Dr. Mazaleski . . . began complaining about the sluggish pace in which his agency had set about designing safety standards for industrial workers exposed to carcinogenic chemicals. The following winter, Mazaleski's criticisms were leaked to the newspapers. Within a few months he was fired. . . . Mazaleski belongs to a haunted little tribe of Federal employees who have transgressed against the bureaucracy—who having seen something seriously wrong in a government operation, made a noise about it.[3]

---

[3] Helen Dudar, "The Price of Blowing the Whistle," *New York Times Magazine,* 30 October 1977, p. 41. © 1977 by The New York Times Company. Reprinted by permission.

CONGRESS AND THE BUREAUCRACY

As mentioned earlier, Congress creates government agencies, authorizes and finances their activities, and oversees those activities through hearings and reviews. Agency heads spend much of their time preparing for congressional hearings and appearing at them. An effective agency head has good relations with the members and staff of the congressional committee that watches over his or her agency.

Yet Congress, like the President, does not have tight control over bureaucratic agencies. Instead, the relationship between Congress and the bureaucracy is best described as a cooperative one. Congress as a whole does not supervise the bureaucracy; this is done by individual committees and subcommittees. Members of Congress are often appointed to committees that deal with matters they are interested in. A member from an agricultural district may be assigned to the Agriculture Committee; a member with a strong interest in military matters may be assigned to one of the Armed Forces committees; and so on. Over the years these members form close ties with the agencies they are supposed to supervise. They become specialists in the agency's area of activity and often represent the agency to Congress.

The "Triple Alliance"

A government agency and the committee that has jurisdiction over it may form a "triple alliance" with the interest group or industry that the agency is supposed to regulate. Examples include the "alliance" formed by the House Armed Services Committee, the Defense Department, and the major arms

Congressional committees often work closely with the government agencies that they are supposed to supervise. Here the Secretary of Defense testifying before the House Armed Services Committee.

manufacturers, as well as the relationship of the House Education and Labor Committee with the Labor Department and the AFL–CIO.

All of the partners in a triple alliance benefit from the alliance. The agency is protected from attempts to cut its budget or reduce the scope of its activities. Members of the congressional committee benefit because the agency can often do favors for them, such as providing services for the member's district or hiring people recommended by the member. The interest group benefits because its preferences are given careful consideration by both the agency and the committee.

Congressional Oversight

Even though congressional committees have friendly relations with particular agencies, Congress does not simply let those agencies have their own way. In many cases the committees supervise the agencies quite closely. This is called *congressional oversight*. Congress is often criticized by agencies for paying too much attention to their day-to-day business. The agencies would rather have Congress set general guidelines and leave them free to fill in the details of government policy. Some committees, however, seem more interested in the details of a policy than in its broad outlines. Often this is because individual members of Congress want to make sure the agency serves the specific needs of their districts.

THE PRESIDENT AND THE BUREAUCRACY

In principle the President is in charge of the executive branch, but in practice he is lucky if he knows what is happening in even a tiny part of it. This is illustrated by the following news item, datelined Notasulga, Alabama, 27 July 1972:

> In 1932, Charlie Pollard, then a 26-year-old Macon County farmer, took advantage of a public health official's offer of a free blood test and was told a few days later that he had "bad blood."
>
> "They been doctoring on me off and on ever since then," Mr. Pollard, now 66, said yesterday. "And they give me a blood tonic."
>
> Mr. Pollard did not know until Tuesday that for the past 40 years he has been one of a constantly dwindling number of human guinea pigs in whose "bad blood" the effects of syphilis have been observed.
>
> U.S. Public Health Service officials revealed Tuesday that under a Public Health Service Study, treatment for syphilis has been withheld from hundreds of afflicted Negroes for the 40-year period. For the past 25 years, penicillin has been generally available to treat it. The purpose of the study was

observation of the course of the disease in untreated persons over a long
period of time.[4]

This study had been carried out by officials of the U.S. government, using
public funds, during the Presidencies of Roosevelt, Truman, Eisenhower,
Kennedy, Johnson, and Nixon. Any of these Presidents would probably
have stopped the program if it had come to his attention. But how can one
man know everything that is being done in the name of the U.S. government
in hundreds of offices, laboratories, agencies, bureaus, departments, programs, and projects?

When we think of the President of the United States and the bureaucracy
of which he is the head, we imagine that the President issues orders and the
agencies obey. But most Presidents have found that this is not the case. This
is how Franklin Roosevelt described his relations with the bureaucracy:

> The Treasury is so large and far-flung and ingrained in its practices that I
> find it almost impossible to get the action and results I want—even with
> Henry [Morgenthau] there. But the Treasury is not to be compared with the
> State Department. You should go through the experience of trying to get
> any changes in the thinking, policy, and action of the career diplomats and
> then you'd know what a real problem was. But the Treasury and the State
> Department put together are nothing compared with the Na-a-vy. The admi-
> rals are really something to cope with—and I should know. To change any-
> thing in the Na-a-vy is like punching a feather bed. You punch it with your
> right and you punch it with your left until you are finally exhausted, and
> then you find the damn bed just as it was before you started punching.[5]

Far from having the bureaucracy obey him, the President can become
highly dependent on his subordinates. He depends on them for two
important things: information and compliance.

Information　The President depends on the federal agencies for information because they are closer to the sources of that information. In making
foreign-policy decisions the President must rely on the State Department,
the CIA, and the military for information. The same is true in domestic affairs: The Agriculture Department has the facts and figures on grain production; the Nuclear Regulatory Commission has the details on the danger of
nuclear power plant operation.

Control over such information can be a source of power. Agencies that
want more money for their programs can supply information showing why
additional funds are needed. They can make their programs look more
successful than they are, or cover up failures. For example, an official investi-

---

[4] *New York Times,* 27 July 1972, p. 18. © 1972 by The New York Times Company. Reprinted by permission.

[5] Richard Neustadt, *Presidential Power* (New York: Wiley, 1960), p. 110.

gation of the My Lai killings—in which a large number of Vietnamese civilians were killed by American troops—found that the number of victims dropped as the information was passed up through the army's chain of command. By the time it reached the top it did not look bad at all.

Compliance   The President also depends on the bureaucracy for compliance. It is the President's duty to see that the laws are "faithfully executed," but the actual execution of the laws takes place at a much lower level. In fact many government programs are criticized because a lot of effort goes into designing the program and very little into seeing that they are properly carried out. Many of the urban programs of the late 1960s and early 1970s were criticized for this. As a result many programs are ineffective or have effects other than those intended by Congress or the President.

Many Presidents have complained that they have no real control over what is going on in various parts of the government. President Kennedy said that he could not count on State Department officials to carry out his foreign-policy directives. No matter what he wanted, they did things the way they always had. Other Presidents have made similar comments about the problem of compliance. As President Nixon put it, "We have no discipline in this bureaucracy."

The Civil Service

The President's control over the bureaucracy is also limited by the fact that most government jobs are covered by civil-service regulations. This means that government employees cannot be fired every time a new President comes to Washington.

The civil service was developed to end the "spoils system" of the nineteenth century. Under the spoils system the main qualification for a government job was membership in the President's party. Whenever a new President took office he fired all the government's employees and replaced them with his own supporters. Needless to say, this system bred corruption and inefficiency.

In 1883 Congress passed the Pendleton Act, which introduced a new system based on two principles: (1) selection on the basis of merit (usually scores on civil-service exams) and (2) job security regardless of the party in power. These two principles required a third one: (3) responsiveness to political leaders or, in other words, political neutrality.

For the most part the civil service works the way it is supposed to. Most government positions are included in the system. An incoming President can appoint only about 2000 of his own people, and of these only about 700 are top executives. The rest are assistants to those executives, ranging from personal advisers to cooks and chauffeurs.

On the other hand, the civil service reduces the President's control over the bureaucracy still further. According to one top official, "The system is rapidly bringing the government to a state of paralysis."[6] It is almost impossible to fire an employee for incompetence, and the seniority system (in which those with the longest service rise to the top) makes it impossible to reorganize a government agency.

The civil service is supposed to be a neutral servant of the administration in power. But it is a servant with ideas of its own, and new administrations find it hard to control. When a new President takes office he appoints a number of top officials. These include not only the heads of the major departments but also assistant secretaries, heads of agencies, and bureau chiefs. These officials are supposed to help the President take control of the bureaucracy. However, this is much easier said than done. The President's appointees are usually new to the job. Their agencies are staffed by career civil servants who have more knowledge about and commitment to "their" programs and procedures than the newcomers. This makes it hard for the new officials to take control.

Presidents and their appointees may be frustrated by an unresponsive bureaucracy. But for the government to function well it is important for many government agencies to be free from direct political control. For example, if there is to be an effective federal program to support cancer research, the decisions on what research to support must be made by experts who will not be swayed by demands that research funds be spent in particular congressional districts. Similarly, the Bureau of Labor Statistics must be able to resist pressure from the White House to "tailor" the unemployment rate to the needs of a President running for reelection.

THE BUREAUCRACY AND THE PUBLIC

If elected officials have trouble controlling the bureaucracy, does the public itself have any way of controlling it? One way citizens can keep government officials responsive to their needs is through their representatives in Congress. As we have seen, one of the main tasks of members of Congress is to deal with complaints or requests for help in dealing with the bureaucracy.

In addition, some government programs are set up in such a way as to get citizens involved in them. Several of President Johnson's antipoverty programs provided for participation by the poor in the administration of the program. However, such participation is not usually very effective. Few citizens take part; they often do not represent the groups affected by the pro-

---

[6] Anonymous official quoted in the *National Journal,* 23 April 1977, p. 617.

gram; and they usually have little impact on the way the program is carried out.

The Government in the Sunshine Act

A recent attempt to give citizens more control over the bureaucracy is the Government in the Sunshine Act. This act requires government agencies to hold their meetings and hearings in public and to give notice of when and where they will be held. The purpose of the law is to allow for more citizen participation; however, at this point it is too early to tell whether it will have the desired effect.

The Freedom of Information Act

The public's lack of control over the bureaucracy is often due to lack of information. Government agencies have traditionally kept their files closed to the public. In 1966 Congress passed the Freedom of Information Act in an attempt to make more information available to the public. However, the agencies still had a lot of control over what they released; besides, they could delay in responding to requests for information and charge high fees for whatever information they provided. As a result the 1966 act was ineffective.

In 1974 Congress amended the act. Agencies now have less freedom in deciding what they will release. They also have to respond within a fixed time and charge reasonable fees. The new law has been much more effective. Public-interests groups and individual citizens have taken advantage of the law, focusing on information in FBI, CIA, and Defense Department files. Their requests have led to the release of information about government spying on political groups such as the Socialist Workers party and black and feminist groups, as well as the CIA's 25-year program of research on mind control drugs. But the main users of the new law have been American businesses, which have been especially interested in getting information from the Federal Trade Commission and the Food and Drug Administration. This heavy use by business was not anticipated by the act's original supporters and illustrates a point made earlier in this book: Those who have the most money and other resources (e.g., legal advice) are in the best position to take advantage of government laws and regulations.

The Freedom of Information Act has given citizens some control over the bureaucracy, but it has been criticized for making it harder for agencies to operate. Agency heads complain about the amount of time and the number of employees they need to handle requests from citizens. They claim that many requests lead to the release of information that should be kept secret in the interest of national security.

PROFESSIONALISM AND THE BUREAUCRACY

Professionals—people with advanced technical training—have a strong influence on bureaucracies. This can make it harder for the public to control the federal bureaucracy, but it can also prevent control of the bureaucracy by special interests.

When the spoils system was replaced by the civil service, the result was government by professionals. As new agencies were created to deal with new problems, they were turned over to specialists: educators, engineers, chemists, foresters, agronomists, and so on. (See Table 12.2.) These specialists believe—probably rightly—that they understand problems in their fields better than people who lack professional training. They share certain standards with other members of their profession and judge themselves and other professionals by how well they live up to those standards. Above all, they want to be free from control by nonprofessionals.

TABLE 12.2 Professionals Employed by the Federal Government

Occupation	Number of Federal Workers
Engineers (all types)	146,940
Scientists (all types)	85,501
Nurses and nurses' aides	67,904
Personnel administrators	35,331
Accountants	31,780
Teachers	26,284
Air-traffic controllers	26,005
Internal Revenue Service agents	21,155
Investigators	21,133
Inspectors	17,427
Forestry workers	14,624
Mathematicians and statisticians	13,550
Attorneys	12,761
Computer operators	11,602
Doctors	8,033
Librarians	6,643
Economists	4,798
Writers and editors	3,577
Psychologists	3,099
Photographers	3,061
Veterinarians	2,284
Pharmacists	1,439
Dentists	925
Chaplains	461

SOURCE: U.S. Civil Service Commission. Data as of October 1974.

The fact that so many agencies are headed by professionals makes it harder for elected officials—or the public—to control them. Professionals believe they know best—better than the people themselves—what is good for the nation. This is a challenge to the authority of the President, which is based on the fact that he is elected by the people and stands for the will of the people.

On the other hand, professionalism can make some agencies better servants of the public. Earlier we mentioned the increased activity of the Food and Drug Administration in regulating the drug industry. A major reason for this change is the increased role of professionals within the agency. These people respond less to pressure from the industry than to the standards of their profession. Similarly, the Consumer Product Safety Commission and the Environmental Protection Agency are staffed by professionals who insist that industries comply with federal product safety and pollution control regulations despite the protests of those industries.

CONCLUSION

For the various reasons discussed in this chapter, many people are concerned about the problems of bureaucratic control. However, any plan to increase control over the bureaucracy would not reduce the size and importance of the bureaucracy by very much. It appears that a large bureaucracy, only partially and imperfectly controlled by elected officials and the public, is unavoidable in any modern democracy, including the United States.

CONTROVERSY

How far should the government go in regulating the lives of citizens? For example, no one objects if the government sets strict safety standards for commercial aircraft, but what about a law requiring motorcycle riders to wear crash helmets?

One Side

The government has no business telling motorcycle riders that they must wear crash helmets. Such a regulation interferes with their freedom, including the freedom to risk injury. It is not like a speeding law. Forcing motorcyclists to obey speeding laws protects not only their lives but other people's as well. Here the government is interfering in a decision that affects only the safety of the motorcyclist. And like all government regulations this one is costly to enforce. Traffic police spend a lot of time stopping helmetless motorcyclists when they could be doing more important things like catching speeders. Laws like this one are an example of the government's meddling where it has no business meddling.

The Other Side

A law that prevents people from hurting themselves is highly desirable. Studies have shown that crash helmets greatly reduce the number of injuries and deaths caused by motorcycle accidents. The average citizen may not realize this—which is why safety experts make such studies and why those studies are translated into laws. Besides, it is not true that motorcyclists who go without helmets are risking only their own heads. Suppose there is a serious injury and the state must pay for medical care. Suppose the motorcyclist is killed and his family must go on welfare. In both cases the taxpayers have to pay. In a modern nation the health and safety of every citizen are social matters, not simply personal ones.

13

"Scarcely any political question arises in the United States that is not resolved, sooner or later, into a judicial question," Alexis de Tocqueville remarked 150 years ago. What did he mean?

In the first place, we have a very complicated government, with three branches (legislative, executive, and judicial), two layers (federal and state), and all sorts of checks and balances to keep one branch or layer of the government from dominating the others. When a conflict arises between two units of the government—say, between the President and Congress—it must be settled by an umpire. This role is played by the courts.

In the second place, Americans have a habit of taking their disagreements to court. This is called *adjudication*. The dispute may be a simple liability case —"I'll sue you for medical costs because I broke my leg when I slipped on the ice on your sidewalk." Or it may be a case that will affect the whole society—such as those that established the right of workers to form unions or the right of blacks to vote.

Finally, the United States probably has more "judge-made" law than any other nation. Laws are made by Congress and the state legislatures, but those laws are interpreted and sometimes reversed by the courts. In addition, we allow judges to propose and carry out certain social reforms, such as school integration plans. This is the courts' policy-making role.

In this chapter we will discuss these three functions of the courts, especially as they are performed by the Supreme Court.

THE COURT AS UMPIRE

Earlier we learned that the writers of the Constitution wanted to create a government that would be able to protect itself against tyranny. This was done by means of two great principles: separation of powers and federalism. But as we will see shortly, the Constitution does not say what should happen when one part of the government comes into conflict with another. Such conflicts have at times been severe—a bloody civil war was fought to settle a conflict between the federal government and the states. Other disagreements have been settled more peacefully through the courts' power of judicial review.

Judicial review is the power of the courts to decide whether a law passed by Congress is constitutional or not. It includes the power to review and overrule lower-court decisions. This power is not mentioned in the Constitution. It was established by a Supreme Court decision early in the nation's history.

To gain the power of judicial review the Court had to overcome two sources of opposition: (1) those who believed that Congress had the right to pass final judgment on the meaning of the Constitution and (2) those who believed that the state supreme courts had the right to interpret the Constitution in relation to the laws of their states.

Judicial Review of Acts of Congress

In the early years of the Republic the Supreme Court did not seem to have much power or influence. In 1801, when John Marshall was appointed Chief Justice, there were few cases before the Court and the other two branches of the government were controlled by Marshall's political enemies. Yet Marshall managed not only to maintain the independence of the Court but also to establish the Court's power to review acts of Congress.

The power of judicial review was established in the case of *Marbury* v. *Madison*.[1] This case developed out of the political rivalry between the Federalists, who were led by John Adams, and their opponents, who were led by Thomas Jefferson. Jefferson was elected President in 1800 after Adams had served for one term. Before leaving office Adams made a series of "midnight appointments" in order to "pack" the judicial branch with Federalists.

William Marbury had been appointed justice of the peace for the District of Columbia, but the Adams administration was unable to deliver his commission before Jefferson took office. Jefferson's Secretary of State, James Madison, refused to deliver the commission. Marbury turned to the Supreme Court for help, asking for a *writ of mandamus* requiring Madison to deliver the commission. According to Marbury, the Judiciary Act of 1789 had authorized the Court to issue such writs.

This case put the Court in an awkward position. It could order Madison to deliver the commission, but if he refused to comply with the order the Court would be unable to do anything about it. Or the Court could refuse to issue the writ, but then it would be saying that Madison had a right to act as he did, and this too would advertise the Court's lack of power. Marshall got out of this situation by declaring that the law on which Marbury's suit was based was unconstitutional.

Section 13 of the Judiciary Act had given the Supreme Court the power to issue writs of *mandamus* in original jurisdiction. *Original jurisdiction* means the power to decide a case in the first instance; that is, another court does not have to hear it first. But according to Article 3 of the Constitution, the Supreme Court has original jurisdiction only in cases affecting ambassadors and consuls and cases in which a state is a party. Therefore, Marshall reasoned, Section 13 violated the Constitution and the Court had no jurisdiction in the Marbury case.

---

[1] 1 Cranch 137 (1803).

Marshall thus ruled that the Supreme Court had the power to declare a law of Congress null and void. He based his ruling on three principles: (1) The Constitution is superior to congressional law; (2) the Court has the power to determine what the Constitution means; and (3) laws that violate the Constitution must be declared void by the courts.

Ever since the Marbury case the power of judicial review has been a subject of controversy. Historians argue over whether Marshall claimed powers that the Court was not entitled to or whether he was simply carrying out the intentions of the nation's founders. Political scientists argue over whether or not judicial review is compatible with democracy. There are no clear answers to these questions. What is clear is that judicial review is accepted, at least in principle, by the American people.

Actually, the power of judicial review has not been used very often: Only 85 congressional acts (or parts thereof) have been declared unconstitutional in the 176 years since *Marbury* v. *Madison*. But the Court has another power that it has used much more often: the power to review decisions of state courts.

Judicial Review of State Court Decisions

The Constitution does not specifically give the Supreme Court the authority to review the decisions of state courts. But one of the first things Congress did was to give the Court that power, which is known as *appellate jurisdiction*. Under Section 25 of the Judiciary Act of 1789, an appeal could be taken to the Supreme Court if the highest state court with jurisdiction over a case ruled that a federal law or treaty was unconstitutional or if it ruled in favor of a state law that was claimed to be unconstitutional or in violation of a national law or treaty. This power was not challenged until 1815, in the case of *Martin* v. *Hunter's Lessee*.[2]

The state of Virginia had passed a law denying aliens the right to inherit property. When one of the richest landowners in the state willed his estate to a British relative, Virginia refused to let the heir inherit the property and began selling it to its own citizens. The heir brought suit, claiming that the Virginia law violated a treaty with Great Britain, but the Virginia Court of Appeals ruled in favor of the state law. The Englishman then appealed to the United States Supreme Court, and the Court reversed the Virginia court's ruling.

The Virginia judges refused to comply with the Supreme Court's ruling, declaring that it violated state sovereignty; in other words, they held that the United States Supreme Court did not have appellate jurisdiction over state courts. The case went back to the Supreme Court. In its decision the Court

[2] 1 Wheaton 304 (1816).

argued that the Constitution was created not by the states but by "the people of the United States." The people had the right to deny the states any powers that were contrary to the basic goals of the Constitution. Therefore it made sense for the federal courts to have appellate jurisdiction over the state courts.

Moreover, it was necessary for federal courts to have appellate jurisdiction over state courts if the Constitution and federal laws and treaties were to be interpreted in a uniform way. Otherwise federal laws would come to mean different things in different states, and according to the Court, "The public mischiefs that would attend such a state of things would be truly deplorable."

The Martin case made the Supreme Court the official umpire in conflicts between the states and the federal government. But three years later the Court was again put to the test, this time in a case that challenged the "national supremacy" clause of the Constitution (Article 6, Section 2).

Judicial Review and National Supremacy

The case of *McCulloch* v. *Maryland*,[3] arose as a result of the creation of the second Bank of the United States by Congress in 1816. In order to protect state and private banks against competition from the national bank, several states, including Maryland, tried to tax the operations of the national bank. McCulloch, who was cashier of the Baltimore branch of the United States Bank, refused to pay the Maryland tax, claiming that it was unconstitutional. The state brought suit, and the state courts upheld the Maryland law. The national bank then appealed to the Supreme Court.

"The Power to Tax Is the Power to Destroy"　There were two constitutional issues to be resolved: (1) Did Congress have the power to charter a national bank? (2) If so, could a state tax such a bank? Chief Justice Marshall answered the second question by declaring that the states' power to tax was not unlimited. Although the Constitution did not specifically bar the states from taxing federal agencies, such a restriction was implied by the "national supremacy" clause. The power to tax, Marshall argued, implies the power to destroy, and if operations of the federal government could be taxed by the states they would be dependent on the will of the states. This was not the intent of the Constitution: No state had the power to "retard, impede, burden, or in any manner control, the operations of the constitutional laws enacted by Congress."

The Implied-Powers Doctrine　Did Congress have the power to charter a United States Bank? The State of Maryland claimed that the federal government was entitled only to the powers that were specifically mentioned in the

---

[3] *McCulloch* v. *Maryland* 4 Wheaton 316 (1819).

Constitution, and the Constitution did not mention the chartering of banks. Therefore Congress had gone beyond its constitutional authority in creating a national bank. Marshall answered by referring to general principles as well as to the wording of the Constitution.

In the first place, he argued, a government must have all the powers it needs to carry out its duties. In the second place, the Constitution states (in Article 1, Section 8) that Congress shall "have the power to make all laws which shall be necessary and proper for carrying into execution the foregoing powers [that is, the powers specifically listed in earlier sections]." It is clear from these words that the nation's founders intended Congress to have other powers besides those mentioned in the Constitution. This is the *implied-powers doctrine*. In Marshall's words,

> Let the end be legitimate, let it be within the scope of the Constitution, and all means which are appropriate, which are plainly adapted to that end, which are not prohibited, but consistent with the letter and spirit of the Constitution, are constitutional.

In the McCulloch case, the *ends* of borrowing money, raising an army, and regulating interstate commerce made it necessary for the national government to use the *means* of chartering a national bank.

THE COURT AS ADJUDICATOR

In this section we will discuss the second major function of the Supreme Court: adjudication. *Adjudication* is the power to interpret and apply the law in order to settle disputes. Suppose one citizen says a law banning school segregation means that public schools cannot discriminate against racial minorities while another citizen says it means that the school board must take action to integrate classrooms? What does the law "really" mean? Once the meaning of the law has been determined, people (or school boards) can be made to comply with the law. Through adjudication we find out not only what the law means but also whether individuals or groups have broken the law.

Judicial Power

The court's authority to interpret the law is its *judicial power*. Anyone who is affected by the court's interpretation of the law is legally required to accept it as final. But what is "the law"?

There are actually several kinds of law: constitutional law, statutory law, administrative law, and common law. *Constitutional law* is the Constitution itself plus the decisions made by the Supreme Court on occasions when it has had to interpret the Constitution. It is superior to all other kinds of law. *Statutory law* consists of all laws made by legislatures in an attempt to solve social problems or establish rules to cover particular situations. These laws too must be interpreted by the courts. *Administrative law* consists of the rules and regulations made by government agencies. These rules and regulations are not made by lawmakers, but they have the effect of law. *Common law* is judge-made law, that is, a set of decisions made by judges and considered binding in similar cases. It can be overridden by statutory or constitutional law.

Rules of Operation

In addition to the power to interpret the law, the courts must have rules of operation to guide them in settling disputes. One such rule is that, unlike legislatures, courts cannot take action to solve a social problem. They must wait for cases or controversies to come to them. For a dispute to qualify as a case or controversy, it must have the following characteristics:

1. There must be an *actual conflict* in which two parties have opposing interests. The courts will not give advisory opinions (e.g., on whether or not a proposed law is constitutional). Nor will they deal with friendly suits, that is, cases in which the parties have feigned a controversy.

2. One party must have a *standing to sue*. You cannot bring suit just because you have money and an axe to grind. To have a standing to sue, you must have a personal interest in a controversy (not simply an interest you share with other citizens), and that interest must be a legally protected right. For instance, a civil rights group could not sue to integrate schools unless it could be claimed that legal rights of students were being harmed by segregated schools.

3. The case may not involve a "political question." It is the courts that determine what is "political," and critics have claimed that this is just a way of passing the buck on issues that are too hot to handle. For example, the Supreme Court will not rule on whether a state has a "republican form of government" or not, although the Constitution declares that the United States "shall guarantee to every state in this Union a Republican form of government" (Article 4, Section 4).

The Adversary Process

The system by which court cases are decided in the United States is known as the *adversary process*. In this process, lawyers on both sides of a case present their clients' positions and a third, independent agent—the judge—decides on which side is the truth. Unlike judges in many other nations, American judges are not expected to find out the facts of a case. Rather, they are expected to make a decision (or instruct the jury to make a decision) on the basis of arguments and evidence presented in court by the opposing parties.

The adversary process has two main parts. First, the lawyers for the two parties present their arguments; then the judge evaluates those arguments. Since the lawyers are motivated by self-interest or their clients' interests and the judge is not actively engaged in bringing out the truth, it is often said that the adversary system does not produce justice. The answer to this criticism is threefold: (1) Other systems do not produce better results; (2) in addition to fighting for their clients' interests, lawyers are "officers of the court" and are therefore bound by certain ethical rules; and (3) whatever their motives, lawyers must prove that their clients' claims are just or are supported by the law.

The Appeals Process

There are two main reasons for having courts of appeal. One is to prevent miscarriages of justice. A large percentage of criminal convictions are reversed by appeals courts. A second reason is that the appeals process makes the interpretation of laws and the administration of justice more uniform.

In the federal system there is a third reason: Federal courts must have the power to review the decisions of state courts.

Appeals courts do not operate under the same rules as trial courts. The appeals court does not retry the case; instead, it works from the record of the original trial, the appeal briefs for the two sides, and oral arguments. There is no jury, but the appeal is heard by a panel of judges, usually three. To win a case on appeal it is necessary to prove that the lower court misconstrued the case, made procedural errors, applied the wrong legal rules, or clearly drew the wrong conclusion from the evidence.

ADJUDICATION AND PUBLIC POLICY

The power to adjudicate gives the courts a role in the policy-making process. You may be surprised at this. First you learn that the power to make laws belongs to the legislature and the power to interpret the law belongs to the courts. Then you are told that the courts also make policy. How can this be?

The answer is that laws are—and must be—very general. This is especially true of constitutions. Words like *unreasonable* (unreasonable searches or seizures), *equal* (equal protection of the law), and *due* (due process) appear in our Constitution. Anyone who has the power to interpret such language has the power to decide what the law means and how it will affect different interests, that is, to make policy. This is why the Supreme Court was able to rule that the principle of equal protection of the law did not prevent the states from creating segregated school systems and later to rule that it *did* prohibit such action—without a single word being added to or subtracted from the Constitution.

The power to interpret statutes passed by a legislature leads to the power to fill in the details of the law, perhaps to stretch the law, and in some cases to block the intent of the lawmakers. This way of making policy is more subtle and less dramatic than interpreting the Constitution, but it is an important aspect of the role of the courts in the American political system.

THE SUPREME COURT'S ROLE IN PUBLIC POLICY

The power to adjudicate, then, can also be seen as the power to make public policy. In the rest of this chapter we will explore the impact of Supreme Court decisions on public policy in the United States.

Establishing National Sovereignty

We have already described the Supreme Court's role in establishing national sovereignty. In the early 1800s the Marshall Court[4] developed the right of judicial review. This right was used to centralize power in two ways: (1) by protecting the government against actions by the states and (2) by interpreting the Constitution in such a way as to give broad powers to the national government. For a long time Marshall's judicial nationalism acted as a check on the tendency toward state sovereignty.

Establishing a Capitalist Economy

Between 1890 and 1937 the Court played a major role in defending American capitalism against efforts to limit its activities. The Civil War had put an end to the idea that the nation could have two different economic systems: a plantation economy based on slave labor and an industrial economy in which people sell their labor power for wages. The Industrial Revolution of the late 1800s shifted power from the countryside to the cities and from small businesses and farmers to bankers and industrialists. These new "captains of industry" often abused their power, and both the national government and the states began to put legal restrictions on their activities. The industrialists turned to the Supreme Court for protection against such restrictions, and the Court came to their rescue.

---

[4] The Supreme Court is often referred to by the name of the person who was Chief Justice at the time.

Substantive Due Process The basis for the Court's actions in relation to economic competition was the Constitution's provision for "due process." The Fourteenth Amendment prohibits the states from depriving "any person of life, liberty, or property without due process of law"; the Fifth Amendment places the same prohibition on the national government.

In the 1890s the Supreme Court gave the concept of due process a new meaning in the form of *substantive* due process. Due process became a means of preventing the government from doing certain things instead of a process to be followed in doing those things. In other words, any law the Court defined as an unreasonable restraint on property or liberty could be declared unconstitutional. Using this standard, the Court became a superlegislature, overturning laws passed by Congress and the states in an effort to control certain questionable business practices. It vetoed laws that set rates for public utilities and railroads, provided for minimum wages and maximum hours, tried to control child labor, and attempted to regulate prices.

Until the 1930s, the Supreme Court ruled that business practices such as child labor could not be prevented by government laws.

The Court vs. the President   In October of 1929 the stock market collapsed. Ruined speculators, bankrupt merchants, unemployed laborers, and farmers threatened with foreclosure joined in demanding large-scale governmental action to get the economy rolling again. President Roosevelt introduced laws to deal with the crisis, but many of those laws were blocked by the Court. Statutes intended to bring relief to the nation's farmers, the oil industry, the coal industry, and other groups were declared unconstitutional.

The Court felt that it had no choice: The new laws clearly violated the Constitution. But it could not ignore the rising tide of public, congressional, and presidential disapproval of its actions. The fact that the justices were appointed for life seemed to protect them against this tide, but in reality it did not.

The first challenge to the Court's anti-New Deal stand came in 1937. Roosevelt proposed a bill providing that whenever a federal judge aged 70 or over refused to retire, an additional judge could be added to that court. The maximum number of Supreme Court justices would be set at 15. If Congress had passed the bill, it would have allowed Roosevelt to "pack" the Court with judges who favored his New Deal policies.

Strictly speaking, it was not unconstitutional to change the size of the Supreme Court. This had been done several times in the past. But Congress did not pass Roosevelt's proposal. Instead, two members of the Court, Justice Roberts and Chief Justice Hughes, made what newspapers called "the switch in time that saved nine." Laws that had been found unconstitutional by votes of six to three were now upheld by a majority of five justices. They included the act by which Congress set up the National Labor Relations Board to deal with conflicts involving labor unions. When the four dissenting justices pointed out that in a long series of decisions the Court had ruled such an act unconstitutional, the Chief Justice simply said, "These cases are not controlling here."

Establishing Social Citizenship

Since the post-world War II years the Supreme Court has been concerned largely with social issues. Indeed, when Earl Warren was Chief Justice (1954–1969) the Court took the lead in promoting social reform. This was especially true in the area of racial segregation.

In the southern states the law demanded segregation of the races in public schools and other public facilities such as libraries, parks, and swimming pools. This policy was backed up by the "separate-but-equal" doctrine, which had been established in an 1896 Supreme Court decision.[5]

---

[5] *Plessy* v. *Ferguson* 163 U.S. 537 (1896).

In the 1950s and 1960s, the Supreme Court ruled that school segregation was unconstitutional, but it sometimes required federal troops to enforce the Court's rulings.

The segregation laws remained unchanged for over 50 years. But during this period the status of black Americans changed greatly. As they became better educated and gained political experience and influence, they began to demand their right of full equality. Many of their demands were made in the courts in a series of cases chosen and prepared by the NAACP. The best-known of these was the famous *Brown* v. *Board of Education of Topeka*.[6]

The schools for black children in Topeka, Kansas were equal to those for white children in every way. This made it possible to raise the question of whether legal segregation of students by race violated the constitutional principle of equality. In 1954 the Court ruled unanimously that "separate educational facilities are inherently unequal."

With this decision the Court changed the agenda of American politics. School desegregation is a complicated problem that cannot be easily solved, as the controversy at the end of this chapter makes clear. But the issue of whether legal segregation is constitutional or not was settled by the Brown decision.

Another area in which the Warren Court was active is law enforcement. The Court made several rulings on *procedural rights* (the right of people suspected or accused of crimes to receive fair treatment) that benefited the poor and the weak. Before the Warren Court's rulings it had been possible in some states for a poor citizen to be sentenced to prison without benefit of counsel, that is, without being defended by a lawyer. The Warren Court refused to tolerate such an unfair situation, and in the case of *Gideon* v. *Wainwright*[7] it

[6] 347 U.S. 483 (1954).
[7] 372 U.S. 335 (1963).

threw out Gideon's conviction because Gideon had not had the benefit of counsel. Counsel for the defense, the court said, is "fundamental to a fair trial," and if the defendant cannot afford to hire a lawyer the state must provide one.

In a related case, *Miranda* v. *Arizona*,[8] the Court ruled that police officers may not question suspects unless they inform them of their right to have counsel present and of their right to remain silent. These rights are intended to protect suspects against self-incrimination. In the adversary system a suspect is assumed to be innocent until proven guilty, and it is the state that must prove guilt. The defendant is not required to help the state make a case against him or her. If the police were not required to give the "Miranda warnings" they might be tempted to trick suspects into incriminating themselves or might try to force them to confess.

The Burger Court   During his 1968 campaign for the Presidency Richard Nixon promised to put "law-and-order" judges on the Supreme Court. Soon after he was elected he was able to keep his promise. Chief Justice Warren resigned, and Nixon appointed a well-known conservative, Warren Burger, as Chief Justice. Within three years Nixon was able to make three more appointments to the Court. (See Table 13.1.)

The Burger Court has taken a cautious position toward constitutional interpretation.[9] It has not pressed for reform, though it has made some rulings that may be viewed as reforms (e.g., decisions that make it harder for the states to use capital punishment, allow the use of busing to desegregate schools, and prevent the government from using wiretaps and similar devices without a search warrant). In some cases it has weakened the impact of the Warren Court's decisions. For example, in a housing discrimination case

---

[8] 377 U.S. 201 (1966).

[9] With one major exception: the ruling that states cannot forbid women to have abortions during the first six months of pregnancy.

TABLE 13.1   Members of the Supreme Court, 1978

Member	Appointed by	Year
William J. Brennan, Jr.	Eisenhower	1957
Potter Stewart	Eisenhower	1959
Byron R. White	Kennedy	1962
Thurgood Marshall	Johnson	1967
Warren E. Burger	Nixon	1969
Harry A. Blackmun	Nixon	1970
Lewis F. Powell, Jr.	Nixon	1971
William H. Rehnquist	Nixon	1971
John P. Stevens	Ford	1975

The Burger Court.

it ruled that white communities are not required to change their zoning laws to allow the construction of low-income housing for blacks unless those laws are specifically intended to exclude blacks.

Expanding Judicial Authority

Today a new chapter in constitutional history is being written. Federal and state courts are taking over the day-to-day operation of prisons, hospitals, and school systems. They are issuing specific court orders and thus are requiring state legislatures to collect new taxes in order to build or improve certain public facilities.

An example is the case of the Jacksonville, Florida jails. A federal district judge, Charles R. Scott, found conditions in those jails to be cruel and inhuman punishment: The cells were without windows, inhabited by rats and roaches as well as suspects, and strewn with filth, including urine and vomit. Sleep was nearly impossible, and muggings and homosexual rape were common. Inmates were not allowed to shower, shave, or brush their teeth. In addition, prisoners were subjected to "arbitrary, capricious and unlawful summary discipline" by prison guards.

Scott ordered numerous improvements: reduction of the number of inmates, hiring of more correction officers and nurses, construction of recreation facilities, purchase of hot trays for food. He also "threatened city and county officials with contempt (of court) if they failed to follow the order," and he appointed a U.S. marshal to make sure the improvements were made.

Florida state legislators complained that Scott was doing things that only the state legislature was entitled to do. Scott answered that if Jacksonville "chooses to operate a jail, it must do so without depriving inmates of their rights guaranteed by the Federal Constitution."[10]

Similar decisions have been made by judges in St. Louis, Baltimore, New Orleans, New York City, and elsewhere. Judges are running state hospitals in Alabama, Louisiana, and Mississippi, and a school district in Boston. Many people believe that we will see more such court interventions and that this is the greatest expansion of judicial authority since *Marbury* v. *Madison*. Others worry about this trend. Former Alabama Governor George Wallace, for example, says the courts are taking over functions of the legislative and executive branches, in violation of the principle of separation of powers. "It is government by the judicial branch," he says. "The judges, in their robes, lean back and say, 'You spend this money.' They don't say how to raise it."

LIMITS ON THE POWER OF THE COURT

Clearly the Supreme Court has had a tremendous impact on public policy in the past two centuries, and will continue to play an important role in American political life. But the court is not all-powerful. Here we will describe some of the limits on its power.

1. *The Constitution*. The Court does not have a completely free hand in interpreting the Constitution. It may decide how freedom of speech may be limited, but it cannot rule that the Constitution does not guarantee freedom of speech.
2. *Past Decisions*. The Court usually uses past decisions as guidelines in dealing with similar problems. This principle, known as *stare decisis,* results in continuity and predictability in the law. Sometimes the Court does not follow past decisions, but in such cases the Court must prove the need for new guidelines.
3. *Political Factors*. As mentioned earlier, the Court cannot isolate itself from the currents of American politics.
4. *Amendments*. The Court's interpretation of the Constitution can be overruled by a constitutional amendment. Thus the Court's decisions may not be final after all. For example, when the Court ruled that the government could not tax income, the Sixteenth Amendment was passed, allowing it to do so.
5. *Noncompliance*. The Supreme Court depends on the executive branch to enforce its decisions. This makes it possible for the President to weaken those decisions by means of a go-slow policy or delaying tactics. State officials can also limit the

---

[10] Quoted by Martin Tolchin, "Intervention by Courts Arouses Deepening Disputes," *New York Times,* 24 April 1977. © 1977 by The New York Times Company. Reprinted by permission.

The Supreme Court justices take a break.

effectiveness of a Court ruling, especially if Congress and the President are not eager to see the ruling enforced. This happened in the years just after the school desegregation case.

6. *Public acceptance.* The Court can be effective only if it has the acceptance of the public. This involves two somewhat contradictory principles. On the one hand, the Court must not get either too far behind or too far ahead of public opinion. On the other, it must not follow public opinion too closely. The goal of the Court is to achieve justice. If it bends too easily to the public's will, it may lose contact with ethical principles. Justice is an ethical goal, not easily achieved but worth the effort.

CONTROVERSY

Within a few years after the Brown decision it became clear that ending legal segregation would not necessarily result in integrated schools. In many parts of the country blacks and other minority groups live in separate neighborhoods from whites. If children go to neighborhood schools, they will go to schools that are segregated as a result of housing patterns (this is called de *facto* segregation). Therefore some courts decided that segregation could be eliminated only by busing schoolchildren to other neighborhoods or other communities. Should they have made this decision?

One Side

According to the Brown ruling, segregated schools violate the Constitution whether the segregation is legal or de facto. To put an end to de facto segregation, white students must be bused into black areas and black students must be bused into white areas. The courts may not be the best place to make such regulations, but the President, Congress, and the state legislatures have their hands tied by political pressures. If they cannot act effectively on the issue, the courts have a constitutional duty to do so.

The Supreme Court is aware that it has taken on a big job that it must do alone, with little help from the executive and legislative branches. It is true that the Court has not made a final decision on how schools should be desegregated, but this may be due to the complexity of the issue and the intense feelings on both sides.

The Other Side

Some courts have ruled that the Brown decision applies only to cases in which segregation is a result of *intentional* discrimination. The only way to end de facto segregation is to get rid of the ghettos. By ordering the busing of schoolchildren from one neighborhood to another, the courts are taking over the lawmaking role of the legislature, ignoring public opinion, and reading the Constitution any way they like.

Besides, court decisions can be avoided. Laws have been passed that limit the use of busing to desegregate schools, and some members of Congress have considered introducing a constitutional amendment prohibiting the use of busing for this purpose. When the Supreme Court made the Brown ruling it was making a sociological decision, and such decisions are hard to enforce—it is not easy to change people's attitudes, beliefs, and life styles.

Finally, there is the question of what the majority of the people want. It is not yet clear whether the courts are going against the will of the majority. If this is the case, we must ask, Do the courts have a right to enforce busing to integrate schools if this policy is not supported by the majority of citizens?

The Court System

The American court system has two parts, the federal system and the state system. The Supreme Court has appellate jurisdiction over both parts. (See Figure 13.1.)

The Federal Judicial System

The federal judicial system has three layers. The Supreme Court is the top layer; below it are the circuit courts, and at the bottom are the district courts.

The Supreme Court. The Supreme Court has both original and appellate jurisdiction. It has original jurisdiction only in cases involving ambassadors and other foreign diplomats and disputes between states. It has appellate jurisdiction in cases appealed from lower federal courts and state supreme courts.

Cases reach the Supreme Court from other courts through one of two procedures: appeal or certiorari. Cases that come by the first route may be appealed to the Court as a matter of right. Others are appealed by a petition for a

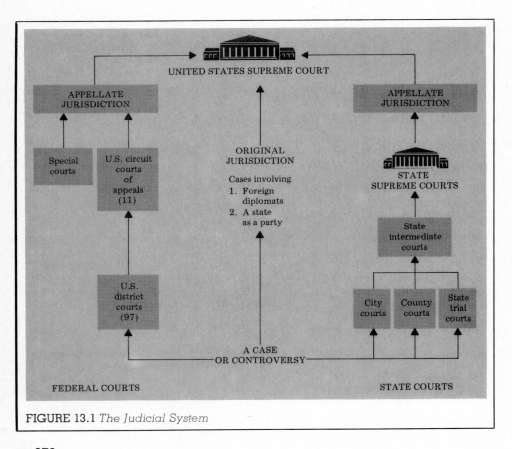

FIGURE 13.1 *The Judicial System*

writ of certiorari, which may be granted or rejected at the discretion of the Court. In both kinds of cases the Court makes a preliminary decision as to whether the case involves issues that are important enough for it to consider. If four or more justices vote in favor of hearing the case, it will be accepted. Otherwise the lower court's decision stands.

Circuit Courts. Most cases come to the Supreme Court on appeal from *circuit courts.* Today there are 11 such courts, each with jurisdiction over a particular part of the country, or *circuit.* The circuit courts were created in 1891 to reduce the Supreme Court's workload and to improve the handling of cases by the federal judicial system. Each of these courts has from 3 to 15 judges, depending on the number of cases generally tried in the circuit. It hears only cases that are appealed from lower courts, and only the Supreme Court can review its decisions.

District Courts. Most of the cases that enter the federal court system are tried by the 97 district and 4 territorial courts. Large states like California have as many as four district courts, but most states have one. A large district court can have up to 24 judges; however, the workload is divided so that only 3 judges hear a case. District courts hear cases involving citizens from different states (e.g., an accident involving an Iowa driver and an Illinois pedestrian). They also try cases involving violations of federal laws (e.g., immigration, income tax, mail fraud, etc.).

State Judicial Systems

Each state has its own judicial system, and some of those systems are very complicated. Generally, however, a state court system contains the following levels:

Trial Courts. These courts are called different things in different areas. They try minor criminal cases such as traffic violations or disturbances of the peace. In rural areas these are justice-of-the-peace courts; in cities they are called police courts, city courts, or municipal courts.

More serious crimes are heard in major trial courts, sometimes called superior or county courts. Here the defendant might have a jury trial. These courts try murder, burglary, rape, and other felony cases.

Appeals Courts. Larger states have intermediate courts of appeal. These courts review decisions of trial courts at the county or municipal level.

State Supreme Courts. Each state has a supreme court that hears cases on appeal from lower state courts and has original jurisdiction in some cases.

The Relationship Between Federal and State Courts

Most cases, both civil and criminal, are tried in state courts, since most crimes involve violations of state laws and most civil cases are covered either by state statutory law or by common law.

The jurisdiction of federal courts is outlined in Article 3, Section 2 of the Constitution. Cases come to federal courts because they involve interpretations of the Constitution, congressional laws, or treaties, or because they are conflicts between citizens of different states, between two or more states, or between a state and a foreign country.

The American judicial system is made more confusing by the fact that Congress has given the state courts *concurrent* jurisdiction with the federal courts over cases of the types just mentioned. The Supreme Court can review state court decisions, but it hears only a small fraction of the cases brought to it. As a result the decision of the highest court in a state often becomes the final decision in a given case—even when a federal question is involved.

Even if the Supreme Court wanted to and had the time, it could not review all state supreme court decisions. Questions involving interpretation of state laws are settled by the state's highest court, and the question of whether a state law is contrary to that state's constitution is also settled by the highest court in the state.

"A democracy is a government that gives citizens the freedom to speak and worship as they wish; in a democracy a person cannot be arbitrarily jailed for unpopular speech or acts."

"A democracy is a government in which laws and regulations are based on the will of the majority."

These two statements describe principles that are basic to democracy: individual freedom and majority rule. These principles often clash with each other, however, and the conflicts that result are the subject of this chapter.

MAJORITY RULE AND MINORITY RIGHTS

Ever since the nation's founding, the principle of majority rule has been in conflict with the principle of minority rights. If majority rule was the only rule for democratic decision making, the majority would be free to do whatever it wished to a minority group. It could take away their jobs, their homes, their freedom, even their lives. And it would all be "democratic" because the majority favored it.

Many writers have warned of the "tyranny of the majority," or democratic tyranny. In many ways it is more frightening than the tyranny of a smaller group, since it is harder to resist a large group. The nation's founders were concerned about this possibility. As we have seen, they designed a government that would limit the power of the majority as well as prevent small groups from gaining too much power.

If majority rule is absolute, tyranny will result. On the other hand, if minority rights are absolute—if minority groups have the right to disobey the government—society will become a war of all against all. Each of us, after all, is a minority of one. So where do you draw the line between majority rule and minority rights?

Historically, several kinds of rights have been protected against majority rule:

1. The right to freedom of speech, a free press, and freedom of assembly.
2. The right to freedom of religion.
3. The right to have one's property protected from arbitrary acts of the government.
4. The right to have one's person protected from arbitrary acts of the government.

Each of these rights has given rise to major controversies, and in many cases the Supreme Court has been called upon to settle the question. In the rest of this chapter we will look at the role of the Court in relation to majority rule and minority rights.

FREEDOM OF SPEECH, PRESS, AND ASSEMBLY

The First Amendment to the Constitution states that "Congress shall make no law . . . abridging the freedom of speech, or of the press, or the right of the people peaceably to assemble. . . ." These three rights are known as *civil liberties* or *First Amendment freedoms,* and many people believe they must be protected if democracy is to survive.[1]

The First Amendment freedoms are central to a democratic system because they are the key to effective majority rule. Effective majority rule depends on knowledge of the possible choices in a given situation and on the ability of people with different views to try to convince others that their solution is the right one. Only if people are free to present all sides of an issue can there be a real choice.

Such freedom is very important to minorities, too. If majority rule were the only accepted way of making decisions, minority groups would have no influence at all. But the freedoms of speech, press, and assembly give minorities a chance to persuade others to join them and form a new majority. To put it another way, the First Amendment freedoms are supposed to prevent any majority from becoming "frozen."

Conflicts Over Freedom of Speech

The First Amendment freedoms have a special place in democratic thought. Indeed, some people claim that they are absolute rights that must not be limited in any way. "The truth" cannot be legislated; it must be found in the "free marketplace of ideas." Therefore a free society should never bar any group from expressing its views, no matter how much harm might come from the expression of those views.

However, there are strong arguments against absolute freedom of speech. For one thing, it clearly violates the principle of majority rule. Suppose a majority of the American people want to prohibit a particular form of speech, such as speeches by communists or atheists or obscene books or movies. What is the "democratic" thing to do—limit freedom of speech or violate the principle of majority rule? This is not a hypothetical question. Situations have arisen in which the majority favored banning speeches by communists or atheists or forbidding the selling of many books and magazines and the showing of many movies. Such situations show that conflicts over freedom of speech usually arise when some other value is threatened. Let's look at some examples.

---

[1] The First Amendment protects these rights against acts of Congress, but the Supreme Court has extended this protection so that it covers acts of state governments as well.

Libel   The right to say whatever you want is a value, but so is the right to be protected against unjustified verbal attacks. Libel laws, which protect citizens against such attacks, put limitations on freedom of speech.

You may agree that such limitations are desirable. In principle, freedom of speech and press should be protected up to the point at which an individual is unfairly hurt or offended. Then the libel laws should apply. But in practice it is not easy to follow this principle. For example, at what point does newspaper criticism of a public official become a libelous attack?

On this issue the courts have recently tended to allow a wide range of criticism, even if it might be damaging. The right to criticize public officials is basic to democracy. In order to make sure the press is free to criticize the activities of the government, it is necessary to risk some weakening of the individual's right to be protected against unfair attacks.[2]

Obscenity   Obscenity is another area in which the courts try to balance conflicting interests. On one side is freedom of the press, the right to publish what one wants regardless of its content. On the other is the right of citizens to protect themselves and their children against material they find offensive. The principle behind obscenity laws is that all literature and movies should be allowed up to the point at which they become pornographic, that is, ap-

---

[2] *New York Times* v. *Sullivan* 376 U.S. 254 (1964).

Recent court decisions hold that local standards can determine what is pornography.

peal only to "base or prurient" interests and have no "redeeming social value."

Most states have laws banning pornography, but it is hard to decide what books and movies are pornographic. Some people believe many great literary works are so damaging to morals that they should be banned. The Supreme Court has long tried to define what kinds of material may be banned by state and local obscenity laws and what kinds are protected by the First Amendment. But because of the difficulty in defining obscenity, it has found itself deciding what is obscene on a case-by-case basis.

In 1973 the Court took a new approach to the problem. It ruled that each community could decide for itself what kinds of material are obscene.[3] Under this ruling a community could decide whether it would allow *Hustler* magazine to be sold or the movie *Deep Throat* to be shown. The issue is far from settled, however. There are no clear guidelines for determining community standards. In addition, publishers of nationally circulated magazines such as *Hustler* and *Screw* have been convicted for selling obscene publications in communities like Cincinnati and Wichita, even though their magazines are published elsewhere. In effect, those communities are being used to set standards for the whole nation.

Thus the laws on pornography and obscenity are still vague, and the Supreme Court is still trying to define the boundary between the right to limit pornography and the right of freedom of speech.

Freedom of Speech and National Security

Many conflicts over freedom of speech are concerned with national security. Freedom of speech protects people with unpopular political opinions, especially opinions that are highly critical of the government. The right to express such opinions, however, may clash with the right of the society to defend itself.

Here again it is easier to state principles than to apply them. In principle, freedom of speech does not give citizens the right to commit sabotage, and Congress has passed laws punishing those who commit or try to commit such acts. In practice, however, these laws are hard to apply because the boundary between speech and action is not clear. Consider the following examples:

1. What if I plan an act of sabotage with someone else? I tell him where to plant the bomb and when to do it. I only "speak." He does the actual bombing. Is my "speech" protected by the First Amendment?
2. What if I make a speech at a public meeting saying that people should sabotage

---

[3] *Miller v. California* 413 U.S. 15 (1973).

government operations? After the meeting some of those who heard me speak go out and plant bombs in government buildings. Is my "speech" protected?

3. What if I make a speech like the one described in Example 2 but no one acts? Is my "speech" protected?

4. What if I make a speech that merely says that "there are times when it would be justifiable to sabotage the government"? (That is, I do not directly advocate such sabotage.) Suppose someone hears the speech, decides that now is such a time, and attempts an act of sabotage. Is my "speech" protected?

5. Suppose I write a book on the history of sabotage and treat some famous saboteurs sympathetically? Is my "speech" protected?

These examples show how hard it is to know whether one is dealing with speech or action. In Example 1 it seems clear that my speech directly advocates action; perhaps it does so in Example 2 as well. But what about Example 4? Is saying that "there are times when one must act" the same as advocating action? Similarly, in Example 1 it seems clear that my speech leads to actual action, but can we say the same for Example 2?

The "speech" in Example 1 probably would not be covered by the First Amendment. It is part of a criminal action and can be punished without violating the Constitution. Example 5, by contrast, is a case of "speech" that is protected by the First Amendment, even though someone might commit acts of sabotage after reading the book.

Examples 2, 3, and 4 are in between. It is not clear whether the courts would consider them speeches protected by the Constitution or activities punishable under federal law. In many such cases the courts have tried to apply the "clear and present danger" doctrine,[4] in which speech is punishable only when it may lead straight to illegal action. But this is just another way of stating the problem of deciding where speech ends and action begins.

Conspiracy and Subversion

Attempts to limit civil liberties are usually made during national emergencies —especially war. At such times the dangers of conspiracy and subversion are of major concern to the government and the public, and civil liberties suffer as a result. In World War II, for example, all Americans of Japanese descent were moved from the West Coast to "relocation centers" in the Midwest, where they were kept until the war was over regardless of whether there was evidence that they were involved in subversive activities.

Since World War II the issue of civil liberties versus national security has centered on a series of laws intended to block conspiracy and subversion.

---

[4] First stated by Justice Oliver Wendell Holmes in *Schenck* v. *United States* 249 U.S. 47 (1919).

Civil liberties have sometimes been suspended in wartime. Japanese-Americans were moved to "relocation centers" in World War II.

These laws were passed during the "cold war" period and were aimed primarily at communists.

The Smith Act of 1940 The Smith Act made it a crime to teach or advocate the violent overthrow of the U.S. government. In 1951 the Supreme Court upheld the conviction of Eugene Dennis, head of the U.S. Communist party, under this act.[5] Critics of this decision argued that Dennis was convicted for speech ("teaching and advocating"), not action, but the Court held that the government has a right to protect itself against the actions he advocated.

In later decisions the Court has generally upheld the Smith Act, but it has interpreted it narrowly and placed the burden of proof on the government. In this way it has limited the extent to which the law can be applied without ever saying that the law violates freedom of speech.

The McCarran Act of 1950 The McCarran Act, passed at the beginning of the Korean War, requires registration of communist and communist front organizations. In 1961 the Supreme Court held that although the registration requirements are constitutional, making party members register would cause them to testify against themselves, and this violates the Fifth Amendment.[6] As in the case of the Smith Act, the Court did not declare the law unconstitutional, but it interpreted it narrowly so as to limit its applicability.

---

[5] *Dennis et al.* v. *United States* 341 U.S. 494 (1951).
[6] *Communist Party* v. *Subversive Activities Control Board* 367 U.S. 1 (1961).

The "cold war" after World War II resulted in a number of court cases about the rights of communists to free speech.

Symbolic Speech

The Supreme Court has defined speech to include symbolic acts such as wearing an armband as a symbol of protest or hanging the American flag upside-down as a symbol of political distress. In 1974 it ruled that a person who sewed the flag on the seat of his pants could not be punished under a Massachusetts law against abusing the flag. According to the Court, the law was so vague that it was unconstitutional.[7] Similarly, the Court overturned the conviction of a student who protested the Vietnam War by attaching a peace symbol to the flag and hanging it upside-down. It reasoned that the value of protecting national symbols was not as great as the value of freedom of political expression.

Freedom of the Press and the Pentagon Papers

One of the most dramatic decisions of the Supreme Court was its ruling in the Pentagon Papers case. The case arose when the government tried to prevent publication of the Pentagon Papers, a series of documents containing top-secret information about the Vietnam War. (The United States was still involved in the war at the time.) Such an attempt to block publication is called *prior restraint*. The government claimed that publication of the papers would do "grave and irreparable" damage to national security. The *New*

---

[7] *Smith* v. *Goguen* 94 S. Ct. 1242 (1974).

York Times and the *Washington Post* argued that the First Amendment gave them the right to publish the papers. The Court ruled in favor of the newspapers.[8]

This decision has been called a victory for freedom of the press. But it was not a clear-cut victory. The newspapers were able to publish the Pentagon Papers, but the nine justices wrote nine opinions on the case—six in favor of the newspapers' position and three in favor of the government's. Most of the justices said that prior restraint could be allowed if publication of the material in question would "result in direct, immediate, and irreparable damage to our nation or its people." In addition, the Court left open the possibility that the newspapers could be prosecuted *after* publication for any damage to the national interest that resulted from publication of the material.

Freedom of speech or of the press, thus, is not an absolute right. The need for national security cannot be used to make it illegal to criticize the government, but the courts' interpretation of the Constitution and congressional law makes it clear that First Amendment freedoms *can* be limited in some circumstances.

FREEDOM OF RELIGION

The First Amendment also guarantees freedom of religion: "Congress shall make no law respecting an establishment of religion, or prohibiting the free exercise thereof." This statement has two parts. The first, known as the "nonestablishment" clause, bars the government from supporting any religious establishment. The second, the "free exercise" clause, bars it from interfering with the freedom of Americans to worship as they wish. These clauses are basic to civil peace, since in a society with many religions, severe conflict can arise if the government favors one over another.

Yet the words of the First Amendment do not settle all issues related to religion. The amendment was intended to prohibit a state-supported religion and to separate church and state. But it is not clear how wide that separation is supposed to be. Does the fact that the government cannot establish a church mean that it cannot give aid to parochial schools or provide buses for children going to such schools? Does the fact that the government cannot prevent individuals from practicing their religion mean that it cannot forbid polygamy or snake handling or require citizens to pay taxes or serve in the armed forces if they try to avoid taxes or military service on the grounds of religious conviction.?

As in the case of freedom of speech, the Constitution leaves such questions unanswered. As a result we have a situation in which the government

---

[8] *New York Times Co.* v. *United States* 403 U.S. 713 (1971).

respects the separation of church and state in general, but not completely. The Supreme Court has ruled that the government cannot give aid to parochial schools but that it can provide buses for children who go to such schools. People who refuse to salute the flag for religious reasons cannot be forced to do so, but they cannot refuse to pay taxes for religious reasons. These and other seeming inconsistencies stem from the need to balance one value against others.

This is especially true in the field of education. The conflict between the rights of minority religious groups and the value of obedience to laws based on the will of the majority has focused on the schools. Examples are the so-called flag salute cases, school prayers, and government aid to religious schools.

The Flag Salute Cases

The flag salute cases arose out of the Jehovah's Witnesses' refusal to worship images; this includes forbidding their children to salute the American flag. Many state laws required a flag-salute ceremony at the beginning of each school day in order to teach children respect for national symbols. In 1940 the Supreme Court ruled that children of Jehovah's Witnesses could be required to salute the flag,[9] but three years later it reversed itself.[10] The Court's reasoning in the second case was that the value of the flag salute ceremony was not as great as the value of freedom of conscience.

The 1943 ruling was a landmark in the attempt to draw the line between freedom of conscience and the right of the government to demand respect for its institutions. The issue has not been settled, however. For example, in 1977 a federal court overturned a New Jersey law requiring schoolchildren who did not take part in the pledge of allegiance to stand at attention during the ceremony. The court ruled that the children could remain seated as long as they were not unruly.

School Prayers

The First Amendment was intended to prevent the government from favoring one religion over another. But does it allow the government to favor religious people over nonreligious people? In recent years the Supreme Court has protected the rights of nonbelievers. For example, in 1972 it ruled that it is unconstitutional to require chapel attendance at the nation's military academies. Perhaps the most controversial issue related to the rights of nonbelievers is the issue of school prayers. Does it violate freedom of religion if the

---

[9] *Minersville School District* v. *Gobitis* 310 U.S. 586 (1940).
[10] *West Virginia State Board of Education* v. *Barnette* 319 U.S. 624 (1943).

government supports school prayers—even if the prayers are nonsectarian and not compulsory?

Many school systems traditionally opened the school day with a prayer of some sort, but in 1962 the Supreme Court barred such prayers.[11] It ruled that a New York school district had violated the Constitution by requiring that the school day begin with a nonsectarian prayer, even though children could be excused from the prayer at the request of their parents. The Court held that such prayers violated the separation of church and state because they were required by the government.

In this and similar cases the Court was taking the side of a small minority. Many polls have shown that the majority of Americans favor school prayers. The parents who objected to the prayers (and took their case to court) were a small and generally unpopular group. Critics of the Court's decisions on this issue argue that nonbelievers have a right to expect tolerance for their views, but that such tolerance is expressed in the fact that their children do not have to take part in the prayers. Supporters of the Court's position argue that the Constitution requires more than simple tolerance.

Again, the issue is not settled. Some people have called for a constitutional amendment to allow prayer in the schools. In addition, the Court's decisions are not always followed in practice. Many school districts still allow some form of prayer despite the Court's ruling.

Government Aid to Religious Schools

Does it violate the separation of church and state if the government gives aid to private religious schools? Opponents of such aid say that it would amount to discrimination in favor of particular religions. On the other hand, those who favor such aid argue that these schools contribute to society by educating children. Parents who send their children to religious schools, for which they pay tuition, support the public schools through their tax payments. Thus they bear a double burden because of their religious beliefs.

The Supreme Court's decisions in this area have been quite mixed. In 1947 the Court upheld a New Jersey law providing payments for bus transportation to parochial schools. These payments helped some children obtain religious training. Yet in its ruling the court declared that "the First Amendment has erected a wall between church and state. That wall must be kept high and remain impregnable. We could not approve the slightest breach."[12]

Other decisions have been equally contradictory. A state can provide transportation to parochial schools and pay for their textbooks, but it cannot pay for the maintenance or repair of such schools. State funds can, however,

---

[11] *Engel* v. *Vitale* 370 U.S. 421 (1962) and *Abington School District* v. *Schempp* 374 U.S. 203 (1963).
[12] *Everson* v. *Board of Education* 330 U.S. 1 (1947).

be used to aid church-related colleges in constructing new facilities. The Court's position seems to be that, while government funds should not be used to support the teaching of religious beliefs, the government cannot limit freedom of religion by denying citizens standard governmental services such as police protection. Free transportation to parochial schools is designed to promote the welfare of children, not their religious education. The reasoning behind the granting of funds to church-related colleges is that college training is less likely to involve religious indoctrination than elementary and secondary education.

PROPERTY RIGHTS

In the 1780s there was no conflict between property rights and human rights. The Revolutionary War was fought to protect the rights of liberty and property. "The true foundation of republican government," wrote Thomas Jefferson, "is the equal right of every citizen, in his person and in his property." This did *not* mean that every citizen should have an equal amount of property. It meant that property was to be protected by the government.

Protection of Property Rights

Protection of property rights was written into the Constitution. For example, the Constitution contains a just-compensation clause. The nation's founders knew that privately owned land might be needed for public facilities, but they provided for compensation for the owner out of the public treasury. This and other laws protect private property, and standing behind those laws is the police.

What do we mean by *property rights*? We mean the right to own something and to prevent others from using it. We also mean the right to sell or trade a thing we own, whether it is tangible property (e.g., a car or a house) or intangible property (e.g., stocks or bonds). In addition, we mean the right to will our property to our heirs. But the courts have placed many restrictions on private property.

The Property Owner vs. the Public Interest

Restrictions on property rights often rest on the claim that the public interest is a greater value than the rights of property. The owner of a 300-horsepower car cannot drive it at its highest speed; the homeowner who has a diseased elm tree in his or her yard must cut it down; the builder of an apartment complex must include parking space for tenants. Each of these property owners might well ask, "Who are they to tell me what to do with my property?"

"They" is the government, which claims to act in the public's interest. But it is not easy to define the public interest. The definition varies from one area to another and from one time to another. Billboards are a good example. For a long time the right to lease land to a billboard company was not challenged, and as a result our public highways were surrounded by private advertisements. Today, however, some local and state governments are restricting this practice. They are responding to a new definition of the public interest, one that objects to having scenery blocked by billboards.

The Property Owner vs. Human Rights

On Election Day in 1964 the California ballot included a proposal for an amendment to the state constitution guaranteeing the right of property owners to sell, lease, or rent their property to anyone they choose. This proposal sounds reasonable enough, but in reality it was a response to an open-occupancy law passed by the state legislature. The law banned racial discrimination in the sale and rental of property. The voters passed the amendment, but it was declared unconstitutional by the state supreme court, and this ruling was upheld by the United States Supreme Court.

Here is a clear case of property rights (the right to do what one wants with one's own home) versus human rights (the right of blacks not to be discriminated against in housing). When two constitutional rights come into conflict, it is the courts that must make the final decision. Sometimes the courts take the side of the minority against the majority. This was the case in California, where the property rights of the majority were restricted in favor of the human rights of the minority. At other times the property rights of a minority are restricted in favor of the human rights of the majority. Inheritance taxes can be seen in this light. They attempt to redistribute the wealth of the richer groups in society to the majority who are less well off. (As we saw earlier in the book, however, this redistribution does not go very far.)

Despite such restrictions on property rights, private ownership has an important place in our society. Thomas Jefferson made this point when he remarked that "everyone, by his property, or by his satisfactory situation, is interested in the support of law and order." By "the support of law and order" he meant the use of the legal and police powers of the government to protect private property.

THE RIGHT OF PRIVACY

Does the Constitution protect the citizen's right of privacy? This is a new area of constitutional interpretation. Until recently many states had laws intended to regulate the sexual activities of citizens. Such laws banned so-called deviant sexual behavior or the use of contraceptive devices. In addition, most states made abortions illegal.

In recent years, however, the Supreme Court has recognized a right to privacy in such matters; that is, it has ruled that the state has no business trying to regulate the intimate behavior of citizens. This right is not mentioned in the Constitution, but the Court has decided that it is implied by the Fourth Amendment protection against "unreasonable" searches and seizures, the Fifth Amendment protection against self-incrimination, and the "other rights" mentioned in the Ninth Amendment. The Court cited these rights when it overturned a Connecticut law that made it illegal to use any drug or device to prevent contraception.[13] The right of privacy has also been used to challenge Virginia's sodomy law and laws prohibiting the hiring of homosexuals. In these cases the courts have expanded the range of private activities that are protected from public control—even though the majority of the people may disapprove of those activities.

The most controversial issue involving the right of privacy is abortion. In 1973 the Supreme Court overturned antiabortion laws in 46 states, holding that the right of privacy includes the right of a woman to end a pregnancy during the first three months after conception. Few Court decisions have aroused as much conflict as this one. The Catholic Church, along with many other groups, opposes abortion. These groups claim to represent the constitutional rights of unborn children. Their opponents claim to represent a woman's right to choose whether or not to bear a child.

[13] *Griswold v. Connecticut* 381 U.S. 479, 490–492 (1965).

The Supreme Court struck down antiabortion laws, but the issue remains controversial.

Since 1973 the Court has expanded the right of abortion. In 1976 it overturned a state law requiring that a married woman obtain her husband's consent before having an abortion, as well as a law requiring that a minor obtain permission from her parents to have an abortion. On the other hand, the Court has upheld a federal law against using medicaid funds to pay for abortions. A woman has a right to have an abortion, but the federal government is not required to pay for it.

It is likely that the controversy over abortion will continue for some time, since both sides have strong feelings about the issue. In fact some antiabortion groups are seeking an amendment to the Constitution to overrule the Supreme Court's 1973 decision.

CONTROVERSY

Should prayer be allowed in the public schools?

One Side

Communities should be allowed to require that the school day begin with a prayer. If some communities do not want to pass such a law, that is all right. But some communities are quite religious, and if their citizens feel that praying is a good way to start the day, they should have the right to require prayer in their schools. Besides, children who do not want to take part in the prayer can be allowed to leave the room, and the prayer can be nonsectarian. In this way no limits are placed on individual freedom. If school prayers are banned, the Supreme Court is restricting the freedom of communities to run their schools the way they wish.

The Other Side

It is true that many Americans would like the school day to begin with a prayer, and in many communities a large majority would favor such a law. But minority groups must be protected against this kind of majority rule. School prayers break down the constitutional barrier between church and state and amount to state support of religion.

Moreover, the rights of minorities are not protected by allowing their children to leave the room during the prayer. Such children will feel pressure to be like the majority. Prayer therefore simply does not belong in the public schools.

White House,
State House,
and City Hall

Throughout this book we have been talking about "the government." It would have been more accurate to say "the governments." A major fact of American political life is that there are many governments in the United States. The federal government, of course, is the biggest and most powerful of these, but it is by no means the only one. There are also 50 state governments and a wide variety of local governments. In this chapter we will concentrate on the relationships among the various levels of government.

TYPES OF GOVERNMENTS

There are three basic types of governments: unitary governments, confederations, and federations. In a *unitary government,* state and local governments are subordinate to the central government, which creates them and can abolish them if it wishes. Policy is made by the central government. Many European nations have unitary systems; the French government is a good example.

In a *confederation,* by contrast, the central government is subordinate to the state governments. It has little power over individual citizens and acts only through the state governments. An example is the system set up by the Articles of Confederation in 1783.

A *federal* system is somewhere between a unitary government and a confederation. Neither level of government is subordinate to the other. Both the central government and the state governments are protected by the Constitution; neither level can abolish the other, and each is independent of the other. Both levels have direct power over citizens.

The government of the United States is usually described as a federal system. But in reality it does not fit neatly into any of the categories we have described. If in a federal system the central and state governments are supposed to be equal, the United States is not a federal system, since the state governments are clearly subordinate to the central government. If in a federal system each level of government has certain powers that the other cannot take away, the United States is not a federal system, since the Supreme Court has ruled that laws passed by Congress are the "supreme law of the land" and override any state laws that interfere with them. In these ways the United States resembles a unitary system.

On the other hand, the states are not created by the central government and cannot be abolished by it. The state governments are independent centers of power. They can raise and spend money, and they have a lot of control over our lives.

The United States, thus, is a federation because the Constitution guarantees the survival of the states and because the state governments have important powers. Yet it resembles a unitary system because the central government is clearly dominant and could increase its powers if it wanted to.

Where are decisions made in such a system? How is power divided? How are the arguments for centralization and decentralization balanced? The nation's founders tried to divide power by assigning different responsibilities to the central and state governments. But in practice there has never been a simple division of labor between the two main levels of government. Instead, we have a system of shared and overlapping powers, made more complex by the existence of a large number of local governments in addition to the central and state governments.

LOCAL GOVERNMENTS

There are many, many governments in America. Besides the central and state governments, there are county governments, cities, towns, townships, and districts for all sort of purposes: education, sewage disposal, recreation, mosquito abatement, and many others. In fact there are almost 80,000 local government units in the United States today: 18,517 municipalities, 16,991 townships, 23,885 special districts, and 15,781 school districts.[1]

[1] U.S. Department of Commerce, Bureau of the Census, *Census of Governments* (Washington, D.C., 1972).

There are almost 80,000 local government units in America.

These units are governments because they have the power to raise money and spend it. Some, such as city and county governments, raise funds and spend them on a wide range of programs. Others, such as special districts, deal with specific problems.

The American educational system provides a good example of the governmental nature of single-purpose districts. In the United States, more money is spent on education than on any other domestic governmental activity. Over four-fifths of the schools are controlled by school districts. These districts, which are independent of other local governments even when they cover the same territory, are run by school boards whose members are elected by local residents or appointed by the town council. They can raise money by means of taxes and bond issues to build and maintain schools and pay salaries. It is true that they must operate within guidelines set by the state, but they usually have a lot of freedom to make policy.

To sum up, instead of two levels of government—the federal government and the states—there are several overlapping levels covering the same territory. It is estimated that there are about 1500 government units in the New York metropolitan area alone. They range from small single-purpose districts with budgets of a few thousand dollars to the government of New York City, which has a budget larger than those of many nations.

Why so many governments, and such a variety? How can they possibly get along with each other? Before we can answer these questions we need to know more about the issue of centralization versus decentralization.

CENTRALIZATION VS. DECENTRALIZATION

In France it used to be said that the minister of education could look at his watch and say, "At this moment every sixth-grader in France is doing the following math problem: . . ." and tell you the problem they were working on. This story is an exaggeration, but it illustrates the *centralized* nature of the French educational system. Schedules, curriculum, standards, and so on are set by the Ministry of Education in Paris and carried out in the local schools.

Now suppose you wanted to find out what every sixth-grader in the United States was doing at a particular moment. You could go to the Department of Health, Education and Welfare in Washington and ask someone in the Office of Education, but you would not get an answer to your question. The American educational system is *decentralized*. Schedules, curriculum, and so on are determined by the states or by the school boards of counties, cities, towns, or school districts. To find out what sixth-graders are doing you would have to visit all of the 15,781 school districts in the nation.

Which is better, centralization or decentralization? There is no easy answer to this question, since there are many arguments on each side.

Arguments for Decentralization

One argument for local control is that pupils differ in different parts of the country. They have different interests, needs, and backgrounds. If you tried to apply the same curriculum to ghetto schools in New York, suburban schools in Michigan, and rural schools in North Dakota, it would not fit any of those schools very well. Only local citizens understand the educational needs of their own district and can create programs to meet those needs.

Moreover, local control lets the community decide how much it wants to spend on education. If the citizens of a particular community can afford an expensive school system, they should be allowed to have it. The supporter of decentralization can also point out that a huge, complicated bureaucracy would be needed to run a centralized school system, and such a bureaucracy would put the schools beyond the control of parents.

Arguments for Centralization

Those who favor a centralized system argue that local control is confused and wasteful. For one thing, there are no educational standards that apply to the nation as a whole. A degree from a French *lycée* (high school) means something specific—you know what the student has studied and what he or she can do. The same cannot be said for an American high school diploma. Sometimes it means the student is ready to enter a university; sometimes it does not. Another problem with local control is that communities vary widely in their ability to provide an adequate education. As a result some children get a much better education than others who happen to be born in the wrong place. New York spends about two and a half times as much on education as Alabama, and the variations within a state can be even greater. (See Figure 15.1.)

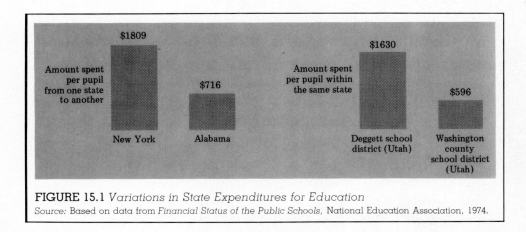

FIGURE 15.1 *Variations in State Expenditures for Education*
Source: Based on data from *Financial Status of the Public Schools*, National Education Association, 1974.

Supporters of centralization place a higher value on *equality* than on *diversity*. It is not fair, they say, for the quality of a child's education to depend on where he or she is born. Supporters of decentralization, on the other hand, value *diversity* over *equality,* claiming that equalization would "drag down" the quality of education offered in good schools.

It can also be argued that centralization would increase the efficiency of the educational system. Local districts do not have the skills needed to run a modern school system; however, those skills could be provided by a centralized school system.

Local control of the schools allows for variety as well as wide differences in quality.

Finally, those who favor centralization could warn their opponents that they may be confusing decentralization with democracy. If decisions are made by each community, it would seem that the average citizen can have more control over local affairs. But this is not necessarily the case. Local government can be democratic, or the community can be run by a political "boss" or a small group of wealthy citizens. The result may be less citizen control rather than more.

Who Is Right?

It is hard to say who is right. Some would say the evidence favors local control; some would say it favors centralization. But few would argue that there is nothing to be said for one side or the other. The same is true of debates over centralization versus decentralization in other areas. In some of those areas—such as libraries or recreational facilities—the arguments for decentralization are more convincing. In others—such as interstate transportation systems—more central control seems desirable. But in all of these areas there are strong arguments on both sides.

The centralization-versus-decentralization debate is also a debate over federal power versus states' rights or big government versus local government. And it is a never-ending debate. Almost any solution stressing decentralization and local control can be criticized because it does not provide coordination. Almost any solution stressing centralization and federal control can be criticized because it does not pay enough attention to local needs and preferences. The crazy-quilt pattern of American government can be seen as a response to this dilemma: If neither solution is right, try both at the same time. This is one reason for the wide variety of governments in the United States.

Note, however, that the mixed pattern of American government is not a result of careful planning. Rather, it developed out of a long historical process, a process dominated not by theories of government but by the *interests* that prevailed at any given time. This point is important. The centralization–decentralization debate can be based on general principles such as the need for coordination or the differences between communities. But at any given time specific interests may cause one group to favor federal control and another to favor local control, no matter what their political philosophies may be. For example, black leaders may call for greater federal involvement in local affairs if they want to challenge white-dominated governments or school boards. But in neighborhoods where blacks are a majority, they may demand local control. In general, any group wants control to be at the level of government it is most likely to influence.

STATE AND NATION

As we saw early in this book, the writers of the Constitution tried to shift power away from the state-dominated system created by the Articles of Confederation. They created the executive branch, gave Congress the power to pass laws that affect citizens directly, and set up a federal court system to settle disputes between the states and the federal government. Thus they created a truly national government.

As with so many other aspects of American political life, the Constitution did not settle the issue of federal power versus state power. Instead, it created a framework within which future changes could be worked out: the framework of a unified central government and a series of partially independent states. In doing so it established the principles of centralization and decentralization without facing the fact that they are contradictory. This is what has allowed the federal system to evolve as it has. The balance of power between the nation and the states has changed over time, but the basic framework of central government and independent states has survived.

The tension between centralization and decentralization was especially strong during the years before the Civil War. As we have seen, during this period a series of major Supreme Court decisions established federal power over taxes, interstate commerce, and many other areas of American life. The implied-powers doctrine, discussed in Chapter 13, made it clear that the federal government was a true national government and not just a creation of the states.

Concurrent Majorities   Meanwhile the pressure for decentralization led the nation into the Civil War. The issue centered on the protection of regional interests, notably the interests of the southern states. John Calhoun, a senator from South Carolina, developed the theory of *concurrent majorities*. According to this theory, neither a majority of the citizens of the United States nor a majority of the states themselves could tell the others what to do. Rather, policies must be agreed to by a majority of the people in the region affected by those policies. This principle, of course, was contrary to the idea of a strong federal government.

Dual Federalism   The Civil War settled the issue of secession: Decentralization could not go so far as to let a state or group of states leave the Union. But it did not settle the issue of federal power versus states' rights. In the post-Civil War period the Supreme Court developed the doctrine of *dual federalism*. According to this doctrine, the states and the national government each have a specific area of jurisdiction. For example, the national government is responsible for regulating interstate commerce, while the states are responsible for regulating some businesses within states. But the Court used this doctrine to block the power of both the national and state governments. Each was blocked to protect the jurisdiction of the other. As a result the Court often prevented both levels from carrying out needed reforms.

New Federalism   Since the 1930s the balance of power has shifted toward the national government. Under what is called *new federalism* the Court has emphasized the Constitution's statement that national laws are "the supreme law of the land . . . anything in the Constitution or laws of any state to the contrary notwithstanding" (Article 6, Section 2). In short, the Court's current interpretation of the Constitution does not treat the states and the nation as equals. If Congress passes a law that conflicts with a state law, the congressional law overrides the state law. The national government cannot abolish the states or change their boundaries without their consent (Article 4, Section 3), but clearly it could take away most of their power if it wanted to.

THE EXPANSION OF FEDERAL POWER

Since the 1930s the federal government has become active in areas that used to be dominated by the states, and in those areas federal law has replaced state law. For example, environmental protection was once a concern of state and local governments; now the federal government is active in this area. Civil rights used to be a local affair; today the federal government is a major force in this area. The states still play a role in these areas, but the federal government has moved in. When you add in the new programs, such as atomic energy and space exploration, that are run entirely by the federal government, you can see how the balance of power has shifted toward Washington.

Why has the federal government's power grown so far beyond what the nation's founders had in mind? Why, at the same time, have state and local governments remained important centers of power? The answer to the first question lies in the development of the United States as a nation. The Constitution gave the federal government the power to regulate interstate commerce and manage foreign affairs. Therefore as the nation became a modern industrial society and a world power, the federal government's power increased.

Development of a National Economy

The development of a national economy made it impossible for any one state to control American economic life. The nation's economic problems affect all the states and can be solved only at the national level. Inflation and unemployment do not stop at state borders; instead, the economy is an interlocking system that must be dealt with by national policy.

The American economy is a national one; the individual states cannot regulate it.

An example is welfare policy. If one state sets up a program that offers much higher payments than other states, it may be swamped by poor families moving in from other states. Under the Constitution the state cannot exclude those families. The state that wants a better welfare program and the states that do not are all part of a single national economy. What one state does affects what the others do. In such a situation pressure for federal standards builds up.

Growth Through Defense

Another reason for the growth of federal power is the need for national defense. Federal power has always grown in wartime, and that power is maintained by high defense budgets. As the defense budget has grown, so has federal power in other fields. The National Defense Education Act gave large amounts of aid to local school boards in the name of national defense, and federal involvement in transportation, space research, and health programs has also been related to defense policy.

Pressure for Equality

The federal government has also grown in response to demands for equal treatment. Equality is a major issue in American politics. Over the years more and more groups have called upon the government to enforce equality —between blacks and whites, for example, or between the sexes. The pressure for equality almost always involves the federal government. For one thing, the federal courts have limited the power of state and local governments in this area. For another, groups seeking equal treatment naturally turn to the federal government. Since equality applies to citizens in all parts of the country, the best way to enforce it is through federal law. As a result federal power has increased in such areas as race relations, equal treatment of the sexes, and voter registration, which were once under state and local control.

The Financial Crisis

The weakness of state and local governments compared to the federal government is increased by the fact that they cannot raise enough money through taxes. There are three main types of taxes: income taxes, sales taxes, and property taxes. Each level of government gets most of its revenue from one of these sources—the federal government depends on income taxes, the state governments on sales taxes, and local governments on property taxes.

The income tax has several advantages over sales and property taxes. First, it raises more money, since it taps personal income directly. Second, it is progressive; that is, it taxes the rich at a higher rate. Sales and property taxes are regressive—they have a greater impact on poorer citizens. Third, income taxes respond quickly to the economy: The amount they bring in goes up when the economy expands.

Another disadvantage of sales and property taxes is that they lead to inequality. This is especially true of property taxes. Wealthy communities can raise much more money through property taxes than poorer communities, though the needs of the poorer communities may be greater.

Federal Aid To State and Local Governments

One way of correcting the imbalance between the federal government and state and local governments is by transferring funds from Washington to the states and localities. And this is what is happening. State and local budgets are depending more and more on federal funds. (See Figure 15.2.) These funds are used for a variety of purposes: welfare, education, highways, pollution control, and mass transit.

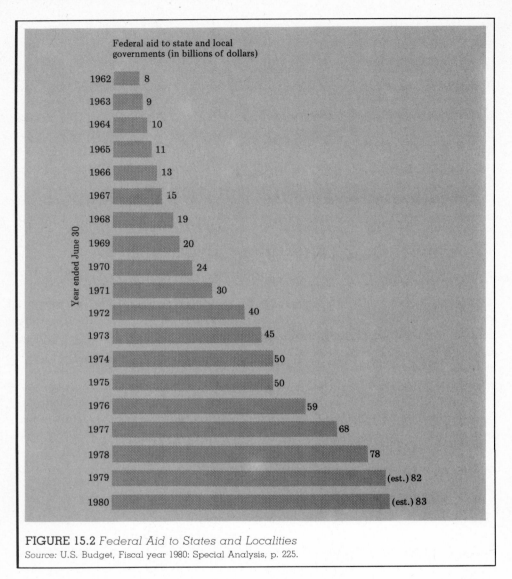

Federal aid to state and local
governments (in billions of dollars)

Year ended June 30

Year	Amount
1962	8
1963	9
1964	10
1965	11
1966	13
1967	15
1968	19
1969	20
1970	24
1971	30
1972	40
1973	45
1974	50
1975	50
1976	59
1977	68
1978	78
1979	(est.) 82
1980	(est.) 83

FIGURE 15.2 *Federal Aid to States and Localities*
Source: U.S. Budget, Fiscal year 1980: Special Analysis, p. 225.

Federal aid comes in many forms, but the main ones are grants-in-aid and revenue sharing. The difference between these two forms of aid lies largely in the "strings" attached to them.

Grants-in-Aid Grants-in-aid are given for specified purposes and usually come with regulations as to how the funds are to be used. *Categorical grants* are for very specific purposes such as building roads or bridges and usually are not very flexible. *Block grants* are also given for specified purposes such as educational improvement, but they are more broadly defined and more flexible.

Revenue Sharing Revenue sharing gives states and localities much more freedom in the use of federal funds. Under this program, which began in 1972, over $30 billion has been distributed to state and local governments with few strings attached. Local governments are supposed to use this money in such areas as health, public safety, and recreation. But these are general guidelines, and they give the localities a lot of flexibility.

Revenue sharing is an attempt to increase the power of the states and localities relative to that of the federal government. As former Secretary of the Treasury George P. Schultz put it, "Revenue sharing is important less for the money it will provide than for the philosophy it contains. Revenue sharing will place the power and the resources back in the state houses and city halls of this country."[2] For this reason revenue sharing has been a subject of controversy. Critics of the program—including some members of Congress— claim that localities do not spend the money on important things like health or welfare. It has been estimated that only 4 percent of the funds go to the poor and the aged.[3] Many local governments have used the federal funds to replace local funds and then reduced their taxes. In addition, civil-rights groups complain that the revenue-sharing program does not include enough protection against racial and sexual discrimination.

It could be said that revenue sharing is being attacked because it has succeeded in giving power to local governments. Critics of the program do not like the way that power is used. They claim that local officials are unwilling to listen to minority groups or the poor. Since those groups have been most effective at the national level, giving funds to localities reduces their effectiveness.

STATE AND LOCAL GOVERNMENTS IN ACTION

The federal government may be growing more and more important, but it is not yet time to write off the state and local units. States and localities still account for over 60 percent of all government spending on domestic programs (i.e., 60 percent of all spending that is not related to defense, foreign affairs, or space exploration). States and localities still have a lot of power in such areas as the protection of life and property; laws covering marriage, divorce, and abortion; and control of land use. In addition, they build highways and maintain parks, make decisions that affect the environment, and

---

[2] Quoted in the *New York Times,* 3 January 1974, p. 30.
[3] Ibid.

run the nation's educational system. It is true that in each of these areas funds often come from the federal government, and with the funds come some controls. But state and local governments still have major financial and legal responsibilities.

Cooperative Federalism

The mixture of federal, state, and local powers that exists in the United States today is called *cooperative federalism*. There is no clear division of power among the various levels of government, and governmental functions are shared by all the levels. One student of federalism has written that this system is more like a marble cake than a layer cake.[4]

This sharing of powers and functions is perhaps best illustrated by public education. Most of the funds for education are raised and spent locally. Yet the federal government has been involved from the very beginning. A 1785 statute provided for federal grants to local governments to build schools. Under the Morrill Land Grant Act of 1862, federal land grants were given to the states to set up agricultural and mechanical colleges. In this century a number of programs have expanded federal aid to local public school systems. We have already mentioned the National Defense Education Act of 1958, which, among other things, gave federal funds to local school districts to improve education in mathematics, science, and foreign languages and provided scholarship and fellowship funds for college students. The Elementary and Secondary Education Act of 1965 provided grants of federal funds to school districts with large numbers of poor students. Recent laws have further expanded the government's role in education.

Despite all these programs, the federal government has not taken over the schools. Instead, it has made grants-in-aid to state educational commissions or local school boards. The educational process itself is still controlled by the states and localities. Most federal aid has "strings" attached to it, usually in the form of guidelines that must be followed if the aid is to be received. These guidelines imply federal involvement in the educational process. However—just to complicate things a little more—the guidelines are often written with the help of the states and localities affected, so in a way the states and localities are setting their own standards.

In sum, the educational system is a mixed one. The federal government is involved through grants and guidelines, but control of the system is shared with the states. This pattern can be found in many other areas of American life.

[4] Morton Grodzins, "Centralization and Decentralization in the American Federal System," in Robert A. Goldwin, ed., *A Nation of States* (Chicago: Rand McNally, 1963).

What Preserves the States and Localities?

We have mentioned that the Constitution puts no limits on federal expansion and that the tax system gives the federal government the resources it needs for continued growth. Meanwhile the states and localities are financially weak, and more and more problems are being solved at the national level rather than at the state or local level. What, then, preserves state and local governments?

The answer to this question lies mainly in the structure of American politics, especially the political parties. If, as in some other countries, the parties were controlled by the national administration, the states could be overwhelmed by federal power. But as we have seen, the American parties are basically state and local organizations. They may unite to elect a President, but this unity is only temporary. Moreover, the White House, state houses, and city halls are not always controlled by the same party, and even when they are, this does not mean that the local organization is controlled by the national organization. Decisions as to who runs in state and local elections— even who runs for Congress—are made locally, not nationally, and this keeps the local party independent from national control.

Thus while financial weakness and recent interpretations of the Constitution make the states and localities subordinate to Washington, political reality tips the balance the other way. The federal government is at least partly a product of the states and localities. Members of Congress are part of the national government, but at the same time they are strongly aware of the fact that they represent particular districts or states. Even the President and Vice-President must recognize the importance of state party organizations in the nomination and election process. In short, the states and localities are preserved by the fact that they have *political power*.

WASHINGTON, THE STATES, AND THE CITIES

The greatest challenge to the American mixture of governments is the growth of large metropolitan areas. Can a constitution that was written for a small agrarian society deal with the modern city?

In metropolitan areas we see all the problems of central versus local control, governments with overlapping functions, and federal–state–local relations. Two things can be said about metropolitan areas: (1) They are socially and economically interdependent and (2) they are politically divided. The first point is illustrated by the Census Bureau's definition: "The general concept of a metropolitan area is one of an integrated economic and social unit with a recognized large population nucleus." This interdependence takes many forms. People move easily from one part of a metropolitan area to another; they may live in one part and work in another. The various communities in the area share roads, public transportation, and shopping centers and depend on the same water supply and the same recreational space. They also share common problems.

The term *spillovers* is used to refer to the activities of one community that affects neighboring communities. Smoke from a factory in one community pollutes the air in the next community; this is a spillover. If one community has a mosquito abatement program and its neighbors do not, it will still suffer during the summer; this too is a spillover. Spillovers can also be beneficial. For example, one community may open its parks to everyone in the metropolitan area.

Metropolitan areas, thus, are social and economic units with shared problems. But those problems must be solved by governments, and there can be as many as 1500 separate governments in a single metropolitan area. What this means is that no solution applies to the whole area. Moreover, there is often a wide gap between those who pay for services and those who benefit from them. For example, the central city provides clean streets, a service that is paid for by the taxes of residents. These streets are then used by people who commute to work from the suburbs and whose taxes are paid to the suburban governments, not to the central city. The central cities often try to tax the suburban commuters to help pay for such services but they do not always succeed, and as a result many cities have dirty streets, poor mass transit systems, and so on.

The "Urban Crisis"

For many years middle-class whites have been moving out of the central cities of metropolitan areas and into the suburbs. Meanwhile the central cities have filled up with poor blacks and other minorities. There are many reasons for the movement to the suburbs. They include the desire for fresh air, green lawns, and other benefits of suburban life. They also include the desire to leave behind the problems of the cities, especially inadequate schools. But whatever the reasons, the result is that the nonwhite poor are crowded into the decaying central cities while well-to-do whites live pleasant lives in the suburbs.

This situation is due at least partly to the boundaries of governments in metropolitan areas. When members of the white middle class leave the city, they enter another community. They no longer vote for city officials or participate in city politics; they no longer share the city's problems; and above all, they no longer pay taxes to the city.

Washington, D.C. opened its first subway five years behind schedule.

Thus there is pressure on the central city to provide services (street repair, garbage collection, welfare, etc.) for a growing population that needs those services badly. At the same time, the city's tax revenues, which pay for those services, are decreasing because wealthier citizens and corporations are leaving. In addition, a larger and larger percentage of the schoolchildren in the central cities are nonwhites. (See Table 15.1.) This makes it harder and harder to integrate the schools, since there are not enough white pupils to go around, and stimulates more whites to move to the suburbs to get away from "ghetto schools."

What Can Be Done About the Urban Crisis?

Suppose moving to the suburbs did not mean crossing a political boundary. This would not solve the problems of the cities, but it would make a difference. The tax base of the cities would not change because the suburbs would be part of the same district. It would be easier to integrate the schools. There would be less reason for middle-class whites to leave the city, since moving to the suburbs would make less of a difference in their children's schooling.

TABLE 15.1   Black Enrollment in City Schools

School District	Black Enrollment	Percent of All Students
Washington	133,638	95.5%
Atlanta	73,985	77.1
New Orleans	77,504	74.6
Newark	56,736	72.3
Richmond	30,746	70.2
Gary	31,200	69.6
Baltimore	129,250	69.3
St. Louis	72,629	68.8
Detroit	186,994	67.6
Philadelphia	173,874	61.4
Oakland	39,121	60.0
Birmingham	34,290	59.4
Memphis	80,158	57.8
Cleveland	83,596	57.6
Chicago	315,940	57.1
Kansas City, Mo.	35,578	54.4
Louisville	25,078	51.0

SOURCE: U.S. Department of Health, Education and Welfare, *Directory of Public, Elementary and Secondary Schools in Selected Districts* (Washington, D.C., 1972).

The Supreme Court considered this issue in 1974. A lower court had ordered cross-busing between Detroit and its suburbs in an effort to integrate the Detroit schools. The Supreme Court overturned the lower court's decision, ruling in favor of local control of the schools:

> No single tradition in public education is more deeply rooted than local control over the operation of schools; local autonomy has long been thought essential both to the maintenance of community concern and support for public schools and to the quality of the educational process.[5]

According to the Court, busing between the central city and the suburbs could be ordered only when there was evidence that the boundaries of school districts had been drawn *with the intent of discriminating* against black students.

What, then, can be done to solve the problems caused by urban–suburban boundaries? Should metropolitan areas come under federal control? Should they become single, unified governments? Many urban problems would be solved by the centralization of metropolitan government—the lack of coordination and unequal tax revenues, for example. But could such a government adjust its policies to the needs of citizens in various parts of the metropolitan area?

---

[5] *Millikin et al.* v. *Bradley* 42 LW 5249 (1974).

On the other hand, maybe decentralization would work; maybe the system of metropolitan governments should be fragmented even further into a large number of separate neighborhoods. This would give local residents more control over their own lives—or would it? The problems they would have to deal with—transportation, housing, pollution, even education—go beyond their neighborhood. They could not be solved by neighborhood governments. Clearly, the dilemma of centralization versus decentralization cannot be solved easily.

CONTROVERSY

The schools in America vary widely in quality. Some communities care more about education; some can afford more because they have more taxable property and can raise more money to pay for schools. Should all communities be required to spend the same amount on education, or is the present system satisfactory?

One Side

The present system is fine. If the quality of schools varies, this simply means that some communities want better schools. They should be allowed to have them. If children in poor districts do not get as good an education, this is just another way in which poor people are worse off than rich people. Besides, any attempt to make all schools equal would discourage innovation or variety and lead instead to bureaucratic sameness.

The Other Side

Children have a right to equal educational opportunity. A child's birthplace and the income of his or her parents should not affect the quality of that child's education. Even if variations in the quality of schools are not a matter of money but a result of the fact that some communities care more about education than others, school policy should be geared to the needs of children, not the preferences of parents. If equality is to have any meaning in America, we cannot let artificial boundaries determine who gets a good education and who does not.

HOW INSTITUTIONS WORK: V

State and Local Governments

What Is the Legal Basis of State Governments?

The basic structure of each state government is set forth in a constitution. All state constitutions are based on the principles of separation of powers and checks and balances. The actions of state officials, the laws passed by state legislatures, and the decisions of state courts may not violate the United States Constitution.

How Are State Governments Organized?

All state governments have executive, legislative, and judicial branches. The chief executive is the governor, who submits the state's budget to the legislature and largely decides the legislative agenda. Most governors have veto power and can call special sessions of the legislature. Other officials of the executive branch include the lieutenant governor, secretary of state, treasurer, attorney general, auditor, and superintendant of education.

All state legislatures except Nebraska's have an upper house and a lower house, with seats in both houses assigned on the basis of population. Legislatures range in size from under 60 to over 400 members. They work through committees, and most are organized along party lines.

Most state judicial systems have three levels: justices of the peace and municipal courts, county or trial courts and special courts, and courts of appeals or state supreme courts. In two-thirds of the states judges are elected by the people. In the others they are appointed or chosen through a combination of appointment and election.

What Are the Main Functions of State Governments?

The states have the primary responsibility for education, public health, transportation, welfare, and the administration of justice. They also have authority over corporations, utilities, and banks, and they regulate political parties and elections.

What Is the Legal Basic of Local Governments?

All local governments are created by the states. Municipalities are chartered by the state; other local units such as counties and special districts are either subdivisions of the state or creations of the legislature. They have only the powers granted them by the state. (About half the states have "home rule," in which municipalities may run many of their own affairs.)

What Are the Three Basic Forms of City Government?

1. Most larger cities use the *mayor–council* form, in which the mayor shares power with an elected city council.
2. The *commission plan* calls for a small board of elected commissioners, who serve both as a legislative council and as heads of the city departments.
3. Under the *council–manager* plan a nonpartisan council hires a professional city manager, who then runs the city subject to the council's approval.

What Are the Other Units of Local Government?

They are counties, townships, and special districts. *County* governments are found in almost all states and are the most important units of local government in rural areas. They are administrative and judicial units, usually run by elected officials: the sheriff, prosecutor, treasurer, and clerk and a board of commissioners. *Townships* are unincorporated, usually rural units of government found in fewer than half the states.

Unlike other local governments, *special districts* are created for specific purposes. Chief among them are school districts. There are also over 20,000 special districts with functions ranging from soil conservation to recreation.

Understanding
Government Policy

16

To understand how activities of the government affect the lives of Americans, we must understand how government policy is made and carried out. Note that a *policy* is a long-term commitment to a pattern of *activity*. We are interested in what the government actually does, not just in what it says. Many general statements about policy may be expressions of hope rather than descriptions of reality. For example, if Congress passes a law stating that all children have a right to receive an equal education, that law has little meaning without funds to carry it out.

In addition, we need to follow a policy from the initial statement of intent through to the actual administration of the policy. We have been told that Congress makes policies and executive agencies carry them out; but this is not always the way it works. The important thing is *how* the policy is carried out. Suppose Congress passes a law to improve inner-city schools and appropriates funds for that purpose. If local school districts use the funds for other purposes, this policy does not do much for inner-city schoolchildren. In other words, a policy does not administer itself. It has to be carried out by someone, and in the process it can be changed.

PROBLEMS IN POLICY ADMINISTRATION

It is not unusual for policies to fail, but the failures may not be noticed. Policies are announced with great fanfare—it is big news when a bill guaranteeing voting rights or setting up a job corps is passed. But the way the program is carried out throughout the nation gets a lot less attention.

Sometimes national policy is simply ignored. The Supreme Court, like Congress, often makes important policy statements, but those policies are not automatically put into effect. For example, a variety of Court decisions based on the First Amendment's separation of church and state have set limits on religious activities in public schools. Yet "school systems in virtually every state violate in some way the legal principles concerning religious instruction in the public schools."[1] If no one minds these violations, little is done about them.

Another factor that can stand in the way of change is *symbolic response*. In a number of cases the government has responded to demands for change with statements such as "No more rotten meat shall be sold" or "Our lakes and rivers shall be clean." But little is done to put the policy into effect. The real policy may be to do nothing. Symbolic policies can have important results, however, especially if those who demanded the change believe it has been carried out.

[1] Frank J. Sorauf, "*Zorach* v. *Clausen:* The Impact of a Supreme Court Decision," *American Political Science Review* 53 (September 1959).

The impact of the interstate highways on big cities has been severe.

Finally, not all policies work out the way they were intended to. Often they have additional, unplanned results. For example, uniform testing of schoolchildren was not intended to discriminate against blacks. But the tests discriminate if they ask questions about subjects that are more familiar to middle-class whites than to blacks or use language that is more easily understood by whites than by blacks.

Indeed, it is hard to carry out a large-scale program without unintended results. Consider the interstate highway program, a huge project begun in the mid-1950s. Twenty years and $62 billion later the nation has 38,000 miles of limited-access highways. The goal was to replace slow, unsafe roads with fast, well-designed highways linking all parts of the country. In this the program succeeded; but it had other results as well: Small towns bypassed by the highways became backwaters, "much like the towns left off the railroads 100

317

years ago."[2] And it became easier for middle-class city dwellers to move to the suburbs, thus contributing to the urban crisis.

Limits on What the Government Can Do

We often complain about such problems as poverty, inadequate mass transit, and low-quality education, and we criticize the government for failing to "do something" about these problems. But there is a long and difficult road from the creation of a general policy to the actual results of that policy. Along this road are many pitfalls that limit what the government can do. They include the following:

1. *We May Not Have Clear Policy Goals.* Policy goals may be vague, either because Congress is not sure what it wants to accomplish or because one goal comes into conflict with another. In the case of busing, for example, the goal of integration clashes with the goal of local control of the schools.
2. *We May Not Know How to Achieve Our Goals.* A lot of money and effort has been poured into improving the education provided by inner-city schools. Many programs have been tried: smaller classes, open classrooms, curriculum changes, and so on. But we still do not know exactly what policies will result in improved education.
3. *Some Things Can Be Changed More Easily Than Others.* It is easier to reduce class size in inner-city schools than to bring in better teachers. And it may be easier to improve the quality of teachers than to change the values children learn at home. If values learned at home determine success in school, there is not much that the government can do. As a result government programs will concentrate on reducing class size, even if this may not get to the heart of the problem.
4. *Other Conditions May Affect the Success of a Policy.* Some conditions are beyond the control of policy makers. If these conditions are favorable, the policy works; if not, it fails. Affirmative-action programs, for example, have a better chance of succeeding in a growing economy. In the mid-1970s an economic slump made it hard to carry out such programs.
5. *It May Be Hard to Tell Whether a Program Has Succeeded.* Suppose the government sets up a retraining program so that workers who have been laid off can train for another job. How can you tell whether the program has succeeded? Do you judge from the amount spent on training? The number of people who apply for the training? The number who complete the program? Their success in finding jobs after completing the program? How long they keep those jobs? The program may be successful by one of these standards but not by others.

Action vs. Inaction

To fully understand government policy we must consider what the government does *not* do as well as what it does. If the government is inactive in a

[2] *New York Times,* 14 November 1976.

Medical care for the aged has been government policy since 1965.

particular area, this is a policy even though it may not be planned. Government officials may not have *decided* to do nothing, but the lack of action can still affect people's lives.

There are many examples of such situations. For many years the government was inactive in the area of medical care. This meant that all citizens had to pay their own medical bills. The government has no "language policy" but does all of its business in English. This puts non-English speakers at a disadvantage. Today we have many laws affecting the wages paid to workers, but for a long time this was viewed as a matter to be settled by private agreements between workers and management. Clearly the government's inaction in this area affected the well-being of citizens.

HOW ISSUES BECOME ISSUES

The impact of government policy on the lives of citizens depends in part on how decisions are made about issues, decisions such as whether to provide funds for mass transit or for highways. But an even more basic question is how issues get onto the political agenda in the first place. How do highways become a subject of government policy? Why should the government have a policy on highways? In other words, how do issues become issues?

The first step toward solving a problem is to recognize that it is a problem. Once a problem has arisen and has been "put on the agenda," citizens can pressure the government; debate can take place in the press, in Congress, and in the executive branch; and proposals can be made.

How Problems Get onto the Agenda

Some people believe problems get onto the political agenda automatically: If the economy is going badly, economic problems get onto the agenda; if it is going well, economic problems do not get much attention. When our rivers and streams were pure, pollution was not on the agenda; now that they are filthy, it is.

There is some truth to this view. It is hard to imagine pollution being an issue if the air and water are pure. But the political agenda does not simply reflect a society's problems. Our lakes and rivers were polluted long before pollution became an issue; Lake Erie became almost hopelessly polluted without anyone showing much concern. Now that the same thing is happening to some of the other Great Lakes, it is an issue. Clearly something besides the problem itself is needed to put an issue on the agenda.

Another view is that any citizen or group can put a problem on the agenda. This is true in a way, but is also misleading. The Constitution guarantees the right to petition Congress or form a political group, and these things are often done. But as we learned earlier, not all social groups are equally organized, and unorganized groups have less chance of getting their problems onto the political agenda.

Of course even if a group raises an issue this does not mean it will get a lot of attention. The Constitution guarantees the right to raise an issue; it does not guarantee a favorable response. In addition, just as some people are less likely to put their problems on the agenda, certain problems are less likely to get onto the agenda. For example, in our "free-enterprise" system it is unlikely that an issue involving government ownership of industry will get onto the agenda.

Who Gets Issues onto the Agenda?

People who are politically active are more likely to get problems put on the political agenda. The reason for this is that by participating they communicate their views to the government. Those who do not participate do not communicate.

Activity may not be enough, however. Among the active citizens, it is the wealthy, the educated, and those with high-status jobs who are most effective in getting issues onto the agenda. Lower-status citizens who participate actively are less successful.

Certain individuals and groups specialize in seeking out issues and publicizing them. These *agenda setters* are part of a long tradition. Around 1900 the "muckrakers" brought many social problems to the attention of the public. Today this job is being done by the leaders of the consumer movement, the ecology movement, and the women's movement.

In recent years an important new type of agenda setter has emerged. Members of Congress—especially senators—often play an important role in bringing new issues to the attention of the public. This is one way in which they become well enough known to become presidential candidates.

Sometimes an agenda setter within the government works closely with one outside the government. For example, the legislation that set up the National Highway Safety Bureau grew out of the activities of Senator Abraham Ribicoff and consumer leader Ralph Nader.

Agenda setters play an especially important role in connection with policies that would benefit a large, unorganized group. Pollution control is an example of this kind of situation. The industries that would have to pay for pollution control by buying expensive equipment can be expected to oppose legislation on this issue. But the people who would benefit from cleaner air are hard to organize. No one citizen would have enough influence to make it worthwhile for him or her to fight for a pollution control law. Since all citizens would benefit from cleaner air whether they fought for the law or not, it makes sense for them to sit back and take a "free ride." Agenda setters, by contrast, benefit more directly from their activity. They become nationally known, and they have the satisfaction of doing a professional job well. So they are motivated to fight against the narrower, more intense interest groups that oppose pollution control and similar legislation.

COMPREHENSIVE VS. INCREMENTAL PLANNING

We turn now to how policy is actually made. Imagine a group of government officials trying to solve the problem of pollution caused by cars. There are two ways of approaching the problem: the comprehensive approach and the incremental approach.

The Comprehensive Approach

If the government officials choose the *comprehensive* approach, they will consider all possible ways of solving the problem. They will state the goal they are trying to achieve and relate it to other goals they think are important. Then they will choose the best possible way of achieving their goal.

A comprehensive approach to automobile pollution would have the following characteristics:

1. *The Past Is No Limit.* The way cars have been designed in the past, the number of older cars on the roads, the past history of the auto industry, and patterns of auto use will not interfere with a new plan.
2. *All Possible Policies Will Be Considered.* The planners will consider other ideas besides simply modifying current models. Nor will they limit their planning to existing means of transportation—they may even consider replacing cars with mass transit.
3. *Connections with Other Policies Will Be Considered.* The planners will consider how their goal relates to other policies and will change those policies if necessary. Does private ownership of cars lead to more pollution? Then maybe it should not be permitted. Would government ownership of the auto industry lead to less pollution? If so, it should be considered too.
4. *All Values Are Considered.* The planners will consider other values besides pollution control. Pollution could be stopped by banning all cars, but such a policy would hurt other values such as full employment, not to mention our desire to get from one place to another.
5. *All Effects Are Considered.* What effects will a particular policy have on jobs? on housing? on other means of transportation? Maybe reducing pollution will produce healthier citizens. Maybe the planners should consider the need for more facilities for the aged, who will live longer in a pollution-free environment.

The Incremental Approach

Incremental planning differs from comprehensive planning in every way:

1. *The Past Sets Major Limits.* The planners consider the number of cars on the road, their economic importance, and current patterns of auto use. Past policies provide the framework within which they work.
2. *Only a Few Ways of Dealing with the Problem Will Be Considered.* The planners will stick to changes that will fit into current designs of cars.

3. *Other Policies Will Not Be Considered.* The planners will stick to the problem of pollution control standards and will not consider major changes such as banning private cars or nationalizing the auto industry.

4. *Other Values and Effects Will Not Be Considered.* The planners will not worry about the effects of their policy in other areas besides pollution. Other government agencies can worry about inflation or full employment.

The policy that results from the incremental approach obviously will be very different from the one that results from the comprehensive approach. The comprehensive planner could almost redesign the world from scratch, while the incremental planner would create a narrow policy designed to deal with a specific problem by changing (but not scrapping) existing policy.

The Government's Approach

At first glance the comprehensive approach looks much more promising. Incremental planning often does not accomplish much, and as mentioned earlier, failure to consider all the possible effects of a policy can produce unintended results. Yet most government policy takes the incremental approach. Policies are worked out step by step, starting from existing policies and focusing on a single aspect of the problem.

There are several reasons for this. One is that government planners do not have the ability to do comprehensive planning. It is impossible to weigh every rule against all other values. Besides, how do you measure the "value" of clean air or full employment?

In addition, most government planners are not in a position to consider more than one aspect of a problem. An official who is assigned to work on automobile pollution and comes up with a plan calling for vast spending on mass transit will be told to stick to his or her job. Of course Congress and the Presidency are supposed to take a more comprehensive view of national problems; but they too use the incremental approach. Congress passes broad legislation, but its committees are geared to specific problems. Even the President can deal with only one problem at a time.

Another reason the government uses the incremental approach is the sheer weight of history. Past decisions cannot be ignored. Once a course has been charted, it cannot be changed easily. Once a government program has been set up, you cannot come along and start all over again without creating a new set of problems.

Decentralized Policy Making

In addition to using the incremental approach, the government tends to divide the policy-making process into small units. Each agency makes policy for a particular group on a fairly narrow range of issues. For example, no one sets policy for the economy as a whole. Instead, different parts of the government specialize in different aspects of the economy—agriculture, commerce, mining, and so on. One result of such decentralized policy making is that no government agency is concerned with broad social issues. Another is that, as we have seen, industries that are supposed to be regulated by the government participate in the writing of the regulations.

Decentralized policy making is partly a result of the structure of the government. Major policy decisions are made by agencies or committees—especially in Congress, with its specialized committees and even more specialized subcommittees. Decentralization also results from the fact that the political parties do not give the people a choice between broad programs to solve the nation's problems, and it is reinforced by Congress's tendency to pass vague, general laws. Someone has to decide how those laws are to be applied, and this is left to executive agencies, each of which is concerned with a narrow range of problems and a particular group of citizens.

Attempts to Centralize Planning

American politics is characterized by the balancing of forces: centralization vs. decentralization, Congress vs. the President, civil liberties vs. national security. This is true in policy making as well: Incremental, decentralized planning is balanced by attempts to develop more centralized, comprehensive planning.

Several institutions have been created with the goal of making policy decisions on a comprehensive basis. The most important of these is the Office of Management and Budget (OMB). The OMB is not a part of any government department but is directly under the control of the President. Its purpose is to coordinate government policy. It prepares the federal budget and tries to fit the budget proposals of the various departments into the President's program. In addition, it tries to oversee the way programs are carried out. The OMB does take a more comprehensive view than the executive departments, but this puts it into a tug of war with the departments as they try to protect their own programs and get their own proposals approved.

Congress, too, has tried to take a more comprehensive approach to policy making. Getting the federal budget through Congress used to be an incremental, decentralized process in which the President submitted the proposed budget and each committee of Congress worked on a separate part of that budget. In 1974, however, Congress set up new budget committees in both the House and the Senate. These committees allow members of Congress to look at the budget as a whole and set target figures before working on the various parts of the budget. It is hoped that this approach will increase Congress' influence on the budgetary process as well as make that process less confused.

GOVERNMENT POLICIES: THREE CASE STUDIES

The federal government is active in almost every area of our lives. To see how policy is made we could look at thousands of issues and at the activities of hundreds of agencies, bureaus, and committees. But since this is not possible, we must choose a few areas to study.

This is not an easy choice. Studying how policy is made in one area may not tell us much about how policy is made in other areas. The way the government makes policy decisions on nuclear weapons may have little in common with the way it makes policy on agricultural matters.

In the rest of this chapter we will discuss how the government makes policy in three areas: taxation, energy, and food (that is, food as a foreign-policy issue). While there is no single process by which policies are made, these three case studies will provide an overview of the policy-making process.

Tax Policy

Taxes are the key to all other government programs, since they are the source of the funds that pay for almost everything the government does. Tax policy touches the life of every citizen.

Purposes of Taxation The main purpose of taxes, of course, is to raise money. But taxes can have other purposes too. They can be used to transfer wealth from one social group to another. This is done to some extent by the progressive income tax. If you look at a federal income tax form you will see that the amount of tax paid ranges from a tiny percentage of the lowest incomes to 50 percent of incomes over $100,000 a year. If these funds are used for government programs that benefit the poor more than the rich, there has been a transfer of wealth from richer citizens to poorer ones.

There is evidence that tax policy does lead to some redistribution of income. But the rich rarely pay as much as 50 percent of their income in taxes. The tax laws are full of loopholes—exemptions, deductions, lower rates for certain kinds of income. Upper-income citizens are in a better position to take advantage of those loopholes, for two reasons: (1) They are more likely to have the kinds of income to which the loopholes apply (e.g., tax-free municipal bonds), and (2) they are more likely to get professional help in preparing their tax returns. Only a professional can fully understand the complicated tax laws and take advantage of all the deductions and exemptions they allow.

Tax policy can also be used to regulate the economy. Higher tax rates may be used to limit spending in inflationary periods or when the economy is expanding too fast. Lower tax rates may be used to encourage spending and stimulate business during an economic slowdown. Taxes may be used as an indirect way of controlling certain activities (examples are the taxes on alcoholic beverages, cigarettes, and gasoline) and to stimulate particular parts of the economy (e.g., reduced taxes on certain kinds of capital investments).

The use of taxes to regulate the economy has been increasing lately. For example, when the issue of pollution first came up, the government passed laws requiring factories to reduce the extent to which they polluted the environment. The Environmental Protection Agency was set up, along with dozens of state and local agencies concerned with pollution. But this approach to regulation was hard to enforce and added to the cost of government. Now the government is turning to tax policy instead of detailed regulations as a means of controlling pollution. A factory that installs scrubbing devices to clean the substances it discharges into the air or water benefits from a lower tax rate.

How Is Tax Policy Made? At first glance, taxation does not look like a good area for decentralized policy making. Taxes affect every citizen and every part of the economy. Tax policy can stir up major conflicts over the principle of free enterprise or whether the government is responsible for the poor. In addition, the public cares about taxes. In any election tax rates are likely to be an issue. In public-opinion polls citizens always oppose tax increases. Government officials try to avoid raising taxes, especially when an election is coming up.

Yet even in this area there is a tendency to decentralize policy making into a series of narrow decisions. One reason for this is that the American tax system is highly complex, combining federal income taxes, state and local taxes, and taxes imposed by school districts and other special districts. In this system decisions are made for each group without considering their impact on other groups. For example, the tax policy of one metropolitan school district may stimulate people to move into or out of that district, thus having an effect on the policies of its neighbors.

Even federal income tax policy is made in a series of decisions, each affecting a particular group. Various industries, businesses, and other economic interests ask the government for tax relief—exemptions, lower rates, and the like. They are often represented by members of Congress who feel that they are defending the interests of their state or district. The complicated nature of tax law makes it easy to respond to such requests. Congress would be strongly criticized if it arbitrarily allowed a certain kind of income to be taxed at a lower rate than other kinds of income. But calling certain kinds of income "capital gains" instead of "regular salary" sounds like a mere technicality—though capital gains are taxed at a much lower rate. Most special tax "breaks" are adjustments of this type, not changes in the basic tax rate.

Tax decisions are made on an "interest-by-interest" basis. When the question of tax relief for a particular group (say, farmers) comes up, Congress tends to consider it on its own merits. It seems easy to give one group some relief without hurting other groups; but there are other questions involved besides the well-being of farmers. Who will have to pay higher taxes to compensate for the lower taxes paid by farmers? What government programs will have to be cut back because of lower tax revenues? Is the tax break given to farmers equal to that received by other groups? These questions are never asked when tax decisions are being made.

Tax policy, thus, is a "technical" matter that does not get much public attention, despite the public's concern over high taxes. One result is that the tax breaks go to the wealthier citizens. They are more likely to pressure Congress for tax relief and more likely to have the kinds of income that qualify for exemptions.

Congress as a whole does not play much of a role in tax policy. Over the years the House Ways and Means Committee has developed ways of pushing through "minor" tax bills that can cost the Treasury millions of dollars. These bills come up as "members' bills" whose purpose is to correct cases of "unfair" taxation rather than to change the basic tax laws. Each year the committee brings a long list of such bills before the House under a rule that allows them to pass by unanimous consent without debate.

The outcome is a hodgepodge of separate benefits with no overall structure. An example is the oil depletion allowance, which gave the oil industry a 22 percent deduction because its resources were being depleted. This "break" was supposed to stimulate exploration for new sources of oil—oil that was needed for national defense, among other things. Over the years similar deductions were allowed for other industries that deplete natural resources, including the gravel and sand industry (though no one argues that we need gravel and sand for national defense). Even the coal industry was given a deduction, but in this case the reason is not that we are running out of coal but that there is *too much coal*—it could not be sold because of competition from gas and oil!

The final result of these various tax loopholes is that billions of dollars of income are exempt from federal taxes. In 1972 it was estimated that $166 billion of income was exempt and that the government lost $55 billion by not taxing that income. (See Table 16.1.)

Returning Tax Policy to Public View There are times when tax policies attract the attention of a wider audience and concern for the "public interest"

TABLE 16.1 Income That Escapes Federal Taxes

Tax Preference or Privilege	(BILLIONS OF DOLLARS)	
	Estimated Income Removed From Tax Base in 1972	Estimated Loss in Tax Revenue
Tax exemption for transfer payments, including social-security pensions	$ 55.1	$13.1
Special deductions, double exemptions for the aged and blind, and the retirement income credit	42.2	14.2
Special benefits for homeowners, including deductions of mortgage interest	28.7	9.6
Special tax treatment of capital gains on sales of securities, other things	26.0	13.7
Exemption of interest earned on life insurance investments	9.1	2.7
Tax exemption of interest on state and local bonds	1.9	1.2
Tax exemption of up to $100 in annual dividends per person	1.9	0.7
Excess depletion and depreciation allowances	1.1	0.6
Total	$166.0	$55.8

SOURCE: "Individual Income Tax Erosion by Income Classes," a study by Joseph A. Pechman and Benjamin A. Okner, Brookings Institution, published by the Joint Economic Committee of Congress on May 8. Reprinted from *U.S. News and World Report*, May 22, 1972, p. 59. Copyright © 1972, U.S. News and World Report, Inc.

offsets the narrower interests that usually determine tax policy. In 1974 and 1975 three events combined to produce a more general concern with tax policy: (1) The energy crisis brought the oil industry's 22 percent depletion allowance to the attention of the public; (2) the Ford administration used tax policy to stimulate the economy during the recession; and (3) the revelation that President Nixon had tried to avoid paying taxes led to a general concern with tax reform. This situation has increased the chances for reform of the basic tax structure. President Carter sent a tax reform proposal to Congress during his first year in the White House, but the bill Congress finally passed was a watered-down version of Carter's proposal, largely because it had been whittled away by special interests.

The main lesson to be learned from tax policy is that decentralized policy making has a better chance of success when few people pay attention to it. When an area of public policy becomes a matter of widespread concern, the dominant position of narrow interests is challenged.

Energy Policy

In recent years it has become clear that the nation faces a serious energy shortage. Presidents Nixon, Ford, and Carter have all called for a comprehensive energy policy, but no such policy has emerged. There are many reasons for this: the complexity of the problem, the lack (until 1977) of an executive agency in charge of energy policy, the pressure of interest groups on Congress, and so on. Let's take a look at some of these obstacles.

A Complex Problem   At least three factors make energy a very complex problem:

1. There is no way of separating the energy issue from other economic issues. The American economy is trying to solve a problem known as *stagflation* in which a stagnant economy is combined with high unemployment and inflation. If the government tried to conserve gasoline by imposing a higher user tax, it would contribute to higher gas prices and, thus, to inflation. If it tried to use more imported oil, it would "export jobs" and thus contribute to unemployment.

2. Energy is both a domestic and a foreign-policy issue. Energy policy must take into account both the uncertain international environment and the demands of domestic interest groups. In the early 1970s, for example, the Arab oil-producing nations increased the price of crude oil by 350 percent. They also used an oil embargo to pressure oil-importing nations to side with them against Israel. In response, President Nixon declared Project Independence, which was intended to make the United States self-sufficient in terms of energy by 1980. The project failed, but many of its details still affect both domestic and international politics.

3. Energy policy is often in conflict with environmental protection. Governments at all levels have been trying to clean up polluted air and water, preserve open spaces, and protect the environment. Strong public-interest groups like the Sierra Club have been quite successful in pressuring Congress to pass environmental-protection laws. Environmentalists oppose several aspects of energy policy, such as offshore oil drilling and nuclear power plants.

The Management Problem   Soon after energy had come onto the political agenda it became clear that there was a management problem in addition to the problems just mentioned. There was no executive agency to provide leadership in this area, and no committee in the House or Senate specializing in energy matters. Thus the problem of what to do was made more complicated by the problem of deciding who was to do it.

In 1973 the Nixon administration sent an Emergency Energy Act to Congress with the request that it be acted upon immediately. Among other things, this act set up the Federal Energy Administration (FEA), which was intended to centralize energy policy making in the White House. In 1974 the Energy Research and Development Agency (ERDA), which was responsible for research on new sources of energy, was created. These two agencies were not enough, however, and in 1977 President Carter decided that even more coordination and centralization were needed in the area of energy.

With the approval of Congress, Carter created the Department of Energy. This new department brought together the FEA and ERDA, as well as the Federal Power Commission, which had authority over electricity and natural gas. In addition, it picked up pieces of the energy puzzle that had been scattered across dozens of other agencies. For example, five different bureaus in the Interior Department were in charge of coal policy. Standards for home heating were set by the Department of Housing. Oil pipeline regulations were set by the Interstate Commerce Commission.

The government now had a strong, well-financed executive department responsible for energy policy. But has this department been able to get a comprehensive energy policy through Congress? Not yet. The Carter administration has found Congress just as hard to deal with on energy matters as the Nixon and Ford administrations did.

The Role of Congress   While the President initiates legislation, it is Congress that has the last word. This "last word" has repeatedly blocked attempts to pass comprehensive energy programs. In 1973 President Nixon proposed a series of laws intended to reduce energy consumption. They included federal power to ration oil and gasoline, lower speed limits, and taxes on excessive uses of energy. These proposals were soon bogged down in Congress. The opposition, led by Senator Henry Jackson, feared that Nixon's proposals would be used to benefit the oil industry. There were good reasons for this fear. For one thing, Nixon had received large campaign contributions from oil company executives in 1972. For another, Jackson believed oil industry lobbyists were directly involved in drafting the President's proposals. At one point he said, "I can't distinguish the White House position from the oil industry's position."

Jackson argued that Nixon's proposals would give the oil industry huge windfall profits. (Oil companies were already making profits of about 20 percent, well above those of most industries.) He insisted that the energy act include a reduction in oil prices. He persuaded Congress, and the bill it sent to the White House called for a reduction in the per-barrel price of domestic crude oil. Nixon, taking the side of the oil industry, vetoed the bill.

After the oil embargo the energy crisis seemed less urgent and the Nixon administration was too busy defending itself against the threat of impeachment to develop a new energy plan. The Ford administration promised to do something about the problem, but it came up with only a few modest proposals. President Carter called the energy crisis "the moral equivalent of war" and sent a number of major proposals to Congress, but again Congress put roadblocks in the way of a comprehensive energy policy. It is not that Congress was opposed to a comprehensive plan. It was just that it did not know how to choose among several alternatives. Both Congress and the White House are subject to intense pressure from competing interest groups.

The Role of Organized Groups   Energy policy, or the lack of it, is so important to the American way of life that it is hard to find an organized group that is not affected by it. Auto makers want less restrictive pollution controls. Bird watchers want environmental-protection laws. Supporters of Israel want less cooperation with Arab oil producers; oil companies want credits for the taxes they pay to foreign governments; consumers want lower fuel prices; and so on.

These groups can be divided into two categories. One set of groups believes that the best policy is to conserve the energy supplies we already have. The other set believes the solution is to develop more sources of energy. These two sets of interests are divided on many issues, but nothing illustrates this division better than the issue of energy vs. the environment.

Today the goals of the environmental-protection movement are bumping into other economic goals. For example, offshore oil drilling offers us a

Attempts by the government to create a comprehensive energy program have run into opposition from public utilities, consumer groups, and other interests.

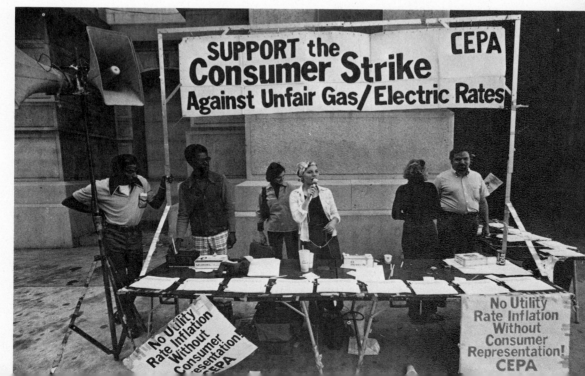

chance to reduce our dependence on imported oil, and the pressure to take advantage of this opportunity is intense. As former Secretary of the Treasury John B. Connally put it, "Let us start leasing, exploring, drilling, pipelining, shipping, refining and using more prudently the resultant clean energy this country needs to keep our people employed, our economy going, and our society alive and thriving." The American Petroleum Institute and many other business and manufacturing associations agree.

The environmentalists are strongly opposed. They remember what happened in 1969, when an oil well in the Santa Barbara channel ruptured. California beaches were covered with oil, and large numbers of birds and fish were killed; ecologists say the area has not yet recovered. The Santa Barbara spill stimulated a lot of public concern over the environment, and as a result the National Environmental Policy Act was passed in 1970. This act requires government agencies to consider the environmental impact of their decisions, including decisions on whether to grant permission to explore for off-shore oil supplies.

Backed up by this act, environmentalists have blocked or delayed millions of dollars' worth of federal projects. But economic interests have been equally intense; among other things, they have succeeded in getting permission to begin drilling for oil and gas off the coast of New Jersey.

There will be no final victory in the battle between the groups that want to sacrifice economic growth for the sake of environmental protection and those that want to sacrifice environmental protection for more jobs or cheaper energy. As a result President Carter—and future Presidents—may find it impossible to develop a truly comprehensive energy policy.

Food Policy as Foreign Policy

It is becoming harder and harder to separate "domestic policy" from "foreign policy." What happens overseas depends on what happens here, and vice versa. We mentioned this fact in our discussion of energy policy, but the interdependence of domestic and foreign policy is even stronger in the area of food policy.

At first it seems strange to think of food as a foreign-policy issue. We think of food policy as having to do with how much farmers will earn when they grow wheat or fatten cattle and how much Americans will have to pay for bread and beef. We are not likely to think of the State Department or the National Security Council as being involved in such matters.

Until the early 1970s food policy *was* basically a domestic-policy issue, but today this is no longer true. Here we will describe the situation that existed before 1970 and the factors that have made food an international issue since then.

Food Policy Before the 1970s   American agricultural policy centers on the production of grain. The American farmer has no trouble growing enough grain to feed the American people. Some of the grain is consumed in the form of breads and cereals, but a lot of it is consumed indirectly by being fed to livestock, which, in turn, become the meat on American dinner tables.

The basic problem of American agriculture is overproduction. The production of food is quite different from the production of manufactured goods. Neither farmers nor manufacturers can predict the demand for their products, but farmers cannot even predict *how much* they will produce. A late freeze or the lack of rain can cut their production sharply. If they plant extra crops in case of poor growing conditions, the result may be overproduction, which drives farm prices down. Then they have to sell their grain or live-stock at a loss, and they are likely to grow less grain in the future. This leads to a grain shortage, which drives prices up and results in inflation and food shortages.

From the late 1940s to the early 1970s agricultural policy focused on this problem. Payments were made to farmers for not growing certain crops when there was a surplus of those crops, and a system of price supports (or farm subsidies) guaranteed a minimum price for some crops. In addition, purchases of farm equipment were subsidized and direct payments were made to farmers when prices for their products were depressed. These were all "domestic" policies. The only "international" aspect of agricultural policy in this period was the Food for Peace program, in which the United States gave away part of its grain surplus to other nations.

The "Food Crisis"   Several things happened in the late 1960s and early 1970s that changed food policy from a domestic issue to one that reflects both domestic and international interests. The most dramatic of these events was a severe drought that caused food shortages in many less developed nations and led to sickness and starvation in parts of India and Africa. There was great pressure on the United States and other food-producing nations to give their surplus food to the needy nations.

The food problem was more complicated than that, however. The increase in oil prices affected food production and prices. It raised the price of oil-based fertilizers, increased the costs of running mechanized farms, and thus increased the cost of grain in the world market to a point at which the less developed nations could not afford it. The wealthier nations were able to buy the grain at the higher prices, thus permitting those prices to be maintained and forcing the poorer nations out of the market.

U.S. Food Policy in the 1970s   Food became a major international issue in the 1970s, and the United States was at the center of this issue because of its dominant position in world agriculture. The United States exports about 40 percent of its crop, enough to feed one-quarter of the world's population one meal a day. Seventy percent of the grain used to feed the people and livestock of Israel comes from the United States; 60 percent of the grain consumed by Japan comes from the United States; and even the Soviet Union gets about 8 percent of its grain from the United States.

Clearly, the United States has an advantage over other nations in the area of food production. This advantage has been used in making foreign policy. An example is the sale of American grain to the Soviet Union. In 1972 the United States sold more than 30 percent of its wheat crop to the Soviet Union at prices well below the market price. This was part of the larger policy of *détente* with the Soviet Union. Another example of the "political" use of food is the use of the Food for Peace program to supply food to America's military allies, whether they are in need of food or not. In the early 1970s about 70 percent of the food distributed by this program went to South Vietnam and Cambodia. The governments of those nations sold some of the food to raise cash to pay for military supplies.

Who Makes Agricultural Policy?   The agencies and interest groups involved in food policy have changed since the 1960s. Of course the Department of Agriculture still plays a major role. Its main concern is to protect the American farmer. Under Secretary of State Kissinger the State Department had a different set of goals: to use American grain to create better relations with the Soviet Union, supply military allies, and cause other nations to be-

Grain surpluses play a role in both domestic and foreign policies of the United States.

come economically dependent on the United States. These goals led to wider markets for the American farmer. However, the Departments of State and Agriculture disagreed on matters such as how grain should be shipped to the Soviet Union.

Interest groups outside the government have challenged the new food policies. Consumers and business groups fear that inflation will result from higher food prices. In 1974 they actually succeeded in getting President Ford to cancel grain sales to the Soviet Union. Other groups are concerned about the threat of worldwide starvation. They call for a policy of sending more food to needy nations, whether they are allies of the United States or not. They also believe less grain should be used for feeding livestock and more should go directly to poor nations. They have not been very successful, however; Americans are used to eating meat, and as a result most grain is still used as animal feed.

Conclusion   The blurring of the line between domestic and foreign policy is bringing new organizations and interests into the policy-making process. Agencies that traditionally were concerned mainly with foreign policy (e.g., the State Department) and agencies that were concerned mainly with domestic matters (e.g., the Department of Agriculture) now have to take into account a wider range of conditions and interests. Foreign policy is more likely to be influenced by domestic pressure groups, while domestic policy will be increasingly affected by the nation's national-security and foreign-policy goals.

The Declaration of Independence

When in the Course of human events, it becomes necessary for one people to dissolve the political bands which have connected them with another, and to assume among the Powers of the earth, the separate and equal station to which the Laws of Nature and of Nature's God entitle them, a decent respect to the opinions of mankind requires that they should declare the causes which impel them to the separation.

We hold these truths to be self-evident, that all men are created equal, that they are endowed by their Creator with certain unalienable Rights, that among these are Life, Liberty and the pursuit of Happiness. That to secure these rights, Governments are instituted among Men, deriving their just powers from the consent of the governed, That whenever any Form of Government becomes destructive of these ends, it is the Right of the People to alter or to abolish it, and to institute new Government, laying its foundation on such principles and organizing its powers in such form, as to them shall seem most likely to effect their Safety and Happiness. Prudence, indeed, will dictate that Governments long established should not be changed for light and transient causes; and accordingly all experience hath shown, that mankind are more disposed to suffer, while evils are sufferable, than to right themselves by abolishing the forms to which they are accustomed. But when a long train of abuses and usurpations, pursuing invariably the same Object evinces a design to reduce them under absolute Despotism, it is their right, it is their duty, to throw off such Government, and to provide new Guards for their future security.—Such has been the patient sufferance of these Colonies; and such is now the necessity which constrains them to alter their former Systems of Government. The history of the present King of Great Britain is a history of repeated injuries and usurpations, all having in direct object the establishment of an absolute Tyranny over these States. To prove this, let Facts be submitted to a candid world.

He has refused his Assent to Laws, the most wholesome and necessary for the public good.

He has forbidden his Governors to pass Laws of immediate and pressing importance, unless suspended in their operation till his Assent should be obtained; and when so suspended, he has utterly neglected to attend to them.

He has refused to pass other Laws for the accommodation of large districts of people, unless those people would relinquish the right of Representation in the Legislature, a right inestimable to them and formidable to tyrants only.

He has called together legislative bodies at places unusual, uncomfortable, and distant from the depository of their Public Records, for the sole purpose of fatiguing them into compliance with his measures.

He has dissolved Representative Houses repeatedly, for opposing with manly firmness his invasions on the rights of the people.

He has refused for a long time, after such dissolutions, to cause others to be elected; whereby the Legislative Powers, incapable of Annihilation, have returned to the People at large for their exercise; the State remaining in the mean time exposed to all the dangers of invasion from without, and convulsions within.

He has endeavoured to prevent the population of these States; for that purpose obstructing the Laws of Naturalization of Foreigners; refusing to pass others to encourage their migration hither, and raising the conditions of new Appropriations of Lands.

He has obstructed the Administration of Justice, by refusing his Assent to Laws for establishing Judiciary Powers.

He has made Judges dependent on his Will alone, for the tenure of their offices, and the amount and payment of their salaries.

He has erected a multitude of New Offices, and sent hither swarms of Officers to harass our People, and eat out their substance.

He has kept among us, in times of peace, Standing Armies without the Consent of our legislature.

He has affected to render the Military independent of and superior to the Civil Power.

He has combined with others to subject us to a jurisdiction foreign to our constitution, and unacknowledged by our laws; giving his Assent to their acts of pretended legislation:

For quartering large bodies of armed troops among us:

For protecting them, by a mock Trial, from Punishment for any Murders which they should commit on the Inhabitants of these States:

For cutting off our Trade with all parts of the world:

For imposing taxes on us without our Consent:

For depriving us in many cases, of the benefits of Trial by Jury:

For transporting us beyond Seas to be tried for pretended offences:

For abolishing the free System of English Laws in a neighbouring Province, establishing therein an Arbitrary government, and enlarging its Boundaries so as to render it at once an example and fit instrument for introducing the same absolute rule into these Colonies:

For taking away our Charters, abolishing our most valuable Laws, and altering fundamentally the Forms of our Governments:

For suspending our own Legislature, and declaring themselves invested with Power to legislate for us in all cases whatsoever.

He has abdicated Government here, by declaring us out of his Protection and waging War against us.

He has plundered our seas, ravaged our Coasts, burnt our towns, and destroyed the lives of our people.

He is at this time transporting large armies of foreign mercenaries to compleat the works of death, desolation and tyranny, already begun with circumstances of Cruelty & perfidy scarcely paralleled in the most barbarous ages, and totally unworthy the Head of a civilized nation.

He has constrained our fellow Citizens taken Captive on the high Seas to bear Arms against their Country, to become the executioners of their friends and Brethren, or to fall themselves by their Hands.

He has excited domestic insurrections amongst us, and has endeavoured to bring on the inhabitants of our frontiers, the merciless Indian Savages, whose known rule of warfare, is an undistinguished destruction of all ages, sexes and conditions.

In every stage of these Oppressions We have Petitioned for Redress in the most humble terms: Our repeated Petitions have been answered only by repeated injury. A Prince, whose character is thus marked by every act which may define a Tyrant, is unfit to be the ruler of a free People.

Nor have We been wanting in attention to our British brethren. We have warned them from time to time of attempts by their legislature to extend an unwarrantable jurisdiction over us. We have reminded them of the circumstances of our emigration and settlement here. We have appealed to their native justice and magnanimity, and we have conjured them by the ties of our common kindred to disavow these usurpations, which, would inevitably interrupt our connections and correspondence. They too have been deaf to the voice of justice and of consanguinity. We must, therefore, acquiesce in the necessity, which denounces our Separation, and hold them, as we hold the rest of mankind, Enemies in War, in Peace Friends.

We, therefore, the Representatives of the united States of America, in General Congress, Assembled, appealing to the Supreme Judge of the world for the rectitude of our intentions, do, in the Name, and by Authority of the good People of these Colonies, solemnly publish and declare, That these United Colonies are, and of Right ought to be Free and Independent States; that they are Absolved from all Allegiance to the British Crown, and that all political connection between them and the State of Great Britain, is and ought to be totally dissolved; and that as Free and Independent States, they have full Power to levy War, conclude Peace, contract Alliances, establish Commerce, and to do all other Acts and Things which Independent States may of right do. And for the support of this Declaration, with a firm reliance on the Protection of Divine Providence, we mutually pledge to each other our Lives, our Fortunes and our sacred Honor.

The Constitution of the United States

[*Preamble*]

We the people of the United States, in Order to form a more perfect Union, establish Justice, insure domestic Tranquility, provide for the common defence, promote the general Welfare, and secure the Blessings of Liberty to ourselves and our Posterity, do ordain and establish this Constitution for the United States of America.

ARTICLE 1

Section 1

[*Legislative Powers*]

All legislative Powers herein granted shall be vested in a Congress of the United States, which shall consist of a Senate and a House of Representatives.

Section 2

[*House of Representatives, How Considered, Power of Impeachment*]

The House of Representatives shall be composed of Members chosen every second Year by the People of the several States, and the Electors in each State shall have [the] Qualifications requisite for Electors of the most numerous Branch of the State Legislature.

No person shall be a Representative who shall not have attained to the Age of twenty five Years, and been Seven Years a Citizen of the United States, and who shall not when elected, be an Inhabitant of that State in which he shall be chosen.

Representatives and direct Taxes shall be apportioned among the several states which may be included within this Union, according to their respective Numbers, which shall be determined by adding to the whole Number of free Persons, including those bound to Service for a Term of Years, and excluding Indians not taxed, three fifths of all other Persons. The actual Enumeration shall be made within three years after the first Meeting of the Congress of the United States, and within every subsequent Term of ten Years, in such Manner as they shall by Law direct. The Number of Representatives shall not exceed one for every thirty Thousand, but each State shall have at Least one Representative; and until such enumeration shall be made, the State of New Hampshire shall be entitled to chuse three, Massachusetts eight, Rhode-Island and Providence Plantations one, Connecticut five, New York six, New Jersey four, Pennsylvania eight, Delaware one, Maryland six, Virginia ten, North Carolina five, South Carolina five, and Georgia three.

When vacancies happen in the Representation from any State, the Executive Authority thereof shall issue Writs of Election to fill such Vacancies.

The House of Representatives shall chuse their Speaker and other Officers; and shall have the sole Power of Impeachment.

Section 3

[*The Senate, How Constituted, Impeachment Trials*]

The Senate of the United States shall be composed of Two Senators from each State, chosen by the Legislature thereof, for six Years, and each Senator shall have one Vote.

Immediately after they shall be assembled in Consequence of the first Election, they shall be divided as equally as may be into three Classes. The Seats of the Senators of the first Class shall be vacated at the Expiration of the second Year, of the second Class at the Expiration of the fourth Year, and of the third Class at the Expiration of the sixth Year, so that one third may be chosen every second Year; and if Vacancies happen by Resignation, or otherwise, during the Recess of the Legislature of any State, the Executive thereof may make temporary Appointments until the next Meeting of the Legislature, which shall then fill such Vacancies.

No Person shall be a Senator who shall not have attained to the Age of thirty Years, and been nine Years a Citizen of the United States, and who shall not, when elected, be an Inhabitant of that State for which he shall be chosen.

The Vice-President of the United States shall be President of the Senate, but shall have no Vote, unless they be equally divided.

The Senate shall chuse their other Officers, and also a President pro tempore, in the Absence of the Vice-President, or when he shall exercise the Office of President of the United States.

The Senate shall have the sole power to try all impeachments. When sitting for that Purpose, they shall be on Oath or Affirmation. When the President of the United States [is tried] the Chief Justice shall preside: And no Person shall be convicted without the Concurrence of two thirds of the Members present.

Judgment in Cases of Impeachment shall not extend further than to removal from Office, and disqualification to hold and enjoy any Office of honor, Trust or Profit under the United States: but the Party convicted shall nevertheless be liable and subject to Indictment, Trial, Judgment and Punishment, according to Law.

Section 4

[*Election of Senators and Representatives*]

The Times, Places and Manner of holding Elections for Senators and Representatives, shall be prescribed in each State by the Legislature thereof; but the Congress may at any time by Law make or alter such Regulations, except as to the Places of chusing Senators.

The Congress shall assemble at least once in every Year, and such Meeting shall be on the first Monday in December, unless they shall by Law appoint a different Day.

Section 5
[Quorum, Journals, Meetings, Adjournments]
Each House shall be the Judge of the Elections, Returns and Qualifications of its own Members, and a Majority of each shall constitute a Quorum to do Business; but a smaller Number may adjourn from day to day, and may be authorized to compel the Attendance of absent Members, in such Manner, and under such Penalties as each House may provide.

Each House may determine the Rules of its Proceedings, punish its Members for disorderly Behaviour, and, with the Concurrence of two thirds, expel a Member.

Each House shall keep a Journal of its Proceedings, and from time to time publish the same, excepting such Parts as may in their Judgment require Secrecy; and the Yeas and Nays of the Members of either House on any question shall, at the Desire of one fifth of those Present, be entered on the Journal.

Neither House, during the Session of Congress, shall, without the Consent of the other, adjourn for more than three days, nor to any other Place than that in which the two Houses shall be sitting.

Section 6
[Compensation, Privileges, Disabilities]
The Senators and Representatives shall receive a Compensation for their Services, to be ascertained by Law, and paid out of the Treasury of the United States. They shall in all Cases, except Treason, Felony and Breach of the Peace, be privileged from Arrest during their Attendance at the Session of their respective Houses, and in going to and returning from the same; and for any Speech or Debate in either House, they shall not be questioned in any other Place.

No Senator or Representative shall, during the Time for which he was elected, be appointed to any civil Office under the Authority of the United States, which shall have been created, or the Emoluments whereof shall have been encreased during such time; and no Person holding any Office under the United States, shall be a member of either House during his Continuance in Office.

Section 7
[Procedure in Passing Bills and Resolutions]
All Bills for raising Revenue shall originate in the House of Representatives; but the Senate may propose or concur with Amendments as on other Bills.

Every Bill which shall have passed the House of Representatives and the Senate, shall, before it becomes a Law, be presented to the President of the United States; if he approves he shall sign it, but if not he shall return it, with his Objections to that House in which it shall have originated, who shall enter the Objections at large on their Journal, and proceed to re-

consider it. If after such Reconsideration two thirds of that House shall agree to pass the Bill, it shall be sent, together with the Objections, to the other House, by which it shall likewise be reconsidered, and if approved by two thirds of that House, it shall become a Law. But in all such Cases the Votes of both Houses shall be determined by Yeas and Nays, and the Names of the Persons voting for and against the Bill shall be entered on the Journal of each House respectively. If any Bill shall not be returned by the President within ten Days (Sundays excepted) after it shall have been presented to him, the Same shall be a Law, in like Manner as if he had signed it, unless the Congress by their Adjournment prevent its Return, in which Case it shall not be a Law.

Every Order, Resolution, or Vote to which the Concurrence of the Senate and House of Representatives may be necessary (except on a question of Adjournment) shall be presented to the President of the United States; and before the same shall take Effect, shall be approved by him, or being disapproved by him, shall be repassed by two thirds of the Senate and House of Representatives, according to the Rules and Limitations prescribed in the Case of a Bill.

Section 8
[Powers of Congress]
The Congress shall have the Power To lay and collect Taxes, Duties, Imports and Excises, to pay the Debts and provide for the common Defence and general Welfare of the United States; but all Duties, Imposts and Excises shall be uniform throughout the United States.

To borrow Money on the credit of the United States;

To regulate Commerce with foreign Nations and among the several States, and with the Indian Tribes;

To establish an uniform Rule of Naturalization, and uniform Laws on the subject of Bankruptcies throughout the United States;

To Coin Money, regulate the Value thereof, and of foreign Coin, and fix the Standards of Weights and Measures;

To provide for the Punishment of counterfeiting the Securities and current Coin of the United States;

To establish Post Offices and post Roads;

To promote the Progress of Science and useful Arts, by securing for limited Times to Authors and Inventors the exclusive Right to their respective Writings and Discoveries;

To constitute Tribunals inferior to the supreme Court;

To define and punish Piracies and Felonies committed on the high Seas, and Offences against the Law of Nations;

To declare War, grant Letters of Marque and Reprisal, and make Rules concerning Captures on Land and Water;

To raise and support Armies, but no Appropriation of Money to that Use shall be for a longer Term than two Years;

To provide and maintain a Navy;

To make Rules for Government and Regulation of the land and naval Forces;

To provide for calling forth the Militia to execute the Laws of the Union, suppress Insurrections and repel Invasions;

To provide for organizing, arming, and disciplining the Militia, and for governing such Part of them as may be employed in the Service of the United States, reserving to the States respectively, the Appointment of the Officers, and the Authority of training the Militia according to the discipline prescribed by Congress;

To exercise exclusive Legislation in all Cases whatsoever, over such District (not exceeding ten Miles square) as may, by Cession of particular States, and the Acceptance of Congress, become the Seat of the Government of the United States, and to exercise like Authority over all Places purchased by the Consent of the Legislature of the States in which the Same shall be, for the Erection of Forts, Magazines, Arsenals, dock-Yards, and other needful Buildings—And

To make all Laws which shall be necessary and proper for carrying into Execution the foregoing Powers, and all other Powers vested by this Constitution in the Government of the United States, or in any Department or Officer thereof.

Section 9

[Limitation upon Powers of Congress]
The Migration or Importation of such Persons as any of the States now existing shall think proper to admit, shall not be prohibited by the Congress prior to the Year one thousand eight hundred and eight, but a Tax or duty may be imposed on such Importation, not exceeding ten dollars for each Person.

The Privilege of the Writ of Habeas Corpus shall not be suspended, unless when in Cases of Rebellion or Invasion the public Safety may require it.

No Bill of Attainder or ex post facto Law shall be passed.

No Capitation, or other direct, Tax shall be laid, unless in Proportion to the Census or Enumeration herein before directed to be taken.

No Tax or Duty shall be laid on Articles, exported from any State.

No Preference shall be given by any Regulation of Commerce or Revenue to the Ports of one State over those of another; nor shall Vessels bound to, or from, one State, be obliged to enter, clear, or pay Duties in another.

No Money shall be drawn from the Treasury, but in Consequence of Appropriations made by Law; and a regular Statement and Account of the Receipts and Expenditures of all public Money shall be published from time to time.

No title of Nobility shall be granted by the United States: And no Person holding any Office of Profit or Trust under them, shall, without the Consent of the Congress, accept of any present, Emolument, Office, or Title, of any kind whatever, from any King, Prince, or foreign State.

Section 10

[Restrictions upon Powers of States]
No State shall enter into any Treaty, Alliance, or Confederation; grant Letters of Marque and Reprisal; coin Money; emit Bills of Credit; make any Thing but gold and silver Coin a Tender in payment of Debts; pass any Bill of Attainder, ex post facto Law, or Law impairing the Obligation of Contracts, or grant any Title of Nobility.

No State shall, without the Consent of the Congress, lay any Imposts or Duties on Imports or Exports, except what may be absolutely necessary for executing its inspection Laws: and the net Produce of all Duties and Imposts, laid by any State on Imports or Exports, shall be for the Use of the Treasury of the United States; and all such Laws shall be subject to the Revision and Control of [the] Congress.

No State shall, without the Consent of Congress, lay any Duty of Tonnage, keep Troops, or Ships of War in time of Peace, enter into any Agreement or Compact with another State, or with a foreign Power, or engage in War, unless actually invaded, or in such imminent Danger as will not admit of delay.

ARTICLE 2

Section 1

[Executive Power, Election, Qualifications of the President]
The executive Power shall be vested in a President of the United States of America. He shall hold his Office during the Term of four Years, and, together with the Vice-President, chosen for the same Term, be selected as follows:

Each State shall appoint, in such Manner as the Legislature thereof may direct, a Number of Electors, equal to the whole Number of Senators and Representatives to which the State may be entitled in the Congress: but no Senator or Representative, or Person holding an Office of Trust or Profit under the United States, shall be appointed an Elector.

The Electors shall meet in their respective States, and vote by Ballot for two Persons of whom one at least shall not be an Inhabitant of the same State with themselves. And they shall make a List of all the Persons voted for, and of the Number of Votes for each; which List they shall sign and certify, and transmit sealed to the Seat of the Government of the United States, directed to the President of the Senate. The President of the Senate shall, in the Presence of the Senate and House of Representatives, open all the Certificates, and the Votes shall then be counted. The Person having the greatest Number of Votes shall be the President, if such Number be a Majority of the whole Number of Electors appointed; and if there be more than one who have such Majority, and have an equal Number of Votes, then the House of Representatives shall immediately chuse by Ballot one of them for President; and if no Person have a Majority, then from the five highest in the List the said House in like Manner chuse the President. But in chusing the President, the Votes shall be taken by States, the Representation from each State having one Vote; A quorum for this purpose shall consist of a Member or Members from two thirds of the States, and a Majority of all the States shall be necessary to a Choice. In every Case, after the choice of the President, the Person having the greatest Number of Votes of the Electors shall be the Vice-President. But if there should remain two or more who have equal Votes, the Senate shall chuse from them by Ballot the Vice-President.

The Congress may determine the Time of chusing the Electors, and the Day on which they shall give their Votes; which Day shall be the same throughout the United States.

No person except a natural born Citizen, or a Citizen of the United States at the time of the Adoption of this Constitution, shall be eligible to the Office of President; neither shall any Person be eligible to that Office who shall not have attained to the Age of thirty five Years, and been fourteen Years a Resident within the United States.

In Case of the Removal of the President from Office, or of his Death, Resignation, or Inability to discharge the Powers and Duties of the said Office, the Same shall devolve on the Vice-President, and the Congress may by Law provide for the Case of Removal, Death, Resignation or Inability, both of the President and Vice-President, declaring what Officer shall then act as President, and such Officer shall act accordingly, until the Disability be removed, or a President shall be elected.

The President shall, at stated Times, receive for his Services, a Compensation, which shall neither be encreased nor diminished during the Period for which he shall have been elected, and he shall not receive within that Period any other Emolument from the United States, or any of them.

Before he entered on the Execution of his Office, he shall take the following Oath of Affirmation:—"I do solemnly swear (or affirm) that I will faithfully execute the Office of the President of the United States, and will to the best of my Ability, preserve, protect and defend the Constitution of the United States."

Section 2
[Powers of the President]
The President shall be Commander in Chief of the Army and Navy of the United States, and the Militia of the several States, when called into the actual Service of the United States; he may require the Opinion, in writing, of the principal Officer in each of the executive Departments, upon any subject relating to the Duties of their respective Offices, and he shall have Power to grant Reprieves and Pardons for Offences against the United States, except in Cases of Impeachment.

He shall have Power, by and with the Advice and Consent of the Senate, to make Treaties, provided two thirds of the Senators present concur; and he shall nominate, and by and with the Advice and Consent of the Senate, shall appoint Ambassadors, other public

Ministers and Consuls, Judges of the supreme Court, and all other Officers of the United States, whose Appointments are not herein otherwise provided for, and which shall be established by Law: but the Congress may by Law vest the Appointment of such inferior Officers, as they think proper in the President alone, in the Courts of Law, or in the Heads of Departments.

The President shall have Power to fill up all Vacancies that may happen during the Recess of the Senate, by granting Commissions which shall expire at the End of their next Session.

Section 3
[Powers and Duties of the President]
He shall from time to time give to the Congress Information of the State of the Union, and recommend to their Consideration such Measures as he shall judge necessary and expedient; he may, on extraordinary Occasions, convene both Houses, or either of them, and in Case of Disagreement between them, with Respect to the Time of Adjournment, he may adjourn them to such Time as he shall think proper; he shall receive Ambassadors and other public Ministers; he shall take Care that the Laws be faithfully executed, and shall commission all the Officers of the United States.

Section 4
[Impeachment]
The President, Vice-President and all civil Officers of the United States, shall be removed from Office on Impeachment for, and Conviction of, Treason, Bribery, or other high Crimes and Misdemeanors.

ARTICLE 3

Section 1
[Judicial Power, Tenure of Office]
The judicial Power of the United States, shall be vested in one supreme Court, and in such inferior Courts as the Congress may from time to time ordain and establish. The judges, both of the supreme and inferior Courts, shall hold their Offices during good Behavior, and shall, at stated Times, receive for their Services, a Compensation, which shall not be diminished during their Continuance in Office.

Section 2
[Jurisdiction]
The judicial Power shall extend to all Cases, in Law and Equity, arising under this Constitution, the Laws of the United States, and Treaties made, or which shall be made, under their Authority;—to all Cases affecting Ambassadors, other public Ministers and Consuls;—to all Cases of admiralty and maritime Jurisdiction;—to Controversies to which the United States shall be a Party;—to Controversies between two or more States;—between a State and Citizens of another State;—between Citizens of different States; —between Citizens of the same State claiming Lands under Grants of different States, and between a State,

or the Citizens thereof, and foreign States, Citizens or Subjects.

In all Cases affecting Ambassadors, other public Ministers and Consuls, and those in which a State shall be Party, the supreme Court shall have original Jurisdiction. In all the other Cases before mentioned, the supreme Court shall have appellate Jurisdiction, both as to Law and Fact, with such Exceptions, and under such Regulations as the Congress shall make.

The Trial of all Crimes, except in Cases of Impeachment, shall be by Jury; and such Trial shall be held in the State where the said Crimes shall have been committed; but when not committed within any State, the Trial shall be at such Place or Places as the Congress may by Law have directed.

Section 3
[Treason, Proof and Punishment]
Treason against the United States, shall consist only in levying War against them, or in adhering to their Enemies; giving them Aid and Comfort. No Person shall be convicted of Treason unless on the Testimony of two Witnesses to the same overt Act, or on Confession in open Court.

The Congress shall have Power to declare the Punishment of Treason, but no Attainder of Treason shall work Corruption of Blood, or Forfeiture except during the Life of the Person attainted.

ARTICLE 4

Section 1
[Faith and Credit Among States]
Full Faith and Credit shall be given in each State to the public Acts, Records, and judicial Proceedings of every other State. And the Congress may by general Laws prescribe the Manner in which such Acts, Records and Proceedings shall be proved, and the Effect thereof.

Section 2
[Privileges and Immunities, Fugitives]
The citizens of each State shall be entitled to all Privileges and Immunities of Citizens in the several States.

A Person charged in any State with Treason, Felony, or other Crime, who shall flee from Justice, and be found in another State, shall on Demand of the executive Authority of the State from which he fled, be delivered up, to be removed to the State having Jurisdiction of the Crime.

No person held to Service or Labour in one State, under the Laws thereof, escaping into another, shall, in Consequence of any Law or Regulation therein, be discharged from such Service or Labour, but shall be delivered up on Claim of the Party to whom such Service or Labour may be due.

Section 3
[Admission of New States]
New States may be admitted by the Congress into this Union; but no new State shall be formed or erected within the Jurisdiction of any other State; nor any State be formed by the Junction of two or more States, or Parts of States, without the Consent of the Legislatures of the States concerned as well as of the Congress.

The Congress shall have Power to dispose of and make all needful Rules and Regulations respecting the Territory or other Property belonging to the United States; and nothing in this Constitution shall be so construed as to Prejudice any Claims of the United States, or of any particular State.

Section 4
[Guarantee of Republican Government]
The United States shall guarantee to every State in this Union a Republican Form of Government, and shall protect each of them against Invasion; and on Application of the Legislature, or of the Executive (when the Legislature cannot be convened) against domestic Violence.

ARTICLE 5
[Amendment of the Constitution]
The Congress, whenever two thirds of both Houses shall deem it necessary, shall propose Amendments to this Constitution, or, on the Application of the Legislatures of two thirds of the several States, shall call a Convention for proposing Amendments, which, in either Case, shall be valid to all Intents and Purposes, as Part of this Constitution, when ratified by the Legislatures of three fourths of the several States, or by Conventions in three fourths thereof, as the one or the other Mode of Ratification may be proposed by the Congress; Provided that no Amendment which may be made prior to the Year One Thousand eight hundred and eight shall in any Manner affect the first and fourth Clauses in the Ninth Section of the first Article, and that no State, without its Consent, shall be deprived of its equal Suffrage in the Senate.

ARTICLE 6
[Debts, Supremacy, Oath]
All Debts contracted and Engagements entered into, before the Adoption of this Constitution, shall be as valid against the United States under this Constitution, as under the Confederation.

This Constitution, and the Laws of the United States which shall be made in Pursuance thereof; and all Treaties made, or which shall be made, under the Authority of the United States, shall be the supreme Law of the Land; and the Judges in every State be bound thereby, any Thing in the Constitution or Laws of any State to the Contrary notwithstanding.

The Senators and Representatives before mentioned, and the Members of the several State Legislatures, and all executive and judicial Officers, both of the United States and of the several States, shall be bound by Oath or Affirmation, to support this Constitution, but no religious Test shall ever be required as a Qualification to any Office or public Trust under the United States.

ARTICLE 7
[Ratification and Establishment]
The Ratification of the Conventions of nine States, shall be sufficient for the Establishment of this Constitution between the States so ratifying the Same. Done in Convention by the Unanimous Consent of the States present the Seventeenth Day of September in the Year of our Lord one thousand seven hundred and Eighty seven and of the Independence of the United States of America the Twelfth In witness whereof We have hereunto subscribed our Names.

Go. Washington
Presidt and deputy from Virginia

New Hampshire	John Langdon Nicholas Gilman
Massachusetts	Nathaniel Gorham Rufus King
Connecticut	Wm Saml Johnson Roger Sherman
New York	Alexander Hamilton
New Jersey	Wil: Livingston David Brearley Wm Paterson Jona: Dayton
Pennsylvania	B. Franklin Thomas Mifflin Robt. Morris Geo. Clymer Thos. FitzSimons Jared Ingersoll James Wilson Gouv Morris
Delaware	Geo. Read Gunning Bedford jun John Dickinson Richard Bassett Jaco: Broom
Maryland	James McHenry Dan of St Thos. Jenifer Danl Carroll
Virginia	John Blair James Madison Jr.
North Carolina	Wm Blount Richd Dobbs Spaight Hu Williamson
South Carolina	J. Rutledge Charles Cotesworth Pinckney Charles Pinckney Pierce Butler
Georgia	William Few Abr Baldwin

AMENDMENTS TO THE CONSTITUTION
[The first ten amendments, known as the Bill of Rights, were proposed by Congress on September 25, 1789; ratified and adoption certified on December 15, 1791.]

AMENDMENT I
[Freedom of Religion, of Speech, of the Press, and Right of Petition]
Congress shall make no law respecting an establishment of religion, or prohibiting the free exercise thereof; or abridging the freedom of speech, or of the press; or the right of the people peaceably to assemble, and to petition the Government for a redress of grievances.

AMENDMENT II
[Right to Keep and Bear Arms]
A well regulated Militia being necessary to the security of a free State, the right of the people to keep and bear Arms, shall not be infringed.

AMENDMENT III
[Quartering of Soldiers]
No Soldier shall, in time of peace be quartered in any house, without the consent of the Owner, nor in time of war, but in a manner to be prescribed by law.

AMENDMENT IV
[Security from Unwarrantable Search and Seizure]
The right of the people to be secure in their persons, houses, papers, and effects, against unreasonable searches and seizures, shall not be violated, and no Warrants shall issue, but upon probable cause, supported by Oath of affirmation, and particularly describing the place to be searched, and the persons or things to be seized.

AMENDMENT V
[Rights of Accused in Criminal Proceedings]
No person shall be held to answer for a capital, or otherwise infamous crime, unless on a presentment or indictment of a Grand Jury, except in cases arising in the land or naval forces, or in the Militia, when in actual service in time of War or public danger; nor shall any person be subjected for the same offense to be twice put in jeopardy of life or limb; nor shall be compelled in any criminal case to be a witness against himself, nor be deprived of life, liberty, or property, without due process of law; nor shall private property be taken for public use, without just compensation.

AMENDMENT VI
[Right to Speedy Trial, Witnesses, etc.]
In all criminal prosecutions, the accused shall enjoy the right to a speedy and public trial, by an impartial jury of the State and district wherein the crime shall have been committed, which district shall have been previously ascertained by law, and to be informed of the nature and cause of the accusation; to be confronted with the witnesses against him; to have com-

pulsory process for obtaining witnesses in his favor, and to have the Assistance of Counsel for his defence.

AMENDMENT VII
[Trial by Jury in Civil Cases]
In Suits at common law, where the value in controversy shall exceed twenty dollars, the right of trial by jury shall be preserved, and no fact tried by a jury, shall be otherwise reexamined in any Court of the United States, than according to the rules of the common law.

AMENDMENT VIII
[Bails, Fines, Punishments]
Excessive bail shall not be required, nor excessive fines imposed, nor cruel and unusual punishment inflicted.

AMENDMENT IX
[Reservation of Rights of the People]
The enumeration in the Constitution, of certain rights, shall not be construed to deny or disparage others retained by the people.

AMENDMENT X
[Powers Reserved to States or People]
The powers not delegated to the United States by the Constitution, nor prohibited by it to the States, are reserved to the States respectively, or to the people.

AMENDMENT XI
[Proposed by Congress on March 4, 1793; declared ratified on January 8, 1798.]
[Restriction of Judicial Power]
The Judicial power of the United States shall not be construed to extend to any suit in law or equity, commenced or prosecuted against one of the United States by Citizens of another State, or by Citizens or Subjects of any Foreign State.

AMENDMENT XII
[Proposed by Congress on December 9, 1803; declared ratified on September 25, 1804.]
[Election of President and Vice-President]
The Electors shall meet in their respective states, and vote by ballot for President and Vice-President, one of whom, at least, shall not be an inhabitant of the same state with themselves; they shall name in their ballots the person voted for as President, and in distinct ballots the person voted for as Vice-President and they shall make distinct lists of all persons voted for as President, and of all persons voted for as Vice-President, and of the number of votes for each, which lists they shall sign and certify, and transmit sealed to the seat of the government of the United States, directed to the President of the Senate;—The President of the Senate shall, in the presence of the Senate and House of Representatives, open all the certificates and the votes shall then be counted;—The person having the greatest number of votes for President, shall be the President, if such number be a majority of the whole number of Electors appointed; and if no person have such majority, then from the persons having the highest numbers not exceeding three on the list of those voted for as President, the House of Representatives shall choose immediately, by ballot, the President. But in choosing the President, the votes shall be taken by states, the representation from each state having one vote; a quorum for this purpose shall consist of a member or members from two-thirds of the states, and a majority of all the states shall be necessary to a choice. And if the House of Representatives shall not choose a President whenever the right of choice shall devolve upon them, before the fourth day of March next following, then the Vice-President shall act as President, as in the case of the death or other constitutional disability of the President.—The person having the greatest number of votes as Vice-President, shall be the Vice-President, if such number be a majority of the whole number of Electors appointed, and if no person have a majority, then from the two highest numbers on the list, the Senate shall choose the Vice-President; a quorum for the purpose shall consist of two-thirds of the whole number of Senators, and a majority of the whole number shall be necessary to a choice. But no person constitutionally ineligible to the office of President shall be eligible to that of Vice-President of the United States.

AMENDMENT XIII
[Proposed by Congress on January 31, 1865; declared ratified on December 18, 1865.]

Section 1
[Abolition of Slavery]
Neither slavery nor involuntary servitude, except as a punishment for a crime whereof the party shall have been duly convicted, shall exist within the United States, or any place subject to their jurisdiction.

Section 2
[Power to Enforce This Article]
Congress shall have the power to enforce this article by appropriate legislation.

AMENDMENT XIV
[Proposed by Congress on June 16, 1866; declared ratified on July 28, 1868.]

Section 1
[Citizenship Rights Not to Be Abridged by States]
All persons born or naturalized in the United States, and subject to the jurisdiction thereof, are citizens of the United States and of the State wherein they reside. No State shall make or enforce any law which shall abridge the privileges or immunities of citizens of the United States; nor shall any State deprive any person of life, liberty, or property, without due process of law; nor deny to any person within its jurisdiction the equal protection of the laws.

Section 2
[Appointment of Representatives in Congress]
Representatives shall be apportioned among the several States according to their respective numbers, counting the whole number of persons in each State, excluding Indians not taxed. But when the right to vote at any election for the choice of electors for President and Vice-President of the United States, Representatives in Congress, the Executive and Judicial officers of a State, or the members of the Legislature thereof, is denied to any of the male inhabitants of such State, being twenty-one years of age, and citizens of the United States, or in any way abridged, except for participation in rebellion or other crime, the basis of representation therein shall be reduced in the proportion which the number of such male citizens shall bear to the whole number of male citizens twenty-one years of age in such State.

Section 3
[Persons Disqualified from Holding Office]
No person shall be a Senator or Representative in Congress, or elector of President and Vice-President, or hold any office, civil or military, under the United States, or under any State, who, having previously taken an oath, as a member of Congress, or as an officer of the United States, or as a member of any State legislature, or as an executive or judicial officer of any State, to support the Constitution of the United States, shall have engaged in insurrection or rebellion against the same, or given aid or comfort to the enemies thereof. But Congress may by a vote of two-thirds of each House, remove such disability.

Section 4
[What Public Debts Are Valid]
The validity of the public debt of the United States, authorized by law, including debts incurred for payment of pensions and bounties for services in suppressing insurrection or rebellion, shall not be questioned. But neither the United States nor any State shall assume or pay any debt or obligation incurred in aid of insurrection or rebellion against the United States, or any claim for the loss or emancipation of any slave; but all such debts, obligations and claims shall be held illegal and void.

Section 5
[Power to Enforce This Article]
The Congress shall have power to enforce, by appropriate legislation, the provisions of this article.

AMENDMENT XV
[Proposed by Congress on February 26, 1869; declared ratified on March 30, 1870.]

Section 1
[Negro Suffrage]
The right of citizens of the United States to vote shall not be denied or abridged by the United States or by any State on account of race, color, or previous condition of servitude.

Section 2
[Power to Enforce This Article]
The Congress shall have power to enforce this article by appropriate legislation.

AMENDMENT XVI
[Proposed by Congress on July 12, 1909; declared ratified on February 25, 1913.]
[Authorizing Income Taxes]
The Congress shall have power to lay and collect taxes on incomes, from whatever source derived, without apportionment among the several States, and without regard to any census or enumeration.

AMENDMENT XVII
[Proposed by Congress on May 13, 1912; declared ratified on May 31, 1913.]
[Popular Election of Senators]
The Senate of the United States shall be composed of two Senators from each State, elected by the people thereof, for six years; and each Senator shall have one vote. The electors in each State shall have the qualifications requisite for electors of the most numerous branch of the State legislatures.

When vacancies happen in the representation of any State in the Senate, the executive authority of such State shall issue writs of election to fill such vacancies: *Provided,* That the legislature of any State may empower the executive thereof to make temporary appointments until the people fill the vacancies by election as the legislature may direct.

This amendment shall not be so construed as to affect the election or term of any Senator chosen before it becomes valid as part of the Constitution.

AMENDMENT XVIII
[Proposed by Congress on December 18, 1917; declared ratified on January 16, 1919.]

Section 1
[National Liquor Prohibition]
After one year from the ratification of this article the manufacture, sale, or transportation of intoxicating liquors within, the importation thereof into, or the exportation thereof from the United States and all territory subject to the jurisdiction thereof for beverage purposes is hereby prohibited.

Section 2
[Power to Enforce This Article]
The Congress and the several States shall have concurrent power to enforce this article by appropriate legislation.

Section 3
[Ratification Within Seven Years]
This article shall be inoperative unless it shall have been ratified as an amendment to the Constitution by the legislatures of the several States, as provided in the Constitution, within seven years from the date of the submission hereof to the States by the Congress.

AMENDMENT XIX

[*Proposed by Congress on June 4, 1919; declared ratified on August 26, 1920.*]

[*Woman Suffrage*]

The right of citizens of the United States to vote shall not be denied or abridged by the United States or by any State on account of sex.

Congress shall have power to enforce this article by appropriate legislation.

AMENDMENT XX

[*Proposed by Congress on March 2, 1932; declared ratified on February 6, 1933.*]

Section 1

[*Terms of Office*]

The terms of the President and Vice-President shall end at noon on the 20th day of January, and the terms of Senators and Representatives at noon on the 3rd day of January, of the years in which such terms would have ended if this article had not been ratified; and the terms of their successors shall then begin.

Section 2

[*Time of Convening Congress*]

The Congress shall assemble at least once in every year, and such meeting shall begin at noon on the 3rd day of January, unless they shall by law appoint a different day.

Section 3

[*Death of President Elect*]

If, at the time fixed for the beginning of the term of the President, the President elect shall have died, the Vice-President elect shall become President. If a President shall not have been chosen before the time fixed for the beginning of his term, or if the President elect shall have failed to qualify, then the Vice-President elect shall act as President until a President shall have qualified; and the Congress may by law provide for the case wherein neither a President elect nor a Vice-President elect shall have qualified, declaring who shall then act as President, or the manner in which one who is to act shall be selected, and such person shall act accordingly until a President or Vice-President shall have qualified.

Section 4

[*Election of the President*]

The Congress may by law provide for the case of the death of any of the persons from whom the House of Representatives may choose a President whenever the right of choice shall have devolved upon them, and for the case of the death of any of the persons from whom the Senate may choose a Vice-President whenever the right of choice shall have devolved upon them.

Section 5

Sections 1 and 2 shall take effect on the 15th day of October following the ratification of this article.

Section 6

This article shall be inoperative unless it shall have been ratified as an amendment to the Constitution by the legislatures of three-fourths of the several States within seven years from the date of its submission.

AMENDMENT XXI

[*Proposed by Congress on February 20, 1933; declared ratified on December 5, 1933.*]

Section 1

[*National Liquor Prohibition Repealed*]

The eighteenth article of amendment to the Constitution of the United States is hereby repealed.

Section 2

[*Transportation of Liquor into "Dry" States*]

The transportation or importation into any States, Territory, or possession of the United States for delivery or use therein of intoxicating liquors, in violation of the laws thereof, is hereby prohibited.

Section 3

This article shall be inoperative unless it shall have been ratified as an amendment to the Constitution by conventions in the several States, as provided in the Constitution, within seven years from the date of the submission hereof to the States by the Congress.

AMENDMENT XXII

[*Proposed by Congress on March 21, 1947; declared ratified on February 26, 1951.*]

Section 1

[*Tenure of President Limited*]

No person shall be elected to the office of the President more than twice, and no person who has held the office of President, or acted as President, for more than two years of a term to which some other person was elected President shall be elected to the office of the President more than once. But this Article shall not apply to any person holding the office of President when this Article was proposed by the Congress, and shall not prevent any person who may be holding the office of President, or acting as President, during the term within which this Article becomes operative from holding the office of President, or acting as President during the remainder of such term.

Section 2

This Article shall be inoperative unless it shall have been ratified as an amendment to the Constitution by the legislatures of three-fourths of the several States within seven years from the date of its submission to the States by the Congress.

AMENDMENT XXIII

[*Proposed by Congress on June 17, 1960; declared ratified on May 29, 1961.*]

Section 1

[*District of Columbia Suffrage in Presidential Elections*]

The District constituting the seat of Government of the United States shall appoint in such manner as the Congress may direct:

A number of electors of President and Vice-President equal to the whole number of Senators and Representatives in Congress to which the District would be entitled if it were a State, but in no event more than the least populous State; they shall be in addition to those appointed by the States, but they shall be considered, for the purposes of the election of President and Vice-President, to be electors appointed by a State; and they shall meet in the District and perform such duties as provided by the twelfth article of amendment.

Section 2
The Congress shall have power to enforce this article by appropriate legislation.

AMENDMENT XXIV
[Proposed by Congress on August 27, 1962; declared ratified on January 23, 1964.]

Section 1
[Bars Poll Tax in Federal Elections]
The right of citizens of the United States to vote in any primary or other election for President or Vice-President, for electors for President or Vice-President, or for Senator or Representative in Congress, shall not be denied or abridged by the United States or any State by reason of failure to pay any poll tax or other tax.

Section 2
The Congress shall have power to enforce this article by appropriate legislation.

AMENDMENT XXV
[Proposed by Congress on July 6, 1965; declared ratified on February 10, 1967.]

Section 1
[Succession of Vice-President to Presidency]
In case of the removal of the President from office or of his death or resignation, the Vice-President shall become President.

Section 2
[Vacancy in office of Vice-President]
Whenever there is a vacancy in the office of the Vice-President, the President shall nominate a Vice-President who shall take office upon confirmation by a majority vote of both Houses of Congress.

Section 3
[Vice-President as Acting President]
Whenever the President transmits to the President pro tempore of the Senate and the Speaker of the House of Representatives his written declaration that he is unable to discharge the powers and duties of his office, and until he transmits to them a written declaration to the contrary, such powers and duties shall be discharged by the Vice-President as Acting President.

Section 4
[Vice-President as Acting President]
Whenever the Vice-President and a majority of either the principal officers of the executive departments or of such other body as Congress may by law provide, transmit to the President pro tempore of the Senate and the Speaker of the House of Representatives their written declaration that the President is unable to discharge the powers and duties of his office, the Vice-President shall immediately assume the powers and duties of the office as Acting President.

Thereafter, when the President transmits to the President pro tempore of the Senate and the Speaker of the House of Representatives his written declaration that no inability exists, he shall resume the powers and duties of his office unless the Vice-President and a majority of either the principal officers of the executive department or of such other body as Congress may by law provide, transmit within four days to the President pro tempore of the Senate and the Speaker of the House of Representatives their written declaration that the President is unable to discharge the powers and duties of his office. Thereupon Congress shall decide the issue, assembling within forty-eight hours for that purpose if not in session. If the Congress, within twenty-one days after receipt of the latter written declaration, or, if Congress is not in session, within twenty-one days after Congress is required to assemble, determines by two-thirds vote of both Houses that the President is unable to discharge the powers and duties of his office, the Vice-President shall continue to discharge the same as Acting President; otherwise, the President shall resume the powers and duties of his office.

AMENDMENT XXVI
[Proposed by Congress on March 23, 1971; declared ratified on July 5, 1971.]

Section 1
[Lowers Voting Age to 18 Years]
The right of citizens of the United States, who are eighteen years of age or older, to vote shall not be denied or abridged by the United States or by any State on account of age.

Section 2
The Congress shall have power to enforce this article by appropriate legislation.

Presidential Elections 1789-1976

Year	Candidates	Party	Popular Vote	Electoral Vote
1789	**George Washington**			69
	John Adams			34
	Others			35
1792	**George Washington**			132
	John Adams			77
	George Clinton			50
	Others			5
1796	**John Adams**	Federalist		71
	Thomas Jefferson	Democratic-Republican		68
	Thomas Pinckney	Federalist		59
	Aaron Burr	Democratic-Republican		30
	Others			48
1800	**Thomas Jefferson**	Democratic-Republican		73
	Aaron Burr	Democratic-Republican		73
	John Adams	Federalist		65
	Charles C. Pinckney	Federalist		64
1804	**Thomas Jefferson**	Democratic-Republican		162
	Charles C. Pinckney	Federalist		14
1808	**James Madison**	Democratic-Republican		122
	Charles C. Pinckney	Federalist		47
	George Clinton	Independent-Republican		6
1812	**James Madison**	Democratic-Republican		128
	DeWitt Clinton	Federalist		89
1816	**James Monroe**	Democratic-Republican		183
	Rufus King	Federalist		34
1820	**James Monroe**	Democratic-Republican		231
	John Quincy Adams	Independent-Republican		1
1824	**John Quincy Adams**	Democratic-Republican	108,740 (30.5%)	84
	Andrew Jackson	Democratic-Republican	153,544 (43.1%)	99
	Henry Clay	Democratic-Republican	47,136 (13.2%)	37
	William H. Crawford	Democratic-Republican	46,618 (13.1%)	41
1828	**Andrew Jackson**	Democratic	647,231 (56.0%)	178
	John Quincy Adams	National Republican	509,097 (44.0%)	83
1832	**Andrew Jackson**	Democratic	687,502 (55.0%)	219
	Henry Clay	National Republican	530,189 (42.4%)	49
	William Wirt	Anti-Masonic		7
	John Floyd	National Republican	33,108 (2.6%)	11
1836	**Martin Van Buren**	Democratic	761,549 (50.9%)	170
	William H. Harrison	Whig	549,567 (36.7%)	73
	Hugh L. White	Whig	145,396 (9.7%)	26
	Daniel Webster	Whig	41,287 (2.7%)	14
1840	**William H. Harrison** (John Tyler, 1841)	Whig	1,275,017 (53.1%)	234
	Martin Van Buren	Democratic	1,128,702 (46.9%)	60

NOTE: Because only the leading candidates are listed, popular-vote percentages do not always total 100. The elections of 1800 and 1824, in which no candidate received an electoral-vote majority, were decided in the House of Representatives.

Year	Candidates	Party	Popular Vote	Electoral Vote
1844	**James K. Polk**	Democratic	1,337,243 (49.6%)	170
	Henry Clay	Whig	1,299,068 (48.1%)	105
	James G. Birney	Liberty	62,300 (2.3%)	
1848	**Zachary Taylor**	Whig	1,360,101 (47.4%)	163
	(**Millard Fillmore**, 1850)			
	Lewis Cass	Democratic	1,220,544 (42.5%)	127
	Martin Van Buren	Free Soil	291,263 (10.1%)	
1852	**Franklin Pierce**	Democratic	1,601,474 (50.9%)	254
	Winfield Scott	Whig	1,386,578 (44.1%)	42
1856	**James Buchanan**	Democratic	1,838,169 (45.4%)	174
	John C. Fremont	Republican	1,335,264 (33.0%)	114
	Millard Fillmore	American	874,534 (21.6%)	8
1860	**Abraham Lincoln**	Republican	1,865,593 (39.8%)	180
	Stephen A. Douglas	Democratic	1,382,713 (29.5%)	12
	John C. Breckinridge	Democratic	848,356 (18.1%)	72
	John Bell	Constitutional Union	592,906 (12.6%)	39
1864	**Abraham Lincoln**	Republican	2,206,938 (55.0%)	212
	(**Andrew Johnson**, 1865)			
	George B. McClellan	Democratic	1,803,787 (45.0%)	21
1868	**Ulysses S. Grant**	Republican	3,013,421 (52.7%)	214
	Horatio Seymour	Democratic	2,706,829 (47.3%)	80
1872	**Ulysses S. Grant**	Republican	3,596,745 (55.6%)	286
	Horace Greeley	Democratic	2,843,446 (43.9%)	66
1876	**Rutherford B. Hayes**	Republican	4,036,572 (48.0%)	185
	Samuel J. Tilden	Democratic	4,284,020 (51.0%)	184
1880	**James A. Garfield**	Republican	4,449,053 (48.3%)	214
	(**Chester A. Arthur**, 1881)			
	Winfield S. Hancock	Democratic	4,442,035 (48.2%)	155
	James B. Weaver	Greenback-Labor	308,578 (3.4%)	
1884	**Grover Cleveland**	Democratic	4,874,986 (48.5%)	219
	James G. Blaine	Republican	4,851,981 (48.2%)	182
	Benjamin F. Butler	Greenback-Labor	175,370 (1.8%)	
1888	**Benjamin Harrison**	Republican	5,444,337 (47.8%)	233
	Grover Cleveland	Democratic	5,540,050 (48.6%)	168
1892	**Grover Cleveland**	Democratic	5,554,414 (46.0%)	277
	Benjamin Harrison	Republican	5,190,802 (43.0%)	145
	James B. Weaver	People's	1,027,329 (8.5%)	22
1896	**William McKinley**	Republican	7,035,638 (50.8%)	271
	William J. Bryan	Democratic; Populist	6,467,946 (46.7%)	176
1900	**William McKinley**	Republican	7,219,530 (51.7%)	292
	(**Theodore Roosevelt**, 1901)			
	William J. Bryan	Democratic; Populist	6,356,734 (45.5%)	155
1904	**Theodore Roosevelt**	Republican	7,628,834 (56.4%)	336
	Alton B. Parker	Democratic	5,084,401 (37.6%)	140
	Eugene V. Debs	Socialist	402,460 (3.0%)	
1908	**William H. Taft**	Republican	7,679,006 (51.6%)	321
	William J. Bryan	Democratic	6,409,106 (43.1%)	162
	Eugene V. Debs	Socialist	420,820 (2.8%)	

Presidential Elections 1789–1976 *(continued)*

Year	Candidates	Party	Popular Vote	Electoral Vote
1912	**Woodrow Wilson**	Democratic	6,286,820 (41.8%)	430
	Theodore Roosevelt	Progressive	4,126,020 (27.4%)	88
	William H. Taft	Republican	3,483,922 (23.2%)	8
	Eugene V. Debs	Socialist	897,011 (6.0%)	
1916	**Woodrow Wilson**	Democratic	9,129,606 (49.3%)	277
	Charles E. Hughes	Republican	8,538,221 (46.1%)	254
1920	**Warren G. Harding**	Republican	16,152,200 (61.0%)	404
	(Calvin Coolidge, 1923)			
	James M. Cox	Democratic	9,147,353 (34.6%)	127
	Eugene V. Debs	Socialist	919,799 (3.5%)	
1924	**Calvin Coolidge**	Republican	15,725,016 (54.1%)	382
	John W. Davis	Democratic	8,385,586 (28.8%)	136
	Robert M. La Follette	Progressive	4,822,856 (16.6%)	13
1928	**Herbert C. Hoover**	Republican	21,392,190 (58.2%)	444
	Alfred E. Smith	Democratic	15,016,443 (40.8%)	87
1932	**Franklin D. Roosevelt**	Democratic	22,809,638 (57.3%)	472
	Herbert C. Hoover	Republican	15,758,901 (39.6%)	59
	Norman Thomas	Socialist	881,951 (2.2%)	
1936	**Franklin D. Roosevelt**	Democratic	27,751,612 (60.7%)	523
	Alfred M. Landon	Republican	16,681,913 (36.4%)	8
	William Lemke	Union	891,858 (1.9%)	
1940	**Franklin D. Roosevelt**	Democratic	27,243,466 (54.7%)	449
	Wendell L. Willkie	Republican	22,304,755 (44.8%)	82
1944	**Franklin D. Roosevelt**	Democratic	25,602,505 (52.8%)	432
	(Harry S. Truman, 1945)			
	Thomas E. Dewey	Republican	22,006,278 (44.5%)	99
1948	**Harry S. Truman**	Democratic	24,105,812 (49.5%)	303
	Thomas E. Dewey	Republican	21,970,065 (45.1%)	189
	J. Strom Thurmond	States' Rights	1,169,063 (2.4%)	39
	Henry A. Wallace	Progressive	1,157,172 (2.4%)	
1952	**Dwight D. Eisenhower**	Republican	33,936,234 (55.2%)	442
	Adlai E. Stevenson	Democratic	27,314,992 (44.5%)	89
1956	**Dwight D. Eisenhower**	Republican	35,590,472 (57.4%)	457
	Adlai E. Stevenson	Democratic	26,022,752 (42.0%)	73
1960	**John F. Kennedy**	Democratic	34,227,096 (49.9%)	303
	(Lyndon B. Johnson, 1963)			
	Richard M. Nixon	Republican	34,108,546 (49.6%)	219
1964	**Lyndon B. Johnson**	Democratic	43,126,233 (61.1%)	486
	Barry M. Goldwater	Republican	27,174,989 (38.5%)	52
1968	**Richard M. Nixon**	Republican	31,783,783 (43.4%)	301
	Hubert H. Humphrey	Democratic	31,271,839 (42.7%)	191
	George C. Wallace	American Independent	9,899,557 (13.5%)	46
1972	**Richard M. Nixon**	Republican	46,631,189 (61.3%)	521
	(Gerald Ford, 1974)			
	George McGovern	Democratic	28,422,015 (37.3%)	17
1976	**James E. Carter**	Democratic	40,828,587 (50.1%)	297
	Gerald Ford	Republican	39,147,613 (48.0%)	240
	Eugene McCarthy	Independent	700,000 (0.9%)	

Glossary

accountability The principle under which the public officials in a democracy are held responsible for their actions by those who elected or appointed them.

adjudication The process by which a judgment or decision is made according to law; adversary proceedings in a court of law.

administrative law The rules and regulations made by government agencies.

affirmative action The hiring of members of a minority group in order to make up for previous discrimination against that group.

agenda The list of items to be considered at a meeting or legislative session; more generally, the politically relevant issues.

amendment A change in or addition to a bill, motion, or constitution.

amicus curiae brief A brief filed by a person who is not a party to a lawsuit but may be affected by its outcome.

appeal A legal proceeding in which a case is carried from a lower court to a higher court for review or reexamination.

appellate jurisdiction The right to try cases on appeal from lower courts.

appropriation A bill granting the actual funds for a program that has been authorized by Congress.

authorization Congressional legislation prescribing a particular program and putting limits on spending for that program.

Bill of Rights The first ten amendments to the U.S. Constitution.

budget A statement of estimated income and expenses.

bureaucratic discretion The situation in which bureaucrats are able to make policy instead of simply carrying it out.

capitalism An economic system based on private ownership of land, natural resources, and the means of production, distribution, and exchange, in which there is a minimum of government interference in the economy.

centralization The gravitation of political power and decision-making responsibility from units or agencies that are geographically small or functionally separate to ones that are larger or more general (cf. decentralization).

checks and balances The system under which each branch of the government has the power to limit the activities of the other branches.

circuit court (of appeals) A federal court with appellate jurisdiction assigned to one of the eleven judicial circuits, or regions, in the United States.

citizens' lobby An interest group that lobbies in behalf of the public welfare (e.g., consumer protection, conservation, political reform, etc.).

civil liberties Liberties guaranteed to the individual by the First Amendment to the Constitution: freedom of speech, press, and assembly.

civil rights The rights to which a citizen is legally entitled, including individual freedoms, economic rights, and due process of law.

civil service The system under which most government employees are hired on the basis of merit and have job security regardless of the administration in power.

coalition A political union containing a variety of political groups.

collective good A benefit that is available to all citizens whether or not they have worked to create that benefit.

commission plan A form of city government in which a small board of elected commissioners serves both as a legislative council and as heads of the city departments (cf. council–manager plan, mayor–council plan).

common law Judge-made law, that is, a set of decisions made by judges and considered binding in similar cases.

communal activity Political activity in which citizens act as a group to pressure the government.

comprehensive planning A form of planning in which all possible ways of solving a problem are considered (cf. incremental planning).

concurrent majority The idea that a majority of the citizens of the United States cannot determine the policy followed within a particular region.

confederation A form of government in which the central government is subordinate to the state governments (cf. federation, unitary government).

conference committee A committee formed to resolve the differences between the versions of a bill passed by the Senate and the House of Representatives. It usually consists of senior members of the House and Senate committees sponsoring the bill.

confirmation The Senate's power to approve nominations made by the President for certain public offices.

congressional caucus A meeting of the members

of one political party in the Senate or the House of Representatives in which various decisions are made such as the choice of congressional party leaders. Also, particular subgroups in Congress based on race, region, and the like.

Connecticut Compromise The compromise in which it was decided that Congress would consist of two houses: the House of Representatives, in which the number of representatives from each state would be determined by population, and the Senate, in which each state would be represented equally.

conservative A political position that favors maintaining a stable society and stresses the need for strong political and social institutions. Conservatives often stress the need to maintain the status quo (cf. liberal, radical).

constituent A person who lives in a legislative district.

constitution The fundamental law—written or unwritten—that sets up the government of a nation, state, or any other organized group of people; specifies the duties and powers of the various government agencies; and describes in detail the relationship between the citizens and their government.

constitutional law The Constitution plus the decisions made by the Supreme Court when it has had to interpret the Constitution.

constitutionalism Belief in government according to a basic law, or constitution, against which all other laws are measured.

cooperative federalism The system in which government powers are shared across the various levels of government—federal, state, and local (cf. dual federalism).

council–manager plan A form of city government in which a nonpartisan council hires a professional city manager, who runs the city subject to the council's approval (cf. commission plan, mayor–council plan).

decentralization The process of transferring political power and decision-making responsibility from larger political units or agencies to ones that serve smaller geographic areas or narrower functional constituencies (cf. centralization).

de facto segregation Segregation that results from housing patterns in which different social groups, e.g., blacks and whites, live in separate neighborhoods.

defendant The defending party in a court case; the person sued or accused (cf. plaintiff).

depletion allowance A tax reduction that may be taken by owners of oil and gas wells and other minerals, supposedly to stimulate exploration for such natural resources.

district court A federal court of original jurisdiction. There are 90 district courts in the federal court system.

documentary research The use of records kept by the government, as well as records published by other sources, in doing research on political questions.

dual federalism The doctrine that the states and the nation have separate areas of responsibility (cf. cooperative federalism).

due process of law The guarantee, contained in the Fifth and Fourteenth Amendments to the Constitution, that an individual cannot be deprived of life, liberty, or property by an arbitrary act of government.

elector A member of the Electoral College. Each state's electors are chosen by the voters in the November election. They usually vote as a unit for the candidate who won the greatest number of votes in that state.

Electoral College The group of electors, representing all the states, who actually choose the new President and Vice-President.

ethnic group A group whose members share characteristics such as national background, religion, customs, or language.

executive agreement An international agreement signed by the President that does not need Senate approval.

executive privilege The doctrine under which only the President can decide what information about the activities of the executive branch can be revealed to the public or to other branches of the government.

federalism A system of government in which power is shared between a central government and state or regional governments.

Federalist Papers A series of essays written by Alexander Hamilton, James Madison, and John Jay to defend the new Constitution.

federation A union of states in which each member agrees to subordinate its power to the central authority in common affairs while retaining authority on other matters (cf. confederation, unitary government).

filibuster A delaying tactic used in the Senate in which a small group can "talk a bill to death" under the rule of unlimited debate.

floor leaders Party leaders, one from each party in each house of Congress, responsible for keeping party members informed and active in legislative battles.

grant-in-aid A grant of funds by the federal government to a state or local government (or by a state government to a local government) to be used for a particular purpose.

House minority leader The leader of the minority party in the House of Representatives.

impeachment A formal accusation of a public official for misconduct in office, made by the lower house of a legislature.

implied powers The doctrine that Congress isn't limited to the powers listed in the Constitution but has all the powers necessary to carry out those that are listed.

impoundment Literally, seizing and holding in legal custody; politically, refusal by the President to spend funds appropriated by Congress.

incremental planning A form of planning in which problems are approached one step at a time (cf. comprehensive planning).

independent regulatory commission An agency set up outside the executive branch and responsible for regulating a particular part of the economy.

independent voter A voter who identifies with neither major political party and votes on a case-by-case basis according to the specific candidates or issues involved in a given race.

inequality of distance A term that refers to the gap in income between the rich and the poor in a society.

inequality of scope A term that refers to the ways in which the rich are better off than the poor.

inflation An economic situation in which an increase in prices is accompanied by a loss of purchasing power.

interest group An organized group that uses various techniques to influence government policy; also referred to as a "pressure group" or "lobby."

Jim Crow laws Laws passed by southern states requiring segregation of blacks and whites.

judicial review The power of the courts to decide whether a law is constitutional or not.

legitimacy of government The belief that the government is legitimate—that public officials deserve support and that the law must be obeyed.

libel Written statements that defame the character of a person without justification.

liberal A political position that supports political, social, and economic changes in order to improve the well-being of the individual (cf. conservative, radical).

lobby A group of professionals that tries to influence the decisions of legislative and executive agencies in Washington and the state capitals in favor of a particular interest group.

majority A number over 50 percent. In a democracy the majority rules in choosing public officials and making political decisions.

mayor–council plan A form of city government in which the mayor shares power with an elected city council (cf. commission plan, council–manager plan).

merchant class A group of leaders who believes that the well-being of citizens and of society as a whole can best be achieved by allowing the competitive marketplace to operate without government interference (cf. social engineers).

monopoly An economic situation in which a single corporation has so much power that it can fix prices and eliminate competition.

national sovereignty The principle that ultimate authority rests with the national government rather than with the states (cf. state sovereignty).

oligopoly An economic situation in which a few corporations have so much power that they can fix prices and reduce competition in a particular part of the economy.

original jurisdiction The right to try a case for the first time; in other words, a case "originates" in a court that has original jurisdiction.

party identification The feeling that one belongs to a particular political party the way one belongs to a particular religion.

party regular Members of local political party organizations who are loyal to the party and want to see its candidates win.

patronage The power to make partisan appointments or to distribute, on a partisan basis, jobs, franchises, contracts, or favors.

plaintiff A person who brings a suit in a court of law; the challenger (cf. defendant).

platform A political party's statement of principles and policies.

pocket veto The President's power to veto a bill by holding it for ten days without either signing it or vetoing it; if Congress adjourns during that time the bill does not become law.

policy A long-term commitment of the government to a pattern of activity.

political efficacy One's belief that he or she has a voice in the government and can influence its actions.

political mainstream The broad policies that most Americans actively support or at least willingly tolerate; also, the belief in the importance of "working within the system."

political socialization The process by which young people learn basic political beliefs.

potential group A group with interests in common but little shared sense of group membership.

president pro tempore The presiding officer of

the Senate when the Vice-President is absent (always a member of the party holding a majority of the seats in the Senate).

pressure group See interest group.

primary election An election held by a political party to determine which of its members should be nominated for public office.

prior restraint The attempt to block publication of material (e.g., by a newspaper) in advance.

proportional representation An electoral system in which legislative seats are apportioned to parties or factions according to the percentage of the vote won by each.

public-opinion poll A survey that finds out the opinions of a representative sample of the public in order to get a picture of general public opinion.

radical A person who advocates immediate and sweeping political, social, or economic changes (cf. conservative, liberal).

realignment A situation in which an election results in a major, permanent change in the makeup of the political parties and/or a shift in which party is dominant.

revenue sharing A program in which the federal government distributes funds to state and local governments to spend where they are needed most.

roll call vote A vote in Congress in which each legislator's vote is put on record.

segregation The separation of blacks and whites in public and private facilities—schools, buses, theaters, restaurants, and so on.

Senate majority leader The leader of the majority party in the Senate (also the recognized leader of the Senate).

Senate minority leader The leader of the minority party in the Senate.

seniority rule The congressional rule under which the member of the majority party who has served longest on a committee chairs that committee.

separation of powers The principle under which government power is shared by the three branches of government—legislative, executive, and judicial.

social engineers A group of leaders who believe that government programs must supplement the operations of the marketplace if individual and social well-being are to be achieved (cf. merchant class).

Speaker of the House The presiding officer of the House of Representatives and the leader of the majority party.

special district A local government unit created to provide a single service.

spillover A term used to describe the activities of a community that affect its neighbors.

standing committee A permanent committee in the Senate or the House of Representatives.

stare decisis The principle that past decisions should be used as guidelines in ruling on similar cases.

State of the Union Address An annual speech to Congress in which the President discusses the problems facing the nation and presents a legislative program to deal with those problems.

state sovereignty The principle that ultimate authority rests with the various states rather than with the national government.

statutory law All laws made by legislators to solve social problems or establish rules to cover particular situations.

tariff A tax on imports that protects products made in this country from foreign competition by raising the prices of foreign products.

tax deduction A subtraction (e.g., the amount of medical payments or interest on a mortgage) reducing the amount of income that can be taxed. This in turn reduces the amount paid in taxes.

tax exemption Income that is not taxed, such as interest on municipal bonds.

unit rule The rule by which the candidate who gets the greatest number of votes in a primary election wins all of that state's delegate votes at the nominating convention.

unitary government A form of government in which all state and local governments are subordinate to the central government (cf. confederation, federation).

whip An assistant floor leader who acts as a liaison between party leaders and party members and makes sure party members are present for important votes.

writ of certiorari A request from a higher court to a lower court for the record of a case for review.

writ of mandamus A court order requiring an individual, corporation, or public official to perform some duty.

Index

80 81 82 9 8 7 6 5 4 3 2